Sustain and Develop
306090 books, Volume 13

D0825193

Sustain and Develop
Published by 306090, Inc.
350 Canal Street, Box 2092
New York NY 10013-0875
info@306090.org
www.306090.org

Editors
Joshua Bolchover
Jonathan D. Solomon

Series Editors
Emily Abruzzo
Jonathan D. Solomon

Copy Editor
T.J. Fitsell

Graphic Design
Thumb: Luke Bulman and Jessica Young
Original design schema by ORG

Advisory Board
M. Christine Boyer
Mario Gandelsonas
David L. Hays
Mark Jarzombeck
Ralph Lerner
Paul Lewis
Michael Sorkin
Christian Unverzagt
Sarah Whiting

**Sustain and Develop is supported by a grant from
the Graham Foundation for Advanced Studies in the
Fine Arts, a Grant from the National Endowment
for the Arts, Princeton University School of
Architecture, The University of Hong Kong Faculty
of Architecture, and the generous sponsorship of
Elise Jaffe + Jeffrey Brown.**

The editors wish to thank Kevin Lippert, Nettie Aljian,
Janet Behning, Jennifer Thompson, Wendy Fuller, and all
of Princeton Architectural Press for their continued
support of 306090; and Stan Allen, Susan Begley, Sara
Herda, and Ralph Lerner for their consistent interest.

About the typeface: Portions of Sustain and Develop,
306090 13, were set in OCR Sine, a typeface designed
specifically for this volume. It uses a common proportional structure defined by a series of modules, in this
case squares. By increasing and decreasing the size of
the squares in a sequential fashion along the vertical
axis a variety of fonts may be produced.

©Copyright 2009, 306090, Inc.
All rights reserved. Printed and bound in China. All
images courtesy the author unless otherwise noted.
All reasonable attempts have been made to identify
owners of copyright. Errors or omissions will be cor-
rected in future volumes. No part of this volume may
be reproduced without the written permission of the
publisher, except in the context of reviews.

Individuals who do not use conventional print may
contact the publisher to obtain this publication in
an alternate format.

Distributed by Princeton Architectural Press
37 East 7th Street
New York NY 10003
800 722 6657 t
718 504 5228 f

First Edition, 2009
ISBN: 978-0-692-00088-5
Please contact the publisher for Library of Congress
catalog-in-publication information.

NATIONAL
ENDOWMENT
FOR THE ARTS

Sustain and Develop

306090 Books, Volume 13

Joshua Bolchover and Jonathan D. Solomon, editors

306090, Inc.
New York 2009

A village in China recycling electronic rubbish dumped from the United States. Photo courtesy Underline Office. See "China's Sustainability: Asynchronous Revolutions" on page 135

Facade of Pharos building, Hoofddorp, *Vanessa van Dam, 2002, never realized. Image courtesy of the artist. Photographer: Gertjan Kocken, image manipulation: Nick Strong. See "Towers, Maintenance, and the Desire for Effortless Permanence" on page 82*

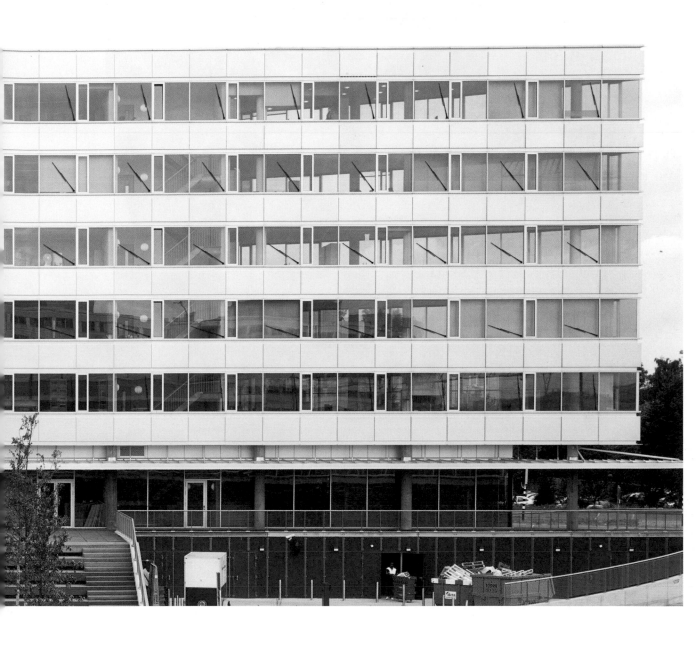

A Model for Sustainable Los Angeles, *James Rojas. This model envisions LA as a more environmentally sustainable city. The plan is based on the Olmstead Parks Plan and the Centers Concept for LA, where urban activities were clustered in certain areas surrounded by potential open space connected by rapid public transit. The model building is an interactive process where participants are given a piece of land to develop as they see fit and build buildings and/or lay out their landscapes. As participants create spaces they develop narratives about what they are creating. However, all developments are temporary so the urban landscape constantly changes with every new idea, much like any urban environment. At the end of the exhibition "A Model for a Sustainable Los Angles" should be a completely built out model of what LA could and should be like if it is to incorporate sustainable practices. James Rojas and a team of environmentalists, architects, urban planners, and landscape architects direct the model building process. The structures are made from small-recycled objects such as pieces of wood, jewelry, sample shampoo bottles, incomplete games, nuts and bolts and an assortment of found objects. Participants can also bring their own objects. Image courtesy the artist*

Burj Dubai, the world's tallest tower. Image courtesy Imre Solt. See "Endurance and Obsolescence: Instant Cities, Disposable Buildings, and the Construction of Culture" on page 57

...the plastic polymers commonly used in consumer products, even as single molecules of plastic, are indigestible by any known organism. Even those single molecules must be further degraded by sunlight or slow oxidative breakdown before their constituents can be recycled into the building blocks of life. There is no data on how long such recycling takes in the ocean—some ecologists have made estimates of 500 years or more. Even more ominously, no one knows the ultimate consequences of the worldwide dispersion of plastic fragments that can concentrate the toxic chemicals already present in the world's oceans.
—*Charles Moore,* Trashed: Across the Pacific Ocean, Plastics, Plastics Everywhere. *Image courtesy Ralph Hockens*

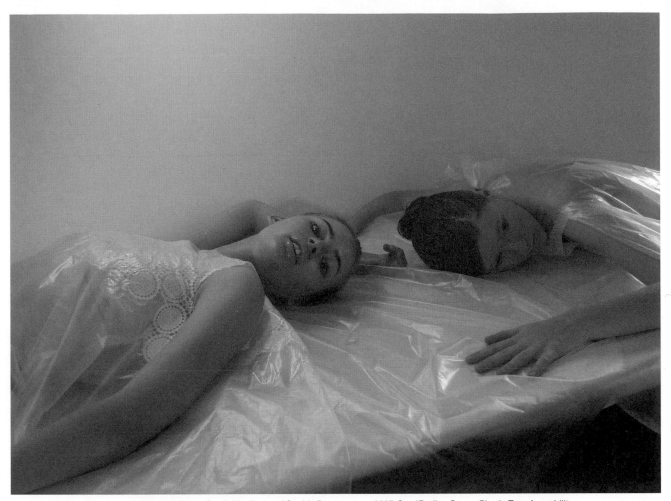

Sbstititsue, *Sarah Martinus and Sophie Braungartner, 2007. See "Feeling Green: Plastic Transformability and Generative Critique" on page 271*

Florient Rise, *Hong Kong. Image courtesy Hong Kong Cultural Imaging Workshop. See "Be Our Guest" on page 73*

Floating Green, *Ling Fan, Zhangjiang Art Park, Pudong, Shanghai, 2008. Four 2 x 1.5 x 1.2 meter stainless steel units are assembled and topped with turf on-site. See "Sitting on a Floating Green" on page 303*

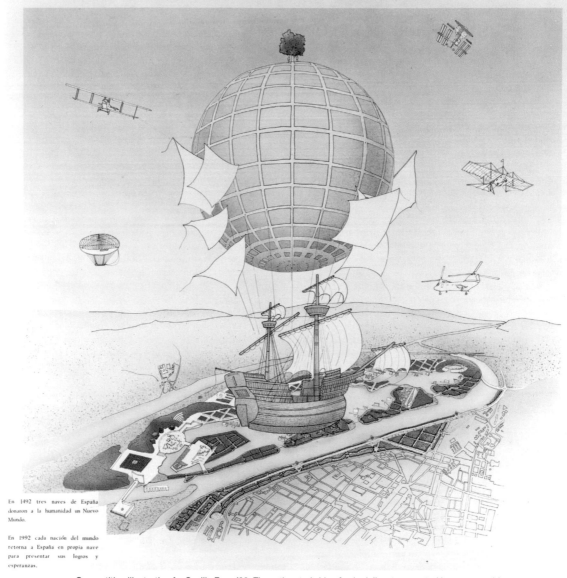

En 1492 tres naves de España donaron a la humanidad un Nuevo Mundo.

En 1992 cada nación del mundo retorna a España en propia nave para presentar sus logros y esperanzas.

Competition illustration for Seville Expo '92. The antiquated ship of colonialism transported by a new world order. "In 1992, every nation of the world returns to Spain in their own ship to present their hopes and achievements." Image courtesy Emilio Ambasz, Hon. FAIA. See "Landmarks in Post-Western Ecology" on page 126

SUSTAIN AND DEVELOP

We will feel mounting pressure to plunder the environ-
ment. We will have a crash program to build more nuclear
plants, strip-mine and burn more coal, and drill more
offshore wells than we will need if we begin to conserve
now. Inflation will soar, production will go down, people will
lose their jobs. Intense competition will build up among nations
and among the different regions within our own country.

If we fail to act soon, we will face an economic, social and
political crisis that will threaten our free institutions.

But we still have another choice. We can begin to prepare
right now. We can decide to act while there is time...[1]

It is 1977 not 2009 and Jimmy Carter is about to
reveal his new energy policy advocating conservation
methods and the invention of new renewable technologies. Resulting from the tumultuous period of global
economic re-balancing during the 1970s in which the
US had already suffered the indignity of the 1973
oil embargo — a protest by the Organization of Arab
Petroleum Exporting Countries against US military support for Israel in the Yom Kippur War — Carter realized
that the continued development of the US economy was
predicated on finding alternatives for its dependency
on oil and becoming more sustainable.

Thirty years on and our predicament is worse
rather than better. But the issue is still the same: how
to sustain and yet continue to develop? This paradox
remains the contentious issue blocking any form of
global agreement on how to facilitate a reduction of
carbon dioxide production and stem global climate
change. The US refused to sign the Kyoto Protocol in
1997 due to China's exclusion from the requirement to
reduce emissions as well as the fear that any reduction of their own would damage economic development.
Despite this, the Protocol's ratification in 2005 set up
a mechanism through which carbon could be traded to
assist developing countries in financing carbon-reducing
projects; in effect the excess of the developed world
would subsidize sustainable projects in developing
countries. The Protocol set out a clear mandate: that
the only way to persuade countries and businesses to
cut emissions was either through set targets or by
providing financial incentives.

The Stern Report of 2006 commissioned by the
British Chancellor of the Exchequer[2] presents the
economics of climate change as an issue that could
jeopardize the global economy. By financially evaluat-
ing climate change Stern argues that the cost to the
world economy would be 5% of global GDP per year every
year compared to an investment cost of 1% of global
GDP per year to reduce emissions to a controllable level.
In effect Stern inverted the problem; in order to
develop, one must sustain.

Both the Stern Report and the Kyoto Protocol
represent a strategic shift emphasizing the economic
imperative of climate change rather than the fear
factor of environmental Armageddon. The threat of imminent meteorological disaster, starvation, drought and

mass flooding do not seem to work. Only the likelihood of
financial demise seems to trigger governmental action.

The Kyoto Protocol is not without problems;
notably those that contributed to dissuading the US
from signing it in the first place: India and China have no
requirement to reduce emissions due to their status as
developing nations, even though China exceeded the US
to become the world's number one emitter in 2006. The
global recession of 2008 reinforced the fragility of
the global economic system while it stimulated promised
investment from China into sustainable infrastructural
projects and renewable energy. In this context if the
Communist Party of China decides to direct policy
towards environmental sustainability and structured
regulation a real and rapid reduction of emissions could
be feasible at a pace that is simply not possible through
the political processes of Western democracy. Current
indications are that China has no intention of reducing
emissions as part of the revised Protocol. This revision
will take place in December 2009 in Copenhagen as part
of the United Nations Climate Change Conference with
the aim of initiating a further framework beyond 2012
with the fundamental challenge to persuade the US to
sign and for China and India to agree to reductions.

China's rapidly growing new prosperity and enormous
population make it both the most active development
economy and the most acute ecological precipice on the
planet. There is perhaps no better place to feel this tension than in Dunhuang, an ancient oasis on the Silk Road
and site of the Buddhist enclave at Mogao Grotto, where
China has built its first municipal solar power plant and
largest wind power array. Since 2007, China has required
large power companies to derive 3% of their output from
renewable sources; projections are for China to produce
30,000 megawatts of power from renewable sources in
2010 — previously the 2020 target.[3] These extraordinary
achievements pale in comparison to the challenge of
providing for the power needs of the 720 million rural
citizens of China in the coming decade. Especially in
China's dry west, development often comes paired with
political agendas that can be as threatening to local
populations as the impending desertification they are
meant to abet. In majority Muslim Kashgar, the Central
Government's development plans call for razing up to
85% of the old city; their implementation comes amidst
rising unrest and ethnic strife.[4] Throughout China,
resistance to development can be seen from the sub-
sistence plots being tilled adjacent to new skyscrapers
to "nail houses" — private residences that refuse to
vacate for commercial development.

As China demonstrates, the practice of architecture and urbanism is entirely intertwined within
the quagmire of global, economic and political forces.
Working in architecture, landscape and urbanism today
means operating in the tension between development
and sustainability. Forms of practice have evolved that
not only respond to the question of sustainability
but propose new positions through which sustainable
strategies catalyze new forms of economic development
and vice versa.

This new practice holds that sustainability and
development are not mutually exclusive, but constantly
overlap and mingle. Their steady state is not as the

Nail houses resist development amid fields of rubble near the ancient city wall, Xi'an, China, March 2009

poor hybrid *sustainable development*—an expression that more often than not exposes the basest opportunism of both terms—but as independent and coextensive fields that together comprise the practice of architecture. Likewise, this practice recognizes that neither sustainability nor development contains a categorical imperative, or demands absolute obedience. The pursuit of either must be considered in a state of protracted poise relative to the other.

This volume of 306090 compiles approaches that are grappling with this problem through specific interventions; investigations on existing phenomena; theoretical positions and cultural responses. Some are serious, some more playful. *Sustain and Develop* is a global poll of urban and architectural actors, from China, US and Europe, on the cusp of a new global direction on climate and resource awareness. With a newly inaugurated US president advocating *Change* there is real optimism for a significant global agreement inciting a new era of architectural and urban strategies enabling development through sustainable invention.

We hope the contents of this volume will be superseded urgently and imminently.

—Joshua Bolchover and Jonathan D. Solomon, Editors

1. Jimmy Carter, "The President's Proposed Energy Policy." 18 April 1977. *Vital Speeches of the Day*, Vol. XXXXIII, No. 14, May 1, 1977, pp. 418–420
2. http://www.hm-treasury.gov.uk/d/CLOSED_SHORT_executive_summary.pdf
3. Bradsher, Keith. "Green Power Takes Root in the Chinese Desert," *New York Times*. January 2, 2009
4. Wines, Michael. "To Protect and Ancient City, China Moves to Raze It," *New York Times*. May 27, 2009

Preface: In the Briar Patch

To ask, How can one escape the market? is one of those questions whose principal virtue is one's pleasure in declaring it insoluble.
—Jacques Ranciere

Environmental ecologies and market economies have always been entwined; such that "sustain" and "develop" present not opposing but interdependent forces. If anything, the portrayal of these ideas as a zero sum game in which collusion or refusal are the only option is probably a mistake in thinking.

Ecologies, economies and polities are frequently theorized as if they had an elementary particle with extensive powers to organize. For Marxist analysis the elementary particle is labor. For some classic forms of economic analysis, it is utility. Some contemporary political economists have constructed arguments that reject these in favor of commodified power as the building block. The technocracy movement of the 1920s in the US promoted energy units. For cyberneticians, the particle was information. In contemporary theories of a digital gift economy, a utopia is spun around non-market, peer production. In territorial analysis of the globalizing world, realist, liberal, neoliberal or noopolitical theoreticians have insisted on parsing the "necessities of history" with everything from states to region states, to civilizations. Management culture aspires to universal rationalization through procedural standards. Environmental theories adhere to the atmospheric and economic chemistries of carbon. The Bouvard or Pécuchet in all of us is kept occupied with many such examples.

Theorizing the elementary particle, however mistaken, is, with its ready rewards and recognition, a durable strategy. The unified theory, as an all or nothing proposition, bumps off the previously popular elementary particle with resolute one-upsmanship. The elementary particle frequently encourages notions of recursion and self-organization yielding, for instance, an invisible hand, a Gaia or a homeostatic system. Indeed, steady-state conceptions of environmental and cybernetic ecologies have become paradigms for market economies in mutually reinforcing utopias. For some forms of activism, it may help to establish a realm of proper activity within which to declare not only non-conforming particles but enemies and innocents. For the most ambitious, the elementary particle has an added bonus: it is so annoyingly persuaded, and the ground around it so littered with contradictory evidence that it is both attractive and easy to refute and so garners much attention.

Those for whom the testbed is space can frequently only see a blizzard of elementary particles in collision at every scale. Many things that are most easily theorized as virtual packets are, in fact, very heavy, spread out over square miles of development and accompanied by technological remainders or obdurate politics. Administrative layers are lumpy and braided with no clear hierarchy, and while their accretion is theorized to blur state boundaries, those entities remain crisp and even multiplied by various proxies. The utopia of digital non-market, peer production meets political and infrastructural obstacles that prevent it from reaching some of the most populous areas of the world. The enclosures that the profession regards as formal objects have become active forms—physical, spatial medias and technologies moving around the world as information.

Despite the lure of the elementary particle, the space of mismatched particles is, for the sly practitioner, a good briar patch. There will always be designers who are attracted to the lure of unified theories, who want to make "pictures" of networks and who want to wire every bird and leaf to every tree. In this sense, "sustain," if it means preserve, would be synonymous with death, not life. The greater political power naturally lies not in fixing organizations but operating in the mongrel space between them and recognizing attributes of how they change—not knowing what they are but what they are doing and what object forms and active forms they need to fuel their change. Unlike many designers who are trying to devise the single most soulful expression of themselves, most entrepreneurial players in most economies or ecologies selfishly survive by figuring out how to keep the desires of others continually changing and ready to absorb more products, more life and more information. While the atmospheric and biological imperatives of contemporary environmental thinking might seem to suggest interest in land or landschaft, the last thing that an inventor wants is a conventional architectural

Image courtesy Ralph Hockens

site. They rather want their forms to circulate, propagate and travel beyond to multiple sites. While the utopian theorist must be allowed to remain right, the resourceful practitioner, flush with the abundances of the briar patch, might become an unexpected and powerful cohort.

The essays collected in this volume seem to be offered in this spirit.

Keller Easterling *is an architect and writer from New York City. Her book,* Enduring Innocence: Global Architecture and its Political Masquerades *(MIT, 2005) researches familiar spatial products that have landed in difficult or hyperbolic political situations around the world. A previous book* Organization Space: Landscapes, Highways and Houses in America *applies network theory to a discussion of American infrastructure and development formats. A forthcoming book,* Extrastatecraft, *examines global infrastructure networks as a medium of polity.*

William A. Garnett, Foundation and Slabs, *Lakewood, California, 1950. Gelatin silver print, 18.9 x 23.8 cm. The J. Paul Getty Museum, Los Angeles, © Estate of William A. Garnett*

William A. Garnett, Finished Housing, *Lakewood, California, 1950. The J. Paul Getty Museum, Los Angeles, © Estate of William A. Garnett*

CUFF, Dana and DAHL, Per-Johan

Rx for the R1: Sustaining the Neighborhood

Ceci tuera cela. Is Zoning Terminally Ill?

Sustainable urban development is often paradoxically equated with new towns, be they in China or Kansas.[1] In large part, this is because retrofitting existing cities is so much more complicated, and takes place incrementally and without an overall plan. Perhaps more than any other ideological orientation toward urbanism, sustainability requires comprehensive coordination. Viable suggestions for updated practices have been made in the realm of urban planning, such as Mark Jarzombek's rethinking the masterplan.[2] For architects, however, sustainability has not been particularly fertile ground for design. Instead, it is a victim of its own popularity—the bandwagon that developers and cities alike jump on to enhance their appeal. Chicago Mayor Daley's insistence that Chicago become America's greenest city has been successful as an urban identity brand, but thus far the impact on design or even livability is negligible.

If sustainable building and development has benefited little from architecture, perhaps we have focused debate on the wrong target. Just like New Urbanism found its footing in new suburban development, ignoring the fact that this strategy fundamentally contradicts its basic intentions, most sustainable development is a form of new suburban construction with some environmental pretense intended to mask the fact that it is residential expansion itself that prevents both urbanity and sustainability. Instead, the focus on sustainability should be put on reclamation in existing urban areas.

Similar observations were made in 2004 when *The New Yorker* claimed that Manhattan was the greenest place in America.[3] Following New Urbanism, the New Suburban Greenism is already facing the same fate: didactic and superficial imagery, oversimplification, developer-appeal and rejection by architectural intelligentsia. It is no coincidence that after its total destruction by a tornado, Greensburg, Kansas is rebuilding itself as a sustainable city cloaked in New Urbanist neo-historicism. The convergence of the two trajectories is occurring because neither effectively challenges the root of the problem. To do this, we must kill the elephant in the room: zoning, and most particularly, the R1.

Zoning as ideology and practice not only stands in the way of sustainable development, but prevents the next era of urbanization in which architectural approaches to this challenge are essential. Looking at this claim through the eyes of the architect, sustainability powers the movement that will unleash architecture's ability to operate effectively within contemporary urban conditions. To begin, we must demonstrate that zoning must die. As we shall see, New York may have been zoning's birthplace, but Los Angeles will be its graveyard.

Edward M. Bassett, called the father of modern zoning, was a lawyer and public servant at the turn of the century in New York City. Bassett describes zoning as a *movement* that would regulate the chaotic growth of cities occurring across the US.[4] Zoning responded to the explosion of speculative building by the newly emerging real estate industry, and capitalized upon the advancements of health advocates in the late 19th century city, whereby tenement regulation met with broad popular support because people were convinced that unhealthy living quarters spawned epidemics that knew no geographic bounds.[5] Thus, public interest intersected with the plight of a segment of the population to create political consensus to improve substandard building conditions. In New York, early zoning goals included stemming the exodus to the suburbs by wealthy households by preventing noxious conditions of adjacency that might endanger the population. As Bassett argued, "zoning must be done with relation to the public health, safety, morals and general welfare. If it is done arbitrarily or by whim or for aesthetics or for purely sentimental purposes or with unjust discrimination, the courts will not uphold it."[6]

Nevertheless, Bassett's main contribution to the history of urbanization was to be made in 1916 when he wrote New York's comprehensive regulatory framework, the first in the US. This ordinance, which marks the birth of modern zoning in the US, describes the three overlapping maps that would guide development toward the public interest: one for height districts, one for lot coverage or what is now known as F.A.R., and the last for land use. The concept of zoning implies a concern for social equality and rights, or as Secretary Hoover's national Advisory Committee on Zoning explains in 1926: "Zoning gives anyone who lives or does business in a community a chance for the reasonable enjoyment of his rights. At the same time it protects him from unreasonable injury by neighbors who would seek private gain at his expense."[7] The intentions shaping New York's zoning resolution were not only contextualized in a concern for public good. On the contrary a significant part of the ordinance was based on accommodating the private interests of a very small part of the New York population, and doing so by means of exclusion.

The way public interest is embedded in New York zoning can be unpacked by consulting the tools of architectural representation used to explain the law: the section and the plan. Each encodes a different and contradictory bias about the city. When looking at the sectional implications of the ordinance, the concern for public interest is apparent. Due to the famous setback codes embedded in the law, height and bulk restrictions "dictated that after a fixed vertical height, a building had to be stepped back as it rose in accordance with a designated angle drawn from the center of the street."[8] A measure of light and air was preserved in the city's canyons, which addressed not only public health concerns but provided a means of urban beautification implicitly advocated by the architects who helped to frame the legislation. Thus, an early form of sustainability was laid out by law: future development in cities with zoning would conform to regulations that sustained access to light and air, property values, and indirectly, a particular population.

So much for section, but what about the urban plan? In accordance with the setback codes, the zoning law divided the city into districts regulated by use. These districts segregated Manhattan by functions that were outlined in a plan. Operating on the premises of land use control they were worked out in tandem by private developers and city government in order to protect property values largely by means of social exclusion. The objective of the plan was the opposite of the section since it can be argued that strict functional segregation ran against the public grain.

Utilizing functional segregation for exclusionary purposes, particularly social segregation, was a basic motive of zoning.[9] During the 19th century builders throughout the US had utilized restrictive covenants, or deed restrictions, as a form of land-use control to attract an affluent clientele to new developments as well as to resist incursions by immigrants and the poor. As covenants usually stay with the land, individual owners signed their deeds hoping to secure investments by "limit[ing] development around their homes." Restrictive covenants were introduced to New York City just before the turn of the 19th century when wealthy citizens began to secure their neighborhoods as elite residential areas. The middle and upper class landowners of Fifth Avenue proactively applied covenants "for controlling the use of property… and to develop stable residential enclaves."[10] Prior to the establishment of the 1916 zoning ordinance, covenants secured the exclusiveness of Fifth Avenue by controlling use and reducing social and behavioral diversity.

The 1916 zoning law reflected the will and practices of the Fifth Avenue Association (FAA). Founded in 1907 the group's goal was to preserve Fifth Avenue as an elite commercial and residential area. "To do so, the association undertook an enormous range of activities including legislative advocacy, policing the streets, awarding architectural honors and placing traffic lights." But with the influx of manufacturing, wealthy families of Fifth Avenue found restrictive covenants too weak "to achieve the spatial security they once enjoyed."[11] In their quest for more potent land-use regulations, zoning held magnetic appeal as it entailed enforcement via police power. And so, the FAA's goals were mapped into the restrictive urban land-use plans.

By dissecting the 1916 ordinance, urban regulations can be understood from a slightly different perspective. Regulations dictate urban development through the dual means of code and zone, where the code controls the setbacks and the zone regulates land use through functional segregation. However the two are lumped under the same term, namely zoning.

Zoning would slowly but effectively convert a heterogeneous urban fabric of land uses and people into the geography of enclaves that characterize the contemporary city and its surroundings. From Jane Jacobs forward, critics have argued that zoning is a blunt tool for shaping the city, but that tool has been sharpened over the past century. Special use districts, overlay zones, historic districts, form-based zoning, enterprise zones and

business improvement districts, are all indications that Bassett's movement grew like an urban virus that was capable of mutating to respond to specific geographic conditions and interests. These myriad sub-zones are patches that attempt to cover over the holes zoning creates by treating the city as an abstract canvas.[12]

The concept of zoning as it originally developed in New York was reconfigured in postwar American suburbanization. In the American suburb, the relationship between code and zone was transformed in concurrence with the decreasing F.A.R. of single-family housing developments. The code, invented as a section in New York City to balance public and private interests by securing light and air circulation, became a plan in suburbia regulating land use favoring the private interests of the American Dream. Rotated from vertical to horizontal, the code was transformed from urban to suburban reinforcing control over functional segregation. Hence in suburbia the code became an amplifier of the zone. This homogenization of zoning explicitly served to preserve the low density character of sprawl, increasing the rigidity of the R1's single-family neighborhoods.

R1 Memories

New York and Boston may have pioneered comprehensive zoning, but in 1908, Los Angeles passed the Residence District Ordinance, becoming the first city to divide itself into residential and non-residential districts, and then to oust pre-existing uses that did not conform within the residential zone.[13] The "single family-only" zone or R1 as a legal entity, was born in Los Angeles. LA's R1 has extended far beyond that original district, into the sprawl of subdivisions, extreme commutes, congested freeways, and a continuous landscape of single-family homes that stretches from the Mexican border north to Santa Barbara.

Zoning was conceived as a dynamic instrument, but its fundamental skeleton has resisted change, particularly when it comes to residential districts. The early first-ring single-use residential zones have been surrounded by further urban growth, extended by what urban historian Dolores Hayden has called "sit-com suburbs" of the 1950s and 1960s that offered a seeming haven from urban ills. These too have been exceeded by exurban tracts built since the 1980s that are more remote, affordable and lifestyle-oriented. Though municipalities generally have numerous residential designations differentiating density or number of dwelling units per acre, the dominant residential zone is the R1, typically known as the single-family zone. The R1 is land zoned for one residential structure per parcel, thus producing a landscape of detached pavilions surrounded by their own property. The R1 has come to stand for suburban development.

Three interrelated factors insist that we revisit what is euphemistically known in the States as the R1. The first is a growing complex of environmental issues that implicate the suburbs; the second is the shrinking pool of large tracts of available land in major metropolitan areas; and the third is the real estate debacle that began to unfold in 2007 with the subprime mortgage crisis, followed by secondary and tertiary effects with no end yet in sight. The interconnectedness of these factors is

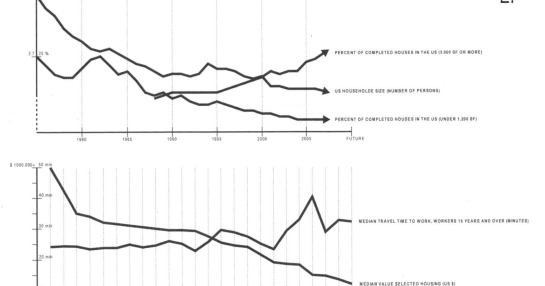

Top: Household size vs Housing size, US Census, 2007; Bottom: Median Travel Time to Work vs Median Housing Value, US Census, 2005

evident in new critiques of exurban R1 tracts. As *New York Times* opinion writer and economist Paul Krugman put it in May of 2008: "And in the face of rising oil prices, which have left many Americans stranded in suburbia— utterly dependent on their cars, yet having a hard time affording gas—it's starting to look as if Berlin [a city of four- or five-story apartment buildings with easy access to public transit and plenty of local shopping] had the better idea."[14]

In his book *Sprawl*, Robert Bruegmann argues that suburban growth has been with us since the beginning of cities, as the natural geography of expansion.[15] A recent change in that pattern however is an indicator that there is trouble in the R1: residential development at the urban fringe has grown denser. At the same time, demand for housing in the traditional (and according to some, non-existent) urban core is rising. Moreover, all kinds of ad hoc housing patterns have arisen in the R1 as means to cope with the high cost of housing, from garage housing and illegal backyard units, to doubling up. The further out into the exurban landscape, the lower house prices are likely to be, yet the longer the commute. If for some reason you find yourself driving out of Los Angeles at 4am on any weekday, you will be greeted by an eerie sight: a continuous river of headlights coming into town. From the north, for example, more than 20,000 residents of Antelope Valley stream 65 miles into Los Angeles every morning and return every evening. They leave early to minimize the commute time; at 4am the drive might take just over an hour and a half, but by 7am it can double. These drivers are among America's 3.4 million "extreme

commuters"—workers who travel 90 minutes or more each way to get to work. The Los Angeles region has two of the top five extreme commute areas—Riverside and Los Angeles.[16] Even with Los Angeles's postmodern geography of multiple city centers, with no center governing the hinterlands, research indicates that the R1 is finished. The most damning factors are environmental: we're running out of water, land, and oil.[17]

Long before the data showed sprawl had "hit the wall," Reyner Banham wrote that LA's deep obsession with a dreamy single-family house was its Id. He interpreted the dingbat, a four- to eight-unit stripped-down apartment building on a single-family lot, as a symbol of disruption in the Plains of Id. "The dingbat, even more than the occasional tower blocks below Hollywood or along Wilshire, is the true symptom of Los Angeles' urban Id trying to cope with the unprecedented appearance of residential densities too high to be subsumed within the illusions of homestead living."[18]

Banham should have seen Pacoima. Or any of a number of first ring suburbs in Los Angeles that have become a cafeteria of shadow housing options, largely because there is no enforcement of zoning or other building regulations. Google Earth images reveal a wealth of backyard activity on lots large enough to make room for the extra units crowding behind a modest house at the street. None of these units is legal because this—like Beverly Hills and Malibu, yet unlike them in nearly every other way—is the R1.

All across the LA basin, the anger that once characterized conversations about traffic congestion has been

Chamberlain Street, Pacoima, 2008

displaced by discussions of density. As the *LA Times* put it, "The density wars in Los Angeles are heating up."[19] Homeowner associations are fighting the construction of more housing in their neighborhoods, while city officials seek ways to accommodate a population that is expected to increase by 6 million, or two Chicagos, by the year 2020. A number of bills have moved successfully through the state legislature that would alter current residential zoning throughout California, but each has met local resistance. Most recently, the state's Republican governor signed into law an anti-sprawl bill that is the first in the nation to link land-use planning with greenhouse gas reductions.[20] To sustain the state's growth, the bill requires regions to set emissions targets and creates incentives for new development that is compact, dense and near transit.

None of the new laws insures the quality of the development, nor sets design-related objectives. While a number of architects are experimenting with regulations as a source of creative design solutions, tackling zoning policy has not proven a productive avenue.[21] If it is difficult to imagine how such goals might be established, the case of Pacoima offers one example. *cityLAB*, a thinktank at UCLA,[22] is tackling a number of problems confronting the post-suburban city in collaboration with architectural practitioners, city planners, developers, local politicians and community activists, and Pacoima is the principle site for rethinking the R1.

10K – Pacoima

Part of the city of Los Angeles, Pacoima sits in northeast San Fernando Valley. Eighty-five percent of its 100,000 residents are Latino, a third of the population is under the age of 18, and nearly 20 percent have incomes below the poverty level. High real estate prices and population pressures have led to a shortage of affordable housing. The majority of Pacoima is zoned R1, but that says nothing about how people in the neighborhood live. Although 80 percent of the 22,000 units of housing in Pacoima are

single-family dwellings, at least one fifth of the residents live in shadow housing—garages, rooms rented in single-family houses, or illegal units.

Like all communities, there are infill sites scattered throughout Pacoima. However, unique to this community, there are over a thousand extra-long single-family lots of more than 10,000 square feet (nearly twice the size of an average Los Angeles residential lot, and hence the "10K" moniker). Of these, a full 95 percent currently have illegal units constructed in the backyard. It is on the remaining 5 percent that *cityLAB* is modeling sustainable, community-responsive, well-designed infill development.[23]

After much study, design and community interaction, a group of students and architects working under the guidance of *cityLAB* Director Dana Cuff have invented a feasible way to provide for-sale, workforce infill housing in the backyards of existing residential sites.[24] *cityLAB* is constructing design, development and finance strategies for the 10K sites that will result in policy recommendations to revise existing approval processes and zoning policies to support quality infill development; the design of three green housing models to serve as templates for development; and collaboratively-shaped development scenarios for typical sites. *cityLAB*'s ultimate goal is to launch a demonstration project that will be constructed in Pacoima, utilizing the design templates and built by a local non-profit developer.

In this scenario, sustainability and community acceptance are working objectives as well as effective development restrictions. The building design invention extends beyond the granny flat, to a prototype that can be implemented on a range of sites, in a range of combinations. The neighborhood scale intervention concerns the incremental implementation of units that can respond to the emergent conditions. The housing templates will receive pre-approval from permitting agencies in the city (currently 12 different agencies must review such housing plans), not only creating cost efficiencies but insuring that infill units are well-designed. Developers who use the pre-approved templates reduce their soft costs

10K corner site at Pala Avenue, 2008

Backyard, Pacoima, 2008

substantially, while avoiding political and entitlement complications. Moreover, they receive the equivalent of a density bonus for building affordable, for-sale units. Working with both lawyers and housing developers, along with community representatives, *cityLAB* is inventing a new system of project delivery that ensures community control over incremental growth. Our workshops in Pacoima indicate that residents want both environmental benefits and contemporary design.

The Pacoima project is expected to become a new policy as well as a built demonstration, which could happen as early as 2010 if federal foreclosure stabilization funds become available. Nevertheless, it already successfully challenges the status quo. With community participation, design innovation, city planning cooperation and physical opportunities for infill, the R1 can be modified in ways that will improve neighborhood quality of life. Indeed, a study of all California cities found residents of every race and every income level willing to live at higher densities provided they can have the housing and services they need. This same research found an abundance of infill sites across California's urban areas, and the data does not count most of the underutilized backyard space.[25] While it is unreasonable to generalize these findings to major urban areas like New York, Boston, or Chicago, there is every reason to imagine that denser neighborhoods could be created by utilizing infill strategies in postwar sprawl throughout the US and beyond. To do so will mean rethinking the R1.

cityLAB's Pacoima-10K project develops innovative, environmentally sensitive and affordable housing models that show the benefits of rethinking community planning from an architectural perspective. It revises those zoning practices that reflect our region's sprawling past for the needs of and opportunities within each of our unique communities. Pacoima-10K is a demonstration that the types of infill sites we'll find in cities are small and unconventional. A blanket land use or F.A.R. strategy is not helpful, whereas more tightly conceived site typologies and solutions encourage fitting growth to existing conditions. This strategy sits squarely between the architecture and planning disciplines, requiring new ideological frameworks that incorporate temporal evolution, that operate at scales between buildings and cities, and that acknowledge a public component (like affordability or sustainability) within private development.

Conclusion

There are good green reasons for infilling the R1 in the contemporary city. First, there are plenty of infill sites available if we proceed creatively, and there are few large tracts of open land remaining in urban areas. Building into cities rather than beyond them saves farmland as well as natural preserves. Second, detached dwellings are being built on smaller sites than in earlier eras without losing the suburban benefits. More dwelling units per acre means lower carbon footprints, densities that promote more adequate services and lower housing costs (by lowering the amount of land attached to each house). Increased densities afford cities the opportunity to require sustainability practices. The intricacies of addressing

the existing R1's deficiencies demand that architecture be brought to bear if planning goals are to be achieved. Surgical interventions at disparate urban sites will be best accomplished by designers who can customize the more standard solutions of builders or planners.

Undoing the R1 is the most complicated part of reclaiming the city from the pathology of zoning. It will not be done all at once, but it will begin in the first ring suburbs and those that have already undermined the prescriptions of R1, through variances, illegal building activity, non-conforming use and informal adjustments. Following that lead, site specific opportunism can move in where zoning failed. The motivation for this transformation will not be the creation of more affordable housing, though the current mortgage crisis could fuel the movement. Instead, perceived risks of change can be quelled by sustainability's goals, both systemic (like reducing global warming) and immediate (like reducing household energy costs). The catchword "density" can acquire implications for both individual and social goods, as is already demonstrated by recent shifts in housing preferences. For the first time in history, more than half the world's population lives in urban areas, and the trend of depopulation in existing urban centers is reversing.

It is important that we not confuse the eradication of R1 with other discredited neo-liberal calls for deregulation. Any city contextualized in the structures of economic accumulation will always be regulated, or as Lawrence Lessig puts it "changes that make commerce possible are also changes that will make regulation easy."[26] Indeed regulations are inherent in urbanization and the failure of zoning cannot be mended simply by abandoning the balance between public and private interests, which to a certain degree is sustained by regulations. Nevertheless, zoning as it has developed during the 20th century has failed and its paralyzed condition requires a radical re-thinking of the codes inherent in its comatose corpus. Indeed the re-coding of contemporary urbanism requires a new mode of flexibility capable of supporting architectural experimentation as well as to reconstitute the outmoded premises of R1, such as the preservation of functional segregation, the maintenance of low density urbanism and the deliberate advocacy for social homogeneity.

The 10K project in Pacoima is but one example of the many site-specific experiments that must be undertaken if we are to develop solutions after zoning. It is indicative of the fact that these experiments will need to be complicated formulae crossing professional boundaries. They will be characterized by opportunism that responds to local ecologies, economies and politics. The advance of R1-busting experiments depends on the momentum that sustainable development provides, and the creativity that architects bring to design.

References

1. For two very different examples, see the plans for eco-cities Dongtan in China and Greensburg, Kansas
2. Jarzombek, Mark. A Green Masterplan Is Still a Masterplan, in Urban Transformation, edited by Ilka and Andreas Ruby, p. 22-29. Berlin: Ruby Press, 2008
3. Owen, David. "Green Manhattan: Why New York is the Greenest

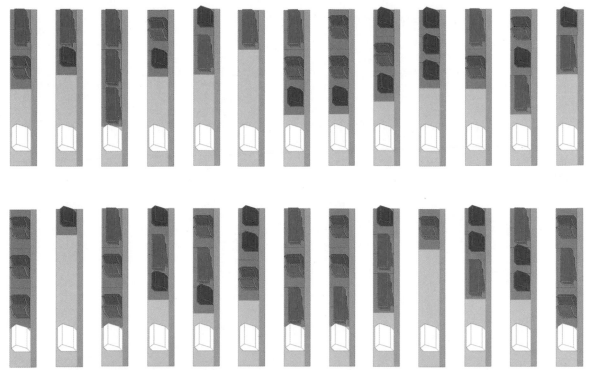

Three housing types and 64 variations

Incremental densification of a Pacolma block

10K site and three housing types

City in America". The New Yorker. *10.18.04.* Popular Science, *however, ranked New York 20th among America's greenest cities. Svoboda, Elizabeth. "America's 50 Greenest Cities."* Popular Science. *2.8.08. Popsci.com*

4. The first comprehensive zoning was in Boston, where a building height limit of 125 feet was enacted in 1892 and upheld by the US Supreme Court in 1909. Subsequent modifications to the blanket building height set limits for different areas in the city (Beacon Hill and Copley Square were limited to 100 feet) and uses (residential buildings were limited to 80 ft). See Murray Bassett, Edward. Zoning. *New York: National Municipal League, 1932, p. 9*

5. Cuff, Dana. The Provisional City, *MIT Press 2000*

6. Murray Bassett, Edward. Zoning. *New York: National Municipal League, 1932, p. 8*

7. A Zoning Primer by the Advisory Committee on Zoning. Department of Commerce. *Washington, 1926, p. 1*

8. Willis, Carol. "Zoning and Zeitgeist: The Skyscraper City in the 1920s," The Journal of the Society of Architectural Historians, *vol. 45, no. 1, March 1986, p. 48*

9. In his handbook, Bassett says "In the great cities especially this danger of invasion of hurtful uses drove well-to-do families out of the city, where in suburban villages they could to a greater extent obtain protected surroundings. Citizens whose financial ability and public enterprise made them most helpful within the city limits were the very ones that would often be tempted to remove their families outside of the city." Hurtful uses included public stables and garages, factories, poorly-built houses and "high apartment houses." Murray Bassett, Edward. Zoning. *New York: National Municipal League, 1932, p. 4. For an analysis of zoning practices through case studies, see Babcock, Richard F. and Siemon, Charles L.* The Zoning Game Revisited. *Boston: Oelgeschlager, Gunn and Hain, 1990*

10. Page, Max. The Creative Destruction of Manhattan. *Chicago: University of Chicago Press, 1999, p. 49*

11. Ibid, p. 53; p. 52

12. For a critical examination of such processes of abstraction, see Scott, James. Seeing Like a State. *New Haven: Yale University Press, 1999*

13. The establishment of single-use districts in Los Angeles evolved over several decades, marked by the first ordinance in 1904 that created three residential districts, followed in 1908 by an expansion of residential districts along with the establishment of industrial districts in 1909 (see map). Not until 1921 did LA adopt real comprehensive zoning. The residential zone in LA led to a lawsuit with a brickyard owner, called Hadacheck v. Sebastian (1915). The case went all the way to the US Supreme Court, and established the constitutionality of retroactive restrictive zoning. The other primary decision, Village of Euclid v. Ambler Realty (1926), gave modern practices the name Euclidean zoning. See Bassett. Zoning. p. 9. Kolnick, Kathy A. "Order before Zoning: Land Use Regulation in Los Angeles 1880-1915," Ph.D. diss., University of Southern California, 2008

14. Krugman, Paul. "Stranded in Suburbia," New York Times, May 19, 2008, p. 25

15. Bruegmann, Robert. Sprawl: A Compact History. Chicago: University of Chicago Press, 2005

16. Howlett, Debbie and P. Overberg, "Think your commute is tough?" USA Today, 11.29.04, http://www.usatoday.com/news/nation/2004-11-29-commute_x.htm

17. See Southern California Studies Center and the Brookings Institution Center on Urban and Metropolitan Policy. Sprawl Hits the Wall. University of Southern California, 2001, p. 57

18. Banham, Reyner. Los Angeles: The Architecture of Four Ecologies. Berkeley: University of California Press, 1971, p. 159

19. Haefele, Marc B. "L.A.'s Anti-Density Warrior." LA Times, April 6, 2008. http://www.latimes.com/news/opinion/sunday/commentary/la-op-haefele6apr06,0,1117979.story

20. SB 1818, passed in 2005, grants density bonuses of 35 percent if some units are priced for low or moderate income residents. Second unit or granny flat laws AB 1866 (2003) and AB 2702 (2004) allow second units in residential zones including the R1 without additional requirements, but local governments have found means to block implementation. Most recently, SB 375, the "anti-sprawl bill" was signed into law in 2008, that revises land-use policy in California to create more compact residential development near transit in order to reduce greenhouse-gas emissions. See Yamamura, Kevin. "Governor Signs Anti-Sprawl Bill." The Sacramento Bee, p.1A, October 1, 2008. http://www.sacbee.com/111/story/1278949.html

21. A good example of architecture experimenting with regulations as a creative design solution can be found at 497 Greenwich Street in New York, an 11-story residential building by Archi-Techtonics, 2004. The significant glass façade facing Greenwich Street is described by designer Winka Dubbeldam as a reinterpretation of the New York regulatory system. Dubbeldam explains that the façade "integrates the strict building setback codes into a new, vertical landscape that folds and twists as it ascends affording differing vistas to each interior." See the website: Greenwich Street [Project], 2002, http://www.greenwichstreetproject.com/index.html

22. cityLAB is an innovative new model for bridging several classic divides: between design and research, between town and gown, between academia and practice. Founded by Dana Cuff with the mandate to bring together design and research to forge experimental proposals for the emerging metropolis, it is supported by private donations and research grants. Cuff, co-director Roger Sherman, and a team of graduate students including Per-Johan Dahl, initiate projects that will contribute to urban theory, advance architectural practices, and form productive collaborations with all arms of the building industry. Housed in UCLA's Department of Architecture and Urban Design, cityLAB is an important channel for bringing real world issues into architectural education, starting with Los Angeles as its focus.

23. cityLAB restricts its infill project in Pacoima to properties where no current resident will be displaced. Aerial and field surveys indicate that of the 1021 10K-XL lots, 54 contain vacant land on 50 percent or more of the lot. With current entitlements, 162 new dwelling units could be built. According to our housing studies, the lots could accept 250 units while still upholding community and sustainability goals, but this would require regulatory changes to current zoning.

24. The multi-disciplinary project team includes two community organizations, Pacoima Beautiful and ICON, senior staff from the LA Department of City Planning, the CRA, for-profit and non-profit developers, a land use lawyer, and staff and graduate student researchers at UCLA's cityLAB. Co-author Per-Johan Dahl has been a leader of the 10K student team since its inception.

25. Landis, John, H. Hood, and C. Amado. "The Future of Infill Housing in California." Frameworks. Berkeley: University of California, Spring 2006, p. 14-21

26. Lessig, Lawrence. Code: And Other Laws of Cyberspace. New York: Basic Books, 1999, p.30

Dana Cuff is Professor of Architecture and Urban Design, and of Urban Planning, at the University of California, Los Angeles. She received her Ph.D. in Architecture from Berkeley, and since then has published and lectured widely about modern American urbanism, the architectural profession, contentious planning debates, affordable housing and spatially embedded computing. In 2006, Cuff founded cityLAB, a thinktank she directs to conduct design and research about architecture in the contemporary metropolis. Dana Cuff has written several books, including Architects' People (with W.R. Ellis; 1989), Architecture: The Story of Practice (1989), and The Provisional City (2000). A forthcoming text on new urban form and theory will be published in 2010 by Princeton Architectural Press.

Per-Johan Dahl has received degrees in Architecture from Lund Institute of Technology and University of Texas at Arlington, and in Engineering from Blekinge Institute of Technology. He worked for Abelardo Gonzalez from 1999 to 2007, and with his own practice since then. He was visiting lecturer and teacher at Lund Institute of Technology Architecture Department 1999-2007, and has been collaborating with RIEA.ch since 2000. He joined the AKAD directed research project "Los Angeles Islands" in 2003 and attended the Doctoral Program at UCLA Department of Architecture and Urban Design in 2007. He has been working with cityLAB since 2007. He has been exhibited in various museums and galleries in Sweden and Denmark.

cityLAB is a thinktank based in UCLA's Department of Architecture and Urban Design charged with exploring the challenges facing the 21st-century metropolis through research and design. Founded in 2006 by its director, Dana Cuff, cityLAB has three initiatives: the post-suburban city, rethinking green and urban sensing. Cuff, co-director Roger Sherman, UCLA faculty, students and Los Angeles area leaders collaborate on problems that hold lessons beyond the specific project at hand. cityLAB is funded primarily through private donations and research grants. For more information, visit www.cityLAB.aud.ucla.edu

Pacoima 10K was initiated by cityLAB in 2007, receiving funding from UCLA's Center for Community Partnerships for a two-year research project that will be completed in 2010. The team is headed by Dana Cuff, with Tim Higgins and Bianca Siegl as associate directors. Contributing UCLA Architecture students include Per-Johan Dahl and Brigid McManama as project leaders, and Rosalio Arellanes, Sergio Miguel Figueiredo, Maria Gomez, and Amelia Wong, with web design by Richard Caceres. An extensive array of local leaders have participated in the project, with special acknowledgment to Jane Blumenfeld of the LA City Planning Department, Nury Martinez of Pacoima Beautiful and Veronica Padilla of ICON. The concepts developed in Pacoima have recently been applied to other neighborhoods in Los Angeles, to determine the vitality of the model, and to take advantage of political will that various Council Members express.

MAHER, Dennis

Towards Un-Building: Sustainable Architecture as Social Enterprise

For three days in November, 2008, a group of 140 activists, community organizers, politicians, architects, planners, artists, entrepreneurs and dedicated volunteers gathered in the city of Buffalo, NY in order to jointly address issues surrounding vacant property management, building de-construction, and the regeneration of blighted neighborhoods. The occasion for this union was the Great Lakes Building ReUse conference, a regional event that sought to creatively confront problems facing former industrial centers of the northeastern United States.

What was fascinating and perhaps most significant about this gathering and its agenda was that, while wholly concerned with the fate of the physical environment, not one session of the conference was focused upon the design or construction of buildings. If there was a common thread which drew the diverse group of attendees together, it was the premise of *un-building* as a viable means of *re-building* both the frayed urban fabric of the struggling post-industrial city and its distressed communities.

Co-sponsored jointly by agencies specializing in material recovery, The Building Materials Re-Use Association and the Buffalo-based social enterprise group Buffalo ReUse, the conference overwhelmingly prioritized the re-use and transformation of existing resources as the basis of business models, strategic governmental policy, public art projects, modes of civic engagement and community development initiatives. Indeed, one of the major themes of the three-day conference was to share knowledge of how buildings may be taken apart, as opposed to how they might be made. As a sustainable alternative to demolition, the process of building deconstruction was at the center of the development dialog in Buffalo.

With no lack of irony, just as the Great Lakes Building ReUse Conference was getting underway, an article focusing upon Buffalo architecture was featured prominently in the *New York Times*.[1] The article, entitled "Saving Buffalo's Untold Beauty," by Nicolai Ouroussoff, firmly situates the origins of Buffalo's rich architectural legacy within an experimental context, providing a thorough analysis of the city's modernist past. It also discusses the problems of preservation and development in a city whose poverty rate is the second highest of any large city in the US.[2] Ouroussoff examines the work being done by activists in order to restore and re-inhabit many distressed areas and rightly cites the actions of local preservation groups to safeguard much of Buffalo's housing stock, as well as to protect gems such as H.H. Richardson's Buffalo State Hospital. Ouroussoff ultimately argues that a context so rich in historical experimentation deserves a revival of those tendencies. While it is unquestionable that the design and construction of contemporary architecture in Buffalo is meager compared to historical precedents, a more nuanced understanding of the local environment would suggest that a progressive architecture has already arrived in the city. This is not an architecture of stand alone new buildings, signature structures, or high profile commissions. The new progressive architecture in Buffalo is so subtle as to be almost imperceptible, an architecture centered on frugality, deconstruction, re-use, and on the networks created among aligned communal partners. In a city of roughly 16,000 vacant properties, the social aspirations of architectural production are a fundamentally different problem than in any thriving, economically advantaged city. With an abundance of derelict buildings and an infrastructure built for a population twice its current size, a city such as Buffalo requires that the goals and practices of new architecture be fundamentally re-thought. Within this context, progressive architectural responses need not emerge through the production of new buildings, but through persistent efforts to transform the least desirable of urban features into unique opportunities. Reconsidered as potential assets, features such as emptiness, absence, decay and neglect might recast the city as a laboratory for experimentation, a city whose raw and rough environment is facilitating strategies of informal communal action and enabling innovative, sustainable results.

What was not explicitly stated but was nevertheless implied by the Re-Use conference was that, in struggling Great Lakes cities such as Buffalo, the design and production of buildings is a far less important determinate of the fate of the physical environment than are other related social arts: those of strengthening communities and of re-using, adapting and re-purposing while addressing the persistent presence of derelict structures and vacant land. A city that has seen relatively few new buildings in the recent past, Buffalo's current new building efforts do not immediately confer status as a particularly progressive locale for the production of new architecture. It is not in conventional architecture offices, nor through traditional, professional practice, nor even through the act of building that the city's progressive tendencies are best defined. Instead, innovative forms of urban development are taking shape through a loosely knit alliance of neighborhood housing activists, building deconstruction specialists, community gardeners, non-profit agencies, sustainable housing co-operatives, urban farmers and concerned citizens. This evolution is not marked by the production of new cutting-edge buildings, but by transforming existing resources through an economy of means.

Deconstructing Home(s)

One organization that is shaping this quiet revolution in Buffalo is the grassroots social enterprise group, Buffalo ReUse. With operations that center on building deconstruction (the sustainable dismantling of derelict buildings as an alternative to demolition), Buffalo ReUse is steadily garnering attention for its efforts to systematically dismantle dilapidated structures and to salvage and re-sell usable materials. By extracting architectural resources from a rapidly deteriorating inner core, this urban mining operation diverted over 150 tons of material from the landfill in 2007, its first full year of work. The organization's mission statement elaborates upon its aims: "The potential of this program is achieved through the development of a social business model for building deconstruction that facilitates the reclamation of quality building materials, preservation of the architectural heritage of buildings that would otherwise be destroyed, and supply of low-cost building materials to enhance the structural and aesthetic quality of existing homes in our city."[3] Although deconstruction has been slow to take hold as a preferable alternative to demolition, its benefits have been widely noted for their economic and environmental impacts.[4] In a recent article by urban planners Leigh and Patterson, the authors note that "Conventional mechanical demolition and landfilling of demolition debris does not meet sustainability goals. Rather, it changes assets (buildings) into liabilities (demolition debris), with valuable construction materials commonly hauled away as waste by demolition contractors at the developer's expense."[5] The value structure that prioritizes liability over asset is precisely that which ReUse interrogates. At every phase of its operations, neglected matter is deemed to be imbued with latent potential. Such ideology is evident not only through ReUse's conversion of wasted material into resource, but also in its efforts to reclaim vacant land in the city, as well to invest, through its job training program, in the future lives of troubled teens and impoverished citizens. The group's work is nothing short of urban alchemy, a practice that specializes in converting the under-recognized into unique, local possibilities. Given ReUse's locally-specific agenda, it is not surprising that its work is

Deconstruction site: facade harvesting

in many ways facilitated by locally-specific environmental conditions. The process of deconstruction, for example, is much easier to accomplish in Buffalo due to the city's abundant supply of vacant lots. Whenever a building is dismantled, adjacent empty parcels become a critical resource as they are converted into factory-like disassembly lines for delaminating, nail-pulling, scraping, sorting and stacking of material.

Although deconstruction lies at the center of their practice, the scope of Buffalo ReUse's work extends far beyond material conservation into an array of social programs, ranging from green-space development to youth mentorship, to art education. The group has led in city-wide tree planting efforts, and it has undertaken a public art campaign that, in a manner reminiscent of Detroit's highly acclaimed Heidelberg project, allowed city school children to reclaim abandoned homes through painted murals.[6] The salvage operations of ReUse have thus constituted a foundation, from which the group has reached out into other community enrichment activities. In addition to the more structured programs of tree planting and youth mentorship, ReUse routinely hosts a variety of less formal events, ranging from art exhibitions to neighborhood barbeques to touch football games. The group has taken every opportunity to insert programs where none previously existed. Simply put, they are filling the void with socially engaging, urban activities. Fittingly, ReUse's logo, which features the caption *"Community. Jobs. Resources."* makes no mention of deconstruction, and instead directs attention to a community-centered agenda. One of the group's principle goals, as stated in promotional material, is "to empower people to build healthy, vibrant, sustainable communities through our deconstruction and salvage efforts." That is to say, taking things apart is seen as a catalyst for regenerating. Embodied in this statement is the idea that the constructed environment might be undone in order to restructure those communal and civic networks that are of primary importance. Deconstruction is thus seen as a piecemeal environmental catalyst: an agent of social, material and cultural change. Accordingly, ReUse's philosophy and activities strategically shift the act of building from the physical environment to the social sphere; the real built environment becomes a network of affiliated groups, rather than physical structures or spaces. Indeed, their advertising campaign proclaims as much, stating that it is these "built partnerships with local non profit organizations and businesses that will allow for continued growth."

In addition to their stated goals of recovering materials and communities, ReUse has also demonstrated an exemplary model of derelict land recovery by reprogramming three distinct properties as their base of operations. Located in an economically

Deconstruction site: interior stair revealed. Buffalo ReUse, 2008. Image courtesy Caesandra Seawell

impoverished and primarily residential neighborhood on the east side of the city, the formerly underutilized territories constitute a veritable compound of post-industrial adaptation that includes domestic, industrial, commercial and green space. Among the appropriated spaces are a 4,000 sq ft storage warehouse/retail store, vacant lots converted to community gardens and a re-habilitated single-family house turned office/meeting space. Each of these properties is a separate lot under different ownership and ReUse has innovatively patched together the parcels through a combination of negotiation, bartering and sanctioned squatting. The disparate nature of the structures is mirrored by an equally various set of functions and users. While the retail store is operated as a commercial establishment by Re-Use management, the garden is tended by volunteers and made available to neighborhood residents, while the house has served as the center for a city youth program, bringing kids and mentors together under its roof. The programming of ReUse's spaces is thus an extension of its social mission; the private single family house and vacant lot have become public and semi-public spaces, and the industrial warehouse has become a destination store within an otherwise struggling urban area.

While the dismantling of homes has constituted a major component of Buffalo ReUse's work, the group's entire project might be more accurately described as re-building through dismantlement. Not only is ReUse undoing the fabric of homes, they are also undoing rigid distinctions between public and private realms, between commercial business and non-profit enterprise, and between individual and collective good. For this group, disassembling the city's houses has required corresponding acts of social restructuring. Accordingly, it has implemented an array of community centered programming in order to advance this aim. The liabilities of abandoned homes have been eclipsed by the restoration of communal functions; un-building and re-building have become fundamentally linked. One consequence of the shrinking that characterizes many rust-belt urban centers is that, in the face of absence, many such grassroots initiatives have asserted a strong presence. The reasons for this may be the opportunities of abundant low cost housing and vacant land, access to government officials and the lack of coordinated, viable public programs. Couple this with a wealth of people who are tired of local government's broken promises and yet still care deeply for their city and the groundwork is laid for grassroots development. Within this climate, informal institutions such as ReUse have become the generators of a progressive, socially responsible urbanism. It is within such nourishing soil that the roots of sustainability may very well lie.

Completing the Cycle

The work that is presented as an accompaniment to this article responds directly to the context of un-building that so characterizes the post-industrial city of Buffalo. It endeavors to complete the cycle of ReUse's un-building project and to give physical form to ReUse's progressive social program. For the past six years, I have been harvesting debris from demolition sites in Buffalo, assembling discarded building materials into large scale public artworks that have often been presented within vacant and underutilized city buildings. From reorganized urban remains, there emerge a range of agglomerate landscapes, restored spaces and densely stratified territories. Within the cracks, gaps and fissures of collected shards, the hints of new urban itineraries may be found.

Many of the materials for the aforementioned projects have been recovered by Buffalo ReUse's deconstruction operations. These materials, however, are the most banal of building components, deemed by ReUse technicians to be unworthy of the effort to salvage. Determined to have no intrinsic reuse value, they have been designated for the landfill. Constituting the picked bones of the un-built city, they include such undesirable leftovers as carpet, wood paneling, wood lath, scrap lumber, and linoleum flooring. Pooled into new amalgams, the forsaken remnants are solidified as the maps for an assembled city of fragments. Streams of waste, diverted into spaces of disuse, coalesce as centers of public art.

Promoting the regenerative capacities of an un-done and re-done urban environment, the assembled city fragments constitute a local response to issues of building demolition, landfill diversion, vacancy and neglect. As a whole, this collection of projects approaches sustainability by symbiotically coupling the city's salient features of waste and emptiness and by resolving to re-inhabit the marginalized spaces of a struggling urban interior. Through the raw and rough contours of detritus and abandonment, the outline of a new city begins to emerge, a city whose re-built image unites the most neglected components of an un-built world.

consider what will become of chosen materials once they are demolished or replaced afterlife

References

1. Ouroussoff, Nicolai. "Saving Buffalo's Untold Beauty." New York Times, Arts/Art & Design, November 16, 2008

2. US Census Bureau, 2006 American Community Survey

3. Buffalo ReUse promotional literature. For more information, see: http://www.buffaloreuse.org

4. "Deconstructing to Redevelop: A Sustainable Alternative to Mechanical Demolition." American Planning Association. Journal of the American Planning Association, Spring 2006, ABI/INFORM Global, p. 217

5. Ibid

6. For more information on the Heidelberg Project, see: http://www.heidelberg.org/

Dennis Maher is an architect, artist, and activist whose work engages the vanishing fabric of post-industrial territories. For the past six years, he has been pursuing critical approaches to demolition, restoration and renovation within the city of Buffalo, NY. Selections from his current project have been exhibited with the Nina Freudenheim Gallery in Buffalo, Artspace II in Birmingham, MI and at the John Hartell Gallery of Cornell University. His work has been featured in Architect Magazine, as well as on the national radio program Smart City Radio. Maher is the recipient of a MacDowell Colony Fellowship for 2008. He has taught in the Department of Architecture at SUNY, University at Buffalo since 2004.

Source, Dennis Maher, 2006. Wood paneling, plywood, hollow core doors, linoleum floor, acoustical ceiling, steel stairs, plaster, fence, peg board, steel mesh, 2x4s, drywall screws, house paint, charcoal. Image courtesy William C. Helm II

Earth, *Dennis Maher, 2003. Wood paneling, plywood, wood lath, hollow door cores, tin, drywall screws, house paint. 98" x 91" x 12"*

Raven, *Dennis Maher, 2006. 2x4s, wood paneling, plywood, tar, light fixtures, drywall screws, house paint. 120" x 170" x 78"*

Queen, *Dennis Maher, 2006. Ductwork, siding, wood floor, drywall screws, house paint. 117" x 241" x 104". Image courtesy William C. Helm II*

Operational Alternatives: (Re-)Configuring the Landscape of Alberta's Athabasca Oil Sands

Syncrude Mine, 2007. View inside active oil sands mine

The Province of Alberta is selling off its natural resources. Increasingly, the provincial government is ceding enormous tracts of Crown Lands over to the interests of the oil industry. Since 1997, Alberta has leased over 26,000 square kilometers of boreal forest for oil sands development, an area equal to the state of Florida. This has spurred the enormous economic investment, infrastructural construction and internal migration front-ending an industrial expansion that has fundamentally shifted the focus of Canada's resource economy to the Athabasca oil sands.

Oil companies, initially dependant on the town of Fort McMurray for labor, housing, civic services and logistics, have begun to distance themselves from the much-publicized negative effects associated with the boomtown atmosphere in this northern-Albertan community. Those, coupled with the ever-expanding geographical extents of the region's resource-extraction activities, have created the perfect conditions for developing privately run industrial enclaves.

Too far from Fort McMurray, the increasingly outlying oil companies have effectively adopted their own private urban planning regimes, constructing their own housing, recreational facilities, field hospitals and private airstrips to service themselves. Extremely remote, secure and often behind concrete Jersey barriers created at the end of isolated gravel roads, multinational oil companies are increasingly in complete control of vast expanses of the Canadian landscape.

But arguably, the companies have always been in control. Canada can be understood as a corporate construct—where land exploration and settlement has largely been dependent upon the activities of industrial interests. Historically, the federal government has ceded its jurisdiction and landscape to private companies (e.g. Hudson's Bay Company, Canadian Pacific, INCO or Imperial Oil) in exchange for modern infrastructure (e.g. charted rivers, railways, reliable gravel roads, secure pipelines) and urbanization (e.g. forts, towns, ports, elevators, bases).

Understanding the wholesale leasing of the oil sands as an extension of this continued exchange, Canadians should begin asking more about the artifacts that these companies will inevitably leave behind. What form will the residual landscape emerging from the excavation and terra-forming of an entire region take on? How will infrastructures, associated with the extraction and transport of a finite resource, transition themselves for a post-oil economy? What forms of urbanization will the industrialization of the oil sands region generate?

To begin addressing these questions, it is necessary to understand the operational activities of the industrial process itself. Oil sands companies have developed an orchestrated set of actions on their landscape based on emerging hydrological, logistical, technological and legal parameters. Initially, while constructing the massive upgrading facilities required to separate bitumen from sand, the primarily forested land is gridded off; its land deforested and cleared; its soil drenched, drained and dried; and its roughly 10-meter-thick layer of overburden (muskeg soil, gravels, rock) removed and stockpiled, before any mining can occur. Simultaneously, massive holding and tailings pond embankments are located adjacent to the future mines to provide the necessary fluids to lubricate the transportation of the crushed sand, which will then have steam pumped into it to separate the oil. Any unfortunate byproducts of the process will be stored in these ponds indefinitely.

It is important to understand that all of the leasable land can be mined, and any particular parcel of land will eventually morph from a holding pond, to an 80 meter-deep surface mine, to a tailings pond which will potentially be replanted and reclaimed when it is no longer spatially required. The orchestration of this process responds to adjacencies; holding ponds locate near water sources, tailings ponds and stockpiles near upgrading locations, surface mining constantly following clear cutting towards the extending edges of development, with landscape reclamation in its wake.

As evidenced in ExxonMobil's Kearl Lake lease evolution plan, mining marches across the lease by outflanking the original watershed to create a landscape of total hydrological control. Initially a landscape of creeks, rivers and a solitary lake, the lease is programmed to morph into a quarantined landscape of water management areas and the loosely defined reclaimed areas expected to somehow regain the ecological characteristics they initially contained. The basic principles of the process are thus clear; oil sands companies will completely transform the ecologic, topologic and hydrologic character of their entire lease holding.

Multiply this transformation by the number of lease holdings and it becomes clear the entire region is undergoing an irreversible change. The breadth of this long-term reality, unfortunately, is seldom discussed, as

process

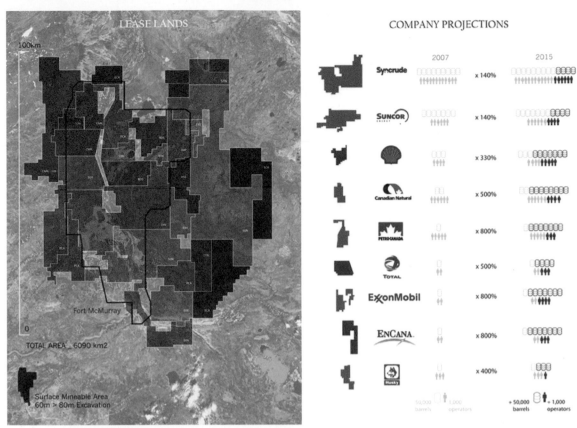

Athabasca Oil Sands Lease Map, 2008. Ownership map and employment projections of oil companies

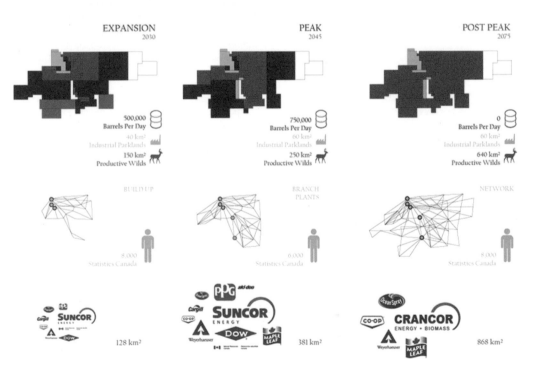

Proposed Lease Phasing, 2008. Proposed lease transformation and tertiary industrial occupations

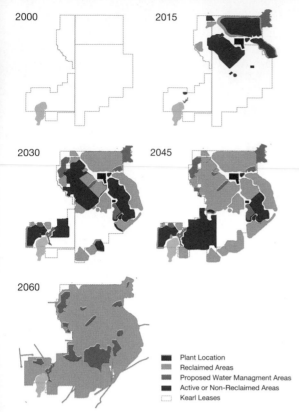

2000　　2015

2030　　2045

2060

- ■ Plant Location
- ▨ Reclaimed Areas
- ▨ Proposed Water Managment Areas
- ■ Active or Non-Reclaimed Areas
- ▢ Kearl Leases

Kearl Lake Lease Evolution, 2007. Exxon Mobil's proposed remediation phasing plan

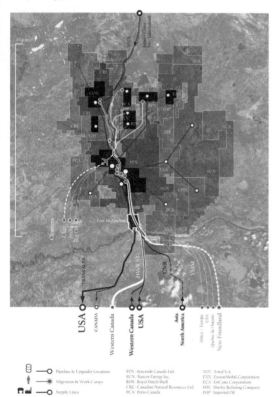

Regional Plan, 2007. Existing regional conditions

more immediate and readily visible ecological, social, infrastructural and governmental issues are at the forefront of the current discourse on the region. Well founded ecological concerns about the long-term effects of industrial water consumption and contamination, wildlife habitat protection, green house gas emissions and suspect reclamation practices are beginning to inform and organize the dirty realities of the oil sands industry.

The complex socio-economic problems associated with the obscenely high wages, rental rates and costs of living resulting in a rapid influx of international labor are only just beginning to be addressed by an overwhelmed municipality's civil services and oil company protocols. For infrastructure, the region is completely dependent upon the narrow band of Highway 63, a pipeline right-of-way and the Athabasca River for the transportation of all heavy equipment, construction supplies, hazardous goods and labor to an expanding archipelago of upgraders. Finally, the failure of the federal and provincial governments to effectively co-ordinate their management of the region has permitted a rate of expansion that has exacerbated all of the previously mentioned issues. Somehow the region needs to begin addressing its short- and long-term futures simultaneously.

A systemic reluctance to adopt or enforce an effective framework has permitted this collection of self-interested companies to set the terms and pace of development to the provincial government. The province's Regional Sustainable Development Strategy and Cumulative Environmental Management Association's have "failed to protect Alberta's environment from rapidly expanding oil sands interests."[1] Fortunately, oil sands companies are structured to enable decisions free from four-year terms; they plan on digging in for another 60 years. Given that they'll be around much longer than any sitting government; it is about time the province transfers the burden of planning back into industrial hands.

Albertans should begin demanding much more, not from their representation, but from the companies that occupy and profit off their public holdings. The historical relationship, where industries acting in self-interest invest into the construction of public landscapes, infrastructures and architectures, needs to be reconstructed. The public, increasingly conscious of the brevity and economy of this development, needs to begin demanding more than watered down royalties to ensure a sustained future for their lands.

Likewise, companies in the business of energy ought to begin viewing their current activities as an opportunity to situate future, alternative productions. The perception of the oil sand industry's enormous abilities to manufacture the landscape, rapidly lay infrastructure and erect architecture, must transition from destruction and catastrophe towards construction and creation. Both spheres, public and private, need to begin recognizing the immense potentials implicit in industrialization of this landscape.

The operations of these companies need revision; the industry has increasingly recognized the need to begin coordinating mine planning, tailings storage, surface water modeling, watershed management, landscape design, reclamation and end land uses across their lease boundaries. Kearl Lake's lease evolution will require multiple modifications to adapt to evolving neighboring

POND 3 tailings pond   POND 4 tailings pond   POND 2 holding pond   POND 5 tailings pond   POND 1 tailings pond   Voyageur Upgrader   Athabasca River

Suncor Voyageur Lease, 2007. Aerial view of Suncor Voyageur Lease, 2007. Image courtesy George Gilks

activities and evolving ecological and legal requirements. The volatility of market forces, currently in retreat,
can help create the conditions necessary to allow the
questioning, recalibration and modification of ongoing
operations. The illustrated fluidity of the mine's orchestral
process allows for the adaptation and augmentation of
operations to occur easily while maintaining production
levels. A coordinated control over an entire region could
produce a self-constructing, bottom-up, infrastructural
landscape capable of breeding post-oil economies.

Fort Suncor

"Suncor is a unique and sustainable energy company
dedicated to vigorous growth in worldwide markets
through meeting or exceeding the changing expectations
of our current and future stakeholders."[2]

Over 30 years of surface mining and upgrading by
Suncor has produced an active landscape containing
the range of distinctive occupations, topographies and
residues of the oil sands operations. On the verge of
doubling its production capacities with the completion
of the Voyageur South upgrading facility, Suncor's operations will soon straddle the highway-pipeline corridor;
thus doubling its public edge. As mining moves away
from this corridor towards the periphery of the lease,
these exhausted, well serviced edges are suited to take
on future occupations. As a publicly traded, relatively
transparent and highly visible occupant (due primarily
to its immediacy to Fort McMurray, Highway 63 and the
Athabasca river) of the oil sands, Suncor is positioned
to implement new sets of behaviors and invite satellite
industries into its field of operations.

The shadow economy of the oil sands extraction
process; the importation, creation, usage and storage of
chemical lubricants and byproducts, could become an integral and visible part of the occupation and reformation of
the landscape. Concurrently, leveraging the value of waste
streams; deforested organic material, soil and overburden
stockpiles, tailings, sludge, emissions and heat, to that
of a resource could attract parasitic productions capable
of capitalizing on an otherwise dirty reality. Finally, the
creative capacities implicit in the replacement of an 80m-
deep hole, permits an unprecedented ability to specify
landscapes tailored for particular modes of production.
Suncor, armed with an immense ability to transform
and service a landscape, could customize its waste and
reclamation streams to permit parasitic occupations, via
a set of Industrial Parklands and Productive Wilds.

Parklands, each tailored to fit into the rounded
embankment geometries of exhausted mining parcels,
are constructed at the pace of excavation further afield.
Annual yields of cleaned sand, at volumes with corollary
barrels per day, are dumped into pre-determined figures
intended to maximize exposures, hydrological gains and
byproduct flows. The resultant variations of slopes and
soil strata are re-enforced with periodic sheet steel piles,
which act to stabilize the sands and provide footings for
future architectures. With the range of organic materials,
sands, gravels, sulphates, nitrates, etc, stockpiled on the
lease; soil cocktails can be mixed to predict species.

Water, the region's scarce resource, is ponded and
provided for via ditches, dykes and banded snow fencing
intended to entrap all surface waters into an interior pond.
Compacted silts, a natural product of sludge, act as pool
liners to encase and prevent water from percolating in
an otherwise porous landscape. This water, at various

Targeted Fill

The Wild

Wetland Rim

Middle Ground Moss

Planted Rim

Fallow

1 tonne of sand ≈ 1 barrel of oil
240,000 barrels per day ≈ 240,000 tonnes of sand or
≈150,000 cubic meters
annually this equates to 54,750,000 cubic meters
or

2.7 km² x 20 meters deep per annum
(2007)

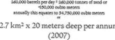

SnowFencing • Monitoring

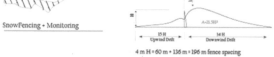

Wind ➔   Fence

A=21.5EP

15 H   14 H
Upwind Drift   Downwind Drift

4 m H = 60 m • 136 m = 196 m fence spacing

The Pond

Floating Edibles

Remediation Reed Beds

Tailing's

Ice

Landscape design parameters, 2008. Set of parameters for the refilling of exhausted strip mines to yield other productions

View of Industrial Parkland, 2027

DORAN, Kelly

POND 3
tree nursery

POND 4
wind generation

POND 2
cranberry farm

POND 5
tailings pond

POND 1
bison ranch

Voyageur
Upgrader

Athabasca
River

Suncor Lease 2027

Aerial view of Suncor Voyageur Lease, 2027

levels of toxicity, is treated through phytoremediation and settlement, to allow for future agricultural uses. Finally, the infrastructures of the upgrader are extended into the Parklands to provide district heat, steam and chemical compounds to new occupants. These new enclaves, each highly programmed and specific, are dually serviced by the ongoing activities of the lease and an immediate adjacency to Highway 63.

Outlying areas, serviced only by Suncor's interior roadway network and increasingly distant from the highway and upgrader as mining activities extend towards the lease's periphery, are similarly constructed but re-programmed as satellite colonies to parkland occupants. Each Productive Wild can serve as an eco-industrial Petri dish, test sites for an alchemic ecology capable of adapting to the quarantined landscape. Companies set up along the highway can buy-up test sites as they become available across the lease, competing for an ever expanding set of specific landscape. Bison ranches, corn plantations, hybrid boreals, glass plants, greenhouses, cranberry bogs and algae farms begin to occupy the lease. Productive Wilds, capable of transforming waste streams into crops, energy and capital, could proliferate to support future regional and northern development.

Suncor, an energy company, will begin to reform itself. As energy reliance shifts from carbon to carbo-hydrate, oil companies will become biofuel, biomass, bio-energy companies. The arduous, energy intensive development of the finite oil sands could be designed to suit new methods of infinite production and conversion. The homogenous, destructive extraction of oil from sand can produce emerging cyclical, heterogeneous as a means to ensure future stakeholders. Existing pipeline infrastructures, easily transformed to transport other fluids, would service an expanding demand for cleaner energy. In short, the unfortunate realities of "dirty oil" could easily begin to inform and reform the oil industry. The Athabasca oil sands simultaneously represent the effects of peak oil, and the possible of futures without it.

References

1. Severson-Baker, Chris; Grant, Jennifer and Dyer, Simon. Taking the Wheel, Correcting the Course of Cumulative Environmental Management in the Athabasca Oil Sand, *The Pembina Institute and the Canadian Parks and Wilderness Society, p. 12, 2008*
2. Suncor Energy homepage, http://www.suncor.com/ (Accessed November 3, 2008)

Kelly Nelson Doran *was born in Winnipeg and grew up observing the economic, industrial and infrastructural transformation of the Canadian landscape. He holds a Master of Architecture degree from the University of Toronto where he was the recipient of the RAIC Medal, the AIA medal and the 2007 Cohos Evamy Travelling Scholarship which funded his research travel to Northern Canada. His work has been published by the MIT Press and by Canadian Architect and has been exhibited at the Harvard Graduate School of Design. Kelly has worked with WilliamsonWilliamson Inc (Toronto), Eisenman Architects (New York), 70'N Arkitektur AS (Norway) and is currently working with the Organization for Landscape Infrastructure (Rotterdam).*

Flow Mechanism: Toyota Motor Manufacturing Kentucky

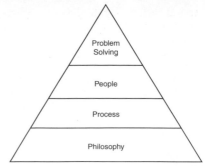

4P Pyramid, redrawn after Toyota Culture: The Heart and Soul of the Toyota Way

Eliminate muda, mura, muri* completely
—Taiichi Ohno, Former Executive Vice President of Toyota Motor Corporation

* Waste, Unevenness, Overburden

At a time when America's Big Three auto makers are struggling, Toyota is thriving in the US in comparison. A clue to Toyota's success may be in the culture that underwrites their production strategy. In 1985, in order to keep up with US demand for their vehicles, Toyota brought a Motor Manufacturing Plant to Kentucky. With its plant Toyota brought its management process, known as the Toyota Production System, and commonly referred to as "Lean" after the 1990s. This system is based on a concept of *flow* or the progressive achievement of tasks organized so that a product proceeds from design to launch, order to delivery, and raw materials into the hands of the consumer with no stoppings, scrap, or backflows.

In order to understand how flow production operates, there are few key concepts that must be defined. In the book *Toyota Culture*, by Jeffery Liker and Michael Hoseus, the management principles of Toyota are summarized in a 4P model: Philosophy, Process, People and Problem Solving. The four Ps form a pyramid, the foundation of which is a "Philosophy" that focuses on adding value to customers and society. Next is "Process," which is the Lean process that seeks to eliminate all *muda*, or waste. Above that is "People," which not only represents the individual workers employed by the company but the culture that unites them towards common goals, and on top is "Problem Solving" which is based on the concept of *kaizen* or continuous improvement.[1]

Kaizen is more readily deployed when adaptation to changing demands of the consumer requires less effort. Toyota continually evaluates and reorganizes assembly lines inside its manufacturing plant to match consumer demand. While other manufacturing industries in the US rely on a push system in which an overstock of product is made and pushed on the consumer, Toyota relies on a pull method where consumer demand controls production quantities. With no overstock, Toyota's production system can adapt quickly based on necessity. The Lean manufacturing concept eliminates any activities that are not necessary for the end result. Relative necessity is judged by the use of a model called the Value Stream. The Value Stream comprises the specific activities required to design, order and provide a certain product, from concept to launch, order to delivery, and raw materials into the hands of the consumer. Flow is defined as the progressive achievement of the Value Stream.[2]

PUSH

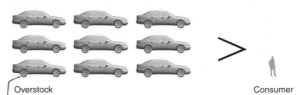

Overstock   Consumer

- Overstock of products to be pushed on consumer creates waste in production, time, and material
- Overstock slows rates of improvement of a product until current stock is sold

PULL

Consumer   Necessary Stock

- Consumer demand drives production. No waste
- Less stock allows for flexibility in system of production and continuous re-evaluation and improvement

Push and pull. Overstock of products pushed to sell to consumer vs. consumer pulling what product is necessary

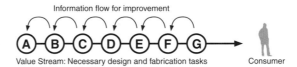

Flow. As each task is fulfilled along the value stream, the product not only moves toward its final stage in the hands of the consumer, but also provides feedback to previous steps

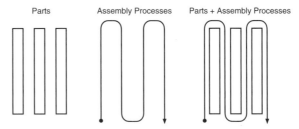

Spatial configuration of just-in-time manufacturing. Previous manufacturing models would separate stock from assembly lines. Just-in-time saves space by weaving assembly processes and the part stock

The spatial dimension of flow deals with programming adjacencies that facilitate just-in-time manufacturing in which processes occur only at the moment they are necessary. This leads to an organization of space in which necessary processes are adjacent to each other. Instead of separating material stock and assembly—which halts the act of assembling while a part is located—processes are implemented that ensure the part is on hand for assembly at just the right moment. When this is combined with the pull concept which eliminates overstock, wasted space is reduced and communication across programs of assembly is more immediate. This immediate communication across programs facilitates *kaizen*.

At the Toyota Motor Manufacturing Plant in Georgetown, Kentucky, there are many processes taking place along the assembly line of the car. Each is laid out in a series of big boxes—an efficient means of shelter for the tightly formed process occurring inside the plant. The circulation of the plant is a three-dimensional network of assembly lines populated and driven by a diverse mix of automated machines and people. Each year under the philosophy of *kaizen* the assembly lines are reorganized in order to adjust to new models of automobiles and to improve the quality and efficiency of production. A maximum flexibility in terms of spatial layout allows programs to shift to maximize flow and leads to maximum efficiency.

Problem Solving: The University of Kentucky

The University of Kentucky (UK) is expanding its campus on to a 735-acre lot at the edge of its host city, Lexington, Kentucky. The Coldstream Research Campus (CRC) was acquired in 1992 and development began that year. In 2007, 15 years after development began; the University has decided it needs a vision for this growth. In the meantime it has already invested $80 million in infrastructure and has partitioned the land into 32 lots

to sell to developers. UK has taken on a problem-solving approach to planning that is symptomatic of many other campus developments in the region which leads to inefficient and inconsistent land use. The CRC is a case in point; if it is to use space efficiently or create a cohesive and comprehensive plan, it must not be organized by the same methods.

In 1992, John Russell Groves Jr completed "An Examination of Major Initiatives in Campus Planning at the University of Kentucky 1919-1991." In it, he traces the history of the development of the UK Campus from its inception in 1865 until 1991. The campus was originally situated at the outer limits of the city of Lexington. It, like the city, grew out from the center over time until the city's growth enveloped it. During this time, four major plans for the campus were developed. However they were implemented only after "compromise, partial fulfillment, abandonment, and reversals."[3]

Two plans that stood out due to their consistency were the Olmsted brothers' Preliminary Plan of 1919 and Crane and Gorwic's Lexington Central Campus Plan of 1965. The Olmsted plan was the first attempt at master planning the University. It suggested an "irregular and picturesque arrangement of buildings in a setting suggesting a rural village or naturalistic park."[4] While it was never fully implemented, the plan influenced the University's rural aesthetic, laying out buildings as objects in a field surrounded by green space.

The Crane and Gorwic plan was much bolder "in its vision and (is) reflective of an 'urban renewal' attitude which typified 1960s growth era."[5] In stark contrast to the courthouse style of the buildings on campus, Crane and Gorwic proposed white concrete monoliths. Groves observes that though comprehensive "planning (in this case) may do a greater disservice to the institution than its absence. Raising large but impractical expectations…[it]

Coldstream Research Campus
Development begun in 1992

I-75

New Circle Road
Completed 1967

Man o'War Boulevard
Begun 1975, latest addition
completed 1988

University of Kentucky Campus
as of 2009

Urban Service Boundary
as of 2007

1 Mile

University of Kentucky and the Coldstream Research Campus located within the Urban Service Boundary of Lexington, KY

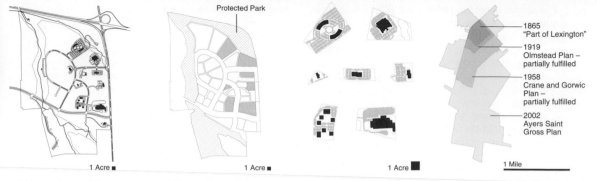

1865
"Part of Lexington"

1919
Olmstead Plan –
partially fulfilled

1958
Crane and Gorwic
Plan –
partially fulfilled

2002
Ayers Saint
Gross Plan

Protected Park

1 Acre ■   1 Acre ■   1 Acre ■   1 Mile

Coldstream Research Campus:
Current Plan

Coldstream Research Campus:
Lot Divisions

Coldstream Research Campus:
Developed Lots

Coldstream Research Campus Plan. Buildings and their parking lots are laid out within the imposed lot divisions (first 3 diagrams); University of Kentucky Physical Development Plans' land use over time (last diagram)

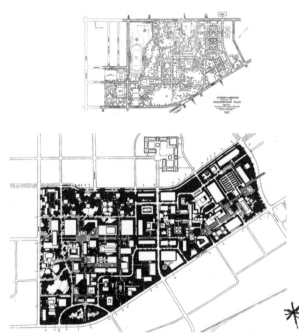

Bird's eye view of Patterson Office Tower Plaza on the University of Kentucky campus. Courthouse style typologies (bottom) and "urban renewal" monoliths, the Patterson Office Tower and the White Hall Class Room Building (top). Image courtesy University of Kentucky

Two University of Kentucky Physical Development Plans noted for their consistency in design. Courtesy University of Kentucky. 1919 Olmstead Plan (top) redrawn by the students of the UK Department of Landscape Architecture, 1965 Physical Development Plan (bottom) by Crane & Gorwic Associates, Inc. Planning and Urban Design Consultants

may create problems where none existed and in general put forth unrealistic objectives."[6] The university—unable to afford demolishing its existing infrastructure and buildings—felt this comprehensive plan was unattainable and this created a disdain for the planning process. "Eventually the Crane and Gorwic plan produced the Patterson Office Tower, the White Hall Class Room Building and two parking structures."[7]

These campus plans were developed decades apart and never fully realized. Rather, they were implemented in a piecemeal fashion to solve problems as they arose. This has led to a sprawling campus filled with juxtapositions of unlike typologies. Groves concludes his research by stating that "a master plan is not an end-product but rather a process which is continuously updated to reflect changing conditions of the University Environment."[8] The issue with these plans is not that they lacked vision, but that they sought a fixed end and that the university could never fully realize. Since Groves' dissertation, UK has developed the 2002 Campus Physical Development Plan. Key to this plan is that all the leftover spaces within the zone defined by the 1991 plan are beginning to be filled. By no means does such a strategy solve the issue of a creating a unified spatial experience, but it smartly addresses the issues of leftover space given the unfortunate conditions.

Adaptive Planning: The Coldstream Research Campus

If a cohesive vision for the Coldstream Research Campus is to be achieved, a more direct model must be implemented that conserves land use and provides spatial consistency. There must be some flexibility in its masterplan if existing infrastructure and existing buildings are to be included. If we look to other large adaptive models of development in Kentucky we may find new sustainable strategies for growth. The current application of lot divisions superimposed on the site allow for individual developers to fill at their own discretion. This will not allow for comprehension of a greater organization or maximum use of space. With buildings and infrastructure already in place, a more flexible mechanism must be implemented to achieve these goals. A more pragmatic approach to design derived from models of efficiency found in industry may be considered. If the industrial flow model, as described in Toyota's Lean process, were to be applied towards organizing the interaction of light, air, and views with circulation and program, this could allow for organization to be arranged and re-arranged out of changing necessity and allow for more opportunistic connections. Spatial flow on the site can be created by aligning programs and activities that facilitate and enhance each other. By breaking down the scale of the buildings that house the programs, smaller typologies could be turned over faster for new programs. By clustering these smaller building typologies together, the need for the automobile and parking lots could be reduced. A greater variety of programs could be achieved within a smaller surface area facilitating pedestrian circulation and this could reduce the need for driving and parking thus reducing transit time between activities. The success of such a strategy could be judged by the emergence of a unique character based on the concept of *kaizen* that allows the masterplan to be adaptive in nature rather than fixed and destined for obsolescence.

[handwritten margin note: Toyota principles applied to University development]

References

1. Liker, Jeffrey K.; Hoseus, Michael and The Center for Quality People and Organizations. Toyota Culture: The Heart and Soul of the Toyota Way. *New York: McGraw-Hill, 2008, p. 25-30*
2. Womack, James P. and Jones, Daniel T. Lean Thinking: Banish Waste and Create Wealth in Your Corporation. *New York: Free Press, 2003, p. 348, 353*
3. Groves, John Russell. An Examination of Major Initiatives in Campus Planning at the University of Kentucky 1919-1991. *Lexington, KY: [s.n.], 1992, p. 152*
4. University of Kentucky. A Plan for a Plan: Considerations for Campus Planning, *Symposium, June 1-4, 1989. Lexington, KY: University of Kentucky, 1989, p. 9*
5. Ibid. p. 11
6. Groves, John Russell. An Examination of Major Initiatives in Campus Planning at the University of Kentucky 1919-1991. *Lexington, KY: [s.n.], 1992, p. 153*
7. University of Kentucky. A Plan for a Plan: Considerations for Campus Planning, *Symposium, June 1-4, 1989. Lexington, KY: University of Kentucky, 1989, p. 11*
8. Ibid. p. 12

Jason Scroggin *is an assistant professor of architecture at the University of Kentucky College of Design. He holds a Master's of Science degree in Advanced Architectural Design from Columbia University. His interest in large-scale planning models has been most recently carried out in the creation of a vision for the masterplan of the Coldstream Research Campus, a 700-acre site in Lexington, KY, a proposal for a development surrounding the lot containing the historic Carnahan House within that campus, and the design of Cherokee Square, a park located along the main street of downtown Guthrie, Kentucky.*

Prosolve

elegant embellishments was formed in 2006 as an architectural start-up, with the aim to self-initiate projects for condition-specific spaces. Previously, we had spent some time working as architects in various London offices, witnessing the often convoluted processes of the production of common buildings. We envisioned a future whereby design intentions would be constantly disfigured and subsumed by the dual processes of value engineering and design and build contracts. We were reluctant to be part of this, and instead began looking for a new concept for an architectural practice that could help integrate these processes for the sake of quality and perhaps creative freedom as well. At the same time, it was becoming evident that many of the world's most pressing ecological imbalances emanated from urban conditions in which architects practice.

We spoke frequently with a consultant friend at the time. A German car part manufacturer had recently opened a factory in Romania. It was producing horrific rates of reject parts of walnut dash boards. The curvy design was completely at odds with the characteristics of the material and its manufacturing process. We talked a lot about process integration as a necessary means to achieve a high quality product and the exemplary Toyota production system and how important it was that designers understood how things were made and put together.

A certain fascination with po-mo classics such as Venturi's *Learning from Las Vegas*, with an emphasis on a semiotic reading of architecture led us to accept a practice limited to the design of facades. In fact, we liked the idea of practicing in this post-modern paradigm of symbols and signs and images—things which are formally flat and refer to other things that are not really there through levels of abstraction and representation. We were more interested in common buildings and less in high-end design. We were looking for a product or a technology that could reintroduce an emotive and aspirational aspect to architecture, much as the iPod did for the conventional hard drive. We were hoping that we could create a product with so much appeal that it could invert the traditional client-architect relationship. Essentially, we wanted to create popular products for buildings that could bypass slow institutional processes and change the face of cities quickly.

Rather than designing our product to attach to specific buildings, we focused our attention on the study of an urban condition: air pollution in cities. This came from a general interest in the immaterial aspects of architecture, such as cell phone networks, surveillance systems, radar, or the weather. These micro-climates seemed to be acquiring more significance than the built environment itself, yet at the same time were being generated by it.

We began to think more in terms of product territories, places where conditions were favorable for a product to thrive and propagate. Rather than corresponding to a design brief of a specific building to which a product is attached, the product could respond to adjacent, more atmospheric and general conditions that are architecturally relevant, but have previously lacked any architectural definition or expression. During this research we stumbled upon de-polluting coating technologies based on photo-active titanium dioxide.

Prosolve370e — Product Concepts

Out of this constellation emerged our first "product," *Prosolve370e*, a set of architectural modules that, when positioned in appropriate spaces, remove air pollutants from the immediate environment.

De-polluting Technology — Technology without Form

Millennium Chemicals patented the active ingredient in 2002, but it wasn't until much later that it became commercially available. Millennium Chemicals lent support to us during the development of our product and partnered with us on several exhibitions.

The superfine, photo-reactive titanium dioxide-pigment is activated by ambient UV light to drive a chemical reaction to absorb and neutralise nitrogen oxides (NOx), volatile organic compounds (VOCs) and pollen. NOx is a product of combustion engines (cars), and is perhaps the single most potent air pollutant in cities: it is in itself toxic, and is also a precursor to the formation of ground-level ozone, acid rain, smog. Targeting NOx is therefore an effective way of tackling tropospheric air pollution occurring in the lower levels of the atmosphere that we inhabit where it directly affects our health.

The technology occurs on a molecular level, yet has spatial implications. While this technology can be theoretically applied to almost anything, we located a flaw in its embodiment: the technology had no link to form. In its ambition to be likened to an ordinary paint, it masked its own critical microscopic activity, embedding it into a traditional building material. The beauty of the chemical reaction is not expressed, and consequently, skepticism gathers as to whether it has any "magic" beyond plain white paint. We were looking for an appropriate architectural form for this process that could increase its efficacy and simultaneously serve as its formal expression. This would improve the appeal of this technology as a product and create a visible embodiment of a new approach towards sustainability. It re-appropriated the elegance of the underlying process for architectural application.

The sustainability of photo-catalytic, pollution fighting technology is arguable, yet we see Prosolve as a discursive piece that raises questions about sustainability. The more common approach towards sustainability at the moment is one of reducing ecological impact, reducing CO_2 emissions, reducing NOx in cars, etc. This is undertaken knowing that the processes that cause climate change have already—and perhaps irrevocably—been set in motion. This is a necessary change in behavior, but conceivably it may come too late to avert the impending climate shifts. And it is why some scientists are proposing the use of active technologies to avert or alleviate the impact of climate change, such as scraping CO_2 from the atmosphere with large artificial trees, blowing sulphur dioxide into the atmosphere to sufficiently block sunlight, or dumping iron oxides into the oceans to fertilize carbon eating algae.

Pollution-eating titanium dioxide technology essentially feeds off of our unsustainable preference for individualized transport propelled by combustion engines in cities. It is more an intermediate step of improvement on the path to sustainability rather than an ideal solution. However, it's probably a necessary one given the complexities of achieving the radical changes that are needed and the time that will be most likely required to implement them. The European Community's Clean Air policy 2005 estimates that urban air pollution in its member states accounts for 100,000 deaths and damage of around 42 billion Euros annually. The EU plans to invest 7 billion Euros per year in reducing air pollution in cities.

The Form of Prosolve —

Tuning Form

Shapes in products are commonly tuned to invisible forces: radiators distributing heat, surfboards meticulously shaped to perform on waves, air plane wings responding to aerodynamics. Their shapes reveal the forces that act on them. No formal expression existed that expressed the conditions of urban air pollution. We found highly decorative, fractalized shapes created more surface area, and more omni-directional exposure to ambient light needed for the reaction, in places with higher concentrations of pollution, such as traffic tunnels. Appropriating the pollution-absorbing coating on to a complex surface could enhance the technology's performance, as well as become a decorative and identifiable architectural device that addresses the invisible problem of pollution in cities. Fittingly, we are doing the opposite of what car designers do: we are designing for turbulence in order to increase the exposure of polluted air to the active surfaces. We wanted to express both aspects of the coating, its de-polluting and self cleaning properties, the former requiring formal complexity, the latter smoothness to facilitate the washing away of dirt by the coating's hydrophilic effect.

Complex Modularity

Prosolve370e is a modular system that achieves apparent randomness, while benefiting from economies of scale. The tiling method is derived from a five-fold symmetric underlying grid, one that appears irregular, yet is made of only two constituent parts. The pattern is aperiodic, creating apparent randomness although composed from only two repeating modules. The tiling method ultimately enables a complex surface, typically associated with the bespoke, to become a modular system that could be implemented as a building product, onto a standard cladding substructure with orthogonal geometries.

Morphology of Polluted Spaces

Our product has only one consistent contextual requirement — air pollution, a problem that has no perceivable form and little association to building. The first application was designed for a building façade, ideal for receiving light and pollution, and providing a large expanse of

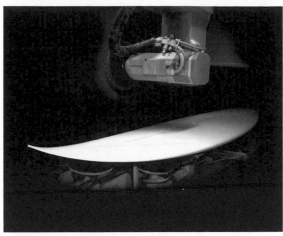

Surfboard tuned to wave dynamics, shaped with a 5-axis cnc machine. Image courtesy cybernetic.net.au

surface to tile. The city is full of opportune polluted and disenfranchised sites: housing estates needing regeneration; marginal architectural spaces overlooked by grand housing schemes; or residual infrastructural spaces. Not only de-polluting, the tiles could create a new identity and sense of ownership in these city spaces. Instead of building new, modify the old. Instead of building, we advocate *building tuning*, calibrating the existing to perform better to new and constantly changing architectural criteria.

Product Development—

Prototyping

Without clear regulations, or a well-defined competitive market to guide the process, prototyping is our only means for signposting progress. Over time, our prototypes reveal the distortions of the processes acting upon them, requirements of manufacturing or fire regulations as one parameter of establishing material thickness. Since the modules create complex shapes, we need to prototype installation processes as well to create a product with realistic installation and transportation conditions.

Prosolve's growth can be marked by three prototypes of 210mm, 420mm, and 1050mm module edge length, corresponding with the a gradual development of the product context, from studio to small exhibition and trade fair stands, to larger exhibition and ultimately to building size. One step enabled the next in gathering a minimum of financial support, feed back on possible demand, and technical feasibility. The 210 module was rapid-prototyped on an advanced stereolithography (SLA) machine, and hand-cast in polyurethane. The 420 series, was vacuum-formed with ABS sheet plastic, resulting in lighter, more pliable shapes that granted tolerances across the pattern. The 1050 series involved prototyping several joint and installation conditions to simulate a façade condition. Here, we made the inevitable leap from studio to factory, merging our role as designers with novice-manufacturers.

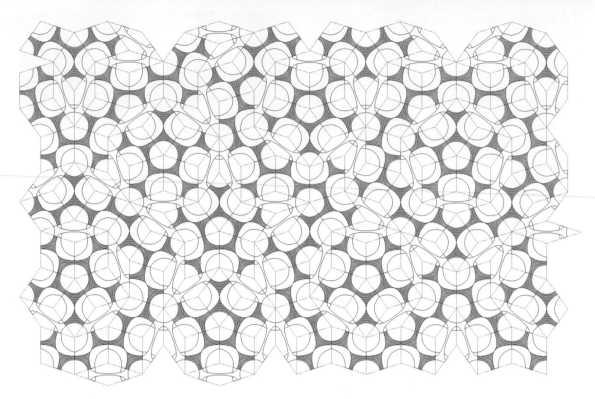

Prosolve370e on a five-fold symmetry underlying grid, composed of two repeating parts. The two modules create an aperiodic pattern that benefits the depolluting technology by providing omni-directional exposure to uv light

Testing/Legitimising

In order to enter a product officially into the European market, it must first obtain the omnipresent CE mark, (*Conformité Européenne*). The CE mark symbolises the need for a market to standardise, to bring a product idea and embodiment into a formal description that can be located against similar and competing products.

In Germany, the route is taken through the *Deutsches Institut für Bautechnik* (DIBt), the national office of building certifications. The DIBt have informed us that Prosolve does not necessarily qualify as a building product according to their definition: products that perform in the conventional sense of building, i.e. shelter, insulation, structures, etc. This definition is further distinguished by how permanently the product is installed onto the building. A purely aesthetic installation may not, according to the DIBt, be viewed as a permanent installation. In this scenario, our product might be deemed irrelevant from the perspective of building technology, and, with this in mind, we could strategically bypass the authorization process without needing any formal building product certifications required for standard products. What is revealing in wading through this informational haze, is that many building products do not fit this definition. Some, for example solar panels, are products *associated* with building, yet may not acquire certifications as building products.

If Prosolve is not defined as a commercial building product, we are then subject to the testing and conformity of all built propositions in public space: fire tests, structural stability tests, wind loading tests, etc. While the tiles suffice for much standard testing, there is no established test for the sustainability aspect of our product. Prosolve is *eco* in its ability to actively reduce pollutants in the air; it is *sustainable* in its ability to harness a renewing energy source to carry out its reaction. Yet it has no direct response to the building it is attached to — it does not support or improve the building's energy abilities, but rather its effect is on the immediate, surrounding environment. One could say its only function, for the building, is to be highly decorative.

DIY Manufacturing

Typically, designers expect to offload their product at the prototype stage, concluding that the processes of production and the intricacies of marketing are better suited to a large production house, preferably one that can take on upfront tooling costs, and absorb potential losses should the product fail. Traditionally, for the handover of a design, a designer can expect a 3-5 percent royalty on sales, having no influence on the promotion of the product to its public.

Prosolve370e has not yet found a manufacturing partner, primarily because we have not found a manufacturing house that can hybridize the processes needed to make it. Manufacturing in the building industry is rooted in expertise with particular materials or processes, new product ventures moving only slightly into like-minded or like-grouped areas. For a better idea of how manufacturers are differentiated, see the RIBA product selector,

DRING, Allison and SCHWAAG, Daniel

where products are listed by materials, with each material being supported by its national federation. In the RIBA listings, we would expect to find de-polluting products next to solar collectors, which are listed in "mechanical heating, cooling and refrigeration"—though our product has no relationship to these services. Instead, Prosolve associates *building* with *air pollution*, much in the same way satellite dishes associate building with media reception—which could suggest a new category: atmosphere-harnessing products?

A consistent characteristic amongst innovative products is hybridisation. With Prosolve, we are re-examining a building material's ability to *perform*—considering the potentials of single-functioned building materials that insulate, strengthen, and protect. New successful products are hybridised across many agendas, to stay lean and carry out multiple activities. Hybridisation reduced the need for extra materials, which in itself is a sustainability strategy. If there is a material expenditure, then why not fuse different requirements in one material, in one installation process?

Not surprisingly, when it comes to developing new sustainable products, we found the common practice of manufacturers is to make an eco version of a process they already perform, or produce for a market in which they already sell. Also noticeable is the inflexibility to perform multiple processes in the making of one part. For example, most standard construction materials are formed and sold as sheets; a three-dimensional or sculptural part would involve new machines, new materials, and with it new perceptions. Yet, these seemingly shocking shapes in the architectural industry have been commonplace in manufacturing for nearly a century in the car industry.

Prosolve370 is a plastic tile; ABS, ABS/PC, ASA all form a selection of materials that meet standards for building. Plastics, though petroleum based, actually have strong eco-potential: they are material-efficient, and can be formed additively, using only what material is needed. They are also formable as alloys from multiple types with varying characteristics from being bullet-proof to bio-degradable. Plastics are advantageously lightweight yet strong, and are still relatively unorthodox as a building material. We chose plastic as a sustainable route over other materials particularly for its *leanness*. Using minimum amounts of material, shapes could be formed as a constant response to needs of context; the resulting minimal, lightweight structures appear bio-mimetic, and the material begins to typify an eco-aesthetic.

Manufacturing with plastics implies designing for moulds: our parts needed to be shaped conducive to single-pull moulds and free of deep undercuts. For example, complex surface geometries that would provide the technology with an increased surface area had to be negotiated with the process, in order to be pulled easily several thousand times from a mould. Production knowledge for moulded shapes cannot be learned from the architecture or building industry—instead, we focused our attention toward the pollution-*causing* car industry. Examples in manufacturing efficiency such as Toyota's Kai Zen (continuous improvement) or Poka Yoke[1] (error-proofing) as a way of managing complexity, became more inspiring than those in architectural cladding.

Product Life

Building product longevity has changed in recent years: lifetimes are now often five years, instead of 20. Corresponding maintenance schemes suggest an active future relationship between owner and building, implying that products are more sensitive, more *alive*, than ever before. *[handwritten: alive? planned obsolesc.?]* Furthermore, environmental technologies evolve more quickly, anticipating more frequent updating, for better performance. The idea of building *tuning* is latent in building *products*, and suggests a continuously symbiotic relationship between building and component.

In this context, product standardisation is elusive. The idea of building products as active, and performing, implies that they are unique to their specific context, and, rather than construction elements, are the management of a condition. Products that perform sophisticated processes might never wholly reach standardisation, because they are tuned to criteria with some degree of open-endedness and ambiguity. Products like Prosolve370e, which are calibrated not to buildings, but to building environments, could signify the end of the off-the-shelf era.

Afterword—

Variation in the Year of Darwin

6 January 2009. We've been invited to attend a discussion on sustainability in the context of building culture. The discussion gravitates around a single theme: how to certify sustainability and sustainable architecture specifically through a single seal of approval that signifies to consumers they are purchasing a product that will not harm the environment There are arguments brought forth by representatives of different standards such as LEED, the American system of certification, and a new German standard, more stringent since it is being introduced at a later point. These standards must take years to formulate. Their focus seems to be on product life cycles and the use of sustainable energy sources and materials.

A brief summary of the theory of evolution: the procreative process is an open one. It allows for permutations to occur constantly. This creates variety. New sets of properties and traits are continuously generated by an open ended procreative process. This ensures diversity and is the precondition of evolution. These permutations and deviations from temporary norms are then tested against territory, which itself is a dynamic field of changing conditions.

Nuclear power was not considered sustainable up until the point that the climate discussion began to move into the center of the sustainability debate. In the context of climate change and the immediacy of that problem, the aspect of nuclear waste storage has receded. The technology territory has changed, and nuclear power is reconsidered.

While a standardisation of sustainability facilitates decisions for consumers, the nature of it reduces the creation of a variety of solutions, which might be exactly what we need given the complexity of a dynamic territory defining sustainability.

DRING, Allison and SCHWAAG, Daniel

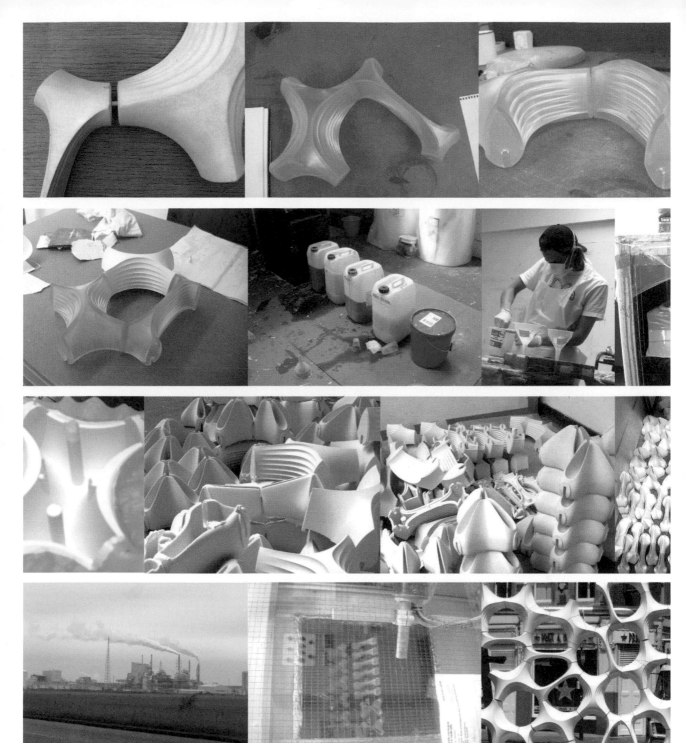

Above: Evolution of prototype 210 for London Architecture Biennale 2006. Facing page, top: Prototype 1050 for a commercial project in Perth, Australia, bottom: Prototype 420 for the Venice Architecture Biennale 2008

420 prototype at the Venice Biennale

References

1. Poka Yoke refers to a method of standardising the conditions, limiting options and possible outcomes, and sometimes marking parts that reduce the likeliness of errors or deviations in a production process, even if it occurs in different factories. This is one of the concepts behind Toyota's envied consistency of quality of their products manufactured in different places of the world. Kai Zen refers to a manufacturing ethos, where there is continuous and constant communication of feed-back up and down the manufacturing process which is used for continuous process improvement.

elegant embellishments *was formed by Allison Dring and Daniel Schwaag in 2006 as an architectural start-up, with the strategy of self-initiating projects for condition-specific spaces. ee investigates new materials and methods for the quick modification of existing buildings and spaces. These modifications are used to "tune" buildings, converting previously inert surfaces into active surfaces that can meet new architectural criteria.*

Our first active product, Prosolve370e, is an example of our interest in new, complex topographies for smart surfaces. We seek new processes that can transcend the current reliance on tooling, and derive new forms for innovative technologies that occur on a molecular level, yet are significant enough to transform spaces.

VEREBES, Tom

Endurance and Obsolescence: Instant Cities, Disposable Buildings, and the Construction of Culture

Recent, prolonged demands for increasing speed of design and construction pose challenges to building longer-lasting, socially beneficial, well performing buildings and cities. Rather than celebrating impermanence and ephemerality, contemporary design research faces a paradox between the seeming parallel necessities of adaptive, evolutionary forms of urbanism and the need for greater cultural, social, environmental and economic endurance of architecture. This research oscillates between political discourses and speculative design work driven by advanced design and productions techniques, on a range of scales dealing with duration and design life of architecture and urbanism. As an alternative to throw-away architecture and the design of instant cities, the economic benefits of high-quality design emphasize innovation in computational and material research, aiming for increasing the design life of buildings, and the capacity of cities to evolve and adapt to dynamic contextual conditions. Key to achieving the objective of greater endurance of the social and material space of future cities is to approach environmental performance as an opportunity for greater local specificity rather than a global problem to solve. Within the (un)fashionable rhetoric of "sustainable architecture" questions arise as to why, when and how did design become an unethical distraction at best, and an immoral vice, at worst? For a building to endure, does it not require its users and the broader population to value it, firstly in cultural terms, so it is deemed more worthy of preservation or re-use, than of demolition?

Wow! So Big! So Fast! So Much of it!

In recent years of booming economies fuelling accelerated global urbanization, current generations of architects have tended to observe, document and comment upon the phenomena of the Instant City. This form of celebratory commentary assumed rapid urbanization was set on automatic, like a movie, where we marvel passively, powerlessly and remotely as spectators, at its impressive, awesome force. Far from innocent in this process, the architect who either honors, or conversely, who condones this mass—or mess—of urbanization, is implicated in what turns out to have been a myopic frenzy of production. In this light, should the architect be either credited, blamed, or rendered impotent, for the state of our buildings, our cities and our planet? The unprecedented

rate and extent of urbanization witnessed worldwide over the last 20 years far exceeds that of any previous era or empire. In the aftermath of the economic meltdown of late 2008, and the increasingly frenetic pace of production of new cities for hundreds of millions of people in recent years, many cranes stand idle, shipping containers empty, banks broke and bailed out, and architects unemployed. The world economy and the entire theoretical basis of neo-capitalism are in shambles; the so-called natural environment damaged to the extent that scientists predict imminent, man-made environmental catastrophes. This is the new 21st century. Nowhere to run and hide, only our demons to confront.

Dubai = Timbuktu

Few other cities than Dubai better exemplify the model of the Instant City. The world's first Free Trade Zone was created by the Sheikh of Dubai in 1901, when the port of Lingah in the Bastak region of Iran raised taxes, and merchants fled to settle in what is now Dubai. The harbor was dredged in the 1970s, with hopes of becoming a major cargo hub, and in 2007, Dubai surpassed Hong Kong as the world's most prolific port. Tourists outnumber the residential population of Dubai by five to one, and the world's largest airport will soon open. The UAE has also recently filled a time gap during a 24-hour day in the world's stock markets, opening the Dubai Financial Exchange earlier this decade.[1] Although global financial systems have been proven to be ephemeral, Dubai has, since 9/11, been regarded as a safe haven for investment and financial services in the Middle East. The UAE produces nothing except oil—but this emerging economic wonder has generated enormous wealth by tapping into the flow of international capital.

Dubai's status as a global hub can be correlated to another City of Gold in the desert—Timbuktu, the ancient fabled city in Mali, whose obsolescence was brought on with the emergence of cargo shipping between coastal sub-Saharan Africa and North Africa during the early colonial period. Timbuktu maintained a population exceeding 100,000 for nearly 500 years—larger than any European city until the end of the 17th century. The city was re-discovered by a European, for the first time in over three centuries, in 1826. Timbuktu is credited with having the world's first university, and commercially, it was the center of the gold and salt markets. For centuries, Timbuktu was also complicit in the transportation of an estimated nine to 13 million sub-Saharan slaves to North Africa and beyond.[2] Like Dubai, Timbuktu did not produce anything. It was a city of contractors and merchants, serving as a node for the warehousing and distribution of goods, transferring to and from the boats of the River Niger, and the camel caravans through the Sahara to North Africa. The Dubai model of the Instant City follows a similar pattern of wealth being generated from the exchange of goods and services. Both cities risk(ed) extinction through threats of desiccation from harsh climatic and geographical environments, and the fragility and non-sustainability of their economies. The difference between the two cities is Timbuktu endured as

Various towers and infrastructure under construction in Dubai Marina, 2008

Aerial photo of Timbuktu. Image courtesy www.sum.uio. noresearchmalitimbuktutimbuktu

Timbuktu, the fallen city of gold in the desert: a view of the central business district, 1992

Plan of Timbuktu. Image courtesy Museum of Timbuktu, Timbuktu, Mali

VEREBES, Tom

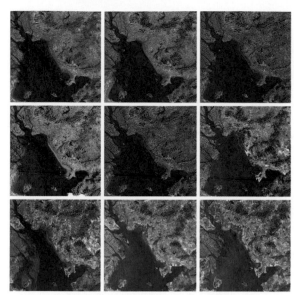

Series of satellite photos of Shenzhen, from 1973-2008. Image courtesy NASA, www.svs.gsfc.nasa.gov

a thriving city for half a millennium. The future holds the history of Dubai.

(P. 49)

The Ancient Chinese Instant City

A clean sheet of paper has no blotches, and so the newest and most beautiful words can be painted on it.
—Mao Tse-tung, 1966[3]

Chairman Mao's words are as sublime as the beauty he so admires in blank paper, yet the actions implied and carried out in the name of revolution serve as a reminder of the violence caused in the pursuit of cultural and material erasure.

Chairman Deng's ensuing One Country-Two Systems communist-capitalist hybrid has propelled great cultural evolutions over the last two decades. Predating the 20th century, two paradoxical tendencies are discernible in the history of the Chinese city. Firstly, the building of cities in the imperial era in China perpetuated three millennia of walled cities, symbolising and ensuring state authority, while exemplifying the will for insularity and permanence. Although not particularly unique to China, the building, rebuilding, altering and extending of city walls were carried out in response to military, administrative, economic, demographic and religious parameters specific to the country's development between the 17th and 19th centuries in China, a great period of development of walled cities provided security and more effective governmental control.[4] Another tendency during the imperial era was for emperors, and central and local governments to unilaterally remove entire cities to new locations. This second tendency to renew, start afresh and relocate cities, demonstrates a parallel view of the city as impermanent, ephemeral and open to radical change. The Instant City has historical roots, rather than representing a new phenomenon in China.[5] Fastforwarding to the turn of the millennium, it has taken China only two decades to urbanize the population and landmass of Europe, which

had endured several centuries. Who could predict the rise of Shenzhen from a fishing village of 25,000 to nearly 10 million in just over a quarter century? Other than the planners in central government offices, who can name the 400 Chinese cities mushrooming from rural landscapes?

Can the Future be Predicted?

Given the current instable state of the global economy, along with planet earth's changing climate, there has never been a more crucial time to challenge, reassess and propose alternatives to conventional urban masterplanning and its associated techniques. By definition, Urban "Planning" assumes the future to be knowable and manageable, and able to be controlled and forecasted with great precision. By all means, the conception of the future need not be farmed out to Hollywood science fiction script-writers and animators, although Hollywood has often been more accurate in conjectures and representations, than the pictures of future urban conditions (hand) drawn by professional Urban Planners. Masterplanning strategies which seek an enduring final state of urban completion tend to lead to dysfunctional cities with limited capability to adapt and change, along with quickly obsolescent buildings. During the gold rush of global urbanization in recent years, the pre-eminent form of representation of future forms of urbanism has been rendered images of 3d digital models. This over-reliance on narrow, singular, inflexible pictures of the future disregards the inherent complexity of the modern world, and the manifold of forces, agents and contingencies which contribute to shape the future. Although staging or phasing is key to the management of large-scale urbanization in time, these methods still intend one singular outcome, rather than a more flexible set of mechanisms leading to various possible futures. Scenario-based planning can yield greater adaptability and hence a multiplicity of eventual outcomes, and these relational forms of urbanism aim for alternatives to masterplans based on stable urban typologies and teleological final states, necessitating the coding of mechanisms with capabilities to adapt to future contingencies. This approach to contemporary urbanism requires new vehicles with which to manage the immensely complex qualities of interaction, communication and exchange that characterise the 21st-century city. These investigations into aggregate, incremental and time-based models of urban growth, correlate top-down and bottom-up systems, played out as both a cyclic set of quotidian, weekly and seasonal phenomena, as well as longer-term timescales of urban growth and change.

Not limited to the scale of urbanism and being always/already relational, associative design methods aim for coherent yet heterogeneous and differentiated forms of architectural, structural and systemic organisation and expression. This approach to urbanism and architecture necessitates computation to manage dynamic information related to the varied performance of urban environments and architectural spaces, and the prototyping of innovations beyond standards and conventions. Parallel to countering the homogeneity of fast-track urbanism, these design methods aim towards an ordered sense of spatial

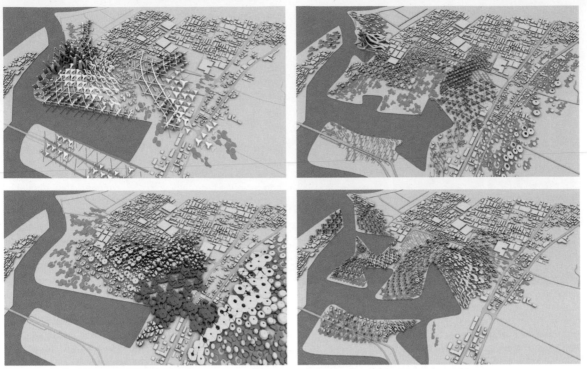

Four scenarios-based masterplans, demonstrating variable future development, with a variety of differentiated massing types, densities, FAR, open space rations, heights and other parameters, modelled in Rhinoceros/Grasshopper. AADRL Sahra team. Tutor: Tom Verebes; Students: Saif Almasri, Suryansh Chandra and Peter Sovinc, Parametric Urbanism 3, DRL v.11 2007–2009, Architectural Association

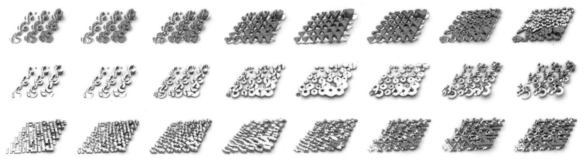

Morphing transformations of massing diagrams, demonstrating the potential to order space with coherent yet differentiated systems, installing a vast array of legible architectural difference, as a robust strategy for endurance and evolution. AADRL Sahra team. Tutor: Tom Verebes; Students: Saif Almasri, Suryansh Chandra and Peter Sovinc, Parametric Urbanism 3, DRL v.11 2007–2009, Architectural Association

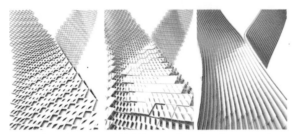

Parametric design systems which bias transformation of components, rather than their mere repetition, as applied to the design problem of generating diverse yet coherent facade patterns, controlling the orientation, duration and exposure to daylight. AADRL Sahra team. Tutor: Tom Verebes; Students: Saif Almasri, Suryansh Chandra and Peter Sovinc, Parametric Urbanism 3, DRL v.11 2007–2009, Architectural Association

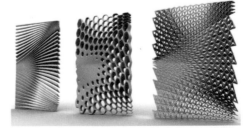

Abstract study of patterns controlling the orientation, duration and exposure to daylight. AADRL Sahra team. Tutor: Tom Verebes; Students: Saif Almasri, Suryansh Chandra and Peter Sovinc, Parametric Urbanism 3, DRL v.11 2007–2009, Architectural Association

VEREBES, Tom

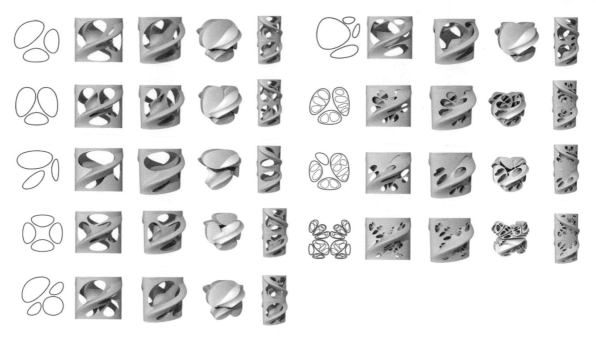

Diagrams of variable formal systems, describing incremental increased complexity of topology, torsion, scale, generating a wide range of specific massing conditions. AADRL 02R team. Tutor: Tom Verebes; Students: Rochana Chaugule, Yevgeniya Pozigun, Ujjal Roy, Praneet Verma, Parametric Urbanism 3, DRL v.11 2007–2009, Architectural Association

Series of massing prototypes, from singular to multiple massing components, with increasingly complex formal properties. AADRL 02R team. Tutor: Tom Verebes; Students: Rochana Chaugule, Yevgeniya Pozigun, Ujjal Roy, Praneet Verma, Parametric Urbanism 3, DRL v.11 2007–2009, Architectural Association

Adaptable masterplans of multiple future scenarios, driven by Maya MEL scripted Floor Area Ratio/density tools, and Catia parametric models; plans of FAR/height and massing views. AADRL 02R team. Tutor: Tom Verebes; Students: Rochana Chaugule, Yevgeniya Pozigun, Ujjal Roy, Praneet Verma, Parametric Urbanism 3, DRL v.11 2007–2009, Architectural Association

differentiation, diversity and difference. The potentials of these new tools and concepts are for mass customisation on the scale of the city—challenging repetitive, Fordist production and the mistakes made for decades in Europe and the Americas, yet still can be avoided in the current mass urbanization in Asia. Individual buildings of a series can be specified to contextual, environmental, user/owner criteria, and other information. Inherent to this position is a new concept of architectural typology, one which is not stable, fixed and static, but rather dynamic, multiplicitous and variable. The projects presented alongside this essay develop recursive, non-linear design methods, based on simple parametric forms of logic, responding to clearly stated performance criteria. Rather than reproducing known typologies, these design outcomes are dependent on prototyping methodologies and an associative, systems-based approach to design.

The 21st-century metropolitan experience is characterised by the complex interaction of associated systems, networks, structures, interfaces and codes. This discourse and these associated design projects are largely speculative, with few conclusions having been reached. This essay presents a set of conjectures concerning the indeterminacy, impossibility, yet paradoxically, the absolute necessity of planning for the future. In this sense, designers in the 21st century must design for endurance in a quickly changing world. If anything is assured, nothing is certain.

References

1. Koolhaas, Rem/AMO. The Gulf. Baden: Lars Müller Publishers, 2007, p. xviii
2. Kryza, Frank T. The Race for Timbuktu: In Search of Africa's City of Gold. New York: Harper Collins, 2006, Introduction, p. xiii
3. Grasso, June; Corrin, Jay and Michael Kort. Modernization and Revolution in China. New York: M.E. Sharpe Inc., 1991
4. Skinner, William. The City in Late Imperial China. Stanford, CA: Stanford Press, 1977
5. Campanella, Thomas J. The Concrete Dragon: China's Urban Revolution and What it Means to the World. New York: Princeton Architectural Press, 2008

Tom Verebes co-directed the AA Design Research Lab (DRL) at the Architectural Association in London, and had taught design studio and seminars in the post-professional MArch course from 1997-2009. He is currently associate professor in the Faculty of Architecture at the University of Hong Kong, and was formerly a guest/visiting professor at ABK Stuttgart. He is the founder and creative director of OCEAN. CN, a consultancy network based in Hong Kong, with links to Beijing, Shanghai, Jakarta and London, working on urban and architectural projects in China and the Asian region. He has written, published, exhibited and lectured extensively in Europe, North America, Asia and the Middle East.

Series of diagrams describing various stages of development of inter-related clusters of buildings, including a variety of different types, possible uses, scales, and densities. AADRL 123 team. Tutor: Tom Verebes; Students: Lindsay Bresser, Claudia Dorner, Sergio Reyes Rodríguez, Parametric Urbanism 3, DRL v.11 2007–2009, Architectural Association

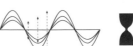

VEREBES, Tom

small components that can come together to create larger/diverse... flexibility

instead of seemingly random forms being placed together what if cities could be structured as a series of building blocks that allow for continuous expansion, overlap and intersection as resources become available?

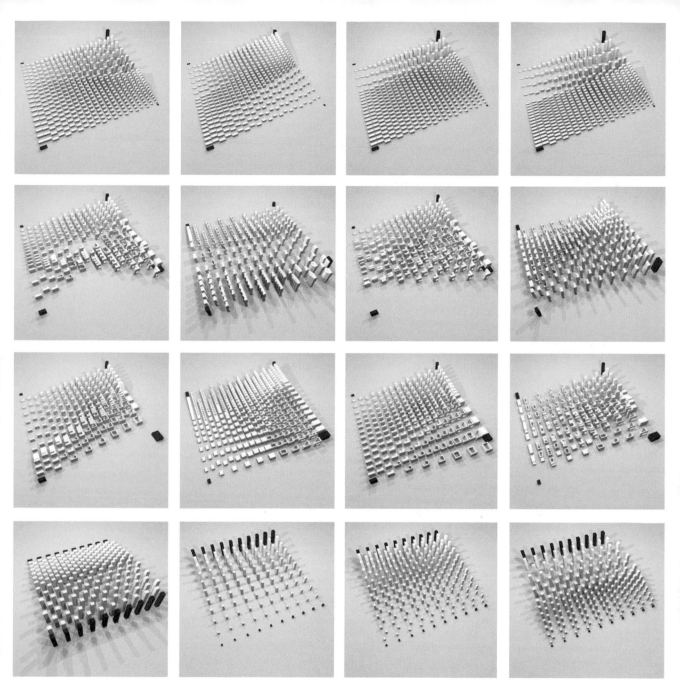

Typology and density studies, emphasising transformation of know massing types, generating hybrid, intermediate conditions of new prototypical massing forms with varied densities and proximities. Courtesy OCEAN.CN: Felix Robbins (Scripting), Tom Verebes, Gao Yan already visible patterns in large cities—just not as regular

DULIERE, Aude-Line and WONG, Clara

Over-Weathering: On Permanence and Resistance in the 2000s

Just as psychoanalysis reconstructs the original traumatic situation in order to release the repressed material, so we are now being plunged back into the archaeopsychic past, uncovering the ancient taboos and drives that have been dormant for epochs… Each one of us is as old as the entire biological kingdom, and our bloodstreams are tributaries of the great sea of its total memory.
—*J.G. Ballard*[1]

Buildings today are accelerated in regeneration, constructed for temporal needs.[2] What happens when these constructed objects persist in time? What if there is no booming economy to replace them? What if another type of program appropriation occurs—how would the users behave?

These graphic explorations focus on such speculative futures. We show not only what the future forms of buildings will be, but also possible adaptations by their users. These speculations glorify the absurdity of architectural forms in the 2000s. They underscore the consequent implications in building permanence and resistance. Contemporary buildings appear to have strong persistent forms in imagery, but weak reliance on any one program. The pretentious hyper-rationalization of "form follows program" is a myth to begin with. The permanence of these forms paradoxically offers low resistance to any new program.

How will these buildings over-live the period for which they have been intended?

In Over-Weathering, preservation is made possible by post-occupancy. Drawings depict a future state where buildings are occupied without being preserved programmatically or physically. The derivative of the survival of the fittest—fictional transformation of the non-adapted to the hegemony of the super-adapted.

Our gaze is evocative of the appropriation of ruins—of the ancient pyramids as well as of future ruins. What could be the result of such a population, willing to conserve iconic structures by appropriated programs?

These drawings represent the work of future archeologists exploring a current architectural trend. Archeologists explain the forms of the past from a rational and functional point of view. The technique of the close-up, theorized by Walter Benjamin[3] and his antecedents, is used to penetrate and understand the real subject. The expansion of space and the unveiling of new structural formations make the close-up a cinematic and architectural method to appropriate space. The result: the unexpected subject.

The depiction of these buildings in a dystopian stage projects us in an imaginable future. Through this dystopian vision, we question the future of architecture and particularly the aftermath of the hegemony of the major buildings that map the architectural landscape of our times. In the spirit of informal economy, we offer a lighthearted critique on contemporary iconic buildings.

References

1. Ballard, J.G. The Drowned World. *Orion Millennium, 1999, p. 41*

2. Mostafavi, Moshen and Leatherbarrow, David. On Weathering: The Life of Building in Time. *Cambridge, MA: The MIT Press, 1993, p. 23*

3. Benjamin, Walter. "The Work of Art in the Age of Mechanical Reproduction," in Illuminations. *New York: Schocken Books, 1969, p. 236*

Building credits: OMA, Rem Koolhaas, Casa da Música, concert hall, 2005, Porto, Portugal; OMA, Rem Koolhaas, CCTV, TV station headquarters, 2002, Beijing, China

Over-Weathering is the prologue of an ongoing project to be published in early 2010 as a book. The project started as an independent study at Harvard, advised by Sanford Kwinter, Michael Kubo, and Antoine Picon. We are indebted to Spyros Papapetros and Timothy Hyde, as well as Monica Ponce de Leon, Stan Allen, and Rafael Moneo. Special thanks to Jonathan D. Solomon and Ralph Lerner. **Aude-Line Duliere** and **Clara Wong** are rebellious daughters of the Koolhaasian 90s. They hold Master of Architecture degrees from Harvard University Graduate School of Design, and together are a model of global collaboration. Aude-Line Duliere is an architect and movie production designer with a Bachelor of Architecture degree from the Institut Superieur d'Architecture La Cambre. Her academic work builds on the dual nature of her experience and explores the crossroads between architecture and cinema. Clara Wong is a practicing architect, artist and academic, currently based in Hong Kong. She received her Bachelor degree *summa cum laude* from Princeton University School of Architecture, and graduated with awards from the Princeton University Program in Visual Arts, with a concentration in Drawing and Painting.

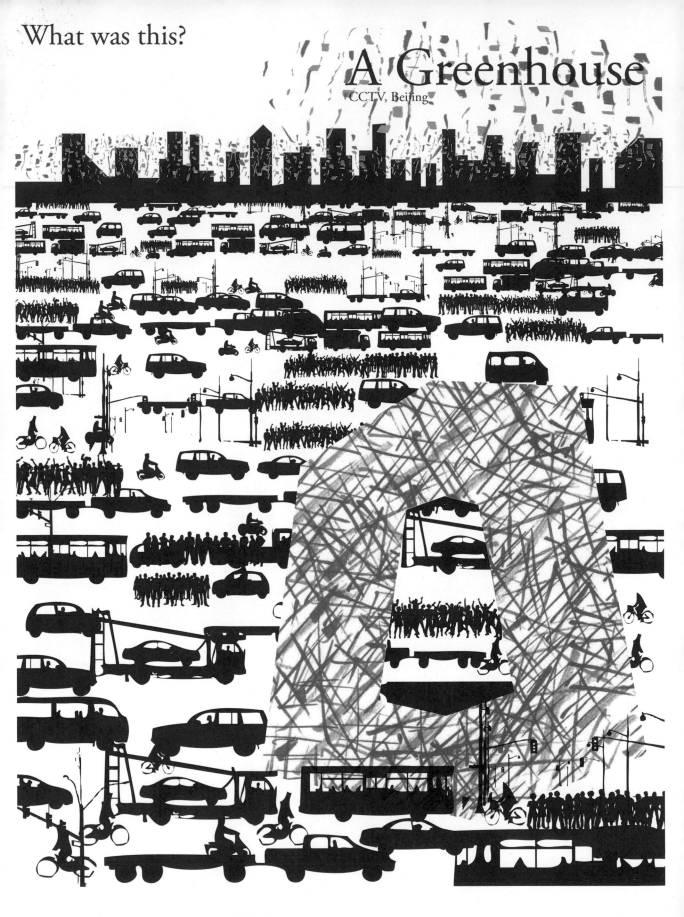

What was this?

A Greenhouse
CCTV, Beijing

DULIERE, Aude-Line and WONG, Clara

HONG KONG CULTURAL IMAGING
WORKSHOP

BE OUR GUEST

Constructing a hyper-real
Hong Kong

This work illustrates the role of
images as architecture in the
spatial manifestation of cultural
imagination. The photographs were
commissioned by developers to
project unique messages that might
have something to do with their
corporate identity, local context
or fantasized life-style.

    Here, image-as-architecture
allows spatial creation combining
real imges in an imaginary setting
that transforms both the original
images and context by lending both
a new meaning.

CHAN YIU HUNG (AH HUNG) has been one of
Hong Kong's most prolific photographers
of architectural design in recent years.
He graduated from Hong Kong Polytechnic
University with a BA(Hon) in Photographic
Design in 1994. He finished his studies with
an MA in Literary and Cultural Studies and
MSċ in Conservation in 1998 and 2009. Chan
is now the director of Hong Kong Cultural
Imaging Workshop Limited, where he applies his personal viewpoint, perception,
and hidden messages to add value to the
environment of commercial image-making,
incorporating artistic aesthetics with
commercial value. He has exhibited in the
Hong Kong Pavilion at La Biennale di Venezia
in 2008 and in "Heritage Branding" at the
Helena May.

The Palazzo, Hong Kong

HONG KONG CULTURAL IMAGING WORKSHOP

Advance Business Park, Beijing

Disney's Hollywood Hotel, Hong Kong

HONG KONG CULTURAL IMAGING WORKSHOP

30b090 13

H Cube, Hong Kong

HONG KONG CULTURAL IMAGING WORKSHOP

H Cube, Hong Kong

Tessa, 27 years old:

Tennis shoes, Van Haert, €12,00; black jeans, H&M, €24,95; vest, Zara, €39,95; T-shirt, American Apparel, €15,00; bag, FREITAG, (second hand), €40; triangle bra, HEMA, €35; g-string, Bijenkorf Basic, €24; socks, HEMA, €2,50; watch, Swatch, €65; mobile phone, Nokia 6120, €0 with two year contract; bike, Gazelle, (second hand), €110; cigarettes Marlboro light €4 per pack; neighborhood, Blijdorp, Rotterdam; average housing price €1850 per m2; public space finishing, granulaat beton klinker, €30 per m2

SVERDLOV, Alexander

LEGS

ALEXANDER SVERDLOV was educated in architecture at the Moscow Architectural Institute and the Berlage Institute, Rotterdam. From 2002 to 2007 he worked as an architect and project architect of large-scale projects at Neutelings Riedijk, West 8, Architecten Cie, and OMA/AMO. In 2007 he established his own design practice SVESMI (www.svesmi.eu) in Rotterdam. In recent years Alexander Sverdlov has won several awards in international competitions. He was a co-curator and a contributor to the Shrinking Cities project by the German Cultural Foundation, as well as to the International Biennale Rotterdam in 2005, 2007 and 2009. Alexander Sverdlov taught, lectured and was a guest juror at various schools in Europe, including The Berlage Institute, Sheffield School of Architecture, AHO and ETH Zurich. He is a lecturer/researcher at the Faculty of Architecture TU Delft.

Svetlana, 27 years old:

Shoes, aPair, €320; leather bag, Prada, €520; dress, Muji €315; push-up bra, Victoria's Secret, €120; g-string, Victoria's Secret, €64; black leggings, Waldorf, €100; bracelet, Swarovsky, €250; mobile phone, Samsung L310, €95; cigarettes, Vogue Menthol Super Slim, €0.85 per pack; neighborhood, Mnevniki, Moscow; average housing price €4900 per m2; public space finishing, asphalt, €.8 per m2, sand, earth, no cost

SAMPLE, Hilary

TOWERS, MAINTENANCE, AND THE DESIRE FOR EFFORTLESS PERMANENCE

Architecture relies upon a never-ending regime of labor called maintenance. The purpose of maintenance is to restore newness to architecture by offsetting the effects of climate, environment and time—it is an ongoing and continuous act. Within crowded urban environments, where maintenance is unavoidably public, it has become a spectacle in its own right, fuelled by new technologies and novel techniques. This spectacle is especially evident at the site of large transparent exterior surfaces, where the distinct machines, apparatuses, materials and techniques of maintenance have become part of the image of the city.

Artists like Mierle Laderman Ukeles, Vanessa van Dam, Sarah Morris and Job Koelewijn have investigated the act of maintenance labor in public institutional and commercial spaces, while others, including Jeff Wall, Iñigo Manglano Ovalle, and Ila Bêka and Louise Lemoîne, have drawn attention to maintenance within the domestic interior. Many of these works are canonic photographs of canonic architecture, but reconfiguring the imagery to draw attention to the arduous, isolated and alienated task of maintenance labor. They destabilize the status of the architectural icon by revealing the laborer, disrupting the privileged subjectivity of most architectural imagery with the difficult, lived-in, messy, exploitative and oppressive. Here architecture is portrayed at its most vulnerable: weak and prone to constant decay, wholly

dependent upon a type of labor and constituency that its enthusiasts typically overlook. While this type of work may satisfy popular suspicions that so-called good architecture is impractical and unsympathetic to its users, especially those tasked with its maintenance, there is also, in fact, much for architecture to learn from a different kind of inhabitation. The act of window-washing, as opposed to its internal counterpart janitorial labor or housekeeping, has become an essential reality affecting performance and aesthetics of architecture.

Artist Vanessa van Dam's window washing installation at the Pharos Office Tower (2003) near Amsterdam by Kohn Pederson Fox Architects, offers one such critique on the anonymous glass office building. To explore the relationship between architecture and maintenance, van Dam proposed the installation of 85 industrial-sized window wipers typically found on airplanes and lighthouses. While the project was never built, the wipers were designed to respond to a programmed script activated by sensors in tune with shifting local weather conditions. The synchronicity of the mechanized façade in action, ever vigilant against the effects of weather and dirt, embodies the modernist injunction of cleanliness in robotic hyperactivity. The addition of the black and heavy arms on the light glass and aluminum façade brings maintenance to the foreground, revealed as an object of a mechanized fantasy that threatens to overtake the architecture itself.

Where maintenance labor is irrepressible from the public view, it poses a major challenge to the status of the architectural object and architecture's projected image. Every method of maintenance labor offers up a social critique of architecture's ambitions. The potential for maintenance labor to disrupt this ambition, particularly in the canonic work of architecture,

is so great that the labor itself is often preemptively transformed into spectacle, a sort of architectural sideshow. This is especially true regarding one of the primary tasks of urban maintenance labor—window washing. It is a spectacle with two main modes: the technologically advanced—usually robotic—and the intensely manual—often involving special skills and re-purposed mountain-climbing equipment. In either case, the newness of the architecture is not only maintained, but symbolically reinforced by innovative techniques publicized as a testimony to the status and uniqueness of the architectural object. This is the case with SOM's Lever House, the first large-scale façade designed specifically to accommodate a window-washing gondola transporting workers. The regime sprang into action once every two weeks, providing a demonstration that underscored the company's soap and detergent products, creating an iconic architectural form in line with the corporate message. SOM's building follows in the tradition of Le Corbusier's Cité de Refuge, technically the first building to promote the concept of window-washing. Lever House goes further, integrating modern architecture and modern advertising, an architectural technology performing ad copy. Like a billboard for Lever soap, the regularly scheduled program of upkeep was integrated into the componentry of the architecture. This project is exemplary for debating the performance of architecture in relation to inhabitation, representation and the maintenance of architecture.

From this precedent, two more recent projects diverge, respectively revealing the trajectories of maximized mechanical technology on the one hand, and maximized ad hoc, low-wage human capital on the other. The images of SOM's Sears Tower (1970–73) in Chicago and the National Aquatic Center (2004–08) in Beijing, known

Facade of Pharos building, Hoofddorp, Vanessa van Dam, 2002, never realized. Image courtesy of the artist. Photographer: Gertjan Kocken, image manipulation: Nick Strong

as the Watercube, each capture acts of urban maintenance, spectacles that belie architecture's traditional notions of effortless permanence. Similar to the Lever House, the Sears Tower, notable for its height and innovative structural design, employs new technologies to achieve optimum, real-time upkeep. Its performance relies on the six roof-mounted robots, all operated remotely by an engineer, that roam continuously, weather-permitting, over its glass façade to clean all 16,000 windows. Building on earlier precedents, Sears Tower eliminates the need for skilled laborers working in dangerous conditions while magnifying a potential technological utopia. Fast-forward 30 years to witness the recent, fast-paced construction of the Watercube's seemingly mysterious building skin, which is made from Ethylene tetrafluoroethylene (ETFE), a non-stick, low friction and stain resistant surface. It is capable of spanning greater distances than glass. The invisibility of the chemically altered material is rendered visible by Beijing's heavily polluted

Engineer inspecting Sears Tower's window-washing robot. Image courtesy of Hedrich Blessing

urban air, which proved less than amenable to the high-performance translucent membrane, depositing unacceptable amounts of grime on the postcard-ready façades. With China's minimal labor costs and abundance of laborers, a low-tech, less-robotic/mechanized solution resurfaced: a team of individually-suspended human window washers with hand-held

China bee extinction

cleaning equipment. This moment was enthusiastically captured by the international press, fascinated with harnessed workers rappelling from bubble to bubble scrubbing the 4,000 "pillows," as if this sort of performance had been planned as a way to further integrate architecture into the spectacle of the Olympics. Where the Lever House building acted as

Maintenance of the Watercube, 2008. Image courtesy of Getty Images

a demonstration of cleanliness associated with the company's products and a particular way of life, the Watercube—prominently visible on the world stage—demonstrates the Chinese government's readiness for cleanliness and skill in amassing workers for a demonstration that is both performance and a spectacle of man over nature.

Decay and ecology upends architecture's ambition for total control and stability over its natural environment. Is it an unavoidable reality, as Le Corbusier's 1929 section drawings of the Cité de Refuge window-washers illustrated? Architecture despite recent efforts still needs to be maintained. But so far, today's sustainable conversation condemns maintenance labor to hiding in plain sight in perpetuity. Maintenance, reconsidered, could be a new trajectory to inform the inhabitation of buildings, as we struggle to understand the new complexity of surrounding transparency.

HILARY SAMPLE is a principal of MOS, and an assistant professor at the Yale School of Architecture.

BRAZIER, J. Cressica and LAM, Tat

Go West, Go Big, Go Green? A Journey through China's "Great Opening of the West"

The Go West campaign, or *Xibu Da Kaifa*, was declared in 1999 by then-Premier Zhu Rongji to attract investment to China's interior, initially via marquee infrastructural projects that would increase connectivity with the coastal provinces, redress economic disparities, and thus ensure social stability.

As a reaction to the Reform and Opening campaign that had heavily favored the Eastern regions, the Go West campaign quickly proved that closing China's East-West gap would not be as straightforward as a pipeline or an irrigation canal: limited central funding, insufficient incentives for foreign investors, human capital drained by emigration and low education levels, and a historically disadvantaged ecosystem posed potentially insurmountable challenges.[1]

Nearly a decade into the campaign, by way of grandiose urban strategies and ill-advised acts of infrastructure, the interior megacities of China remain a critical battleground for negotiating between development, ecology, and social justice. In the summer of 2008, we turned our backs on the model cities of Beijing, Shanghai and Shenzhen, to re-evaluate the intentions and consequences of the Opening of the West, in the campaign's "dragon's head" urban centers of Chongqing, Chengdu, and Xi'an.

We sought to document what the mega-strategy looked like at ground level, while reading the subtexts of big infrastructure and big development. These three megacities are visibly struggling to redefine themselves. With one foot in the realm of real estate and the other in architectural research, we encountered three recurring scales of challenges for China's interior urbanization: the burdens of regional governance hierarchies and socioeconomic inequalities, the adoption of coastal development strategies in the interior and its consequences, and individual resistances and aspirations to modern development.

Xibu Da Kaifa: Regional Ideologies with Natural Consequences

The Reform and Opening campaign, announced by Deng Xiaoping in 1978, paved the way for the implicit sanctioning of the expansion of the *Kaifa*, or development, concept in the modern political context of mainland China. The instantiation of the methodological *Kaifa* in the economic Development Zones, or *Kaifa Qu*, added a layer of instrumentality to the ideology of the Reform and Opening. It also recast the large-scale success of the

Special Economic Zones as a replicable model for foreign direct investment throughout China, with the first Development Zone in Dalian, in 1984. However, it was not until 1987, when trailblazing private developer Luo Jinxing made his first solo moves,[2] that the physical practice of *Kaifa* in the context of real estate development could be accepted as reality in mainland China. The ideological *Kaifa* started the game, the methodological *Kaifa* operates the game, and the practical *Kaifa* plays the game.

The ideological development of the Go West campaign, *Xibu Da Kaifa*, suggests the exploration and pioneering of a piece of empty land. This *Kaifa* has assumed that *Xibu* (Western China) is an undeveloped, unmodernized and even uncivilized frontier. The government desires to *kaifa* the periphery to become more aligned with the center. This *Kaifa* is the ideological layer: to unify the natural resources and human capital and rectify the popularly-perceived backwards situation of Western China. The terminology of the *Xibu Da Kaifa* can operate both as a slogan to align public opinion and as large-scale marketing propaganda to attract investment.[3]

The structure of the Go West campaign follows a hierarchy of centers and peripheries in the classic propagandist strategy of the CCP: "centered around x." This structuring hierarchy traces the transmission of the overarching objectives from the central government, as mandated by party ideology, through the national, provincial, municipal and Development Zone levels, down to the local operators. Individual subjects, both migrant and local, may not participate in the operation, but rather respond to the local interpretation of objectives, such as in the countertrends of suburbanization of urban residents and urbanization of migrants. The source of this "centered" rhetoric is Deng Xiaoping's speech, immediately following the Cultural Revolution, in which he shifted the focus of the country from class-struggle-centered to economic development-centered. He declared that all institutions, units, and individuals should obey and serve this center.

Due to recent interpretations of development, however, this centered hierarchy has been criticized as gradually losing its significance, devolving from Deng's "economic development-centered" ideology (*yi jingji jianshe wei zhongxin*) to a "GDP-centered" model (*yi GDP wei zhongxin*). The hierarchy is further diminished at the local level by the interpretation of development as a myopic emphasis on individual "project-centered" goals (*yi xiangmu wei zhongxin*), at the expense of environmental protection, social advancement, health and cultural development. Eventually, both slogan and policy will lose their meaning.[4]

The Go West policy ostensibly was set out with the intention of holistic development. Even the 2009 World Development Report continues to herald the interior campaign as an "area approach" that will "reap the benefits of scale economies, promote the mobility of goods and workers, and improve the well-being of migrants to cities."[5] However, the stated goals—namely of "speeding up infrastructure construction, strengthening agriculture's position as the basic industry, adjusting the industrial structure, developing tourism, developing science and technology education, cultural resources, and public health work, and ecological construction,"[6]—found their implementation only through the state mandate of large-scale infrastructure projects.

These targeted projects were easily subsumed into the "infrastructural imperialism" that would serve the overarching ideology of the construction of a "harmonious society" while ensuring the economic stability of coastal provinces. The requisite four-character slogans clearly spatialized these intentions of the national-scale infrastructure: Electricity from West to East, Water from South to North, Natural Gas from West to East, Qinghai-Tibet Railway (or, Minerals from High Plateau to Coastal Industry). The 10 spearhead projects consisted of transportation links for Xi'an and Chongqing, highways that could span nearly half the circumference of the Earth, followed by the natural gas pipeline, a dam in Sichuan and an irrigation works in Ningxia. The reforestation project spans 13 provinces, and fertilizer development takes advantage of Qinghai's resource reserves. Finally, greater support for universities has been extended.

In 2005 and 2008, the scope of infrastructural and industrial projects attached to the Go West campaign was even further extended, with the addition of oil refinement, coal mining and health and social projects.[7] Despite the continued concentration on interior development, the gap between both Eastern and Western China and rural and urban areas is widening.

The characters kaifa can be interpreted in three ways: "opening," "development," and, significantly, "exploitation." Mao's belief in "man over nature" was only slightly softened by Deng Xiaoping's declaration of economic development as "the absolute path." Even as emphasis is shifted to the development of "harmonious society," there is mounting tension between the level of economic stimulus needed to sustain the harmony and the environmental exploitation that is destabilizing rural communities.

The vast majority of China's environmental degradation is occurring in the Western regions, and "preliminary evidence is that the campaign framework is largely inadequate and even inappropriate for the environmental protection needs of the region."[8] Logging bans have driven Chinese loggers to the forests of Burma. Not only did the afforestation strategy create a subclass of former farmers who are now dependent on central government handouts,[9] but the scope of the project was fabricated as well: "half of the reported national afforestation claim was false, and the survival rate of planted trees was no higher than 40 percent."[10] As will be explored further in the case of the Zipingpu dam, campaigns to clean up water supplies are leaving voids in the economies of areas, both urban and rural, that are dependent on the polluting industries. Elizabeth Economy summarizes the shortcomings of such area approaches in the context of environmental protection: "the campaigns tend to be highly politically charged with significant investment up front but little follow-through past the stated target of completion; central government officials rarely consult local officials to engage them in the campaign; and the environmental components do not employ the best policy approaches, technologies, or incentives to change behavior."[11]

issues w/ top-down

Kaifa Qu: Development Zones as Methodology

In China's West, the localized moves—the "policy engine driving economic growth"[12]—of the development game are playing out not at the scale of superblock allocation to developers, nor under the nearly nonexistent umbrella of urban planning, but primarily at the large-scale, peri-urban level of Development Zones (DZs). The *Kaifa Qu* becomes a methodology by which local governments can respond to the ideological *Kaifa* of central policy. The *Kaifa Qu* is project-centered, with particular themes named by the government, which also implies political support, beneficial conditions for development, infrastructural improvements, and government-invited enterprises.

The Development Zone phenomenon could be described as a form of accidental urbanism. Impressed by the economic growth of the special economic zones (SEZs) during his visits of Shenzhen and Zhuhai in 1984, Deng Xiaoping noted that he would consider designating more zones for foreign investment, but would not call them SEZs.[13] In May of that year, the central government promptly translated Deng's words into the Development Zone strategy, starting in some 14 cities and working inward from the coast. The functions of DZs were articulated as the "four windows": the window of technology, the window of management, the window of knowledge, and the window of opening beyond China.

Southern Hi-Tech DZ of Chongqing

The second overarching policy directive was the "three prioritizations, and one enforcement" (*san wei zhu, yi zhi li*), which were the prioritization of industrial development, attraction of foreign investment and exportation, and the enforcement of advanced and innovative technology. The local governments' response to all of these political principles was easily predictable: DZs grew dramatically in size and spread throughout China, with similar slogan-goals—"attracting commerce, drawing capital"-(*zhaoshang yinzi*). A decade after Deng spoke in 1984, there were already over 4,200 DZs in China.[14]

The Go West program has adopted this Development Zone as its dominant marketing and urban space methodology. The DZ, in its most beneficial sense, attaches to the transportation hub of the city, and takes advantage of infrastructural resources to pull development into surrounding areas. The strategy, "*yixian chuandian, yidian daimian*,"[15] literally means to connect the points with a line, then to fan out from these points to the area. Xi'an, Chengdu and Chongqing are the designated nodes, and the peri-urban areas extending outwards from the traditional industrial bases—heavy industry, plus computer and biomedical technology on the Chengyu (Chengdu-Chongqing) axis, and equipment manufacturing, aerospace and modern agricultural technology to unify the Xi'an-Xianyang system—become the targets of the DZ demarcation.

The map of clearly-demarcated Development Zones becomes an image of ambition rather than possibility, superimposed on the sprawl of each city. This dissonance between the Development Zone boundaries and the built-up urban area defines Western China's manifestation of the edgeless city. Their layout is driven by the demands of investment, which has rarely led to the optimized clusters of cooperative industries that the zones anticipated. Moreover, the DZs are not harmless boundaries on a map. Speculative real estate sprawl is the visible indicator of the loss of open space, but the Development Zones are the initial perpetrators of the conversion of what is often the most productive farmland to non-agricultural land use—or to be left idle.

In 1997, even before the establishment of most of the Go West DZs, a study determined that only 20 percent of the 12,357 planned area of Development Zones was being utilized, and 55 percent of that total area had formerly been cultivated farmland.[16] The establishment of a DZ

also rapidly re-centers the priorities of public projects, drawing funding away from the city center to serve business interests. Well-watered green parks and mass transport systems that service the farthest reaches of the zones are characteristic, while older suburbs such as eastern Chengdu rely on a single limited bus service.

Kaifa Shang: Real Estate Practicalities

The *Kaifa* of real estate development (*Kaifa Shang*) connotes the ways in which private operators utilize the official methods and political ideology of *Kaifa* to impose developments on the urban system. The current practice of this development—using existing infrastructure to accumulate people (either residents or speculators) into significant profits through real estate projects—plays out within the *Kaifa Qu*, or DZ. Taking advantage of the DZ's positioning, the *Kaifa Shang* may package the development in different terms, such as tourism, hi-tech communities, or ecology, but the end result is development driven by and producing practicalities.

An official may make use of a project to operate within the bureaucratic system, and the developer will share interest in that project to operate within the market system. The relationship between these operators is more complex, however: the developer-official may join into a single entity when exploiting the *kaifa* project, but certain changes within the system, such as a shift in the central government's policy, may cause the single entity to "become" two entities again. The dualism of conflict is thus commuted to the dualism of harmony, so that all three interpretations of *Kaifa* may operate in concert.

Each of the three major development models—Beijing, Shanghai and Shenzhen—reacts to and emphasizes very different building criteria, such as housing orientation in northern Beijing and natural views for southern Shenzhen. The real estate development model of Chongqing follows the southern instant city of Shenzhen. Longhu Development, one of the largest local developers in Chongqing, began sending their staff to study the most successful Shenzhen developer, Vanke, at the beginning of the 21st century. Their takeaway lessons went beyond execution strategies; they also learned how to manage their housing as an after-sold service.

Western Hi-Tech DZ of Chengdu

View east towards Chanba Ecological Zone, Xi'an

Eventually, more local developers adapted the Shenzhen style, synthesized with the local market context, and even transformed the style to accommodate their unique topography. Chongqing has been made an example for the dynamics between developer and official: money is often exchanged for better development criteria, such as higher FAR, which results in instant market benefits for the developer, areas that are entirely unreasonable in terms of urban planning theory—and, with increasing frequency, prosecution for corruption, as in the case of the former Chongqing Planning Department principal's arrest.[17]

The spatial structure of state-owned enterprises has had a lasting effect on the urban system of Chengdu. In contrast to coastal cities, Chengdu was the object of the reconsideration of Mao's Third Front strategy of remote placements of industries, in which the factories were relocated to the urban zone.[18] As the resident population has doubled and the floating population tripled, the built area of the city has increased from 60 to 228sq. km.[19] High-end residential development is shifting to the sub-center in the south, where the government is building a new municipal administrative complex. The brand new sub-city is surrounded by numerous multi-use development projects and public megastructures, including the gigantic exhibition and convention center.

Xi'an transformed from gritty to glamorous in eight years, but it still frames its planning in the nine-square construct, replicating the Princely City diagram on a massive scale, with the Tang dynasty Chang'an still at the core. In updated terms, its strategy is an immense "multi-center" network, with sub-centers that will compete and compensate for each other's functions and programs. The old city core maintains its centrality, and five directions have been predefined by historical development and DZs: the new administrative center, airport and ETDZ to the north; the technology center to the southwest and tourism zone to the southeast; the west maintains its manufacturing gravity; and the east is transformed into a tourism and high-end residential zone.

The dominant trend of real estate development branding focuses on historical and cultural image-making, as the marketing value of and confidence in local culture increases.[20] The high incidence of superblocks with near-identical names, such as "royal" and "imperial" attached to some form of gardens, speaks to the monoculture into which the real estate industry has diluted the complexity of Xi'an culture.

Xi'an: Ecological Propaganda

From the seat of a bicycle—we imagined cycling was the only satisfactory means to observe an Ecological Zone—the vision of the Chanba DZ was bleak. As we criss-crossed the Chanhe river on highway bridges, we peered through the haze to find little more than trash collecting on the riverbanks. None of the promised villas had sprouted yet, but fortunately we couldn't see any traces of the eco-zone's only concrete claim to fame, as host to the 2007 Powerboat Racing World Championship, either.

The intersection of environmental crisis and development is clearly visible on the eastern edge of Xi'an. Due to urban expansion, the Chanhe and Bahe rivers that once formed a natural boundary were severely polluted, and this environmental degradation subsequently became the barrier for further, desirable development. Local officials were determined to *yi du gong du*—fight poison with poison: "After deliberation, the city government decided on the strategy of building an industrial development zone in the polluted area, using development to curb pollution."[21] Road access was quickly in place—"infrastructure has been built at such an amazing rate that local people say they can see changes every day"—and such innovative strategies as constructing hills out of chemically-treated garbage were inflicted on the landscape.[22]

The loss of the ecological green belt of the Chanba sub-center would be a matter of course, if it were not commonly known that it had formerly been part of a more responsible strategy to create measured surrounding development and protect its ecosystem. To relieve the pressure of the expansion of Lintong, a city beyond the Chanba zone, towards the Terracotta Warriors site, a new urban center would be developed just outside the Chanba area so that Lintong would be attracted towards Xi'an proper. The west bank of the Chanhe river could then be locked in as a green belt. This is the point at which the local officials re-considered their profits and promoted the strategy of shifting the center closer to Xi'an, and directly on to the scenic riverbank.[23]

The Chanba planning failure is also a demonstration of the problematic interaction of systems of governance and development, via a well-tested strategy that traveled from the Eastern provinces: control of media. Competition between Development Zones for scarce (or nonexistent) investment sources requires a massive propaganda budget to reach its target audience of provincial leaders. The Xi'an Hi-Tech DZ, in the southwest sector, purchased large advertorials that claimed a major corporation had signed on, when in reality no significant corporations had yet to commit to setting up bases there. But the propaganda successfully served the secondary function of fueling real estate speculation in the zone, where "land

Slum surrounded by high-rises in Yuzhong, Chongqing

and housing prices were the highest in all of Xi'an" and land leases were controlled by the Gaoke real estate group, in which the local officials were primary stakeholders. To compete in image, the Chanba Ecological Zone "successively bought whole pages in local newspapers to applaud the government's achievements… publishing so many advertisements that other zones sent representatives to Chanba to beg for relief from the cut-throat competition."[24]

Chongqing: Accessible Consumption

At Yangren Jie (Foreigner Street), we could purchase bottled water on the honor system, depositing one kuai into the lockbox. We could gaze across the Yangtze river into Chongqing's Northern Economic and Technological Development Zone—it is absolutely barren—while snacking on mutton skewers selected from the dozens of vendors lining the riverbank. We could swing across the Lover's Bridge on our way to the Largest Public Toilet in the World, housed in a Sphinx-faced adobe palace. We didn't do any of these things, but we observed thousands of weekenders who traveled to the remote development to experience this alternate reality.

The flamboyant *Yangren Jie* theme park, the gateway tourist attraction to the hinterland housing developments of the Meixin Corporation, targets a population in between the ecological gentrification of Xi'an Qujiang's garden

city and the sustainable poverty of Chengdu's eastern suburbs. For this growing group on the verge of middle-classdom, it represents an accessible alternative to the glitzy consumption of Liberation Monument Plaza in the center of Chongqing. The theme park was conceived as a novel marketing tool for the next phases of housing development, and the model attracted the support of local government and large-scale investors.[25] With the construction of the new Chongqing Central Business District spreading into the ETDZ directly across the Big Buddha Temple Bridge from Foreigner Street, the project will soon receive even greater attention. Its current big-ness is only the beginning: 1,500 high-end towers and the largest tennis training base in Asia are planned to round out the Meixin empire.[26]

Foreigner Street's unique brand of propaganda has reached out to and captured the attention of both society and government, even as it has been criticized for devaluating culture in its branding strategy.[27] Most of the attractions are gimmicks—Western bars, French weddings, stores, mostly vacant, with free rent to small vendors and craftsmen. However, the use of the honor system for payments, the openness and anything-goes attitude of the park, and even the acceptance of partici-pation in a mass public display (although the vision of "the capacity for over 2,000 people to use the facilities at the same time"[28] is neither likely nor desirable) mean

that the consumer experience has been conflated with an alternative, but not necessarily devalued, cultural space.

This gateway to consumerism leaves open the possibility of developing the theme park concept to further transform attitudes towards ecological participation, if not responsible consumption. Could the Sphinx toilet complex be retrofitted as the world's largest demonstration of the benefits of on-site human waste recycling? What kinds of sustainable vendors could infiltrate the free stands and interface with this class of producers who are fast becoming consumers?

Chengdu: Recycling Migrations

Beyond the Chengdu Industrial Culture Museum (closed for reconsideration), we pause to watch a demolition crew working to flatten the vast Sanhe district; they are amused to have an audience for the dramatic toppling of a two-story brick wall. Past the Fluorescent Tube Factory's smokestacks and the Chengdu Electric Company's dormitories, we enter the warrens of the recyclers' village. Apart from the one bystander who scolds us for needlessly photographing people's homes, they are uncannily friendly and curious, as if they hadn't received a new visitor in ages.

If the Development Zones artificially inflate the spatial impact of these megacities, then the mass labor migration is the densifying force, largely unacknowledged

and unaddressed at any level of development strategy, despite the dependence of both DZs and real estate construction on cheap labor. In a total nationwide migration of 200 million, 1.7 million arrive in Chengdu (still only one-third of the amount who exit the province), Chongqing's urban population grows by nearly 50 percent when accounting for its 3 million migrants, and Xi'an receives 850,000 rural workers.[29] The vast majority in all these cases are intra-provincial movements, in contrast to the coastal provinces. They occupy a similar mix of employment areas as well: about 30 percent in self-employed (*getihu*) retail, 20 percent in the service industry, and 50 percent in construction and manufacturing. As a more localized population, these migrants tend to have greater mobility, spending up to half the year on farms and rural enterprises, than their counterparts from outside the province.[30]

The Sanhe area first appears as a frozen image of *danwei* urbanism, or the superblock organization system of state-owned enterprises (SOEs). The area does still operate in the work-unit lifestyle, with factories, housing and streets lined with *getihu* storefronts. In the 1960s and 1980s, there were two waves of construction of state-owned factories, one of which was the restructuring of Third Front strategy. The area is undergoing yet another adjustment phase, an upgrading of the factory types and the clearing of space for new development, which has precipitated major relocations and layoffs.[31] This evacuation is directly linked to the outlying eastern Shuangliu zone via the adoption of the DZ methodology as urban plan: "Spatially, the Chengdu ETDZ strategy is typical in China in that it represents a destination site for firms being relocated from the core city (in this case the northeast quadrant), a wise policy."[32] It may be an advantageous move for regional economic systems, but in terms of sustainable development, it has given rise to yet another phase of demolitions and migration pressures.

These two eastern areas can also be compared by their migrant labor systems. A concentration of the floating population in Sanhe has added an organic and constructive dimension to the area's otherwise disintegrating economy. The area's proximity to the city, mixture of metalworking and other heavy industries, and the endless supply of demolition debris have combined to enable a unique *getihu* class: the small-scale metal recycling industry. The size of the state-owned enterprises, and the increasing voids between them, allow for the *getihu* economic system to operate distributed agencies between the SOEs, juxtaposing macro and micro-scale scenarios.[33]

The recycler *getihu* system also tends to absorb many of the new incoming provincial migrants, while the ETDZ attracts both new migrants and those returning from the coastal provinces. In the latter scenario, there is some evidence that Go West marketing may begin to equilibrate the flows of inter-provincial migrants. The challenges of accommodating this returning population also appear to be balanced by both social and economic benefits: "Returned migrants have a stronger intention to work in the home province, where they plan to put down roots, after being an "outsider" elsewhere. These returned workers can play an ambassador or linkage role between the Inner West and the Coastal East in terms of technology transfer, and market information sharing, based on their (former) personal networks in the coastal area."[34]

Chengdu: Bottom-up Reactions to Unnatural Disasters

Two months after 5/12, the aftershocks of the Wenchuan earthquake are tangible, visible, audible: we feel a slight tremor while crossing the street, in the Shahe industrial area we discover an abandoned building taken over by an art benefit for earthquake survivors, and we hear the buzz of millions of Sichuanese still sifting through the myriad ways in which they are coping with the consequences. "The earthquake has accelerated the urbanization process," leaving one transportation planner to contend with the new migrants who have been propelled into the city. "People from nearby counties feel it is safer to move to Chengdu instead of living in the earthquake area." Another architect, in Liu Jiakun's studio, relates how he has reconfigured his working days around trips to the temporary camps, in his role in the rebuilding process.

The Zipingpu dam, just 70km from Chengdu's center, numbered in the 10 marquee projects of the Western Development campaign. It is an object lesson in the ideological operation of the Go West strategy: the Sichuan and Chengdu city governments had repeatedly lobbied the central government to approve the dam, but only after the announcement of the campaign did the project win support and seed funding. With this favorable attention, the local governments were successful in attracting the balance of investment, the standing of the provincial officials was in turn bolstered, and the province was further enabled to secure more centrally-mandated projects.

The byproducts of this cycle were increased intra-regional economic asymmetries, notably through the severance of livelihoods in industry, forestry and farming: Wenchuan's factories—many of them relics of the Third Front—were taken offline to ensure an unpolluted reservoir, and greater access allowed for enforcement of logging bans, implementation of reforestation campaigns and closer integration of this minority-populated area.[35]

As the reservoir filled in 2004, Sichuan officials hoped that the Zipingpu project would place Wenchuan on the investment map, and it soon did: in December 2008, it was proposed that the reservoir's weight had hastened the Wenchuan fault rupture.[36] Government expenditure on earthquake reconstruction has been pledged to surpass $440 billion;[37] the total public investment promised to the Go West campaign to date is $170 billion[38] (At least there was one Western Development project, the highway to

Recyclers' village in eastern industrial area of Chengdu

Dujiangyan, that was indispensable for Chengdu's disaster response). The build-up to this crisis also contains a troubling reality: the government had wanted to clear out the bad assets in these outlying cities, and the earthquake accelerated that agenda.

Beyond the campaign for water security that had brought the dam to the city's doorstep, the earthquake's effect on popular attitudes is causing major shifts in the development of Chengdu. Overnight, structural quality became a major branding point, if not an obligation, for the local real estate market.[39] The Chengdu government then voiced its dedication to providing a supportive environment for the sustainable development of real estate in the post-5/12 era.[40]

But these seemingly positive consequences are coupled with a cascading effect of detrimental development pressures. The post-earthquake Chengdu real estate market is believed to face a short period—less than a year—of contraction, as individual buyers weigh questions of construction safety against affordability, which may still disadvantage pre-earthquake housing stock and lead to further demolition.[41] But for those who can afford it, the prediction is a gradual movement towards Chengdu due to its perceived good performance during the earthquake.

A survey conducted by the Central Real Estate Development Ltd (*Zhongquan Dichan*) revealed that 51 percent of their interviewees would choose apartments lower than the fifth floor and only 5 percent of them would live on the 20th story or higher. For the sake of this lower-density architecture, there will be waves of suburbanization around Chengdu, most likely favoring the Southern Hi-Tech DZ and the eastern suburbs, which conveniently had already been slated for demolition and redevelopment.[42] Thus the earthquake inverted development trends—"local preferences of both residential and business decision-makers (based on factors such as higher status) to locate to the west if possible" and the establishment of Hi-Tech DZs in the south and west that "created market forces that well-intentioned (and rational) plans are unlikely to counter"[43]—and advanced the agenda of the Eastern ETDZ instead.

After cycling 10km up the northern axis of Xi'an, through the recently built-up ETDZ, we make a detour into the market street of the Youjiazhuang "urban village." As we move down the alley, a sequence of realizations creeps in: the street feels claustrophobic, the storefronts all appear to be only a meter deep and are squeaky-clean stuccoed and tiled. In a few exchanges with the residents, our suspicions are confirmed: this is demolition-ready construction, thousands of bricks piled in anticipation of the village's inevitable buy-out for the land grab.

At the regional scale, securing uninhabited land for the forced resettlement of populations, to make way for infrastructure and development projects, is an implied line in the Go West campaign playbook.[44] But the highly individual responses to the threat of this relocation have often characterized the era of Western Development policy. Chongqing's "most stubborn nail house"—its occupants resisted demolition from 2004 until 2007—was a secondary effect of the original Go West infrastructural project, an island within a new mall's construction pit, directly next to the light rail station. The "tallest box of nails," an entire housing block over which a freeway just north of the Nanping DZ had to be rerouted, barely a meter overhead,[45] was another product of localized response in Chongqing. These events made national headlines, and there is anecdotal evidence that the resistance of these stubborn nails galvanized other populations to stand up to developers. These residents were often criticized as being overly greedy, but most often they are popularly viewed as taking the only recourse to equitable compensation.

More serious questions of social justice, greed and systemic mishandling of the relocation process are raised in cases in Xi'an and Chengdu. The system of compensation depends on the size of the usable area of the houses, and in order to gain maximum compensation from redevelopment, the residents of Youjiazhuang village built walls against the property line to eliminate the set-back design of the houses. This addition between the original and new walls, however, was not used by the inhabitant. When resources are spent on unusable enclosures constructed solely as an "insurance policy"

Youjiazhuang Village in northern ETDZ of Xi'an

94

for future compensation, at the expense of useful communal space, is the action justified? This spatial phenomenon is not functional, ritual, or even meaningful, but the creation of the space reveals how these citizens operate within the system of rapid urban development. Unlike many stubborn nails, the residents have collectively accepted their removal, and may even desire to be demolished: on one hand, the compensation is not sufficient for relocation in the same area, but on the other hand, the compensation is a considerable amount of money for these individuals.

What is humane housing in the context of a city's constructed floor space growing at two to three times the speed of the population—and to live in humane conditions, is there really an alternative to relocation? With the forces of modern development closing in on them, their act of construction can be read as a documentation of the income inequalities that Western Development has perpetuated. It could even be construed as a critique of the unsustainable development model: not only is the response in kind to the top-down, profit-driven system that opens no space for negotiation, but the environmentally unsustainable act of laying a useless brick wall is a payment in kind for large-scale demolition as well.

The problems of demolition and forced relocation extend far into the past ideological framework of the shifting development strategies—"the first reason for such extensive demolition is planning deficiencies...old plans are often discarded for new, the effect of which is the same as having no plan at all"[46]—and the problems are perpetuated long into the future as well. The decision to relocate the Xi'an administrative center from the inner city to the ETDZ was driven by consideration for preservation and the overpopulation of the historical center.[47] Under the strategy of "city as business" (*jingying chengshi*), the new administrative node would lead to layers of developmental activities, such as urban services, commerce and real estate development.

On the periphery, however, there was no space for preservation and commercial leveraging of villages. Moreover, the cohesion of the village community is destroyed by resettlement, and post-relocation support never extends beyond the one-time compensation: "The system is not sustainable enough. Through relocation, and especially in farmland conversion, the residents lose not only their housing and land, but also the tools for sustaining their livelihood. Therefore, instead of huge amounts of compensation, the government should start professional educational programs to help the relocated population to adapt to their uprooted life."[48]

Kaifa-Zhongxin: Opening up for Re-Centering

In Chengdu, we nearly walk past without noticing a concept green wall system, crouching, outmatched, by a massive street intersection. Across the main thoroughfare from the Youjiazhuang Village in Xi'an, we see its future in an expanse of open park, populated by the ubiquitous exercise equipment and hundreds of enthusiastic citizen-athletes, and we hop off our bikes to participate. In Chongqing the alarm on our air quality monitor sounds off and cannot be silenced—it has been exposed to damaging levels of CO, an order of magnitude higher than we had experienced anywhere else in China—and then we look up to find an LED ticker of real-time, local air and sound pollution readings—again a public accounting we'd never seen before in a Chinese city.

These episodes of our journey became both the optimistic signs and instructive warnings of the Go West policy's intentions and realities. Later, we would continue to reconstruct the linkages between scales and interpretations of *Kaifa*: one cannot piece together the actions of municipal officials without accounting for the dependence of their livelihood on projecting an image, visible from as far away as the Central Politburo and even foreign investment, via the medium of the real estate markets. One cannot sketch out the development firm's overlap without drawing in the city administration or their stake in the dynamics of migrant labor. In this period of economic instability, one certainly cannot identify the intentions of central policymakers without considering the direct linkage of their fates to those of the fast-disappearing migrant labor forces. Without a map of this web, one also cannot even attempt to locate the potential openings for reconfiguring operations.

On the ideological front, one could look out for the reframing of the social agenda as a harmonious ecology, to more firmly capture the objectives of sustainable development within the interests of political stability. Better integration of SEPA into the Go West policymaking network,[49] in addition to decoupling the local environmental

Northern Hi-Tech DZ of Chongqing

protection bureaus from local government funding and re-centering these oversight agencies around SEPA, could also be visible shifts in the conceptual strategy.[50]

At the *Kaifa Shang* (developer) level, the Western provinces may continue to follow the lead of their model cities. The speculative environment, in which real estate is one of the few investment avenues for individuals, the profit-driven market, and the uncertainty of land tenure and planning, are all barriers to real progress in adopting sustainable construction or rehabilitation measures. Previous research into promoting more responsible design has targeted the technical experience of local design institutes, suggesting the creation of a replicable model sustainable superblock and design standards could enable the developer to follow through on green designs. The study also pointed to legislation-based (energy efficiency laws and green construction oversight), financially-based (tax incentives for developers and buyers, and market pricing of utilities for consumers), and knowledge-based strategies (industry networks and educational programs for city officials as well as consumers), which all target the pragmatic operation of development.[51]

The shifts with the widest reach and greatest affect could quickly be absorbed at the methodological level, in which "anecdotal evidence such as 'hollow villages' and idle land in numerous encircled 'development zones' suggests that there exist ways for China to use its non-agricultural land more efficiently and economically than hitherto."[52] The megacities' maps reveal that it is not too late for revision of the DZ model, to allow for more spatial flexibility and to adopt the tenet that densification of established built-up areas is less destructive than the indeterminate extension of the edgeless city. Can the DZ phenomenon respond to both investment and public interest? What are alternative spatial strategies for balancing economic development and making livable cities? Chinese cities have long been deficient in a scale of planning that could effectively mediate between the DZs and urban environment at large, and these omissions are readily apparent in the Western megacities: "Chongqing lacks an overarching organization; there is no coherence between one development and another. This is because the urban planning requirements for the developer are too general, and once the developers successfully own the land, there is very limited control from the government.

The city needs another scale of planning and design, between the big scale of city oversight and the scale of individual architecture."[53] There are already signs that the integration of multiple scales of planning is possible within the urban economic and governance systems of these cities, as in the case of Dongguan, which "has recently adopted a new rescaling strategy to group industries into parks, merge individual housing estates into urban districts and link scattered towns to form urbanized regions."[54] With this understanding of the interdependencies and multi-layered perceptions of development, *Kaifa*, we can continue to watch for these openings for re-centered negotiations between development and ecology.

References

1. Tian, Qunjian. *"China Develops its West: motivation, strategy and prospect,"* Journal of Contemporary China, p. 611, November 2004
2. 李昉, "谁建成了中国第一个商品房小区," 25 September 2008, http://lady.people.com.cn/GB/8104841.html
3. McNally, Christopher A. *"Sichuan: Driving Capitalist Development Westward,"* China Quarterly Special Issue, p.447, 2004
4. 陈叶军, "'为中心'与'惟中心'," 新华网, 8 December 2008, http://theory.people.com.cn/GB/49150/49152/8480971.html
5. The World Bank, *2009 World Development Report,* Washington DC, The World Bank, p. 26
6. Economy, Elizabeth. *"China's Go West Campaign: Ecological Construction or Ecological Exploitation?"* China Environment Series, Issue 5, 2002, p. 6
7. Wikipedia.org, *"China Western Development,"* accessed 7 January 2009
8. Economy, Elizabeth. *"China's Go West Campaign: Ecological Construction or Ecological Exploitation?"* China Environment Series Issue 5, 2002, p. 4,
9. McNally, Christopher A. p. 442
10. Economy, Elizabeth. p. 7
11. Ibid
12. Saalman, Lora L. The FDI Paradox: China's Socialist Market Economy and the "Develop the West" Campaign, *Monterey Institute of International Studies,* 2005, p. 3
13. The original speech by Deng was '可以考虑再开放几个点, 增加几个港口城市, 这些地方不叫特区, 但可以实行特区的某些政策.'
14. Lin, George C. S. *"Reproducing Spaces of Chinese Urbanisation: New City-based and Land-centred Urban Transformation,"* Urban

Southern Hi-Tech DZ of Chengdu

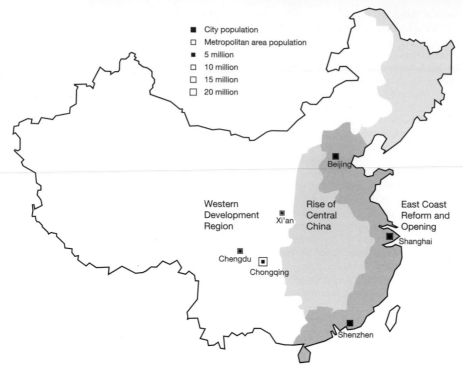

The areas affected by recent environmental crises in China are primarily concentrated in the target region of the Western Development campaign.

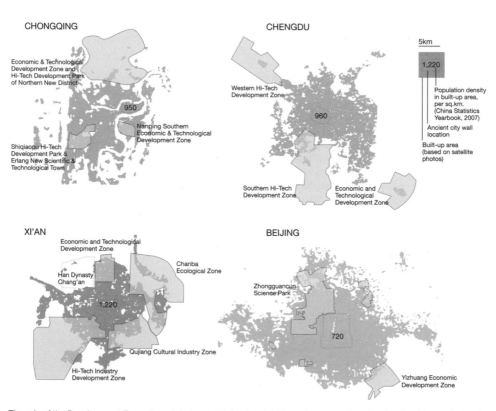

The role of the Development Zones in reclaiming arable land and driving urban sprawl can be visualized by overlaying the officially sanctioned and desired extent of these Zones on each city's built-up area.

BRAZIER, J. Cressica and LAM, Tat

Studies 2007, no. 44, p. 1848

15. 国家发展和改革委员会, 国务院西部地区开发领导小组办公室,西部大开发"十一五"规划, 2005

16. Lin, George C. S. p. 1848

17. Interview with Zhou Duoduo, architect in developer's office, Chongqing, July 2008

18. Webster, Douglas R., Cai, Jianming et al, Peri-Urbanization in Chengdu, Western China: From "Third Line" to Market Dynamics, Asia-Pacific Research Center, May 2004, p. 8

19. Zhiliang, Jia (贾自亮), "三环路建设与加快成都乡村城市化," 成都经济发展 2002, Vol. 3, p. 7

20. Interview with Li Fei, architect and real estate consultant, Xi'an, July 2008

21. Feng Jianhua, "Tang Renaissance," Beijing Review, 27 September 2007, http://www.bjreview.com.cn/quotes/txt/2007-09/20/content_77190.htm

22. Ibid

23. Interview with Li Fei

24. Zhang Yanlong and Ren Yujie, trans., "Confessions of a Propaganda Hitman," in Nation, 387-8, 29 September 2008, p. 9

25. Di Baojiang (耿宝江), Peng Li (彭利), "基于SWOT分析的重庆洋人街旅游发展对策", 商场现代化, 2007, Issue 12S, p. 333

26. Ibid

27. Yang Zhenwei (杨振威), "为"人文奥运"净化耳目", 中国老区建设 issue 8, 2008, p. 26

28. "重庆斥资打造"最牛厕所", 廉政瞭望 2008, Issue 3, p. 60

29. Tang Peng (唐鹏), "成都平原城市群流动人口特征及影响," 四川建筑, Vol. 26, September 2006, pp. 35-38; http://www.sc.gov.cn/zwgk/jjjs/tjsj/tjfx/200805/t20080505_275321.shtml; 重庆市发展及改革委员会社会处, 重庆社会科学院, "重庆市流动人口现状及其对策," 重庆经济, November, pp. 27-30, 2006; 贾小玫, 张坤, "西安流动人口与经济和谐性实证分析," 西北人口 2008, Vol. 29 Issue 2, p. 84

30. Lu Zhicai and Ren Lu (刘智才 任璐), "浅析西安城市边缘区流动人口特征及住房条件," 山西建筑, September 2007, p. 52-53

31. Ma Renqing (马仁清), "凤凰是这样涅槃的: 成都东郊工业区结构调整实录," 公司 Issue 5, 2004, p. 97

32. Webster, Douglas R. p. 35

33. 時蘌明, 體制的突破, 北京: 中國社會出版社, 1993, p. 1-2

34. Webster, Douglas R. p. 37

35. McNally, Christopher A. p. 442

36. LaFraniere, Sharon. "Possible Link Between Dam and China Quake," New York Times, 5 February 2009

37. Jacobs, Andrew. "Garbled Report on Sichuan Death Toll Revives Pain," New York Times, 21 November 2008

38. Wikipedia.org, "China Western Development," accessed 7 January 2009

39. 焦点成都房地产网, 22 May 2008

40. Zhou Du (舟渡), Shunan Maizi (蜀南麦子), "变灾为利 重建机遇—全面思考灾后成都发展新格局," 广西广播电视 2008, Vol.8, p. 38, 2008

41. 焦点成都房地产网 22 May 2008

42. Guo Yushen. (郭玉坤), "汶川地震对成都房地产的影响分析," 四川省情 Vol. 9, 2008, p. 29-30

43. Webster, Douglas R. p. 35

44. Saalman, Lora L. p. 8

45. 南方新闻网, "高速桥下六层楼", http://newsqq.com/a/20080626/000731.htm, 26 June 2008

46. Pan Jiahua. "Building a frugal society", 5 November 2007, http://www.chinadialogue.net/article/show/single/en/1453

47. Zhou Haihong (周海虹), Zhou Haixia (周海霞), "从西安行政中心搬迁想到的," 北京规划建设 No. 6, 2005, p. 117

48. Interview with Huang He, relocation manager and city planner, Chengdu, July 2008.

49. Economy, Elizabeth. p. 9

50. Green Dragon Media. "How the Chinese Construction Industry Works." http://www.green-dragonfilm.com

51. Ibid

52. Lin, George C. S. p. 1827

53. Interview with Zhou Duoduo

54. Lin, George C. S. p. 1848

J. Cressica Brazier is based in Shanghai and is a research scholar for China Lab, Columbia University Graduate School of Architecture, Planning, and Preservation. She studied architecture, structural engineering and computer science at Princeton University, UC Berkeley and Columbia University. She has also researched traditional Chinese housing at Tsinghua University and practiced engineering in California.

Tat Lam is a PhD candidate at the Bartlett School of Architecture, UCL. After graduating from the architecture programs at the Chinese University of Hong Kong and Columbia University GSAPP, he has been appointed as a research scholar for China Lab.

China Lab, an experimental research unit at Columbia's Graduate School of Architecture, Planning and Preservation, is a platform for student and faculty-initiated research projects. The Go West project was proposed and developed with the support of China Lab and GSAPP, and the field studies for this research project were sponsored by a Kinne fellowship from Columbia GSAPP. This ongoing project focus is a regional approach to China Lab's core research initiative, the Megablock Project, which surveys the environmental, economic, and design implications of large-scale development in China.

98 Rural-Urban Ecology

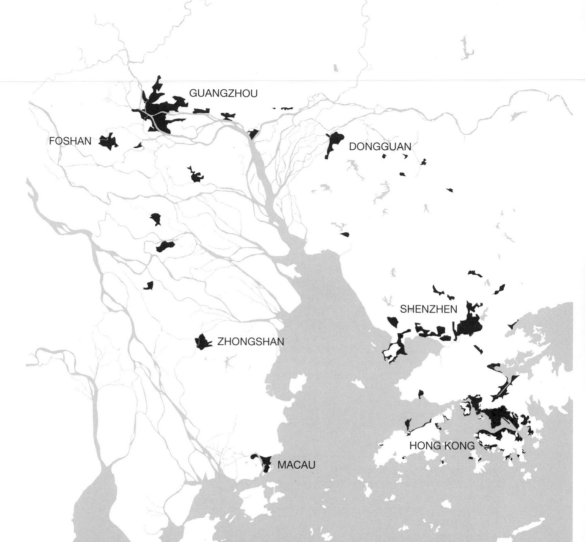

GUANGZHOU

FOSHAN

DONGGUAN

SHENZHEN

ZHONGSHAN

HONG KONG

MACAU

The Rural-Urban Ecology concept originated in a journey that we took to a project site for a rural school construction in a village near the border of Guangdong and Guanxi province. In an eight-hour drive originating in Hong Kong, the journey passed through seven official urban zones and countless in-betweens and otherwise indeterminate territories before arriving at the rural site in Qinmo village. The journey exhibited various conditions of development, many of which exploited grey areas in current government policies and were indicative of the degree of market savvy and entrepreneurship among people who were all simply farmers 30 years ago. There were also clusters of abandoned buildings and projects—bi-products of the extreme influence of the market economy—which were simply halted the moment the market shifted. In the first stage of Shenzhen's transformation from rice fields into a 12 million-inhabitant city, the edge between rural and urban was brutally distinct. Now, as the PRD develops from a region which in 1990 had only four urban areas with over a half million inhabitants into an area today with more than 20 such cities, the entire regional dynamic has become much more complex. What becomes evident is that urban processes are intertwined with rural processes to the extent that the rural is a key agent in the creation of urban fabric. These mechanisms produce specific forms of differentiated urban fabric, creating incoherent adjacencies between banana trees and high-rise developments, remnants of fishponds and factories. The following is a selection of images along this Rural-Urban scan with key issues that factor into the continuing transformation of the PRD.

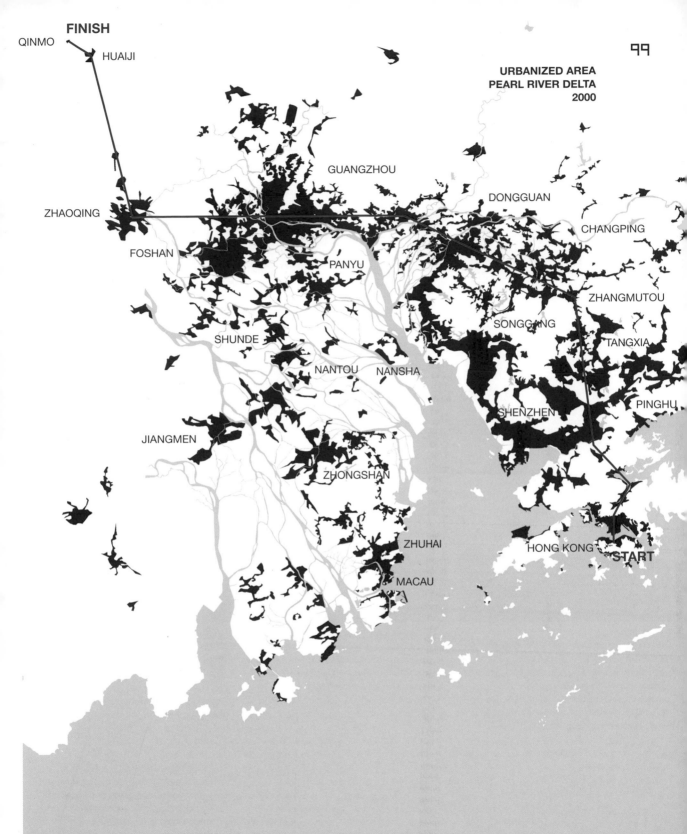

FINISH

QINMO

HUAIJI

URBANIZED AREA
PEARL RIVER DELTA
2000

GUANGZHOU

DONGGUAN

CHANGPING

ZHAOQING

FOSHAN

PANYU

ZHANGMUTOU

SONGGANG

TANGXIA

SHUNDE

NANTOU   NANSHA

PINGHU

SHENZHEN

JIANGMEN

ZHONGSHAN

ZHUHAI

HONG KONG   START

MACAU

306090 13

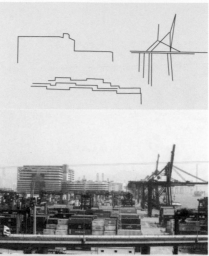

0'15": Hong Kong Real Estate

0'25": Logistics Port

0'45": Lok Ma Chau (HK)

Lok Ma Chau-Huanggang is one of five land border crossings. It has become the busiest border crossing in Asia, with 150,000 cross-border passengers a day on average.

The Frontier Closed Area in HK is a 2,800 hectare buffer zone created in 1951 to prevent illegal migration from mainland China to HK. In 2010 it will be reduced in size, freeing over 2,000 hectares for future development.

1'35": Massage

Huge spa and massage complexes form new leisure attractions for tourists, foreign and local businessmen, and overseas Chinese from Taiwan and Hong Kong. Dongguan is made up of a strange mix of factories, 5-star hotels, and entertainment with 450 licensed karaoke outlets and more than 1,000 bars, clubs and discos.

1'55": Urban Periphery

The urban periphery is a contested zone where the different desires of factory owners, farmers and real-estate developers are played out. This is the zone in which rural territory is transformed into urban substance through the forces of global capital.

2'05": Suburban China

The numbers of the middle class are rising in China concurrent with the country's continued economic renaissance. As their wealth rises more are seeking out high-end Western-style villa developments in the suburbs, often in the form of gated communities.

urban-rural conditions

The years preceding October 2008, when it was generally acknowledged that the world was entering a global recession, could be considered the apotheosis of the extremes of market capitalism. In many developing countries the rapid transformation of rural territory directly into industrialized urban

BOLCHOVER, Joshua and LIN, John

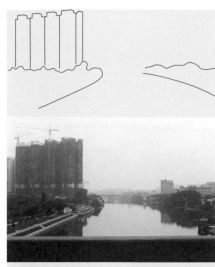

0'50": HK-SZ Border: No Man's Land

0'55": Huanggang (SZ)

1'00": Logistics Port

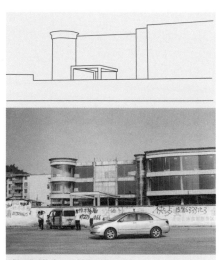

2'15": Highway Urbanism

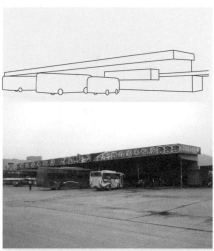

2'20": Mass-Migration

substance was accompanied by mass migrations of workers to these new urban centers. Now those millions of workers are going home. It is estimated that in China alone over a six-month period, 20 million workers have left cities and returned to their rural homes. This represents a crisis not only for cities but for the established relationship and co-dependency between rural and urban territory.

The traditional relationship between the countryside and the city, the farm and the factory has become exploited and increasingly complex within the processes of globalization. Nowhere is this more evident than in the Pearl River Delta in China. Here globalization's incessant search for cheaper land and labor, combined with the specific local conditions of Chinese socialism, with its inherent inequality between Urban and Rural citizens has produced a phenomena of urban migration and urban production that is unparalleled.

Under the original set up of Mao Zedong's collective farming system, the relationship between the countryside and the city was clear and distinct. In exchange for their land rights, farmers contributed a portion of their food production as tax. Food and raw materials were then distributed by the government to the non-agricultural population. As a result, the notion of balance between the roles of rural dwellers and urban dwellers was established in the system of Hukou or household registration, and it has continued to this day. This system defines every citizen as either an urban dweller or a rural dweller with distinct rights and responsibilities. This strict legal separation of its entire population exemplifies China's deep-rooted belief in not only the division but the co-dependency of its urban and

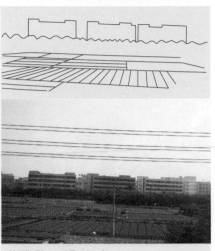

2'35": Residential Abandonment

2'45": Blurred Territories

2'50": Dongguang Vacant Factories

3'30": Guangzhou Super-Highway

3'40": Guangzhou
Guangzhou (formerly Canton) is the capital city of Guangdong Province and has a permanent population of 10 million, out of total population of 14 million. In 1978, the floating population of migrant workers was approximately 235,000, but rapidly grew to 1.7 million in 10 years and stands at 4 million today.

4'45": Bourgeois Villas

rural parts. However the nature of this relationship continues to evolve.

One of the chief architects of China's economic rise, Deng Xiaoping, recognized not only the failure of the commune system but the potential for China to act as fertile territory for the expression of late capitalism in built form. The continued commodification of goods, worldwide consumption and expanded field of production centers made possible through globalization, prioritized affordable and available land, co-operative governmental controls and an abundance of cheap labor. By simultaneously opening up key

areas to foreign investment and loosening the tie between farmers and their land, Deng produced the basic conditions for unprecedented urbanization directly linked to the globalization of markets. In 1978, Shenzhen was named one of five Special Economic Zones, strategically located directly across the border from

Hong Kong, which was already established as a global financial center. A year later, Deng began the emancipation of the farmers by transforming the collective farm system to shift productivity from the collective to the individual. The farmers could choose what to grow and had the right to sell any excess for individual profit. Then in 1983, the huge temporary migration from rural areas to sites of production was legalized by a policy that allowed rural citizens to work in designated urban areas without changing their citizen status.

BOLCHOVER, Joshua and LIN, John

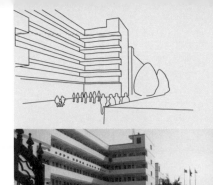

3'00": Live-In Factory Complex

3'05": Gated Factory Town

One of the largest factory towns in Dongguan, Yuyuan Industrial District was founded in 1993, by Taiwan Baocheng Group, the largest shoe manufacture enterprise in the world. It has an area of 3,300 mu (about 543.63 acres), and a total investment of US$1 billion. Now 18 Taiwan factories, mainly shoe and electronic manufacture enterprises, have moved into its complete town facilities, with residential complexes, recreational grounds, local shops, restaurants and on-site medical care.

3'20": Rural Capitalism

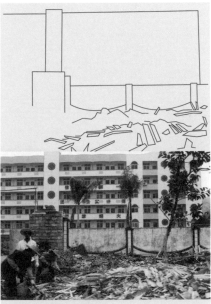

5'15": Zhaoqing

5'45": Truck Town

The blue transporter trucks congregate in a single town implying that this is the town of truck drivers. It seems strange that such specificity, or differentiation of labour would be so explicit.

6'05": Rural Production

In 1978 policy changes allowed for individual businesses and non-agricultural production in rural areas. The 1990s and continued economic development encouraged further investment in rural commerce and industry. Up to 2006, rural and township enterprises account for 40 percent of total GDP in the PRD. In more rural areas some of these industries include the production of construction materials: bricks, concrete, sewage pipes and wood veneer.

Currently the rural continues to play an unequivocal role in the growth of cities and economies of the Pearl River Delta. Massive migration had created a temporary population of 147 million rural workers in the PRD before the recent downturn and current counter-migration. Ironically this temporary population inhabited the cities of Guangzhou and Shenzhen in clusters of densely packed and loosely regulated enclaves called "Urban Villages." These areas, imbedded into the urban fabric are the resultant tradeoffs between the government and villagers when claiming large tracts of

farming plots for urban development. The rights of rural dwellers to build a dwelling and the demand for cheap migrant worker housing transformed local farmers into property developers. The city of Shenzhen has grown so vast in 30 years that many of these areas have become entrenched into the very center of the urban fabric. However due to the legal separation between rural and urban territory, these Urban Villages have

become an intractable problem for city planning, or seen another way as islands of resistance containing a form of informal urbanism that is simply not possible in the

6'20": Rural Industry

6'25": Recycling

7'05": One-Child Propaganda
The government banner reads: "Sex selection is a natural process. Artificial selection will jeopardize social safety."

7'15": Rural Development

7'25": Village Density
As migrant workers send money back to their hometown villages, some families build new homes or renovate their existing houses often with tiles indicating a new social standing amid the typical brick homes.

formal-grid urbanism that predominates Shenzhen's city fabric.

The fact that rural land is owned collectively—something not possible for urban dwellers—gives the farmers of China an inherent capitalistic edge. Originally the collective ownership of property led to the rural welfare distribution system. Since the 1990s the PRD cities of Guangzhou, Shenzhen, Zhuhai and Foshan have begun reforming this system as a method to speed the conversion of farmland into urban land. These actions transformed the existing "collective ownership system" into what was strategically termed the "rural shareholding co-operative system." In the administrative region of Dongguan, as a result of implementing these reforms from 2004-2006, nearly 3,000 shareholding co-operatives have been established. The co-operatives are essentially business entities with shareholders, thus allowing the farmers to conduct business freely with outside investors and developers. One might say that nearly overnight 3,000 new corporations were formed with substantial assets in the form of prime land.

Though essentially urban, the official rural status of most of Dongguan has allowed it to develop in a uniquely capitalistic manner far in advance of the other cities in the PRD.

The continuing conversion of rural territory into urban substance through various means is blurring the lines, which define not only their physical boundaries but their economies. The areas which are outside the cities, the large expansive

BOLCHOVER, Joshua and LIN, John

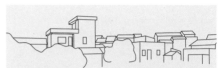

6'50": Rural Infrastructure

The Central Government proposed to increase its spending on agriculture and rural development to 716.1 billion yuan this year, an increase of 120.6 billion yuan from 2008, in order to reduce the gap between rural and urban residents. Rural inland areas are particularly impoverished: in 2006, only 48 percent of rural households had tap water, and 87 percent did not have flush water.

6'55": Investment Farmers

There are approximately 30 million migrant workers in Guangdong Province. The recent recession has left approximately 4.8 million unemployed of which 3.5 million have returned to their hometowns.

7'50": Qinmo Village

8'00": Project Site

Qinmo is a small rural village, which is mainly populated by the very young and very old as most young people, men and women, have left to work in the factories or service industries of the PRD's emerging cities. The set of intertwined relations between the city and the village describes an ecology, always in flux, and liable to change. The current economic recession will no doubt impact several layers within this ecology, its exact ramifications as yet unknown.

peripheries once occupied solely by rice paddies, are rapidly and simultaneously transforming into a generic territory, neither strictly urban nor rural, dotted with factories, isolated residential towers amidst the farmland. This land is still under the legal designation of "rural" territory and continues to developin a haphazard manner through coalitions of rural committees, developers, individual farmers and village governments. The growth of this peripheral zone is much faster, more ruthless and seemingly devoid of planning control even compared to the infamous growth of Chinese urban areas. This proto-rural territory is a contested space, organized along territorial lines of traditional farming plots, being speculated simultaneously as new residential communities and high-end industrial parks. As opposed to the past development of cities, which were government organized and led, this wave of development is propagated by individual farmers and village co-operatives eager to catch up.

Joshua Bolchover *is an urban researcher, academic and architect. He is currently an Assistant Professor in architecture at Hong Kong University. He recently exhibited* Utopia Now: Opening the Closed Area, *a research project on the Hong Kong and Shenzhen border at the Venice Biennale 2008. He has curated, designed and contributed to several international exhibitions including* Get it Louder, *a touring exhibition in China;* Airspace: What Skyline Does London Want; Hydan; Can Buildings Curate *and has exhibited at the HK-SZ Biennale. Joshua was a local curator for the Manchester-Liverpool section of Shrinking Cities between 2003 and 2005. He has collaborated with Raoul Bunschoten, Chora researching strategic urban projects and has worked with Diller + Scofidio in New York. Joshua has previously taught architecture at the Chinese University of Hong Kong, London Metropolitan University, Cambridge University and the Architectural Association. He was educated at Cambridge University and at the Bartlett School of Architecture.*

Opposite: Batou Village, Dongguan, photo by Joshua Bolchover

John Lin *is an architect based in Hong Kong and is a graduate of The Cooper Union in New York City. His experimental constructions have been published in FRAME magazine (2003) and exhibited in the Kolonihaven (Architecture Park) at the Louisiana Museum of Modern Art in Copenhagen (2004) and at the Venice Biennale (2008). His current projects include the design of several school buildings in China. Located in rural areas of Guizhou and Guangdong, the designs integrate local and traditional practices with contemporary technologies. The projects co-ordinate between Mainland and HK universities, the Ministry of Construction, the Education Bureau, and local village governments along with N.G.O.'s and charity organizations from Hong Kong. He has taught at the Royal Danish Academy of Fine Arts, School of Architecture, and the Chinese University of Hong Kong, and is currently an Assistant Professor at the University of Hong Kong.*

DAVIS, Juliet

Towards *Sustainable Communities*? Community, Consultation and the Compulsory Purchase of the Site for the 2012 Olympic Games

According to the International Olympic Committee Evaluation Commission report dated June 6, 2005, London's Bid Team's "Olympic Games concept and legacy" were key to its success in securing the 2012 Games.[1] In an article for *The Guardian* on 12 January 2003, Greater London Authority (GLA) Mayor Ken Livingstone argued that the prospect of an Olympic Games presented London, as it did Barcelona in 1992, with a unique opportunity. This hinged on a view that an Olympic Games had the potential to attract huge levels of investment which could be harnessed toward the long-term regeneration of the East End of London's "economy and physical environment [and] the transformation of the city's, and even the nation's social capital."[2] Livingstone reiterated this view pledging a package of *legacy* benefits for London in the wake of the Olympics which include "mak[ing] the Olympic park a blueprint for sustainable living."[3]

Livingstone's commitments fit within a corpus of British New Labour urban policy relating to the creation and promotion of so called *sustainable communities*. This policy is widely viewed as reflective of a paradigm shift in relation to perceived goals of contemporary urban regeneration. It is developed in response to criticism of the regeneration efforts of the 1980s in particular which, in focusing heavily on growth in terms of the private property markets, have been seen to have failed to adequately tackle issues of social and economic disadvantage. However, debates surrounding new *sustainable communities* policy, its ideological underpinnings and instrumental effects through development practices, are currently throwing up a new set of critical issues. These tend to cohere, firstly, around difficulties in terms of defining *sustainable communities*; secondly around how its ideology coheres with ways in which communities are actually constituted; and thirdly, around the efficacy of tools currently proposed for their delivery. It is recognised that *sustainable communities* is a slippery term, understandings of both words having evolved historically and vary according to context, including the contexts in which they are brought together.[4] An acknowledged consequence of this linguistic slipperiness is that although policy provides a directive framework for the development of *sustainable communities*, what these actually are and how they may be forged relies on the specific, multiple and evolving circumstances in which urban renewal actors both interpret, apply and develop it.

In relation to the third point above, urban policy geared to the creation of sustainable communities often advocates participatory approaches to regeneration. While public consultation has, in these terms, come to be seen as one of the key tools for achieving *sustainable communities*, a quite different instrument advocated concurrently and somewhat ironically for realizing physical regeneration at the scale of neighborhoods is the Compulsory Purchase Order (CPO). It is by means of the CPO powers invested in development corporations or regeneration agencies by central UK government that significant transformations represented by mega-projects such as the 2012 Olympic Games and Legacy can be developed on inner urban sites. The site for the Olympic Park is situated within the Lower Lea Valley—a substantially post-industrialised though nevertheless densely occupied part of East London—and borders the emerging region known as the Thames Gateway, viewed as a major recipient for London's growing urban population over the next 20-50 years.

Authors writing for the London-based think tank Demos have argued that the UK government's assertion that the Olympics can help generate *sustainable communities* is, from the outset, contentious. Many Olympic Games sites, far from catalysing regeneration, are populated with *white elephants* which show little capacity for consistent legacy reuse and take host cities years to repay.[5] Vigor et al argue that questions of how, where and for whom benefits might be directed remain significantly unaddressed. In response to this, the broad aim of this essay is to consider the effectiveness of the CPO as a tool in initial stages towards the development of *sustainable communities* as a legacy to the 2012 London Olympics. I focus particularly on consultation exercises undertaken by the London Development Agency (LDA, an executive arm of the GLA concerned with urban regeneration) in their process of assembling land for the Olympic Park. The first part provides an overview of the site and the CPO process led by the LDA. In the second part, I focus on practices of community consultation with five former occupants of the Olympic site who were relocated from it in 2007: Eton Manor Allotments, the business H. Forman & Son, the residential groups known as Clay's Lane and Waterden Road Travellers and the Eastway Cycle Center. Analysis draws predominantly on material gathered through a number of in-depth, structured interviews with these former occupants in 2008. These interviews shed light on areas in which the links between CPO and consultation appear to be tenuous, particularly in view of the broader aim to create *sustainable communities* in the long term. I explore how a *sustainable communities* vision becomes complicated in reality through contestations over what they are and how to deliver them. The article concludes with a brief assessment of how CPO and consultation strategies employed by the LDA appear to conflict with the aim or contribute to the development of *sustainable communities*.

superbowl & the like.. taking temporary events/gathering spaces & rethinking how they are built & how they can be transformed after their "time" has passed.

Communities, Consultation and Compulsory Purchase

Official accounts and assessments of the site and its locale, prior to demolition, frequently emphasise conditions of economic, social and environmental depression resulting from decades of marginality and underinvestment. In accordance with the Government's *Index of Multiple Deprivation 2004*, the LDA describe it as one of the most deprived in the UK and Europe,[6] while Capita Symond's *Environmental Statement* for the LDA highlights the contamination of the site's degraded physical landscape left by waste and chemical industries of the nineteenth to mid-twentieth centuries.[7] Without discrediting these accounts, they and related others were clearly used to create a strategic case for the social, economic and environmental transformation of the site. This case, in turn, was used to underpin the London 2012 Olympic bid, gave legitimacy to the Compulsory Purchase of the site and informs emerging visions for the Olympic Legacy. In so doing, the accounts, in different ways, serve to downplay aspects of the site that, while not inherently negative, do not cohere with the aims of the broader strategy being adopted. The brief account that follows is underpinned by a different kind of intent. It does not seek either to romanticise the past nor to hold the site, as it was, up as a viable urban model for the future. It is intended to render visible the now vanished complexity of the site in simple terms of relationships between spaces and uses and thus to form a background for exploring some of the effects of the CPO.

The Pre-Olympic Site, 2007

Communities and community life on the Olympic site at the time of the Compulsory Purchase was extremely diverse. The LDA's *Compulsory Purchase Order Lands 2005* document lists 792 separate parcels of land under different ownerships and up to 2200 property interests. The three hundred and twelve hectare site encompassed two hundred and eight businesses and a diverse range of cultural, recreational and agricultural user groups and uses. While some of these groups were more or less permanently based on the site, others made use of particular spaces within it intermittently. The cross-section of uses and built forms were reflective of a series of historical if partial transformations of the site through processes as wide-ranging as nineteenth industrialisation and philanthropy, World War II destruction, and late twentieth century post-industrialisation. De-industrialisation of the chemicals and materials manufacturing of the late nineteenth century made way for transport, communications, supply-and-distribution based industries—whether of foods, building materials or waste.

Maps produced as part of this research reveal the diverse nature of its spaces and uses. In creating these, a range of official sources of information about the site—from the Ordnance Survey to London Development Agency surveys—were drawn upon. In producing them, I also made use of knowledge gained through extensive walks across the site between 2005 and 2007. Although the site was predominantly industrial, the diversity of business uses and their distribution suggest a distinct lack

of zoning. Businesses ranged between scaffolding pole suppliers, smoked salmon producers, newspaper printers, waste recyclers, Chinese cash-and-carry shopkeepers and Halal butchers. Residential use formed a small proportion of the total area of the site but encompassed nonetheless a variety of types, from Traveller (of Irish and Romany Gypsy descent) pitches to single person cooperative dwellings to a gated, private residence. Open space accommodated allotments, an informal market and private club grounds for cycling and athletics as well as a wide range of illicit activities. In many instances, apparently divergent uses existed adjacent to one another—churches next to bed makers, news printers next to Barnardo's offices. There was no fixed relationship between open space and community use or between buildings and private use. Private yards used for hoarding scrap metal or parking cars occupied a large proportion of the open landscape, whereas some buildings were used for congregational—if not strictly public—uses, such as churches. Some spaces could be characterised more in terms of collective disuse than by use—such as derelict railway sidings—others by use and disuse simultaneously such as a dog racing track turned into an informal market. While different "rhythms"[8] of activity intersected, the site often appeared vacant. This related to the low proportion of residential and retail use relative to industry and to the low-rise nature of the built fabric. In spite of the diversity of places of work, few of these drew a steady flow of customers. Open spaces—streets, paths and river ways—were often far less populated by pedestrians than by articles of fly-tipped waste. Though the market attracted enough cars to cause congestion in the surrounding roads, it was convened only once a month, the rest of the time lying destitute. Community groups such as the churches congregated sporadically, producing moments of intensity punctuating episodes of quiet. While Jane Jacobs generally associates diversity of use with intense and continuous public life, this link was not explicitly evident on the pre-Olympic site. Uses included many of the kind that Jacobs refers to as "destructive" for urban life, such as transport depots and scrap yards. The fringes of the site were, what Jacobs calls, "border vacuums" formed at river, rail and road boundaries.[9]

Social spaces such as churches allotments and cycle clubs, though existing in close proximity with each other, complied with many of the characteristics of "intimate communities"[10] as described by Sennett and revealed complex and variable relationships between community and place. Representatives from two of the residential groups reported that while their own communities were tightly knit, they retained a guarded distance from one another. Apart from open space, almost all work, leisure, shopping and education undertaken by members of these groups took place beyond the site. Many of the cultural and or recreational users of the site belonged to other communities within London or beyond. Routes taken by Kingsway International Christian Center (KICC) combi vans, for example, articulated connections within the African community living around the site, suggesting that the church formed a spatial node in a dispersed community network. Allotment holders, though apparently distanced from neighboring uses on

PRIMARY BUILDING USES

- Residence
- Religion
- Sport
- Infrastructure
- Business: Waste
- Business: Financial / Legal Services
- Business: Chemical Industry
- Business: Packaging
- Business: Communication and Distribution
- Business: Media
- Business: Paper and Printing
- Business: Cars
- Business: Construction Industry (including interiors)
- Mixed Use Building (businesses and cultural uses)
- Business: Culture / Entertainment Industry
- Business: Food (manufacturing and retail)
- Business: Property
- Business: Textiles
- Charity Sector
- Public Transport: Buses
- Public Transport: Rail
- Vacant / Derelict

0   100   500   meters

Diagram showing types of building use on the Olympic site in 2007. Ordnance survey data reproduced with permission of: Ordnance Survey © Crown Copyright. All rights reserved. © Juliet Davis 2008

306090 13

OPEN SPACE TYPE AND USE

- Productive landscape
- Market
- Mixed hard / soft derelict landscape
- Derelict hard landscape
- Construction site
- Car parks, road ways, forecourts, yards
- Disused railway sidings
- Road ways
- Public towpaths and pedestrian / cycle track
- Paths / tracks on privately owned land
- Public recreational soft landscaping
- Soft landscaping in privately owned land
- Verges
- Trees / shrubbery
- Campsite
- Rivers
- Tennis court

meters

0   100   500

Diagram showing types of open spaces on the Olympic site in 2007. Ordnance survey data reproduced with permission of: Ordnance Survey © Crown Copyright. All rights reserved. © Juliet Davis 2008

DAVIS, Juliet

the site and forming a tightly prescribed interest group with a special connection to the land, also each belonged to work and neighborhood communities in the wider East End. Businesses mostly attracted employees from neighboring areas and were well-positioned in terms of road access to both Central London and the broader South East of England region. Many firms—whether small printing enterprises or construction material distributors—drew on a highly spatially dispersed if specific client base. In a few instances, spatial arrangements of proximate uses within the site created small places of social exchange. A venue called Club Dezire, for example, was situated to catch the passing trade of night-time bus drivers concluding shifts in lonely hours. In general, the pre-Olympic site appeared to reflect a curious inversion of the positive ways in which Sennett describes "urban disorder"[11]: a complex topography formed from different kinds of social introspection and isolation.

The CPO process

The London Development Agency (LDA) was endowed with statutory power to compulsorily assemble the land designated for the development of the Olympics. The assembly of land forming the Olympic site involved two separate Compulsory Purchase Orders: the first related to power lines and the second to all property interests. In accordance with recent national level policy, the LDA stressed the importance of consultation in relation to the CPO and strategies they developed for the relocation of site occupants. This recent policy has emerged under the shadow of criticism of the typically adversarial nature of CPO processes conducted in the 1980s and 1990s, and their tendency to signify the disempowerment of local people—often already disadvantaged—at the hands of state-sponsored organisations.[12] In interview, an LDA representative of its "Consultation and Engagement" division confirmed that the agency were indeed keen to avoid the kinds of criticism levelled at the London Docklands Development Corporation (LDDC) in the 1980s which hinged on the lack of opportunity offered to land-owners to benefit from enormous profits accruing through the redevelopment of the Isle of Dogs.[13] The LDA's *Relocation Strategy* explains that a package of financial and advisory support and compensation was to be offered, including "offer[ing] landowners a market value for their sites."[14] The strategy also suggests that "it is vital to talk to each [landowner] individually to establish detailed requirements and clarify need" in these terms. In fact, the LDA sought to altogether avoid having to draw down their CPO powers by negotiating towards private agreements for relocation with each legal occupant. The LDA's website reports that a major advantage of negotiation is that solutions can be "found to the satisfaction of all parties—making relocation [and compensation] a real opportunity." Arguably, the LDA's internal policy, developed through the experience of executing the land purchase process, actively seeks to confront heterogeneities of community need and, in these terms, may be said to go beyond current requirements at national policy level.[15]

In spite of the deliberative nature of this approach to land purchase, a number of occupants, most prominently, if not without exception, the non-business users

campaigned vociferously against relocation and their negotiations with the LDA became protracted. As a result, in 2005, the Secretary of State for Communities and Local Government announced that a Public Inquiry would be held before deciding whether or not to confirm the CPO. This was held between May and August 2006. The LDA allege that by the time the hearing commenced, ninety percent of the land was in their possession and seventy percent of jobs on the site were safeguarded, leaving a relatively small number of individuals objecting. While the redevelopment of the site was contingent on the outcome of the inquiry,[16] influencing its outcomes were both the success of the LDA in acquiring most of the land already and the unmovable dates of the Games. The need to have the Olympic Park complete by August 2012 virtually obliged the LDA to deliver a vacant site in July 2007. This deadline was met, despite negotiations with several user groups—including allotment holders, cycle center, residential groups and a church—remaining incomplete after the Public Inquiry. For representatives of these groups, this served to significantly undermine any notion that negotiation was being conducted as a conversation between people on equal footings.

Negotiation and Relocation

In interviews carried out over the past year, I have focused on developing insights into how particular users experienced the Compulsory Purchase Order and the development of strategies for their relocation. Answers to interview questions revealed a spectrum of understandings—that clash with official accounts—of the motives behind the CPO, the meaning of *sustainable communities* with respect to the CPO and the effectiveness of consultation and negotiation as a means of delivering them.

Respondents argued that the LDA's conception of *community* was reductive and suggested that this became reflected in their failure to accord certain groups with the same level of respect as others. As a representative from the residential group at Clay's Lane argued, "The LDA see communities [as] very special groups, i.e. you're an ethnic minority of some kind… [so] the Travellers have a particular designation. To my mind, they don't actually have a concept of community outside of that very narrow definition." He claimed that a major reason why negotiation with his group became protracted was "because we kept on going on about the fact that we wanted community moves" against the LDA's apparent keenness to disperse members to different locations. A representative from the Eton Manor Allotments also suggested that the LDA were resistant to viewing her group as a community. She relayed how she kept insisting in negotiations with the LDA that "we're a community, we're an old one and… we go back two or three generations." The question of whether plot holders could be relocated together or have to be dispersed among existing allotments sites around East London relied on the LDA agreeing that they were a community. She reported that the LDA's position in relation to this was "'you're not allowed to do that'—this because we're not relatives, we're not, you know, real neighbors, we just garden alongside each other." As a result of being pushed toward defending a community position, she said, "I think that what a lot of people find themselves doing [is] just kind of disappearing into the ether," rather than taking it on. A representative for the Waterden Road Travellers gave the impression that, while her community was acknowledged by the LDA, the significance of losing her home where "we were very, very much at home" was not.

For all the interview respondents, the "cataclysmic"[17] nature of change underscored their scepticism of the Government's aim to create a *sustainable communities' Olympic Legacy*. A representative from the Eastway Cycle Centre questioned the meaning and implications of the term. As he put it:

They don't use the words "sweeping away," they don't say "neighborhood cleansing," stuff like that. They say, "regeneration," they say, "new opportunities," they say, "sustainable communities," all of that sort of tosh, which, actually for the people who're being most directly affected by it, just is nothing but bad news... These planners dress up what they do in all sorts of positive language, but really, when it comes to it, they want your land, they want your community, they want it out of there because it doesn't fit their dream, [but] actually, who the bloody hell are they?

For the director of the smoked salmon producer, H. Forman and Son, the use of terms *sustainable communities* and *regeneration* serves to conceal real and insidious motives behind the CPO. He suggested that:

The grounds on which they were making the CPO were completely false and invalid... They didn't have the power to compulsory purchase the land for a sporting event. They didn't have the legal powers to do that. So they did it in the name of "regeneration."

For him, the tragedy, which the current credit crunch only serves to underscore is:

...a national thing really [lying in] that they didn't value manufacturing. This was the greatest concentration of manufacturing land in the whole of London—being wiped out for three weeks of sport! It's been a real problem over the last 10 years with this government—they've destroyed a million jobs in manufacturing [saying] "we don't need a manufacturing base because we've got the... financial services sector earning all our money for this country."
undervaluing blue collar over white collar

Forman argued that delivery time was critical for his business in preserving a niche in city's food industry, enabled by easy access to Central London's hotels and the House of Commons. For him, as for many small business owners, the combination of an un-regenerated site implying low property overheads combined with its inner-city location was strategically important given the competitiveness of national and international markets. For the Clay's Lane residents' representative, the demolition of mature allotments flew in face of sustainability agendas regarding the provision of locally grown food in the city. For the allotments representative herself, it seemed to point to failure in the LDA's understanding of how to create sustainable communities, for which time and continuity are of the essence. As she put it, "I mean

...here we've got this organisation who are talking about *sustainable communities* being the legacy and then at the same time talking about dispersing us, a ninety year-old community, all over the place!" The Clay's resident echoed this, saying:

I mean to me, this stuff about sustainability... I just can't take it seriously because, if you're looking at a programme which is meant to be delivering benefits to the population at large, surely the first people you deliver benefits to are the people who are directly affected!

For the Traveller's representative, *creating sustainable communities* should involve trying

...to help more homeless people... and trying to make more jobs and more careers for people. Instead of even ever bidding for them Olympics from day one, why not—with money for the London Games that they had—put it in something better? It's only lasting for six weeks!

Asked specifically what she thought of the Mayor's "Legacy Commitment" to make the Olympic Park a "blueprint for sustainable living," she responded, "It's a lie... it's common knowledge. The credit crunch... there's hundreds of thousands of people that's out of jobs at the moment, that they're queuing up at Jobseekers," For her, these present realities suggested the ultimate undeliverability of this commitment, which she summed up by saying: "so, I know he's just talking through his hat."

The fact that the development of the Olympic Park on the site was non-negotiable from the time that the bid was won has significantly, if variably, colored perceptions of former user groups on the site of the roles they had in the process. As the Eastway Cycle Center's representative argued that "a lot of the consultation stuff was just not asking the questions, it was putting the questions in a way to get the answers you want." For him, a major step forward in his groups' campaign happened when "we were able to demonstrate that there was a viable community there but that community had not been consulted with in any way, shape or form and that they should jolly well get that sorted." The director of H. Forman and Son argued that the process was more dismissive of local people's objections than other large-scale development processes, even other controversial ones:

Unlike most Compulsory Purchases where these things go to Public Inquiry—you know, Terminal 5: four hundred objections, it took five years—here you had four hundred objections, it took six weeks because you can't have the 2012 Games in 2016!

However, the Traveller and Clay's Lane group representatives argued that a problem with the negotiation process was not lack of engagement from the LDA but excessive, unproductive communication, producing what is known colloquially as consultation fatigue. The Traveller group representative added that what bothered her was not the relocation *per se* but the time it had taken to reach agreement on it. The allotments representative argued that a major problem for her group was that, in spite of having the opportunity to negotiate in unthreatening spaces such as local cafes, so many people "would

Eton Manor Allotments, left, and Waterden Road Traveller site, right. Both photos by Juliet Davis, 2007

be so cowed by authority that they would just agree to anything." She argued that this was because the LDA's key concern was not to establish how best to sustain this community, but what minimum would be required to make them go quietly. To this extent, consultation seemed a token democratic gesture, belying the decisions that had already been made. The Eastway Cycle Center's representative said:

So anybody starting now to look at the planning process, I think, I hope they will realise that… if you want to have a community-orientated planning system, first talk to the communities that are there. Sure, have your own conception of what you want, but…

Each of the representatives argued that the power imbalance between them and the LDA meant that recourse to support from external agents—whether in the law or media—became an essential negotiating tactic. Owing to the energy and commitment of a number of plot holders, the case of the allotments drew particular support in the national press as well as from social commentators such as Iain Sinclair, and restaurateurs Rick Stein and Sam Clarke and became highly publicised. The allotments representative was of the view that:

… those groups that in a way were more successful for various reasons… were those that managed to engage the media, they were the Travellers—the Gypsies—and us. And the reason for that is that we were both highly political areas. We were riding on a wave of, well, green sustainability.

Sinclair derided the arrogance of public institutions claiming to be able to "imagin[e] for us" what communities and their spaces might be, and how to make them.[18] The Waterden Road Travellers' representative reported that while on a number of occasions they felt that their privacy was being infringed by journalists wanting to capture and make use of their story, interest in their plight—which led to a High Court hearing—ultimately advanced their position. The representatives also each claimed that social ties between groups were strengthened by the common aim of opposing the LDA's proposals during 2005 and 2006. As the process wore inexorably on,

certain members of these groups began to pull apart. However, others remained strengthened, participating in active demonstrations of solidarity on the site in the run-up to its closure in 2007. Allegedly, all negative propaganda was promptly pulled down, seeming to reflect the assertion of law and enforcement over public opinion and suggesting that even the right to objection that is legitimated in CPO law is only so within certain contexts.

In spite of the LDA's emphasis on communication with user groups, outcomes of consultation were perceived in variable lights. For some businesses, the strategic relocation of their activities and *market value* compensation was adequate and advanced their situation. One of the former waste businesses reports on the LDA's website that "[w]e're delighted with our new premises, as they allow us to develop our business in a way which would not have been possible were it not for the Olympic Games." For other groups, particularly the residential groups and allotment holders, it was not *market value*, but relationships, established over time within their group and with their sites that were important. For the director of H. Forman and Sons, *market value* is, like *sustainable communities*, a tricky term that discounts the amount of time required for negotiating with the LDA, the disruption of economic activities through relocation and the effects of relocation on staff. For him:

The problem with Compulsory Purchase Law is that you're not allowed to benefit from the reason why you're being acquired. You're not supposed to be worse off, but you're not allowed to be better off.

In spite of this, the site to which his firm has been relocated, a stone's throw away from the Olympic stadium and closer to the city clearly presents advantages in the long term. The Eastway Cycle Center's representative was dismissive about *market value* saying that "it's all just part of the funny money that goes around with the Olympics." For him, the position of the cycle center within the broader pre-Olympic site was relatively insignificant. What drove the centre's campaign was desire to promote their sport within East London and create the best opportunities for their club members to excel in 2012. The

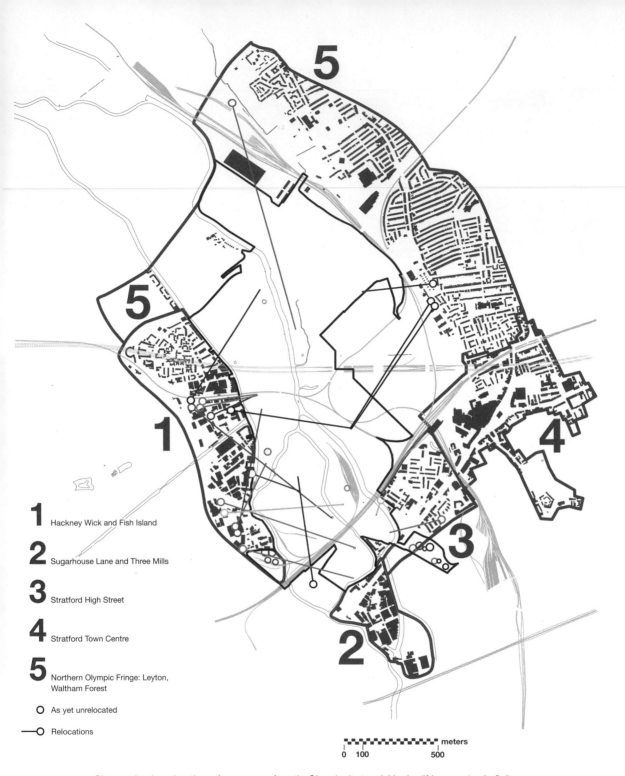

1 Hackney Wick and Fish Island

2 Sugarhouse Lane and Three Mills

3 Stratford High Street

4 Stratford Town Centre

5 Northern Olympic Fringe: Leyton,
Waltham Forest

O As yet unrelocated

—O Relocations

meters
0   100   500

Diagram showing relocations of user groups from the Olympic site to neighboring "fringe masterplan" sites by 2008. Ordnance survey data reproduced with permission of: Ordnance Survey © Crown Copyright. All rights reserved. ©Juliet Davis 2008

DAVIS, Juliet

Diagram showing relocations of user groups from the Olympic site by 2008. Ordnance survey data reproduced with permission of: Ordnance Survey © Crown Copyright. All rights reserved. © Juliet Davis 2008

site to which they have been relocated is considerably better than their former home, though they claim that this is only by dint of an exhausting campaign. The Clay's Lane representative described how he ultimately failed to reach a negotiated solution for the relocation of his dwindling group and wound up accepting terms for individual relocations to neighborhoods bordering the site. At the Public Inquiry, the allotments representative objected to the CPO on the grounds that the loss of their site would catalyse the breakup of their community. Although the correct number of sixty seven plots were offered as replacements for those lost, a series of factors—proximity to a busy road, a standard layout of sheds, a different soil—have conspired to sever ties between community and land. The Waterden Road Travellers' representative reported that their relocation to three separate though proximate locations was ultimately positive—"we got good out of it, but really"—as each of these groups now includes a smaller number of families who have things in common with each other and their bespoke, brick houses allow them to feel more established and legitimated within East London. In spite of this, the thirty five Traveller families, at the time of writing, await completion of these houses and, in the meantime, continue to camp on the Olympic construction site.

Conclusions: From Policy to Practice

The aim of this article has been to consider the effectiveness of the CPO as a tool in initial stages in the delivery of a *sustainable communities'* legacy for the 2012 Olympics. I looked at disparities between how consultation conducted as part of the CPO process was intended to operate and how representatives of five former user groups experienced it. I also considered some of the outcomes of the CPO and relocation processes from the perspectives of these representatives. Although these perspectives don't represent all the views of former occupants of the pre-Olympic site, they do serve to suggest some early conceptual cracks in the LDA's approach to creating a *sustainable communities* legacy through the London 2012 Olympics.

The LDA clearly recognised the need for consultation and engagement to take place in different ways and in different spaces, suited to the heterogeneity of use and community on the site. Nevertheless, experiences of consultation processes of former occupants of the site reveal a number of problematic issues: with respect to how communities are both defined and define themselves; to the difficulties of equating a comprehensive strategy with a diverse set of needs and perspectives; to the problems of relocating communities which have

Opening day at the new Cycle Centre, left, and the new headquarters of H Forman and Son, Hackney Wick, right

been forged strongly in relation to place and/or location; and to inherent power imbalances in negotiation. These experiences help to highlight a broader point: that the translation of *sustainable communities'* policy through CPO and consultation practices is far from direct, relying on multiple actions and interpretations that, inevitably, produce varied and situated outcomes.

While advocates of the Olympics Games argue that it provides a means for attracting the capital investment needed for long-term regeneration in East London, the spatial requirements of an Olympic Park mean the foreclosure of possibilities for incremental, contextually subtle approaches to development. If community groups, as respondents to my interviews suggest, require continuity and time to evolve, then consultation, as a community-building exercise, appears to marry problematically with development processes which are about rapid, drastic change. Similarly, as a number of the above interview respondents suggest, the gradual and diverse ways in which communities are formed and the values people come to attach to these are hard to equate with the market values of an urban economic system. Not only has the pre-Olympic site been completely demolished, but there is now an interlude of seven years before it can, in theory, begin to be re-occupied by local users. Such an interlude, required for the development of the site for the Games, appears to diminish the possibility that *sustainable communities* of the future include people who inhabited the site before it. Despite the LDA's assertions to the contrary, a concern that arises over and again in ongoing consultation exercises on the development of the *Legacy Masterplan Framework* is that the need for the LDA to recoup investments in land purchase before the Games through reselling it afterwards will create conditions for the exclusion of all but the wealthiest locals and, moreover, require that new communities are formed to a significant extent by non-locals. Skepticism also often arises that the kinds of image of London as a World City that the Olympics helps to promote are even compatible with regeneration—as a form of rehabilitation, and even over time—of a local place. Who, in these terms, will the constituents of *sustainable communities* of the future be? Will they be large-scale developers and wealthy city dwellers, whose interests lie in creating an exclusive

enclave in the midst of the social diversity and complexity at its fringes? How could they otherwise, include a broader social and economic mix, becoming a "blueprint for sustainable living" in an inclusive, heterogenous and more empowering sense? The LDA certainly emphasise the need to create ongoing opportunities for the public to be involved in decision-making and community-building exercises through the development of the spatial frameworks and economic models for 2012's Legacy. Watch this space.

References

1. International Olympic Committee Evaluation Commission (IOCEC), Report of the IOC Evaluation Commission for the Games of the XXX Olympiad in 2012 *(International Olympic Committee, 2005), p. 71.*
2. Ken Livingstone, "We Must go for Gold with London's Olympic Bid," The Observer *(2003) <http://www.guardian.co.uk/uk/2003/jan/12/ olympics2012.sport> [accessed 15 January 2009]*
3. Greater London Authority (GLA), 5 Legacy Commitments (2007) <http://www.london.gov.uk/mayor/olympics/docs/5-legacy-commitments.pdf> [accessed 02 February 2009]
4. See, for example:
Julian Agyeman and Tom Evans. "Toward Just Sustainability in Urban Communities: Building Equity Rights with Sustainable Solutions," Annals of the American Academy of Political and Social Science, *Vol. 590, Rethinking Sustainable Development, 2003, 35-53*
Claire Edwards. "Participative Urban Renewal? Disability, Community and Partnership in New Labour's Urban Policy," Environment and Planning A, *40, 2008, 1664-1680*
Gerald E. Frug. City Making: Building Communities without Building Walls. *Princeton: Princeton University Press, 1999*
Rob Imrie, Loretta Lees and Mike Raco. Regenerating London: Governance, Sustainability and Community. *London: Routledge, 2008.*
Richard Sennett. The Fall of Public Man. *London: Penguin, 2002 [1977]*
Mike Raco. Building Sustainable Communities: Spatial Policy and Labour Mobility in Post-War Britain. *Bristol: Policy Press, 2003.*
5. Vigor, A., Mean, M., Tims, C. After the Gold Rush: a Sustainable Olympics for London. *London: IPPR and Demos, 2004.*
Also see, for example:

ShiNa Li and Adam Blake. "Estimating Olympic-Related Investment and Expenditure," International Journal of Tourism Research, *11, 2009, 1-20.*

6. London Development Agency (LDA). "Olympic Site Land Assembly," London Development Agency: Places and Infrastructure *<http://www.lda.gov.uk/server.php?show=nav.00100h003001> [accessed 01 January 2009]*

7. Capita Symonds. Environmental Statement. *London: Capita Symonds and the London Development Agency, 2004.*

8. Henri Lefebvre. Writings on Cities. *Selected, translated, and introduced by Eleonore Kofman and Elizabeth Lebas. Cambridge, MA: Blackwell, 1996, p. 229*

9. Jane Jacobs. The Death and Life of Great American Cities. *Harmondsworth: Penguin, 1972 [1961], p. 336-352*

10. Richard Sennett. The Fall of Public Man. *London: Penguin, 2002 [1977], p. 259-268*

11. Richard Sennett. The Uses of Disorder: Personal Identity and City Life. *Harmondsworth: Penguin, 1973.*

12. See, for example:

Rob Imrie and Huw Thomas. "Urban Redevelopment, Compulsory Purchase, and the Regeneration of Local Economies: the Case of Cardiff Docklands," Planning Practice and Research, *4(3), 1989, p. 18-27*

Rob Imrie and Huw Thomas. "Law, Legal Struggles and Urban Regeneration: Rethinking the Relationship," Urban Studies, *34(9), 1997, p. 1401-1418*

13. For example, Peter Hall. "The City of Capitalism Rampant: London 1979-1993," in Cities in Civilization: Culture, Innovation and Urban Order. *London: Weidenfeld & Nicolson, 1998*

14. London Development Agency (LDA). Relocations Strategy: Lower Lea Valley Olympic and Legacy Planning Applications *(Appendix to the Environmental Statement). London: LDA, 2004, p. 6*

15. As set out in the following key documents:

Office of the Deputy Prime Minister (ODPM). Sustainable Communities: Building for the Future. *London: ODPM, 2003*

Office of the Deputy Prime Minister (ODPM). Planning Policy Statement 1: Delivering Sustainable Development, *London: ODPM, 2005*

Sustainable Communities Act, *2007, Chapter 23*

Planning and Compulsory Purchase Order Act, *2004*

16. David M. H. Rose. London Development Agency (Lower Lea Valley, Olympic and Legacy), CPO 2005 Inspector's Report to the Secretary of Trade and Industry. *Bristol: The Planning Inspectorate, 2006*

17. This expression was used in interview by the Eton Manor Allotments' representative but refers to Jane Jacobs analysis of the effects of "cataclysmic money" investments on urban areas in The Death and Life of Great American Cities.

18. Iain Sinclair. "The Olympics Scam," The London Review of Books. *30(12), 2008 <http://www.lrb.co.uk/v30/n12/contents.html> [accessed 23 January, 2009]*

Juliet Davis *is undertaking a PhD entitled* Framing an Olympic Legacy: Mediations in Urban Change in London's Lea Valley *at the Cities Programme, LSE, where she also has a tutorial fellowship. This focuses on the public's role in shaping pre-planning application stages of design development of the masterplan framework for the 2012 Olympic legacy. It considers how notions of the public are constituted through participation, how, through it, local and past contexts are ascribed value and also how relationships between public ownership and urban form evolve over time. Prior to commencing this project, Juliet practiced as an architect, also running design studios at Cambridge and Canterbury architecture schools.*

KOHN, David

A Brief History of the Fortunes of Deptford Creek: An Interview with Mark Brearley

Deptford Creek is a tributary of the River Thames just upstream from the more famous Greenwich, home to the Prime Meridian. It has a comfortably derelict appearance that attracts kestrels, Chinese mitten crabs, aggregate barges, artists and black redstart. Recently however, the seemingly inexorable property boom meant that even the Creek became, albeit briefly, prime real estate. Next door to the Laban Centre (Herzog de Meuron, 2003) the catchily named Creekside Village is currently under construction and due for completion in 2010. Including 800 residential units and 220,000 square feet of commercial space the development represents a serious change to the density and fortunes of the area. Around a further 50 property freeholds surround the Creek. If it had not been for the credit crunch the fortunes of many of the local property owners might also have been seriously changed. But the market has stalled so the cranes have stood still and everyone, from developers to local residents, has had a moment to reconsider their future.

Despite its current dereliction, Deptford too had its heyday. Henry VIII was attracted to the Creek's deep waters when siting the first Royal Dockyards in the early 16th century and the East India Company ran its operations for nearly 100 years from its banks. During the 19th century, the area rapidly industrialised becoming home to one of the world's first suburban railway station in 1836 and largest power stations the following year. Deptford Power Station was expanded several times during the 20th century and was described as "monstrous and magnificent" by one visitor in 1947. However by the 1960s it was facing closure and by 1992 it was razed to the ground.

The area's economic rise and fall has been mirrored by its political fortunes. The Metropolitan Borough of Deptford, a local government district and subdivision of the then County of London, was established in 1900 with a lavish baroque town hall built on New Cross Road in 1903. When London's local government infrastructure was reorganised in 1965, the Borough of Deptford was split in two, down the length of the Creek, and divided between the boroughs of Greenwich and Lewisham. Once having been physically, economically and politically a center, Deptford Creek became, officially, a margin. Fittingly, Deptford Town Hall is now home to Goldsmiths College, one of London's leading art schools.

Returning to the present, the recent property boom brought the Creek's marginal status into sharp relief. Being of peripheral concern to two local governments, and in the last half century, down on its luck, there was no strategic plan in place for how the area might change. As planning permissions were granted for larger and larger developments, local awareness grew that, if left unchecked, the artists, kestrels and crabs would be forced to flee once again until the next economic bust. Fortunately for some, the bust promptly arrived which is where this story really begins.

Mark Brearley leads Design for London: a design advisory body and part of the London Development Agency that works on behalf of the Mayor of London. They work to ensure design is an essential component in the transformation of the city's urban spaces, as well as working with local borough councils on strategies or proposals for difficult sites such as Deptford Creek:

David Kohn: Can you describe Design for London's role in promoting sustainable development?

Mark Brearley: We work to realize policy. This may sound really dull, but we are enthusiastic about the policies defined by the Mayor of London, which aim to shape London's growth. They are bold and tough policies. The most significant of these policies constricts land supply, so that as the city grows it remains compact, with some areas of heightened intensity. There is a requirement that intensification occurs in places with good public transport, in order to shift the transport balance away from private vehicle use. These policies are being applied to a city that is, by European standards, growing fast, and this leads to a whole series of design issues. It leads to conflicts that require design resolution. To squeeze more uses in bigger quantities into a fixed size place is not easy. It's a challenge that has not been faced up to before in London.

Alongside these issues, we work to improve the liveability and the quality of the city we live in, asking how we can shape change and growth to make places better. You asked about sustainability, well the quality of life in London has a relationship with economic sustainability. London is in competition with other cities across the world, in a battle for economic growth. We need to attract and retain sectors such as financial services, tourism and tourist-based retail, corporate headquarters, creative industries, all of which could choose to go elsewhere. If London isn't a good place then the jobs will not come and we'll all be in trouble.

DK: Another aspect of sustainability that I am interested in is ecology. As the distinction between city and countryside around London becomes increasingly blurred, what effect do you see this having on London's ecology?

MB: London is a mature city with a self-aware attitude to development. There is a good understanding of the effect of development on the immediate context of the city, and those policies I mentioned, holding us in, have strong popular support. London's growth is not rolling out destruction across the landscape it sits in, nor is it destroying its internal spaces and ecology. In fact, there is a steady enhancement of spaces and bio-diversity going on; hard-won, but still steady. There are exciting opportunities around the edge of the city, in the spaces between the chunks of the wider conurbation, in those more dispersed places. Here the priority given to ecology can dovetail with other priorities. For example, a new wilderness can incorporate better management of water, mitigating the increased threat of flooding, and alongside we can find space to expand urban food growing, and we can lay down the simple infrastructure to connect Londoners with these in-between spaces, to allow them to enjoy more of their city, satisfying their need to play. So, we are pushing forward projects which will encourage people to spend their recreation time in landscapes they don't need to drive to, luring them, for example, to the end of the tube line for picnics in the Green Belt.

DK: How do those working in development react to policy? Does your relationship to developers feel oppositional? Or is there more-or-less a broad consensus?

MB: The development process in London can be tough, but by and large it does not feel like we need to be oppositional. There is a familiarity with, and a friendly embracing of the day-to-day conflict between different parties with different objectives, but I don't have the sense that, at some bigger scale, there is a fight between fundamentally different priorities. No doubt this would be different if the city was expanding out over agricultural or wild spaces, or if there was widespread demolition and displacement. But in London now the conflicts are more local, more good-humored.

DK: Does this mean that creating an ever more sustainable city is simply a matter of resources?

MB: There is a need to keep London's economy strong, so that the resources can be there. Are there enough resources to do things better than they have been done before? Well, if London was not growing, if it was poor, we would not be able to do many of the things we would like to. Retrofitting buildings to reduce their energy consumption, restructuring logistics to lower congestion and reduce emissions, renewing the waste-processing infrastructure, sorting out the network of public spaces; these are all expensive. We like to point out that "you can't make a snowman unless it's snowing." We're part of the effort to keep the snow falling, to keep the resources rolling.

At Design for London we focus on physical projects and the shaping of places. We help steer and shape our city, by deploying small budgets, through persuasion and planning. The whole way that steering and shaping works would be different if it wasn't snowing, if the city wasn't growing. So it is sobering in the current economic downturn to recognize how different the parameters of action and influence would be if London stopped thriving. As it happens, we are assuming that we are experiencing a hiatus rather than a transformation of fortunes. However, the current economic crisis reminds us that urban growth is not an inevitable fact of life. It can't be taken for granted.

DK: I would like to touch on an issue related to recent urban projects in my office. Is there an active debate surrounding narratives of place and how they can help different parties pursue common, sustainable goals? This kind of work is difficult to enshrine in policy being as it is about stories, fictions, identities, images.

MB: Yes, a lot of what we are engaged in involves telling stories about places: "This is how this place can be understood." "This is what this place can be." "This series of spaces can be understood as a single piece of the city, and this is how it can be adjusted." Many of the places we are involved with are tough places that people have not been feeling good about, and that's been holding them back. Even though they have much that's good already, it's not always obvious. In these situations photography becomes a great tool. People see a photographer's response to the places they know, and then they can begin to realize that those places are in fact diverse and beautiful. Once people are more able to see the good in a place, start to appreciate particularities, possibilities and ambitions, then we can help weave stories, by making a few simple drawings which state an ambition, for example, and then help re-shape the place to match the story, making real the potential.

DK: Social sustainability, therefore, is dependent on a participatory process involving telling stories backwards and forwards between those trying to steer change and those who will live with that change?

MB: At the first stage of a project those stories can create the enthusiasm to act and move forward. For example, by the Thames in Rainham, we noticed a good place for a cafe; in an industrial area, next to a marsh and the river. We learnt that it had once been a visited place; that there had been a ferry and a pub called The Three Crowns. We knew there were local people who remembered the history, and enjoyed it and connected with it. It became obvious that you could work with this. We called the cafe proposal The Three Crowns, and made sure the photomontages had the Three Crowns sign on them. This has helped people connect with and embrace the idea, and so we're now confident we can make it happen.

DK: Do you see the methods that you use here as being pioneering or do you look to other cities in Europe as being leaders? How do you contextualise what you do?

MB: We have glanced at other cities, hoping to discover that we are not alone in our way of going about the job. We've made plenty of friends, but not found any leaders. We realize that we are doing something quite particular and yes, if you like, pioneering. We have embraced the development process in an unusual way, choosing to work through negotiation, being ingenious and entrepreneurial in order to influence and nurture change. We constantly use the leverage of modest funding to show how something could be, or the leverage of being able to persuade bigger funders, or having some relationship with the process of planning negotiation. We work with an awareness of the levers we can pull, gently, to affect change. This all requires creative opportunism, seizing the chances to steer. We call this process "catch and steer." It's very different from say "own and deliver" or even "own, pay and deliver!" We are a small team working with small means and a persuasive manner to have a big effect. We argue and encourage, working in the context of the convoluted processes which re-shape London. Of course, this way of working isn't unique, but we have pushed it to a special place.

In June 2008, I joined a team of consultants in the Creekside Centre, a nature education resource on the banks of Deptford Creek, for a week-long design charrette looking at the future of the area. Ecologists, artists, sustainability specialists, architects, planners and real estate economists—all-in-all 25 consultants, had been appointed to consider how Deptford Creek might change if all interested parties looked to a longer-term sustainable future, beyond the possible short-term gains of piecemeal property development. The event was organised by Creative Process, a local regeneration agency, and funded by a broad consortium including Design for London, Lewisham Council, Deutsche Bank, the Stephen Lawrence Charitable Trust, Lewisham College and the Creekside Village.

Chaos in the Creekside Centre ensued. Meetings were held almost continuously between local residents, interest groups, property developers, planners and the consultants. At the same time, the team attempted to compile a comprehensive survey of

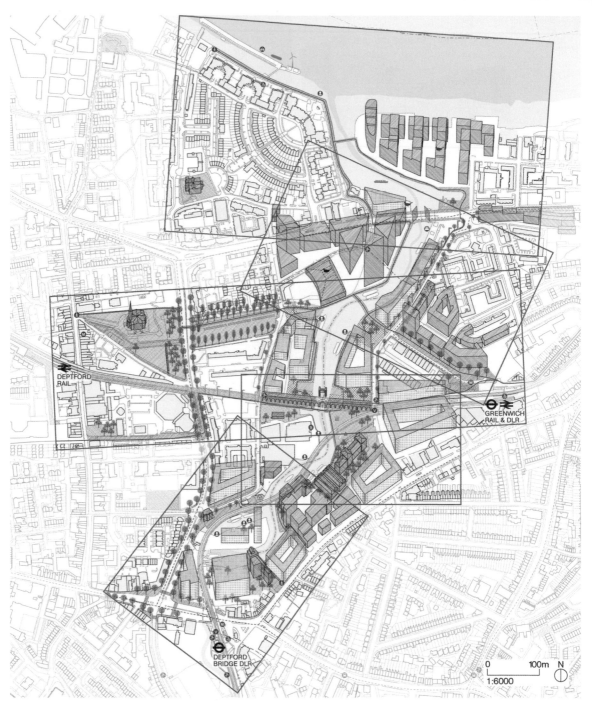

DEPTFORD
RAIL

GREENWICH
RAIL & DLR

DEPTFORD
BRIDGE DLR

0   100m   N

1:6000

*All the proposals represented on a plan of the area. The black outlined rectangles indicate the five sections
of the Creek that were considered as a series of individual rooms, each with its own distinct character.*
*Lower Creek: Lower Creek is characterized by the darker, deeper waters of the River Thames, high steel
embankments and long views to the Isle of Dogs*
*Middle Creek A: With the Laban Centre currently at center-stage, Middle Creek A is soon to be transformed
by the high-rise dense urban living of the Creekside Village development*
*Middle Creek B: Middle Creek B is at the heart of the charrette's proposals, characterized by a string of
exciting new public spaces, connecting Creekside to its neighbors*
*Middle Creek C: Middle Creek C is dominated by the sweeping Docklands Light Railway viaduct overhead
and the potential of the Waterworks to become a public park*
*Upper Creek: As the Creek wends its way south, its twists and turns become shorter and tighter, conse-
quently Upper Creek is warren-like and in need of careful adjustment to ensure legibility and enjoyable use*

Top left: Semi-wild character of the Creek at low tide, with the Docklands Light Railway crossing above. Top right: Charrette participants explore the Creek at low tide, with the Laban Centre in the distance, image courtesy Creative Process; Middle left: At present the Creek is under-used and largely inaccessible to pedestrians. Middle right: The landscape of Deptford seen from roof level. Bottom left: Skips behind the Laban Centre. Bottom right: Mumford's Mill, one of the last remaining 19th-century mill buildings

the area in terms of ecology, use, transport, art, energy resources and market viability. Gradually proposals began to emerge in different forms. Some were very local, highly specific changes that residents had been concerned about for years. Others were less immediately apparent and grew out of conversations that took place over several days.

A consistent frame of reference for all involved was the Creek itself. We had met in a building by its shores and would have meetings outside, on a slipway that descended to the muddy Creek bottom. The void it created in the city fabric allowed the long views that artists enjoyed from their studios and developers credited to their towers while at the same time providing the habitat for a wide range of flora and fauna that gave the area its semi-wild identity. Its constant twisting and turning meant that, despite having one name and one form when viewed from above, from its banks the Creek was transformed into a string of changing spaces each with its own character and possibilities.

In discussing Deptford Creek and its surroundings, parties with differing and sometimes competing interests needed a shared imaginative language with which to positively describe the area. This would at least achieve a consensus about the value of the place, the basis on which future decisions could be made and a platform for ongoing discussion—a form of intellectual framework for urban change. After various descriptions were recounted in conversation, the idea of Deptford Creek being a series of rooms began to take hold. The idea was tested through drawing, modelling, writing and

Model describing the Creek landscape as a series of rooms. Image courtesy AModels

proved both resistant and sufficiently open to interpretation to invite further elaboration. At the core of the charrette proposals, was a statement about the appropriate scale of intervention in the development process. Considering the whole Creek at once could lead to super-sized developments harboring the possibility of both large mistakes and the likelihood of only partial realization. On the other hand, planning focussing on each individual plot leads to over development and a rapid destruction of the public environment. Between these two ills lies the possibility of scales that relate to experience, to how we understand the spaces between us, landscapes, territories, boundaries, the public and the private.

Plans of each Creek Room were published in March 2009 and are beginning to inform the future of the place with an exhibition in November 2009 offering an opportunity to assess their ongoing influence. Time will tell if the concept outlives the economic slump to affect a re-ascendant property market. Until then, several more modest conclusions can be drawn from the process of the charrette and the development of the rooms concept. Firstly, the telling of stories about places can be highly effective in linking a number of otherwise disparate factors, be they the scale of a landscape, the economic viability of individual properties, the history of the place or changing demographics. They are also highly cost-effective in that they do not require the purchase of land, the drawing up of masterplans, or the commissioning of projects to necessarily achieve currency. Secondly, narratives require a spatial aspect if they are able to connect places and imaginations through recognition of the individual's experience of the city.

As use of the word sustainability increases exponentially and correspondingly our ability to distinguish its different purposes diminishes, so our need to expand on the stories we want to tell about our cities grows. Perhaps it is fair to say, then, that sustainability has become a useful lever to prize open previously closed narratives about places and to inject into them the concerns of a new generation.

David Kohn *is an architect and teacher based in London. His practice, David Kohn Architects, is currently working on projects at a range of scales from urban design studies for London to interiors. Across all of the projects is an interest in the relationship of social interaction to architectural language and urban form. Recent projects include a prize-winning strategy for a forest in East London to house art events, a temporary restaurant at the Royal Academy of Arts, which won a D&AD Yellow Pencil, and a gallery for Stuart Shave Modern Art. The theoretical development of the practice's work is supported by research at London Metropolitan University where David is a Diploma Unit leader. David studied architecture at the University of Cambridge and at Columbia University as a Fulbright Scholar. www.davidkohn.co.uk*

DE LOOZ, Pierre Alexandre

Landmarks in Post-Western Ecology

The fear that sustainability will eschew commercial viability now seems long gone. Green design in the United States, for one, has elicited a specialized and increasingly commonplace lexicon of products, technology and architectural devices that lend the issue an identifiable profile. With new found currency comes a sense that in the very near future, sustainable design will be able to satisfy consumer desires equally or better than standard goods. But when it comes to stoking the market, even in matters of sustainability, the US has found a competitive partner and an unexpected mirror in the United Arab Emirates (UAE). Sustainability and sex met there in 2008, promising an aggressively green product—playgirl Pamela Anderson, reportedly at the bequest of Abu-Dhabi's royal family, began plans for an ecologically themed hotel. The leading Emirate has also begun spending petrodollars on renewable energy research and publicizing its plan for a zero-carbon city—all together hijacking sustainability from the policy pages.

If the Anderson Hotel is any indication, the UAE will sell environmentalism as an international attraction. With a population that is majority foreign, this is not altogether surprising. The pull of tourism has historically served as an antidote to the Emirates dependency on the oil trade and also as a deft political strategy. By the early 1990s American journalists reporting on the UAE, heartily described a traveler's marvel, of which lush urban parks and golf courses were a favorite example, a "green revolution" of sorts. 70 million new trees had been planted, according to one report, dropping the local temperature by several degrees. That same report also picked up on the other side of the coin: "The rulers care more about their parks than about their people," a young emirati soldier was quoted as saying.[1] The reader was left with the implication that fast-paced development which catered to Western consumers might camouflage a lack of democratic process and unanswered social grievances. The race for sustainability in the Emirates appears much less utopian from this angle. True to the mainline of development, codes of rivalry, prestige and showmanship propel sustainability in the UAE more so perhaps then notions of social justice.

Of all the Emirates to announce a vision of sustainability to the world, neither Dubai nor Abu-Dhabi can match the emotional appeal of Ras al-Khaimah. The lesser emirate is planning an entirely new sustainable capital with an architectural gravitas that might seem misplaced elsewhere. A rebel-rousing underdog in the early years of the federation, Ras al-Khaimah has historically taken its sovereignty more than lightly. In a recent documentary covering the emirate's initiatives, the crown prince said he found inspiration in architecture's monumental past, recognizing in the pyramids of Egypt "a reminder that

we have a choice: how we channel our energy, how we become useful."[2] He set the millennial task of channeling this energy on OMA. Echoing the crown prince, OMA turned to the pages of architectural history, "not out of nostalgia, but out of absolute necessity," they argue.[3] Their proposal takes the form of an ideal city, a hard edged footprint that cuts a square geometry from the desert sand. It is crossed by a grid of roadways and dense low-rise structures anchored around a monumental center and park. Schematically, the 300-acre plan reads less like an afterimage of LeCorbusier's Plan Voisin, then a graft of imperial Beijing in part because it revives the image of the ancient fortified city and its network of internal streets. More germane than the origin of the design however, the architects suggest that the capital city will be the new face of development in the region, a short to the "ecological time-bomb" the 20th century set ticking around the world.

Hit hard by "rampant global modernism," OMA observes, cities like Abu Dhabi and Dubai are wired for disaster. Avoiding global modernism on the contrary would offer a sustainable solution. Applied to these cities the term "global modernism," functions as a catch-all for contemporary architecture which has cloyingly spread along with another diffuse and large scale phenomenon, globalization. But before modernism went global—international style now sounds ironic at best—it was Western. It is a particular burden of modernism that its transformation of foreign environments, whether driven by nationalism as in Istanbul or colonialism as in Maputo, can be read as a grander process of Westernization. With this in mind, the task of avoiding global modernism not only shifts architecture's attention from global flows towards local realities, but more importantly pulls architecture out from a historical dénouement that, the assumption goes, has led to ecological collapse. OMA's formulation of sustainability calls not only for casting modernism aside but for relinquishing its inherent historical narrative. There is a coy allusion to this in OMA's renderings. On the outskirts of the plan what looks like a big-box retail outlet appears to be sinking into the sand, the drowning vessel of modern capitalism perhaps, against which the sustainable city must rise. Though OMA manages architectural recognition the way Pamela Anderson can muster celebrity headlines, there is nothing new or sexy in OMA's vision of sustainability. For that reason, OMA's design illuminates notions of sustainability inherited from the history of architecture, particularly in the American context.

Sustainability in architecture, it can be said, has emerged from a reform of industrial modernism, architecture's perennial obsession in the US, but not as a stylistic or technological paradigm. On the contrary, it has been rooted in an attempt to relocate modernism's political and historical program somewhere outside its original confines, as OMA does with its design for a City in the Desert. On many other occasions, architecture has projected this horizon, which is distinctly post-Western in outlook. Three landmarks in a sequence of critical and self-reflective moments like this follow, hastening the advent of a properly post-Western ecology:

Dense, low rise and earthy: sustainable planning the old fashioned way. Image courtesy Office for Metropolitan Architecture (OMA)

Aerial rendering of City in the Desert, new capital city for Ras al-Khaimah. The contemporary fortified city marches around a sacred center, while at the horizon, big box retail sinks into the sands of time. Image courtesy Office for Metropolitan Architecture (OMA)

Bernard Rudofsky, "Architecture without Architects," MoMA, 1964, p. 27. No imagination required to recognize "nature as architect" in the African Baobab wrote Rudofsky. It's soft wood is hollowed out and used as dwellings.

DE LOOZ, Pierre Alexandre

Pulizie di Primavera (Spring Cleaning), Superstudio, from "Italy: The New Domestic Landscape," MoMA, 1972, p. 246. "Life will be the only environmental art." Adolfo Natalini, Cristiano Toraldo di Francia, Roberto Magris, G. Piero Frassinelli, Alessandro Magris, Alessandro Poli (1970-72)

1964

In 1964, Bernard Rudofsky made the case that we had lost sight of the good life with our fixation on modernity. Our most fulfilling hours, he mused ironically, elapse through the informal architecture of cabins and tents or about remote locations like fishing villages and hill towns. If we can draw any conclusions from the magnetism of these settings in popular media from the 1960s, then he had a point. Rudofsky showed settings like these at the Museum of Modern Art, in an exhibit called *Architecture without Architects*, an abstracted black and white montage worthy of *National Geographic* (which had in fact supplied some of the imagery.) The exhibition included rural Mediterranean and Eastern Europe to a degree, but concentrated heavily on countries farther afield, like Sudan and Zambia, Iraq and Pakistan, China and Japan. Having composed a kind of expanded Grand Tour, Rudofsky was wary of seeming the accidental tourist with a penchant for exoticism and alerted the viewer to his polemic intentions. He intended the exhibit to oust architectural prejudices, triggering an intentionally strident comparison between "the serenity of the architecture in so-called underdeveloped countries with the architectural blight in industrial countries."[4] Rudofsky was pointing to the sorts of places that some 20 years later the UN-convened World Commission on Environment and Development would invoke in the Brundtland report.

The report, also known as "Our Common Future," had the combined agenda of overhauling international development aid and protection of the environment.

The Brundtland report would surely be a sign for Rudofsky that modernity had gone too far. Yet in 1964, the serenity of the non-industrialized world was already on its way out. The material that comprised *Architecture without Architects* represents 40 years of travel, research and happenstance, noted Rudofsky in the catalogue. It would be practically impossible, he added, to procure the same images again given the contemporary political climate (communism had sealed off entire swathes of the world in the name of progress.) In this and other ways Rudofsky let his viewer know that the material on display was already visual history, a precious record of places slipping from the present. In the preface to the catalogue, he calls these places "old world communities," which embodies his effort to actualize the past. The term directly echoes architect Pietro Belluschi's definition of communal architecture, also quoted in the preface, as "a continuing activity of a whole people with a common heritage, acting under a community of experience."[5] The idea that architecture should be thought of across generations and continuously through time was not for Rudofsky a defense of historical or vernacular style. It was rather an intimation of sustainability. These communities, he emphasized, successfully understood the need for confining growth and the "*limits* of architecture itself."

"The wisdom to be derived goes beyond economic and esthetic considerations, for it touches the far tougher and increasingly troublesome problem of how to live and let live, how to keep peace with one's neighbors, both in the parochial and universal sense."[6]

1972

In 1972, the UN conference on the Human Environment convened a spectrum of nations, rich and poor, to sow the seeds of environmental change in Stockholm. Despite the absence of the former USSR, the resulting declaration established discourse and principles on an internationally recognized level. In particular, the idea that poverty exerted detrimental pressures emerged and development, as a cure, was enshrined as being essential to environmental protection. The absence of the Soviets underscored, however, the question of competing world views. Development might be necessary to protect the environment, but development according to whom? That same year at MoMA, Emilio Ambasz opened the epic 1972 exhibition *Italy: A New Domestic Landscape*. With it's kaleidoscopic display of home furnishings, decorative objects, appliances and gadgets it was proof of the expanding consumer revolution that had symbolically sparred against communism in the person of Richard Nixon, then vice president, at the famous kitchen debate with Khrushchev in 1959. Schematically speaking, capitalism had nurtured a system where technology was propelled by culture, bettered by competitive design and made exciting and relevant to society. The Brundtland report would later, and perhaps unintentionally, reinforce this idea by pitting the cheap, portable kerosene stove of the developing world against the gas range of the first. It was in the Domestic Landscape's "counterdesign" section however, which challenged the consumer menagerie unrolled in the rest of the exhibition that environment and development combined in the clearest and most radical formulation.

Along with legitimizing development, the Stockholm declaration of 1972 defined natural resources as a web knitting first- and third-world economies, a shared commodity to be safeguarded. It is a vision which resonates in Superstudio collages, one of the most memorable examples of Ambasz's counterdesign program, a moniker the Italian group might have inspired with statements like this: "When design as an inducement to consume ceases to exist, an empty area is created, in which slowly, as on the surface of a mirror, such things as the need to act, mold, transform, give, conserve…come to light."[7] In their famous images, human life plays out on a hallucinatory ground plane, a double exposure of what resembles a cybernetic power grid and a rough natural landscape. According to Superstudio, the images depict architecture at its maximal and minimal limits; maximal, because a universal life-supporting system, the grid, extends in every direction and is everywhere accessible; minimal, because there is no obvious architecture, no walls or roofs to shelter human gathering. Instead, Superstudio presumes that when people decide to congregate, producing what they called a "microevent," the environment will respond in kind, offering the event just the right

"microenvironment," but no more no less. They reduced architecture to the smallest ecological footprint imaginable. As the clearest indication of this architecture to come, Superstudio pointed to the *plein air* refuges of the 1960s—camping sites, drop-out cities and geodesic domes. Though through their words and images Superstudio unmistakably took stock of the self-reflexive, back-to-nature ethos of the hippies, they also pointed to an emerging notion of sustainability. They referred to the shanty towns of the poor, using in particular the word "bidonvilles," with its connotations of post-colonial squalor.[8] But, they used it positively. The informal architecture of shanty towns could, they implied, be an efficient and recyclable model for a planet without architects. The idea that the backwardness of a shantytown or kerosene cooker is not the real problem, underpinned their argument. Fault lay in the larger system. Their fascination with archeological objects, particularly talismans and magical objects makes this even more evident. They called their vision a world without objects, and yet there was no ban on inherited objects of sentimental or poetic value, and especially on objects that reverse the progressive logic of Westernization. This draft for a fresh covenant between man and his environment not only recast thinking about architecture, but also subverted its traditional role in a narrative of modernization and westernization.

1992

As the Brundtland Commission neared completion of their report, Emilio Ambasz produced a winning design for the site of the Universal Exposition in Seville, Spain. The Expo was set to open in 1992, 20 years after the New Domestic Landscape, marking the 500th anniversary of a fabled milestone in the annals of Westernization, Christopher Columbus's discovery of the New World. A perfunctory theme like this could have been downplayed, if not totally sidelined, but Ambasz adopted it with gusto. He produced many evocative illustrations to accompany his entry, modulating the theme of Western progress playfully. In one case, Ambasz placed the cartoon of a monkish scribe filling the pages of a large book in the corner of his site plan. A large terrestrial globe serves as the scribe's table. This is most likely a caricature of Columbus penning the story of the West, a story which Ambasz sought symbolically to rewrite through his design for the expo.

Dominating the allotted site was the man-made island of La Cartuja, in Seville's Quadalquivir River. Ambasz proposed emptying the landfill, returning it to the river by flooding it and creating three large internal lakes. Following standard practice, participating nations would contribute individually designed pavilions, however they would be built on barges. At the end of the expo, the nations would in effect sail their pavilions home. Ambasz's scheme offered participants an opportunity to undertake a reciprocal journey to that of Columbus; this time, however, the rest of the world would set sail and, in a sense, rediscover their origins. The European hosts on the contrary, had nowhere to go; their expedition had come full circle and they could now memorialize the past, as if writing a concluding chapter. Behind them the foreign

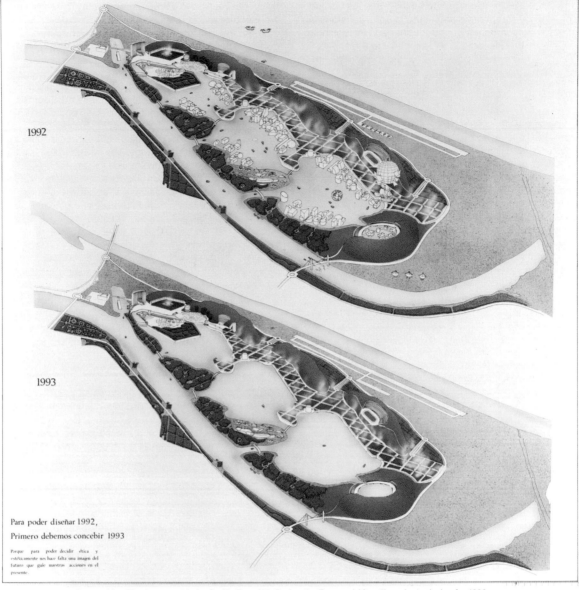

1992

1993

Para poder diseñar 1992,
Primero debemos concebir 1993

Porque para poder decidir ética y
estéticamente nos hace falta una imagen del
futuro que guíe nuestras acciones en el
presente.

*Competition Site Axonometric for Seville Expo '92. During the Expo and After. "In order to design for 1992
it is essential to design for 1993." Image courtesy Emilio Ambasz, Hon. FAIA*

nations would leave an idyllic park for the European city, as if bestowing on civilization the lost gift of nature.

Years later, architect Shigeru Ban, who early in his career designed a retrospective for Ambasz, pledged the Seville plan to environmentalism's official cause. He called it a "green idea." Ambasz, however, had expressed his concept for Seville in terms reminiscent of sustainability: "in order to design for 1992 it is essential to design for 1993."[9] Looking forward was an integral part of Ambasz's architectural oeuvre and interests, as Superstudio and the general tenor of "The New Domestic Landscape" demonstrate. Ettore Sottsass, whose work was also featured at the MoMA in 1972, once stated: "Emilio's architectural landscapes seem to be the remnants of a place… a thousand hours after the cataclysm; those thousand hours that will have given time to Nature to calm itself and to assume the density of silence."[10] According to Sottsass, Ambasz's work assumes that civilization's grand finale lies behind us; that we've made it to the other side of disaster. Wielding the power of erasure, the great cataclysm has cleansed the earthly slate. In his plans for Seville, Ambasz wanted to orchestrate a similar cleansing. His ground plane was water, which was meant to mirror the clarity of the sky; the lakes he envisioned obviated the need for roads, foundations and most significantly national boundaries; he limited enclosures to space frames and tents; visually open and physically demountable these light frames were further erased by a dense overgrowth of plants. He planned to impregnate the structures with a network of cold-water mist nozzles to acclimatize the air while nourishing the landscape, bringing his architecture even closer to a gaseous state, so to speak. Once the

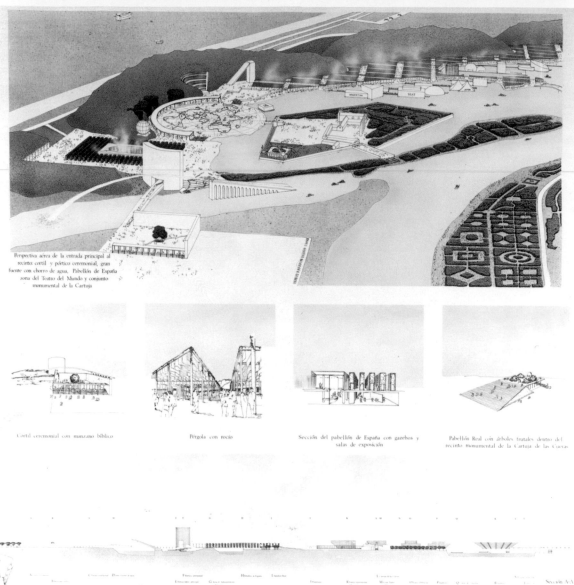

Perspectiva aérea de la entrada principal al
recinto cortil y pórtico ceremonial, gran
fuente con chorro de agua, Pabellón de España
zona del Teatro del Mundo y conjunto
monumental de la Cartuja

Cortil ceremonial con manzano bíblico

Pérgola con rocío

Sección del pabellón de España con gazebos y
salas de exposición

Pabellón Real con árboles frutales dentro del
recinto monumental de la Cartuja de las Cuevas

Sección A-A

*Aerial view of the Seville Expo '92. Main entrance and detailed views of other structures on site. Image
courtesy Emilio Ambasz, Hon. FAIA*

Expo was completed, Ambasz could return his site to architectural silence and the natural elements would be his greatest tool.

Though Seville decided in the end not to implement the Ambasz plan, many of his ideas defined the site and buildings that finally greeted the public in 1992. Though not the official theme, Seville 1992 was the first universal Expo with a universally sensitive approach to the environment. It also happened to be the first Expo after the fall of the Soviet Union, coinciding with a moment of political re-alignment that was euphorically branded by US President Bush as "The New World Order"—a term born from the first war fought over Middle East oil reserves involving direct Western interference.

With nuclear détente came a sense that there new priorities could be openly pursued. In the US, architectural critics lavished attention on the environmental aspirations of the 1992 Expo, its innovative water-cooled curtain walls, retractable shading systems and passive temperature-regulating methods. The fair also marked the arrival of *green*, a word the press media had now appropriated. Lifted from the campaigns of anti-nuclear political parties in Europe and in Canada, whose rise in the 1970s and 1980s paralleled a series of international conferences on the environment, the word exploded in architectural and design writing in the 1990s. The term "sustainability," on the other hand, had a hard time catching up with the color-fast design moniker, as did the substantive set of geo-political and socio-economic narratives Ambasz tried to program for Seville.

Contemporaneous with the fair, the troubled life of another great "green" idea, Biosphere in the Arizona

DE LOOZ, Pierre Alexandre

Aerial view of the third lake, other structures and a section through the planted pergolas. Image courtesy Emilio Ambasz, Hon. FAIA

desert, emphasized how environmentalism now turned almost exclusively on ecological and technological questions, producing a kind of monoculture. Biosphere's internal environments, microcosms of the planet at large, were to grow self-sufficiently and largely free of human settlement, a zero impact bubble. Ecology, it seemed to argue, should be divorced from social and urban content. By 1993 Biosphere's air-tight enclosure had started to fail. Ironically, what is possibly the first pejorative use of the word green appeared that same year in a review by the *New York Times* critic Herbert Muschamp. Reporting from the conference *Architecture at the Crossroads: Designing for a Sustainable Future* (organized by The World Congress of Architects in conjunction with the AIA), Muschamp described the proceedings as well near "an exercise in deceptive green packaging."[11] To illustrate his

point, he recounted a squabble between Helmut Jahn and William McDonough. To his dismay and to the audience's amusement, each accused the other of modernist delusions. The architects, Muschamp observed, seemed patently unable to talk about sustainability, skirting around the topic as if it had vacated the premises. In the end, the single most captivating moment of the Congress Muschamp remembered was neither Peter Eisenman nor Jean Nouvel, nor even William McDonough, but an architect turned revolutionary mayor of a mid-size Brazilian city. Tangible, large-scale sustainable change was happening. It was urban, political and architecturally informed and it was happening in Brazil: post-Western ecology had arrived.

References

1. Schmetzer, Uli. "Enigmas Blosso in Arid Cornucopia," Chicago Tribune. Oct 2, 1990, p. 16

2. Gjørv Eirin. The Sand Castle. *Educational Broadcasting Corporation, Wide Angle series, 2007, documentary video*

3. Office for Metropolitan Architecture. "City in the Desert-Eco Riddle," fact sheet, 2006

4. Rudofsky, Bernard. Architecture without Architects: A Short Introduction to Non-Pedigreed Architecture. *New York: Museum of Modern Art, 1964, p. 9*

5. Ibid. p. 9-10

6. Ibid. p. 13

7. Ambasz, Emilio. Italy the New Domestic Landscape: Achievements and Problems in Italian Design. *New York: Museum of Modern Art, 1972, p. 246*

8. Ibid. p. 244

9. Kimmelman, Michael. "Waste Not: the Accidental Environmentalist," New York Times, *May 20, 2007 and Ambasz, Emilio.* Emilio Ambasz: The Poetics of the Pragmatic. *New York: Rizzoli, 1998, p. 196*

10. Sottsass, Ettore, essay quoted in Ambasz, Emilio. Emilio Ambasz: The Poetics of the Pragmatic. *p. 9*

11. Muschamp, Herbert. "Design vs. the Environment: a Debate Among Architects," New York Times, *June 23, 1993*

Pierre Alexandre de Looz *is an architect and writer. He is co-founder and editor-at-large of the magazine* Pin-Up, *and also serves as contributing editor for Berlin based magazine 032c. Besides writing for these and other publications on architecture, art and fashion, he has worked with Mesh Architectures since 2005 in New York.*

JIANG Jun

China's Sustainability: Asynchronous Revolutions

[handwritten annotation: limiting factors — more than just the land]

The recent opening ceremony of the Beijing Olympics widely broadcasted China's "Four Great Inventions" symbolizing China's role as an ancient, creative power. However, the historical distinction among the four inventions, as well as the differentiation in their global after-effects, has long been ignored. Two of the four inventions—gunpowder and the compass—were clearly oriented towards military power and war, while the other two—paper-making and type printing—were more about cultural cultivation. The suffering and exhaustion of consecutive warring between separatist states prior to unification over 2000 years ago, must have compelled continental civilization to finally choose a more sustainable way to develop itself. Paper-making and type-printing facilitated civil services that were advocated by Confucianism to ensure the relative long lifespan of each dynasty, as well as cultural continuity between dynasties. On the other hand, gunpowder and the compass precipitated wars and colonialism on the Western side of the Eurasian landmass, which in turn unlocked the potential for industrialization and globalization—a revolution that put sustainability in danger.

Sustainability, a modern description of long life, had been the latent principle behind all dynasties of pre-modern China. It was based on three aspects of the civilization: united politics as the organizational mode of the state; agricultural economy as the social mode of production; and Confucian culture as its ideology. United politics minimized the internal exhaustion brought about by national collectivism, the agricultural economy stabilized local power through land-oriented production and local collectivism, while Confucian culture synchronized the two into "oneness" through its isomorphic relation between the state and the family. The stability and sustainability of pre-modern China was defined by this trinity.

The loss of demilitarized local power was compensated through the relative freedom granted by the state for families to develop and maintain a given territory over consecutive generations. The sustainability of the state was therefore resolved via the collective sustainability of all those local families. The absence of military repression and the increase of extrication from self-organization resulted in periodical, massive population increases. Traditional Chinese belief in "more offspring, more blessings" could be translated into "more productivity" or "more power" prior to machine power, which in turn was intentionally suppressed, along with the marginalization of military inventions. Most inventions in machinery were supposed to be merely the reinforcement of human power rather than its replacement.

The massive emphasis on sheer population numbers later used by Mao in fighting against his machinery-armed enemies, was a double-edged sword. On the one hand human power appears more sustainable than the mass consumption of fossil fuels, used intensively by the Western world, after, and because of, the Industrial Revolution. However, given the upper limit of the productivity of land, the population is congenitally confined by the ability of this land to support it. Throughout Chinese history, population growth always surged with economic growth, which was followed by massive reclamation and cultivation, until the demographic dividend was exhausted, leading to economic depression. Civilization itself performed like agriculture, experiencing the ups and downs of seasons while the vitality was reserved for the future—a more oriental notion of eternity.

The Chinese civilizations' refusal to utilize high-end machinery, the over-proliferation of population, as well as an ideological subjection to nature, generated a highly developed handicraft industry. Its low-cost maximized accessibility for the masses, while its low-tech nature minimized exploitation and pollution of the environment. Pre-modern China became defined by the intertwined relation between agricultural production, land, political organization and the suppression of industrialization. The sustainability both in society and nature not only imprinted the most valuable quality of pre-modern China, but also endlessly detained the industrial revolution whose subversive nature would interrupt sustainability itself. To this extent pre-Modern China exhibited a form of sustainable society. The self-sufficiency of this inward developing empire couldn't have been broken but for the influence of external forces.

In the official discourse of late pre-modern China, the Industrial Revolution was seen as a mere tactic "playing one barbarian state against another." This could be understood as the last statement of an imperial civil government, symbolized by paper and printing, on high-end technology that was symbolized by gunpowder and the compass. The offensive term "barbarian" came from *Classic of Mountains and Rivers*—the most ancient Chinese book on geography—in which China was thought to be the orthodox center of both the geographic and the mental world. Barbarians were those uncivilized tribes living in the peripheral nowhere that were constantly attempting invasion. Historically, China falled several times to fight against these "barbarians" and was subjected to minority rule: seemingly a victory of gunpowder and compass over paper and printing. However, these temporary rulers were ultimately de-saturated due to China's massive population and were assimilated by words. Given a long enough timeline, sustainability could be found more in words than in wars.

The handicraft industry is centered on human power, while modern industry is centered on machine power. It is the sheer difference between "machine is part of human being" and "human being is part of machine." The ultimate ambition of the Industrial Revolution was to construct a mechanical utopia through which human beings are liberated from physical labor because of the automation of the machine. The first phase of industrialization was an accelerating process of technological innovation and advanced mobility, until its un-sustainability was unveiled through the energy crisis. Unlike agriculture production, industrial production is not linked to the seasons, nor is it

World Atlas in A Chinese Bestiary, with China at the center. From Shan Hai Classic *(book on ancient Chinese geography), author unknown, appeared in Warring States Period (403-221 B.C.)*

Human-power-oriented development had stifled the development of technology in a direction that could replace manpower and hence change the organizational mode of Local Collectivism. From Tian Gong Kai Wu (The Exploitation of the works of Nature), *Song Yingxing, 1637*

constrained by the amount of local energy supply available. Before the Industrial Revolution transformed agricultural processes, agriculture transforms solar energy into bio-energy through farming on a given piece of land, while industry consumes fossil energy—a more intensified form of bio-energy—to fabricate a myth of automation based on the assumption that the energy supply will not run out. The intensity of energy use reflects the speed of consumption. Industrialization was actually a shift in the speed of consuming what is given by nature. As a revolution, it discarded the sustainable cycles of production and consumption necessary for "slow culture," relying, instead, on the assumption that a new sustainable energy could be found to support mobility-oriented modernization, before fossil fuels were exhausted.

The dependence of industrialization on energy and the uneven distribution of fossil energy thoroughly changed global geopolitics and even triggered two world wars. The impact on China—a country with a deep-rooted tradition in agriculture and the handicraft industry—was profound. Not only was the land-oriented nature of Chinese local society subverted, but also the vertical relationship of families was transformed into a horizontal relationship of classes, resulting in increasing disparity between urban and rural areas as well as massive numbers of people migrating from the impoverished countryside to the city. These fundamental changes motivated potential revolutions that attempted to establish new regimes for the new social economic relationships. Modernization in China was supposed to carry out two revolutions parallel to its western paradigms: the industrial revolution and a democratic revolution. The former takes mobility as the main form of modernization, while the latter emphasizes the equal distribution of mobility as part of human rights. However, the two revolutions were not synchronous in China: the industrial revolution was nearly completed through the Westernization Movement in the 1870s, the national industry development in the 1920s, and the Great Leap Forward in the 1950s; while the democratic revolution, successively led by the

bourgeoisie and the proletariat, was finally consolidated through Communism in the 1950s—an alternate model of national collectivism and a denial of the Western notion of democracy.

The non-synchronicity of the two revolutions has resulted in a paradoxical situation of urbanization. The People's Republic of China is a country where public spaces are supposed to be of, and for, the people. Given the fact that the distribution of mobility is directly linked to the possession of resources in a modern city and the decisions of this distribution are always made in a top-down system of government acting as land owners, urban planning commissioners and infrastructural developers, it is no surprise that "people's space" becomes "rich and powerful people's space." Urbanization is materialized on the basis of the industrial revolution, however, the insufficiency of the democratic revolution leads to the prioritization of the rich and powerful and thus causes an unequal share of the revolutionary achievements. This polarized urbanism risks the sustainability of both the environment and society, and finally to mobility per se.

The global polarization in manufacturing and consumption has shifted China's sustainability issue to a global level since the 1980s. It's dramatic to see billions of peasants migrating seasonally from their land of origin to the world's factories. It's no less ironic to see how the Chinese land-oriented family model also contributes to industrialization and globalization. Agriculture is no longer sustainable when social programs such as education and medical care are prioritized in cities and public resources are exhausted from the countryside. The low-tech, low-cost and slow way of life has been substituted by a see-saw battle between the industrialized coastline and the agriculture hinterland. The rural is the source of labor for low-skilled, low-paid jobs in sweatshops manufacturing global products to satisfy the demands of Western consumers. The model of supply and demand as produced by *Made-in-China* and *Consumed-in-the-West* also produces *Polluted-in-China*. This has proven to be highly unsustainable both in terms of economy and

(lack of farming subsidies effect on job prospects

A Village recycling electronic rubbish dumped from the United States. Image courtesy Underline Office

ecology as demonstrated by the recent effects of the global crises of climate, energy and economy. China's reliance on *Consumed-in-the-West* has meant it has turned its back on its hinterland at a point when the export-oriented economy is crashing, and the global reliance on *Made-in-China* and *Polluted-in-China* has to figure out a more sustainable model of globalization before further disasters occur.

China used to be one of the revolutionary powers against capitalism, whose evil side described by Karl Marx has ultimately resulted in a general crisis after several golden decades. What had been unlocked by gunpowder and compass in Pandora's Box of capitalism, was the desire for consumption and expansion, or the expansion of consumption. As global capitalism proliferates consumerism throughout the world, the world is further beset with inevitable crises: if the consumption of things ends up in climate and energy crises, the consumption of the future ends up in financial and economic crises. As the global consumption of things is cooling down because of our over-consumption of the future, the voluntarily hijacked Chinese economy is compelled to relieve its over-capacity of production into

the hinterland. However, more climate and energy issues can be expected in promoting consumption within such a huge domestic market. To keep sustainable a way of consumption with no return will be a risky adventure in the non-linear labyrinth of interacted crises.

Given the unique historical sustainability of the Chinese civilization, perhaps more elements could be extracted from the antiquity of pre-modern China to reshape our contemporary condition. The farming civilization takes a recyclable form of productivity as its leading industry, while the industrial civilization is going to launch a "green industrial revolution" and "green energy revolution" to match the recyclability and sustainability of agriculture. As pre-modern China took paper and printing to enact its orientation to culture instead of gunpowder and compass, the culture industry might be the last sustainable way for the continued expansion of consumption into the interior of humanity instead of the exterior of space and time, as well as culture's ability to slow the stalling vehicle of modernization.

"Harmonious Society" is also officially quoted from the *Book of Rites*—an ancient book on the diversity-orderly structure of an ideal society—as a delayed make

A Village recycling electronic rubbish dumped from the United States. Image courtesy Underline Office

up for the unaccomplished democratic revolution half a
century ago. An equilibrium of diversities is where vitality
is reserved, and also where all efforts for sustainability
could be started.

Jiang Jun *is a designer, editor and critic. He has been working on
urban research and experimental study, exploring the interrelation-
ship between design phenomenon and urban dynamics. He founded
Underline Office in late 2003 and has been the editor-in-chief of* Urban
China Magazine *since the end of 2004. He is currently working on the
book* Hi-China. *His works have been presented in exhibitions such as*
Get It Louder *(2005/2007),* Guangdong Triennale *(2005),* Shenzhen
Biennale *(2005/2007),* China Contemporary in Rotterdam *(2006),*
Kassel Documenta *(2007). He was the curator of the international
exhibition* Street Belongs to... All of Us! *in China in 2008. He has
been invited to lecture in universities such as Sun Yat-Sen University,
Beijing University, CUHK, Harvard University, UCL, Tokyo University,
Seoul University, Princeton University, Columbia University. Born in
Hubei in 1974, he received a bachelor's degree from Tongji University
in Shanghai and a master's degree from Tsinghua University in Beijing,
and now teaches at the Guangzhou Academy of Fine Arts.*

A Village recycling electronic rubbish dumped from the United States. Image courtesy Underline Office

BUNSCHOTEN, Raoul

Taiwan Strait Atlas, Xiamen Incubator and Beckton Loop Project

The Taiwan Strait Climate Change Incubator started with a workshop in TungHai University in Taichung (Taiwan) in 1996, and a visit with students to Xiamen (in Fujian Province, China) in 2006. Since then the two cities have commissioned masterplans for the management of energy efficiency and CO_2 emissions reductions, in the case of Xiamen through an initial exhibition of the concept for a plan. We are working on both masterplans and increasingly choreograph the dynamics of both plans in such a way that they join up by sharing the same catalogue of policies and applied technologies where possible and even bring in the same investors for similar projects. Xiamen University and TungHai University both have expressed a firm desire to initiate institutes that will address the issues of energy and urban development and bring together the different disciplines necessary to start serious research. This was initiated originally through the work on the *Taiwan Strait Atlas*, initiated by Joost Grootens and myself, and has been pushed into direct action by Chris Huang, my new partner and co-founder of *Green Action*, a new company based in Shanghai and Xiamen with a better Chinese name than the English version suggests. The Taiwan Strait is a Liminal Body, and at the moment one of the most powerful symbolic territories in China. Its physical nature, boundary and connective sea body, forms the context for the first urban Incubator we have been able to instigate and direct. It is work in progress but has found a window of opportunity that is little short of miraculous. The opportunity was the gradual onset of Climate Change as a recognized crisis and the sudden emergence of the financial crisis, pushing the Central Chinese Government, as many others, into vigorous action to direct emergency funds towards green technology and its development.

Taiwan Strait Atlas

The *Taiwan Strait Atlas* is a unique cross-strait collaboration produced by CHORA Research, the sister organization to CHORA Architecture and Urbanism lead by Prof. Raoul Bunschoten, together with award-winning Dutch graphic designer Joost Grootens and teams at Xiamen University in Fujian province, and TungHai University in Taichung.

The Atlas maps the complex web of economic, cultural and ecological connections across the politically sensitive Taiwan Strait: from mapping cross-strait investment flows and environmental conditions to the spread of different varieties of traditional tea. Focusing on Xiamen and Taichung, two cities facing each other across the Taiwan Strait, the book then outlines an operational plan for how the two cities can become incubators of prototypical climate change projects.

The *Taiwan Straits Atlas* forms the basis for CHORA's Taiwan Strait Incubator, a cross-strait urban renewable energy initiative of climate-change projects in two major cities, Xiamen and Taichung. CHORA has already set up a network of collaborators and stakeholders in the region, and in May 2008 held a symposium attended by top local officials, developers and the press, on the instigation of the Taiwan Strait Climate Change Incubator, which would harness direct investment and Kyoto Protocol "Programmatic CDM" funding to bring about a range of energy efficiency and renewable energy projects in both cities.

There is already a great deal of interest in the Atlas, from government officials from both sides of the Taiwan Strait to property developers, the business sector and carbon brokers: people with the capacity to instigate new CDM projects.

Articles about the *Taiwan Strait Atlas* have been published in both Taiwan and mainland China, in the architectural and general press. The Taiwan Strait Atlas will be published in English by 2010 in Rotterdam, and in both simplified Chinese text in mainland China and traditional Chinese in Taipei.

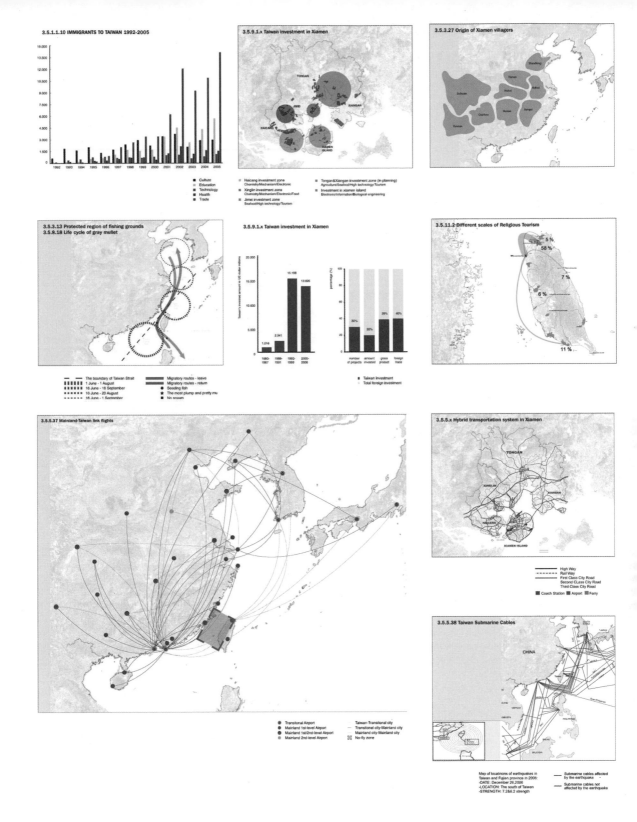

Samples of the Atlas Database, which touches on various cross-strait connections from art to pop culture, transport to ecology, religion to heritage

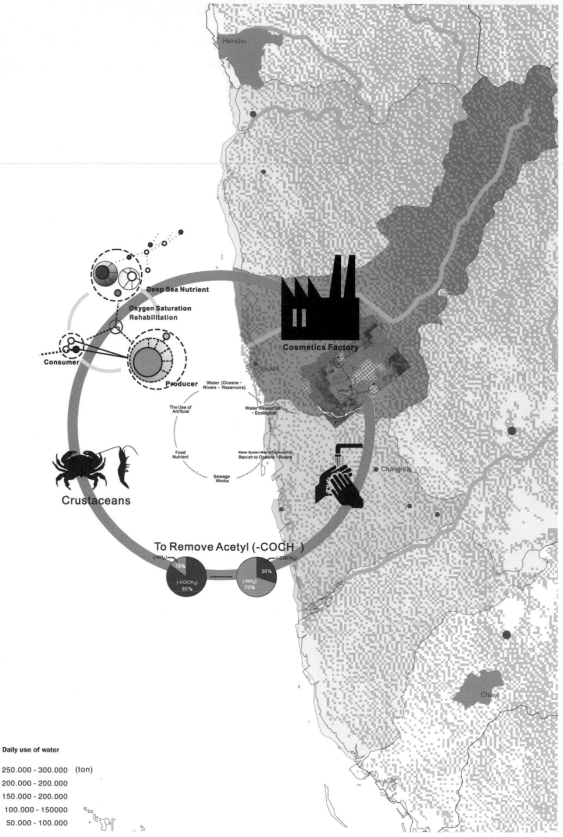

Deep Sea Nutrient

Oxygen Saturation
Rehabilitation

Consumer

Producer

Cosmetics Factory

Water (Oceans ›
Rivers › Reservoirs)

The Use of
Artificial

Water Resources
› Ecological

Food
Nutrient

Water System Map of Taichung City
Banish to Oceans › Rivers

Sewage
Works

Wuchi

Changhua

Crustaceans

To Remove Acetyl (-COCH)

(-NH₂)
15%

(-COCH₃)
85%

(-COCH₃)

(-NH₂)
70%

30%

Hsinchu

Chiayi

Daily use of water

250.000 - 300.000 (ton)
200.000 - 200.000
150.000 - 200.000
100.000 - 150000
50.000 - 100.000

Prototype projects are systems that relates industrial and city development with other dynamics and cycles

BUNSCHOTEN, Raoul

▬▬▬	E (erasure)	activity and services disappear after a certain time of the day
	消失	行为和服务将会消失在一天中某特定时间之后
▬▬▬	O (origination)	pedestrian activity, services used and products purchased feed the economy of this district
	产生	服务被使用和产品被购买哺育了这个区域的经济
▬▬▬	T (transformation)	billboards and signs changes rapidly
	转换	广告牌和标志会迅速的改变
▬▬▬	M (migration)	public transportation enables travel and movement
	位移	公共交通使旅行和行动成为可能

Mini scenarios: closer look at the local dynamics of the area provokes insights into new forms of pilot projects

An indispensable part of the Atlas involvement, Scenario Games sessions map out the effects and proliferation of pilot projects at a regional, national and global scale. Scenario Games at the HK/SZ Biennale 2008

Scenario Games at the HK/SZ Biennale 2008

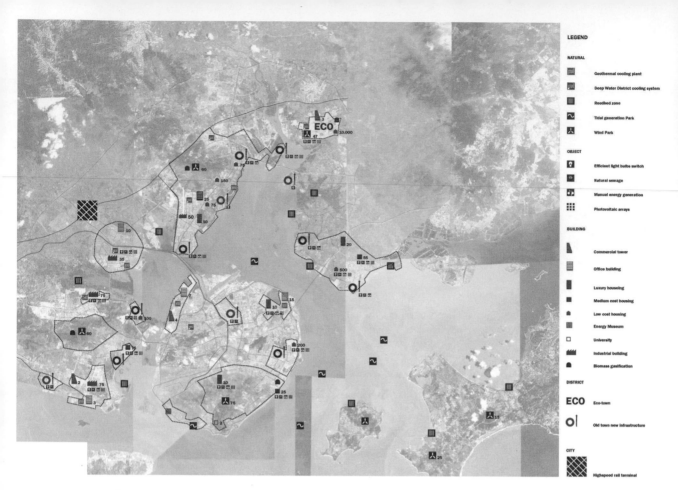

LEGEND

NATURAL

⊞ Geothermal cooling plant

⊞ Deep Water District cooling system

⊞ Reedbed zone

∼ Tidal generation Park

⅄ Wind Park

OBJECT

▢ Efficient light bulbs switch

▣ Natural sewage

▦ Manual energy generation

⦂⦂⦂ Photovoltaic arrays

BUILDING

◣ Commercial tower

▤ Office building

▮ Luxury houseing

▪ Medium cost housing

◉ Low cost housing

▦ Energy Museum

▢ University

⌇⌇ Industrial building

◆ Biomass gasification

DISTRICT

ECO Eco-town

O| Old town new infrastructure

CITY

▨ Highspeed rail terminal

Taiwan Strait Climate Change Incubator

While the majority of the earth's population now lives in cities, it is through cities and their urban culture that the main issues of climate change and energy use have to be tackled. It is both a global issue within a complex cultural and political context, as well as a global economic issue linking local dynamics to global forces. While much depends on global treaties and national laws, much can be done through urban planning and management. Urban projects can be simple, and can be closely linked to the consumer, both economically as well as emotionally. The dynamics of urban environments link these relatively simple projects to the complexity of urban ecologies. This complexity can link the user to global processes and give form to the emotional tension between local problems such as employment, financial security, health and safety issues etc, and the large issues of climate change and energy dependency.

The Taiwan Strait Climate Change Incubator is a masterplan that generates in its entirety a certain number of carbon credits, as well as benefiting the city as a whole, individual developers, owners and users. Investors can finance a single project through the plan or get involved in several projects simultaneously. The plan creates the opportunity for diversification of investment by using carbon credits as the currency. Through pre-financing and investment-in-kind, the partners become shareholders of the potential income in terms of carbon credits generated by the plan.

The proposal creates an operational platform to manage a range of energy efficient and renewable energy projects within the context of an urban masterplan. The masterplan co-ordinates and interconnects the range of projects where possible. Projects range from large-scale, such as wind farms and district cooling distribution grids, to waste treatment plants and systems, individual buildings and biomass plants; to small scale projects that have a socio-economic significance. All projects perform individually but also function as prototypes. CO_2 emission reduction calculations range from immediate gains to gains generated through projected proliferations of prototypes.

BUNSCHOTEN, Raoul

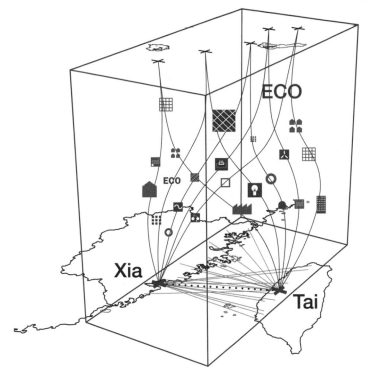

Metaspace for the Taiwan Strait Climate Change Incubator

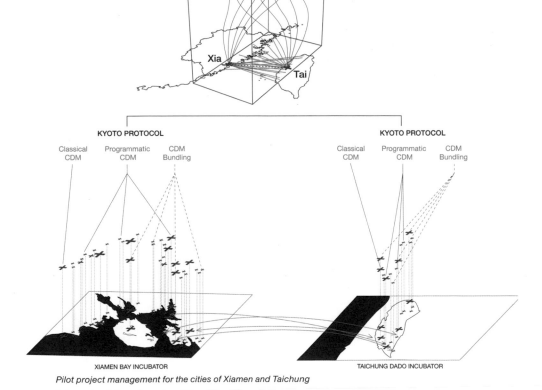

KYOTO PROTOCOL

Classical CDM
Programmatic CDM
CDM Bundling

KYOTO PROTOCOL

Classical CDM
Programmatic CDM
CDM Bundling

XIAMEN BAY INCUBATOR

TAICHUNG DADO INCUBATOR

Pilot project management for the cities of Xiamen and Taichung

COMBINED ENERGY TOWER [12*]

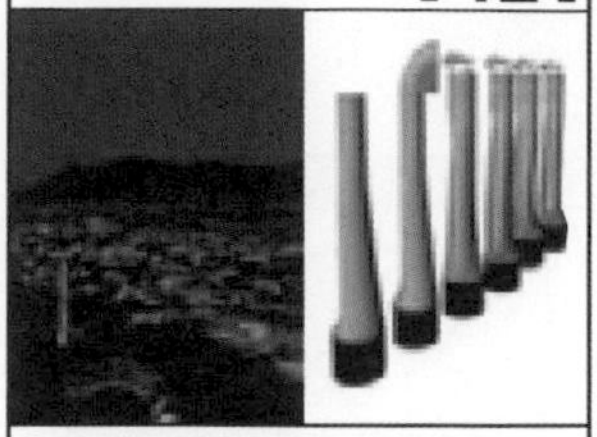

The tower departs from conventional wind towers with its consistency in supply and adaptability within the urban context. Utilising chimney effect to draw in wind energy, as well as solar enery collection, the electricity gemerated is consistent and stable to be consumed through immediate means, instead of feeding back into electricity grid. The tower generates different levels of electricity, depending on the parameters which it is built.

BRANDING DEVICE

The tower produces consistent energy supply through its combined use of different renewable sources. This allow immediate use of electricity. The tower would also become a physical landmark with its aerodynamic form.

INITIAL CONSTRUCTION ALTERNATION COSTS (£)

The tower would be located on open ground, locations where solar and wind energy are available.

PRODUCT INITIAL COST (£)

the estimate cost would include the prototyping and testing of the wind tower, as well as it's production and implementation on site. Wiring for new electricity supply is also necessary as it is separated from the grid.

CARBON REDUCTION EFFICIENCY

If successful, one 40m energy tower would be able to serve 700 households continually, and this wouold in urn reduce carbon emission through electricity production.

GEOTHERMAL HEATING [01]

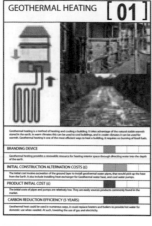

Geothermal heating is a method of heating and cooling a building. It takes advantage of the natural stable warmth stored in the earth. In warm climates this can be used to cool buildings, and in cooler climates it can be used for warmth. Geothermal heating is one of the most efficient ways to heat a building. It requires no burning of fossil fuels.

BRANDING DEVICE

Geothermal heating provides a renewable resource for heating interior space through directing water into the depth of the earth.

INITIAL CONSTRUCTION ALTERNATION COSTS (£)

The initial cost involve excavation of the ground layer to install geothermal water pipes, that would pick up the heat from the Earth. It also include installing heat exchanger for Geothermal water heat, and cool water pumps.

PRODUCT INITIAL COST (£)

The initial costs of pipes and pumps are relatively low. They are easily sources products commonly found in the market.

CARBON REDUCTION EFFICIENCY (5 YEARS)

Geothermal heat could be used in numerous ways, it could replace heaters and boilers to provide hot water for domestic use when needed. At such, lowering the use of gas and electricity.

VERTICAL AXIS WIND TURBINE [11*]

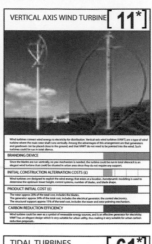

Wind turbines convert wind energy to electricity for distribution. Vertical-axis wind turbines (VAWT) are a type of wind turbine where the main rotor shaft runs vertically. Among the advantages of this arrangement are that generators and gearboxes can be placed close to the ground, and that VAWT do not need to be pointed into the wind. Such turbines could be run in total silence.

BRANDING DEVICE

Since the blades are run vertically, no yaw mechanism is needed, the turbine could be run in total silence.It is an elegant wind turbine that could be situated in urban area since they do not require any support.

INITIAL CONSTRUCTION ALTERNATION COSTS (£)

Wind turbines are designed to exploit the wind energy that exists at a location. Aerodynamic modeling is used to determine the optimum tower height, control systems, number of blades, and blade shape.

PRODUCT INITIAL COST (£)

The rotor: approx 20% of the total cost, includes the blades.
The generator: approx 34% of the total cost, includes the electrical generator, the control electronics.
The structural support: approx 15% of the total cost, includes the tower and rotor pointing mechanism.

CARBON REDUCTION EFFICIENCY

Wind turbine could be seen as a symbol of renewable energy sources, and is an effective generator for electricity. VAWT has an elegant design which is very suitable for urban utility, thus making it very suitable for urban carbon reduction proposals..

SOLAR PANELS [21]

Photovoltaics are is the field of technology and research related to the application of solar cells for energy by converting sunlight directly into electricity. Solar cells produce direct current electricity from light, which can be used to power equipment or to recharge a battery. Building-integrated photovoltaics (BIPV) are increasingly incorporated into new domestic and industrial buildings as a principal or ancillary source of electrical power, and are one of the fastest growing segments of the photovoltaic industry.

BRANDING

Our to its high level of use throughout the world, Photovoltaics are now seen as a branding symbol for renewable energy production.

EXISTING CONSTRUCTION ALTERNATION COSTS

Solar panels are designed with high level of flexibility, which could be located anywhere efficiency reach sunlight. It requires very little building alternation.

PRODUCT INITIAL COST

Initial costs include acquiring solar panels, as well as rechargable cells and necessary structure for holding up the panels. If they are building integrated, roof re-design and construction may have to be taken into account.

CARBON REDUCTION EFFICIENCY

Photovoltaics has evolved into one of the most widely used renewable energy source. The effective use of solar panels to capture sun could produce electricity that charges cell battery for immediate demands.

BIOTOPES [51]

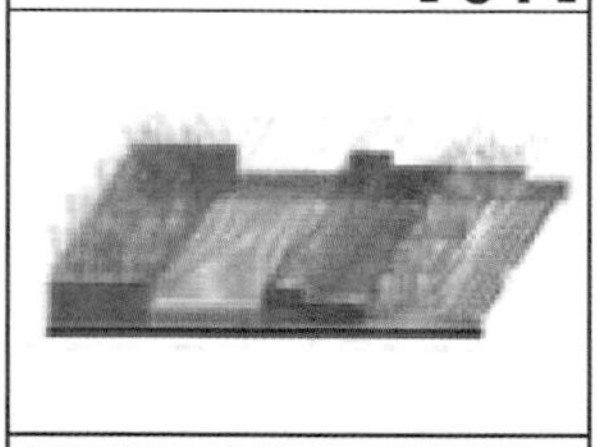

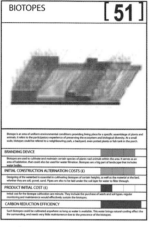

Biotope is an area of uniform environmental conditions providing living place for a specific assemblage of plants and animals. It refers to the participatory experience of preserving the ecosystem and biological diversity. At a small scale, biotopes could be refered to a neighbouring park, a backyard, even potted plants or fish tank in the porch.

BRANDING DEVICE

Biotopes are used to cultivate and maintain certain species of plants nad animals within the area. It serves as an area of habitation, that could also be used for water filtration. Biotopes are a big part of landscape that includes water bodies.

INITIAL CONSTRUCTION ALTERNATION COSTS (£)

Designing of the waterbed is essential in cultivating biotopes of certain heights, as well as the material at the bed, whether they are soil, gravel, sand. Pipes are also to be laid under the soil layer for water to filter through.

PRODUCT INITIAL COST (£)

Initial cost for the biotope cultivation are minute. They include the purchase of seeds and soil types, regular monitoring and maintanence would effectively sustain the biotopes.

CARBON REDUCTION EFFICIENCY

Such biotopes could be cultivated anywhere as long as water is available. This water brings natural cooling effect the the surrounding, and needs very little maintanence due to the prescence of the biotopes.

REED BEDS [52]

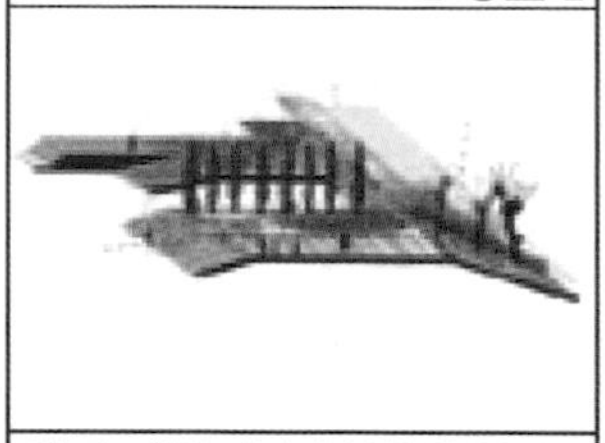

Reed beds are 'temporary' habitats. They are designed to optimise the microbiological, chemical and natural processes that take place in wetlands. Reed bed technology is based upon the cleansing power of the soil dwelling microbes, the physical and chemical properties of the soil, sand or gravel, and finally the plants themselves.

BRANDING DEVICE

Reed beds are effective 'stepping stone' ecologies that involve water filtration, biomass production, and as natural habitats for numerous species living near water, birds and microbes.

EXISTING CONSTRUCTION ALTERNATION COSTS (£)

Existing waterfronts and reedbed areas would have to be redesigned, allowing specific plants to grow, as well as allowing effluent to flow through specific area for cleansing.

PRODUCT INITIAL COST (£)

The initial costs include excavating top soil layer of the reed bed, replanting suitable crops for water filtration.

CARBON REDUCTION EFFICIENCY

Through time, reed beds could serve as an integral part of numerous dynamic cycles, including for secondary water treatment, resting grounds for seasonal birds, as well as producing biomass for energy production.

TIDAL TURBINES [61*]

Tidal turbines are turbines that operates under water of tidal sea, river current area. Each turbine is 30 meters (100 feet) tall, with blades of 20 meters. They can operate in depths up to 100 meters. It generates electricity through the turning of the motor by tidal forces, which provide constant and predictable flows and result in efficient energy resources.

BRANDING

One the greatest untapped energy resources in the world is the motion of the ocean. Tidal power provides a predictable and constant energy source, unlike solar or wind power.

INITIAL CONSTRUCTION ALTERNATION COSTS

Initial construction include deep water excavations that would provide necssary anchorage for tidal turbines.

PRODUCT INITIAL COST

ScottishPower Renewables has announced the largest tidal turbines in Scotland and Ireland water, combining 60MW plant underwater, and the initial cost has come up to about £1 billion.

ENERGY PRODUCTION

The tidal power resource is estimated at some 150 billion kilowatt-hours per annum globally. The Chinese share has been estimated at 19 billion kilowatt-hours, over 80% of this is located in Scottish waters.

WAVE FARM [62*]

Wave power refers to the energy of ocean surface waves and the capture of that energy to do useful work — including electricity generation, desalination, and the pumping of water (into reservoirs). The north and south temperate zones have the best sites for capturing wave power.

BRANDING DEVICE

Wave farm has very low environmental impacts, and takes up minute urban space, as they are situated offshore and under water. They are also provided consitent electricity supply as deep water wave is predictable and consistent.

INITIAL CONSTRUCTION ALTERNATION COSTS (£)

Initial construction include deep water excavation that provide the necessary anchors for wave farm Pelamis machines.

PRODUCT INITIAL COST (£)

Funding for a wave farm in Scotland was announced on February 20, 2007 by the Scottish Executive, at a cost of over £4 million, producing an estimate of 20MW generated by four Pelamis machines (22,000 chinese homes).

ENERGY PRODUCTION

Suitable plants, after several generations, could be used as biomass for energy production and recycling. Well designed green roofs could also be used for phytoremediation of rain water and grey water of the building.

TROMBE WALL [11]

Trombe wall is a sun-facing wall built from material that can act as thermal mass, combined with an air space. Insulated glazing and vents to form a large solar thermal collector. During the day, sunlight would shine through the insulated glazing and warm the surface of the thermal mass. At night heat would escape from the thermal mass.

BRANDING DEVICE

Properly designed Trombe Wall provide passive heating to the building, providing thermal comfort to the users of the building during night time without any extra use of electricity. This could significantly reduce electrical output.

EXISTING CONSTRUCTION ALTERNATION COSTS (£)

Trombe Wall has to be designed and built, according to the dimensions and orientation of the facade. The interior has to also be equipped with necessary ventilation (window or skylights) to create draft for effective heat convection.

PRODUCT INITIAL COST (£)

The initial cost would include acquiring Trombe wall construction material. Thermal mass could range from stone, concrete, water and aerogel, with varying costs according to needs.

CARBON REDUCTION EFFICIENCY

During cold nights, tromble wall could effectively transfer heat to the interior through convection. This could reduce the use of fireplaces and radiatior, thus reducing carbon dioxide production through use of biomass and electricity.

ADJUSTABLE SUN SHADING DEVICE [21*]

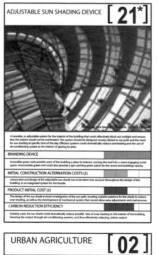

A movable, or adjustable system for the interior of the building that could effectively block out sunlight and ensure that the interior would not be overheated. The system should be designed closely related to sun path and the need for sun shading at specific time of the day. Efficient systems could dramatically reduce overheating and the use of air-conditioning system to the interior of glazing facades.

BRANDING DEVICE

Accessible green roofs provide users of the building a place to interact, turning the roof into a more engaging social space. Unaccessible green roof could also provide a eye-catching green patch for the street and buildings nearby.

INITIAL CONSTRUCTION ALTERNATION COSTS (£)

constuction and design of the adjustable sun shade has to be taken into account throughout the design of the building, as an integrated system for the facade.

PRODUCT INITIAL COST (£)

The design of the sun shade include investigation of the sun path, locating suitable patterns for the shade to reduce over-shading, as well as the development of mechanical system that would allow easy adjustments and mainanence.

CARBON REDUCTION EFFICIENCY

Suitably used, the sun shade could dramatically reduce possibil ities of over-heating to the interior of the building, lowering the output through air-conditioning systems, and thus effectively reducing carbon output.

name

EDUCATIONAL PLANTER

index [EP 1]

scale
- ● local
- ○ national
- ○ regional
- ○ global

actors/ agents
1. school groups
2. adult learners
3. apprenticeships
4. green tourists
5. local residents
6. community groups
7. assembly line workers
8. engineers
9. academic researchers
10. teachers

BRANDING

How does it change the identity of the area?
The prototype provides a new dynamic educational system for the expanding Cross River Park population. It creates a centre for excellence in emerging technologies contributing to reducing global carbon dioxide emissions

EARTH

What is the program?

LEARNING NETWORK: The system is made up of existing educational facilities [schools, adult learning centres, institutes of higher education], Green Industries and designated infrastructural links. The learners can utilize the Industries within the system, going to a different component for specialist education.

HYDROGEN ENGINE FACTORY: This is one component within the Learning Network. Practical learning takes place in the teaching workshops [basic metal work, engine maintenance, advance metal design, creative metalwork], which share the factory floor with the hydrogen engine assembly line. Theory and academic learning happens in the roof space above. Emerging technology research and development also occupies this roof level with teaching and demonstration laboratories. Appropriate spaces within the building are open to local community groups and the wider public [auditorium, bookshop, library, cafes, seminar and meeting rooms].

FLOW

What is the infrastructure?
Pedestrian access to the scheme is through designated fast track infrastructural links; Hydrogen bus routes, water trams, the proposed DLR extension, cycle paths and footpaths. Servicing for the factory is via waterways.

INCORPORATION

Who are the stakeholders?
Ford Motor Company, Hydrogen Energy Centre, Barking & Dagenham Local Education Authority, Learning and Skills Council, University of East London, Barking Community Forum, London Port Authority. Secondary schools within a 2km range [e.g. Langdon School, Abbey Wood School, Woolwich Polytechnic School]. Primary schools within a 2km range [e.g. Gascoigne Primary School, Galleons Primary School, Windsor Primary School]

Anna Holden

HEMP WORKS

index [Hw]

scale
- ● local
- ● national
- ● regional
- ○ global

actors/ agents
1. DEFRA
2. Home Office
3. Hemcore
4. Farmers/ factory workers

BRANDING

The prototype has its own unique visual identity, derived directly as a result of a new type of construction system which address climate change through woodless construction and the use of hemp.

EARTH

Crops are grown in a strip organization, brining a set of crops together in visual proximity, allowing the viewer to see the entirety of crops forming their consumer goods. For instance, they may see hemp and dye crops growing along side one another and consequently being manufactured and sold on the same grounds.

FLOW

The organisation of the building allows for flow between different industries by means of shared spaces between the hemp, soap and dye industries allowing products to be exchanged and raw materials shared. The building also establishes a variety of routes for shoppers for them to view industrial processes.

INCORPORATION

For the hemp factory to operate, licenses and legal issues need to be addresses though contact with the Home Office, DEFRA and the local police. It would also be of interest to form a collaboration with Hemcore, the only present operating hemp industry in the UK. In addition to this, 'Hemp Work's' provides an opportunity to create a self sustainable industrial community on the Cross River Park site.

GARDEN TOWER [01]

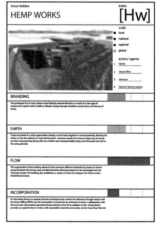

Indoor gardens could be incorperated into existing building fabric, where these gardens could be grown hydroponic, allowing crops that are not allowed to be grown in local soil to be grown. This creates an engaging indoor green space, and if suitably growing crops, could significantly reduce to traveling distance of these crops, reduces carbon emissions through a reduction of imports.

BRANDING DEVICE

The prototype consists of components that can convert an urban area into an garden, or even agricultural landscape. It allows cities to produce food using hydroponics on existing unused land.

EXISTING CONSTRUCTION ALTERNATION COSTS (£)

The indoor gardens could be incorperated into existing residential buildings. Existing construction alternations would include framework constructions for hydroponic gardens and agricultural areas, as well as the necessary watering and maintenance devices.

PRODUCT INITIAL COST (£)

Laying-out of the indoor garden should closely relate to the needs of the garden, whether it is as garden landscape, or urban farming. The initial costs would also include hydroponic preparation, and seeding.

CARBON REDUCTION EFFICIENCY

Through funding and co-operating with local supermarket chains, these indoor gardens could be treated as sources of local produce, thus reducing carbon footprint of the food intake by locals.

URBAN AGRICULTURE [02]

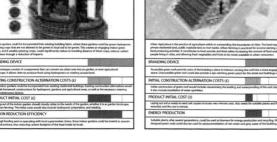

Urban Agriculture is the practice of agriculture within or surrounding the boundaries of cities. The land may be private residential land, public roadside land or river banks. Urban farming is practiced for income-earning or food-producing activities. It contributes to food security and food safety increasing the amount of food available to people living in cities, and allowing fresh vegetables and fruits to be made available to urban consumers.

BRANDING DEVICE

Accessible green roofs provide users of the building a place to interact, turning the roof into a more engaging social space. Unaccessible green roof could also provide a eye-catching green patch for the street and buildings nearby.

INITIAL CONSTRUCTION ALTERNATION COSTS (£)

Initial construction of green roof would include reexamining the loading and waterproofing of the roof cladding layer. It also include installation of water sprinklers.

PRODUCT INITIAL COST (3)

Laying out soil or ready-to-seed soil carpets includes very minute costs. Also seeds for suitable plants and flowers is essential, and the cost is minute.

ENERGY PRODUCTION

Suitable plants, after several generations, could be used as biomass for energy production and recycling. Well designed green roofs could also be used for phytoremediation of rain water and grey water of the building.

PLUG-IN ENERGY FARM [03]

A plug-in energy farm combines conventional renewable energy harnessing techniques, and combining them onto an organised system for combined energy collection. A plug-in system provides the necessary flexibility for the use of different renewable technology, and could be use to accommodate any programme for the field.

BRANDING DEVICE

The plug-in system would become a highly visible grid with combination of different renewable energy sources. They could be used for different demands of the building, as well as accommodate varying use and growth of users.

INITIAL CONSTRUCTION ALTERNATION COSTS (£)

The initial system comprise of the building of a grid system that becomes the 'mother board' for the energy farm plug-in system.

PRODUCT INITIAL COST (£)

The initial costs of the system varies in terms of the size of the complex, combination of renewable energy technology, as well as the combined energy they produced.

ENERGY PRODUCTION

Combining different energy sources could ensure predictable and consistent energy supply, that could provide enough onsite electricity and other energy supply, bringing the complex towards self-sufficiency and zero-carbon.

PASSIVE COOLING [11]

Passive cooling refers to technologies or design features used to cool buildings without power consumption. These techniques include superinsulation, crossed ventilation, airtightness, advanced window design, alternative building facade material.

BRANDING

Passive cooling is an embedded system within building design and construction. Following simple principles for material use and design principles, buildings could achieve a high degree of thermal comfort without the use of extra energy.

INITIAL CONSTRUCTION ALTERNATION COSTS (£)

Initial considerations into design and construction is crucial to ensure building factors provides effective means for passive cooling. These include building orientation, window locations, passive ventilation system, etc.

PRODUCT INITIAL COST (£)

Actual material used for passive cooling could be conventional material, or materials that has low embedded energy and specific thermal mass (which could be cheaper than conventional building material)

ENERGY PRODUCTION

With effective construction techniques, and conscious use of building material designed for specific passive environment, building could achieve a very high degree of thermal comfort with love emergy demand.

SOLAR TROUGH [22]

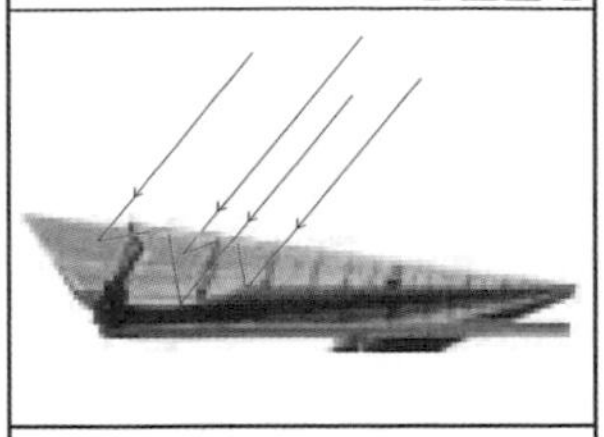

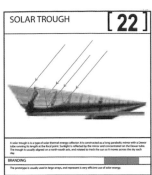

A solar trough is is a type of solar thermal energy collector. It is constructed as a long parabolic mirror with a Dewar tube running its length at the focal point. Sunlight is reflected by the mirror and concentrated on the Dewar tube. The trough is usually aligned on a north-south axis, and rotated to track the sun as it moves across the sky each day.

BRANDING

The prototype is usually used in large arrays, and represent is very efficient use of solar energy.

INITIAL CONSTRUCTION ALTERNATION COSTS (£)

The initial alternation cost is relatively low, since solar troughs could be located in any open ground/ brownfield sites.

ENERGY PRODUCTION COST (£)

A 500 MW plant built in Israel had an extimate buiding cost of $1 billion, with the current cost of electricity from these plants is US$0.10 to US$0.12 per kWh.

ENERGY PRODUCTION

The overall efficiency from collector to grid (Electrical Output Power)is about 15%, similar to Photovoltaic Cells. As this renewable source of energy is inconstant by nature, methods for energy storage have been studied.

HELIOSTATS [23]

Heliostat is a type of solar furnace using a tower to receive the focused sunlight. It uses an array of flat, movable mirrors to focus the sun's rays upon a collector tower (the target). The high energy at this point of concentrated sunlight is transferred to a substance that can store the heat for later use. The most recent heat transfer material that has been successfully demonstrated is liquid sodium.

BRANDING

Undoubtedly an immense structure, combining high level of scientific expertise, high efficiency in renewable energy production, It is a phenomenal system that represents commitement to reacting against climate change.

INITIAL CONSTRUCTION ALTERNATION COSTS

Initial construction alternations are relatively low, since the structure requires a lawrge open area with access to solar radiation, such as sururban outskirts, industrial and brownfield sites.

PRODUCT INITIAL COST

A 200MW Solar Tower recently built in Spain had an estimate cost of US$1 billion. It has gathered 4000 to 5000 heliostat mirrors, each having an area of 140 m².

ENERGY PRODUCTION

In March 2008, Pacific Gas and Electric Company(US) has comitted in building a solar tower with 900MW energy production, revealing the efficiency and potential in the prototype to generate electricity.

PERMEABLE PAVING [31]

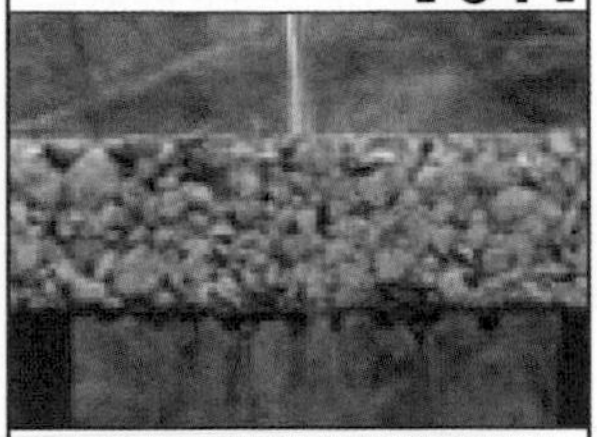

Permeable paving allows the movement of water and air through the paving material in roads, parking lots and walkways. Their effects are important because pavements are two third of the potentially impervious surface cover in urban areas. Porous pavements are potentially the most important development in urban watersheds since the invention of the automobile.

BRANDING

The permeability of the paving allow water to filter from the road immediately, and helping to reduce or eliminate "clogging" found in pervious or porous systems. It is a key component of low impact development, whci hcould help protect pristine watersheds.

INITIAL CONSTRUCTION ALTERNATION COSTS

Initial construction would include the replacement of conventional paving, and the redesign of the storm water BMP network.

PRODUCT INITIAL COST

Some estimates put the cost of permeable paving at two to three times that of conventional asphalt paving. However, it can reduce the cost of providing larger or more storm water BMP's on site and these savings should be factored into any cost analysis.

CARBON REDUCTION EFFICIENCY

Permeable paving surfaces are highly desirable because of the problems associated with water runoff from paved surfaces. As a result, erosion and siltaion in the stream caused by unnatural volume of runoff from precipitation could be reduced and regulated.

James Stopps

BIO-ENERGY NETWORK

index [BeN]

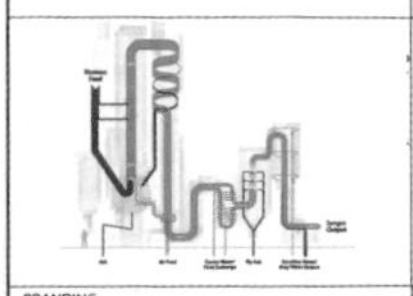

scale
- ● local
- ● national
- ○ regional
- ○ global

actors/ agents
1. Fuel-crop farmers
2. Waste utility companies
3. Energy distributors
4. Dept of Trade and Industry

BRANDING

The prototype seeks to integrate the processes of energy production into everyday society. The industrial components provide a springboard for identity, supplying opportunities for social program and offering a visual key to an area. The anamorphic fins project imagery into the prototypes local context becoming a tool of propaganda or an opportunity for individual expression

EARTH

The network consists of agricultural croplands which are integrated into open parks, gasification plants for the conversion of the collected biomass into a usable fuel, and CHP plants which are fully submerged into local neighbourhoods to supply energy. The gasification plant's integration into the urban context rely on layers of social program and an anamorphic 'clipped-on' identity

FLOW

Central to the prototype's operation is the continuous recycling of carbon, which is absorbed by plant life during photosynthesis and released during combustion. The use of fluidised-bed gasifiers also allows the integration of public waste streams into the process. Waste heat from the gasification plants provide opportunites for social interaction by supplying energy to leisure and educational facilities

INCORPORATION

The utilisation of biomass and gasification will enhance the localised production of energy as the region becomes less dependent on external sources of fuel. This is reliant on the succesful delivery of biomass from farmers in the rural and parkland zones and the cooperation of developers and energy supplies

name

CARBON RESPONSIVE ORGANISM

index [CRO]

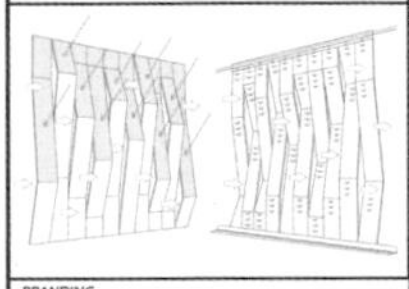

scale
- ● local
- ● national
- ● regional
- ● global

actors/ agents
1. Government
2. Universities
3. Online communities
4. Research bodies

BRANDING

The area becomes a catalyst for the development of advanced digital technologies and climate change awareness.
Direct action against climate change by removing CO2 from air in order to compensate for equally sized emissions elsewhere and at different times.

EARTH

The laboratory develops an infrastructure of high-performance visualization computers and shared file systems that helps scientists and videogame developers explore and share their data through interactive post-processing, analysis, and visualization.

FLOW

The prototype is virtually plugged into a global cyber-infrastructure of scientific data and online gaming networks.
A sodium hydroxide solution is poured through the system and becomes sodium carbonate by capturing carbon dioxide from the air.

INCORPORATION

The system proposes a method of creating tradable carbon credits which comprises extracting carbon dioxide from ambient air at a location remote from where the CO2 was generated, and selling, trading or transferring the resulting carbon credits to a third party.

KINETIC-ELECTRICAL ENERGY CONVERTOR [32]

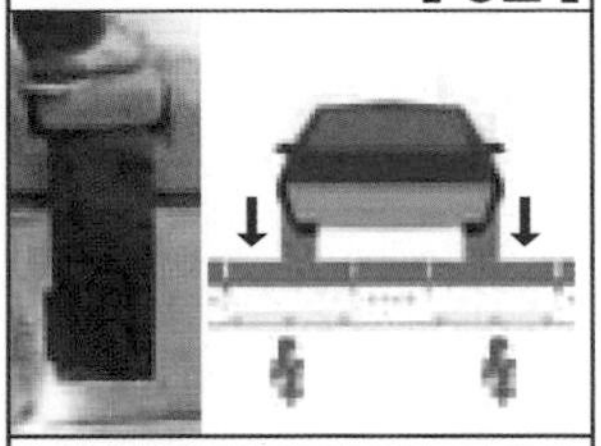

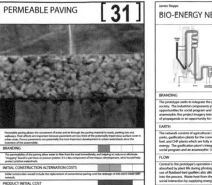

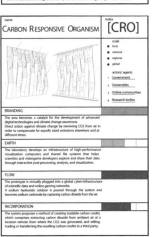

The prototype will reduce the environmental impact of transportation routes through a system of recycling wasted kinetic energy via energy harvesting surfaces. The energy generated along the route is stored at nodal points along the system, that would act as energy transformation points.

BRANDING

It demonstrates a physical commitement to the sustainability of the area, promoting the use of public transport, as well as developing new forms of energy production.

INITIAL CONSTRUCTION ALTERNATION COSTS

Initial construction of green roof would include reexamining the loading and waterproofing of the roof cladding layer. It also include installation of water sprinklers.

PRODUCT INITIAL COST

Laying out soil or ready-to-seed soil carpets includes very minute costs. Also seeds for suitable plants and flowers is essential, and the cost is minute.

CARBON REDUCTION EFFICIENCY

Suitable plants, after several generations, could be used as biomass for energy production and recycling. Well designed green roofs could also be used for phytoremediation of rain water and grey water of the building.

SOLAR WATER HEATER [01]

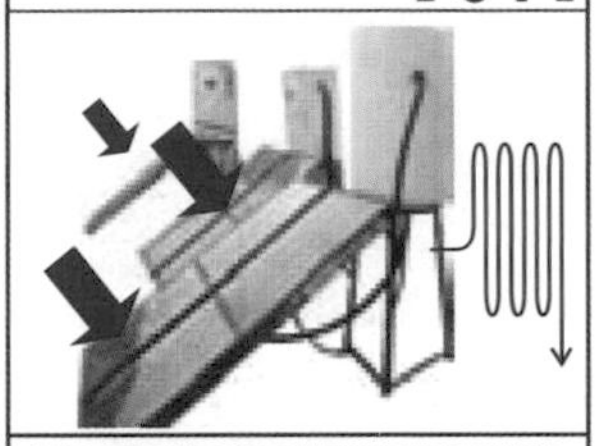

Solar hot water is water heated by the use of solar energy. Solar heating systems are generally composed of solar thermal collectors, a fluid system to move the heat from the collector to its point of usage. The system may use electricity for pumping the fluid, and have a reservoir or tank for heat storage and subsequent use.

BRANDING DEVICE

A solar heating system could provide up to 85% of domestic hot water energy. combined hot water and space heating systems are used to provide 15 to 25% of home heating energy. zero-carbon pumped solar thermal systems use solar electricity which is generated onsite using photovoltaics to pump the fluid and to operate its control electronics.

INITIAL CONSTRUCTION ALTERNATION COSTS (£)

Construction alternation include the installation of the solar water heaters, solar-energy pumps, as well as alternations to the boilers into water collectors.

PRODUCT INITIAL COST (£)

Solar hot water systems have become popular in China, where basic models start at around 1,500 yuan.

CARBON REDUCTION EFFICIENCY

Solar water heaters lower the cost of electric bills. A typical consumer can save about 30%-50% on his or her electric bill, while lessening the use of oil and the impact on the environment.

BIOMASS ENERGY [13]

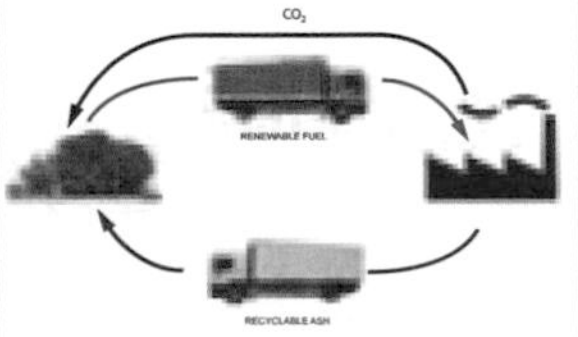

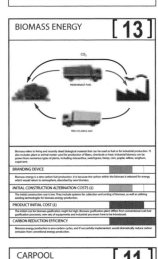

Biomass refers to living and recently dead biological material that can be used as fuel or for industrial production. Tt also includes plant or animal matter used for production of fibers, chemicals or heat. Industrial biomass can be grown from numerous types of plants, including miscanthus, switchgrass, hemp, corn, poplar, willow, sorghum, sugarcane.

BRANDING DEVICE

Biomass energy is a zero-carbon fuel production. It is because the carbon within the biomass is released for energy, which would return to atmosphere, absorbed by new biomass.

INITIAL CONSTRUCTION ALTERNATION COSTS (£)

The initial construction cost is low. They include systems for collection and sorting of biomass, as well as utilising existing technologies for biomass energy production.

PRODUCT INITIAL COST (£)

The initial cost for biomass gasification might be high. Biomass gasification plant differs from conventional coal-fuel gasification processes, new sets of equipments and industrial processes have to be introduced.

CARBON REDUCTION EFFICIENCY

Biomass energy production is zero-carbon cycles, and if succesfully implemented, would dramatically reduce carbon emission from convetional energy production.

INSTANT EVENT SPACES [21]

The prototype proposes a transient and nomadic event space, traveling through different parts of the area bringing with it instant public event experience. This mobility allows public event to be held anywhere, anytime, with infinite variations of scales and composition to suit the local conditions.

BRANDING

It attracts mass movements of population for this momentary, event, centering unique aspects of that community. Large public events with participatory and interactive methods can be stages to generate social climate change awareness through entertainment and education programmes, all without leaving your neighbourhood.

INITIAL CONSTRUCTION ALTERNATION COSTS (£)

The prototypes could be seen as a mobile event that makes use of public spases, closely related to the concepts of expandability and nomad lifestyle of the instant City, developed by Archigram in the 60s.

PRODUCT INITIAL COST (£)

In terms of infrastructure, the Instant Event Spaces descents from the sky, transported by air balloons and so required no ground transport system.

CARBON REDUCTION EFFICIENCY

The prototype provides instant educational, cultural and leisure events for the neighbourhood, without increasing carbon emission through transport. It serves as a prominent tool for raising awareness of climate change.

name

Hydroponic Supermarket

index [HyS]

scale
- ● local
- ● national
- ● regional
- ○ global

actors/ agents
1. ASDA supermarket
2. Defra
3. Mayor of London
4. Local councils

BRANDING

My prototype consists of components that can convert an urban area into an agricultural landscape. It allows cities to produce food using hydroponics and existing unused land.

EARTH

The building consists on a hydroponic tower that will grow a range of tomatoes (plum, beefsteak and cherry), and will meet the yearly demand of 50,000 people. The tower also incorporates residential units and a ground floor supermarket.

FLOW

The prototype relies heavily on existing motorways and roads to link various agricultural components. In the case of the Cross River Park site, the new bridge is integral to providing access from areas North of the river Thames.

INCORPORATION

The operation is funded and developed through a large supermarket chain. The supermarket will sell and distribute the resulting produce, and will also benefit from the publicity such a scheme is likely to create.

URBAN ALGAE FARM [23]

Algae cultuvation, or algae farm for biofuel, has been an emergent technology for future use in vehicles and aircrafts. The urban environment provides the perfect scenarios for cultivation of algae. With a relatively warmer environment, with a relatively higher carbon concentration, as well as large surface area and access the sunlight, urban space could become an energy farm, and the greening of the city would also create a spectacle.

BRANDING DEVICE

vertical algae pools that are attached to the building facade produced greening effect to urban environment. This is a bold statement to the drive against climage change. The algae cultivation could also generate revenue through biofuel technology.

INITIAL CONSTRUCTION ALTERNATION COSTS (£)

Initial constrction alternation could be minute. Algae pools are attached onto the surface of the building, or could be planted on the surface of the ground. Inital excavation and pumping costs should be taking into consideration.

PRODUCT INITIAL COST (£)

The initial cost include structural scaffolding for the buildinf facade, algae pool and pumping devices. It also include biofuel factories that turn algae into useable biofuel.

ENERGY PRODUCTION

Algae biofuel is a highly profitable business for energy production, as the ingredient is extremely cheap, and the biofuel produced could be as efficient as convential fuel, but cleaner.

CARPOOL [11]

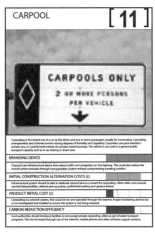

Carpooling is the shared use of a car by the driver and one or more passengers, usually for commuting. Carpooling arrangements and schemes involve varying degrees of formality and regularity. Carpoolers use pool member's private cars, or a jointly hired vehicle, for private shared journeys. The vehicle is not used in a general public transport capacity such as in car sharing or share taxis.

BRANDING DEVICE

Carpool is an infrastructural device that reduce traffic and congestion on the highway. This could also reduce the overall carbon emission through transportation system without compromising traveling comfort.

INITIAL CONSTRUCTION ALTERNATION COSTS (£)

Infrastructural system should be able to dedicate carpool lane as a reward for carpooling. Other initla costs include central listing facilities, defined pick-up points, preferential parking and general advice.

PRODUCT INITIAL COST (£)

Carpooling is a network system, that could be run and operated through the internet. Proper monitoring devices has to be investigated and installed to ensure the system is not being misused.

CARBON REDUCTION EFFICIENCY

local authorities should introduce facilities to encourage private carpooling, often as part of wider transport programs. This has increased through use of the Internet, mobile phones and other software support systems.

BUILDING MATERIAL RECYCLING [12*]

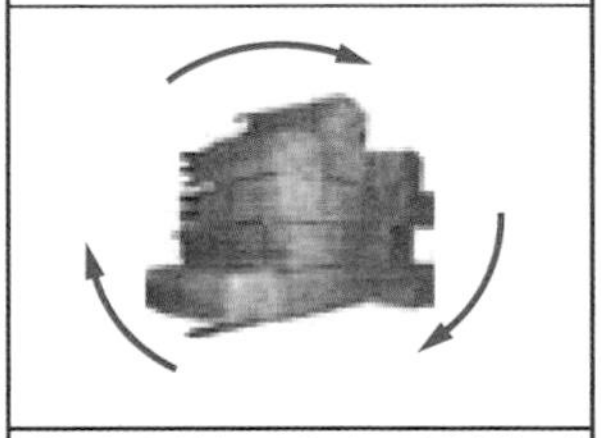

Building materials constitute 45% of total waste produced. They are also waste that has high embedded energy, such as concrete. Most building materials have high recycling values, such as steel, glass, wodden construction materials.

BRANDING

Building material recycling could lower building waste treatment costs, and becomes a significant step towards zero-carbon building construction. It could also lower the cost of building material through recycling.

INITIAL CONSTRUCTION ALTERNATION COSTS

Initial alternations include governmental legislation into the necessary building waste treatment and compulsory building material recycling through construction.

PRODUCT INITIAL COST

Proper collection and sorting procedures should be set up with regard to the mix of building materials to be found. The recycling process should also be closely regulated to ensure high quality of recycled materials for use.

ENERGY PRODUCTION

Recycling do not necessarily produces energy. However, during the time of high oil prices and climate change, alternative ways of waste treatment would be a crucial direction for future production and manufacturing.

PASSIVE RESEARCH CENTRE [13]

Passive energy research centres would make use of Natural ventilation and climate adjustment through indoor gardens. The building should also make use of low impact materials, together with adjustable sun shading devices to provide suitable thermal comfort to the interior.

BRANDING

Research centres as public buildings should take initiatives in terms of using design and construction techniques to achieve passive energy efficiency. It provides suitable and comfortable environments for research and learning.

INITIAL CONSTRUCTION ALTERNATION COSTS

The initial construction should take into account the building design and construction, sourcing appropriate building materials with low embedded energy levels.

PRODUCT INITIAL COST

The research centre design should surrond the basic principles of passive thermal comfort for the interior. By incorperating suitable materials, water bodies and internal garden to regulate humidity, heat flow and ventilation.

ENERGY PRODUCTION

Well-designed passive energy complexes could achieve a high degree of thermal comfort without high energy demand. This would reduce the operational costs of the building.

ZERO-CARBON PUBLIC BUILDING [14]

A Zero Carbon public building makes use of multiple technique to achieve zero net carbon production in terms of building and construction, energy use and demands. It is an up and coming tread throughout the world in deriving new building techniques incorperating renewable energy supply for homes that provide affordable and comfortable habitation.

BRANDING

Current Zero carbon houses may still low peculiar in terms of the building techniques and technologies incorperated. It produce is significant visual difference to the conventional built environment, raising awareness to new building techniques and how construction changes effects of climate change.

INITIAL CONSTRUCTION ALTERNATION COSTS (£)

zero-carbon house could be built on any buildable environment. The building should take into account the sunpath, prevailing wind orientations, as well as the electricity and gas supply through grid.

PRODUCT INITIAL COST (£)

Materials used for building zero- carbon building could be cheaper than conventional buildings. It is due to the carefully chosen material with low embedded energy coefficient, with less construction waste.

ENERGY PRODUCTION

Suitable plants, after several generations, could be used as biomass for energy production and recycling. Well designed green roofs could also be used for phytoremediation of rain water and grey water of the building.

CARBON TRADING [01]

Carbon emissions trading is emissions trading specifically for carbon dioxide (calculated in tonnes of carbon dioxide equivalent or tCO2e) and currently makes up the bulk of emissions trading. It is one of the ways countries can meet their obligations under the Kyoto Protocol to reduce carbon emissions and thereby mitigate global warming.

BRANDING

Carbon emissions trading has been steadily increasing in recent years. According to the World Bank's Carbon Finance Unit, 374 million metric tonnes of carbon dioxide equivalent (tCO2e) were exchanged through projects in 2005

INITIAL CONSTRUCTION ALTERNATION COSTS

Carbon trading is a virtual market system, and does not require any construction alternations. It requires, however, the structural composition of governmental departments in co-operation to the global carbon trading economy.

PRODUCT INITIAL COST

The set up cost include taskforce and think tanks that could develop and sustain regulatory principles for the development of carbon trading projects.

ENERGY PRODUCTION

Carbon trading is sometimes seen as a better approach than a direct carbon tax or direct regulation. It can be cheaper, and politically preferable for existing industries. In addition, more money would be spent on environmental activities through carbon trading.

Panoramic views of the Beckton Loop area

Scenario Game sessions for the Cross River Park and Thames Gateway, with participants from Design for London, Environmental Agency and Thames Water

Algae Industrial Park, proposal, Natalia Andriotis, CHORA-London Metropolitan University studio

Cross River Park (now Beckton Loop Project)

The Thames Gateway has the potential to become a major European incubator, part urban territory, part rural, part mixed industrial and agricultural zone, it is a vast threshold space linking the natural environments of the North Sea and the skies above it, to one of the largest metropolitan areas in Europe. It has a strong emotional aspect: it embodies the fear of flooding as it is a window on the increasing consequences of the changing climate—How can the Thames Gateway become an incubator for climate change related prototypes?

We propose a pilot project to demonstrate how innovative architectural projects can be developed to reduce carbon emissions, increase economy and create benefits to local communities. We will design architectural prototypes that can reduce carbon emissions and create strategies to increase physical activity and healthy lifestyles in a community. Our proposal is to make the Beckton Loop into an attractor of pilot projects related to energy efficiency and the reduction of CO_2 in general. The Beckton Loop can form the center of a test bed for experimental climate change projects. It can become an incubator for future change in the entire Thames Gateway.

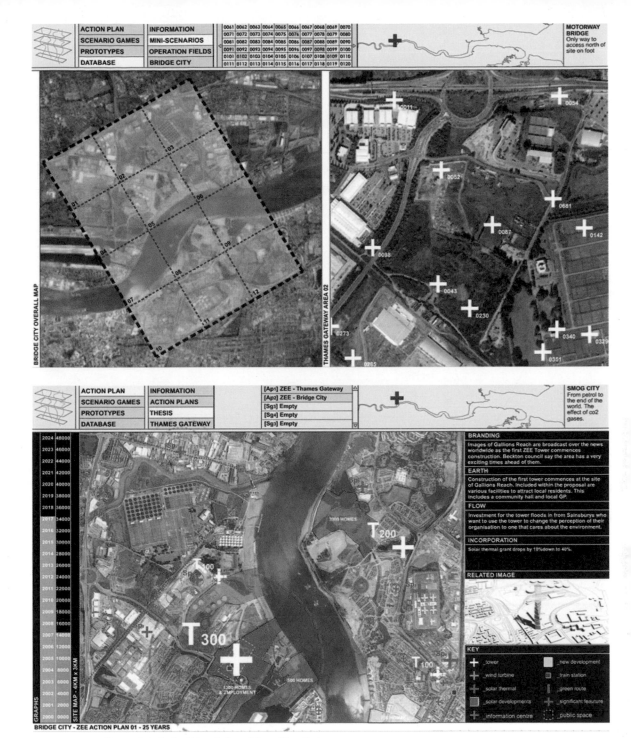

Screenshots for the Urban Gallery at Cross River Park

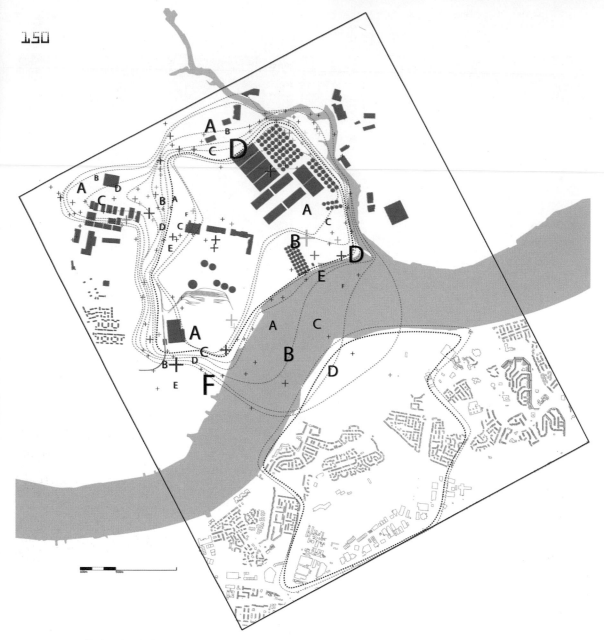

Beckton Loop Lifecycle Park, with a range of climate change prototypes

We have worked together with Design for London and other partners to try to identify the potential of the Beckton Loop as an attractor for prototype projects involving energy efficiency and renewable energy generation, or other climate change related projects, and to select three prototypes that could be realized in the Beckton Loop area as a catalyst for the more ambitious incubator project.

Raoul Bunschoten *is Professor of the Systematics of Urban Planning, landscape and design at the University of Applied Science in Duesseldorf, Germany, and is founder of both CHORA architecture and urbanism and CHORA research. He has been involved in teaching at the London Metropolitan University, the Architectural Association and has lectured or conducted workshops at many other universities. CHORA architecture and urbanism has just won the shared first prize for the ideas competition to redevelop the former Tempelhof Airport in Berlin with a project to create an inner city energy incubator.*

WONG, Julian L.

China's Food-Energy-Water Nexus—A Terrifying Triple Threat

China's Yangtze River is the third longest in the world and stretches over six thousand kilometers from the Qinghai in the west towards the East China Sea at Shanghai. Throughout China's history, it has played a central role culturally, socially and economically. It is the unofficial dividing line between the north and the south, flows through deep gorges in Yunnan province that have been designated as a UNESCO World Heritage Site, and serves as the lifeblood upon which much of China's agricultural and industrial activity has, and continues to depend on. All told, the Yangtze River system produces 40% of the nation's grain, a third of its cotton, 48% of its freshwater fish and 40% of its total industrial output value.

The Yangtze has now become a victim of its own success. With China's rapid economic industrialization over the past two decades, the Yangtze has evolved from a source of life and prosperity to a symptom of the limits of China's unabated economic pursuits. It has become a depository for 60% of the country's pollution, making it the single largest source of pollution in the Pacific Ocean. The Yangtze is also home to two massive and highly controversial hydraulic projects—the Three Gorges Dam, the world's largest hydro-electric power facility, and the South-North Water Diversion (SNWD) project, an unprecedented, multi-decade effort to channel water from the water-rich south to the arid north—each a symptom of a larger ill. The former project points to China's struggles to maintain energy security and desire to use cleaner sources of energy in a carbon-constrained world, while the latter points to its sheer desperation to address a gross imbalance in the distribution and use of water resources across the Chinese sub-continent. Neither project comes cheap; the Three Gorges Dam bore a price tag of US$30 billion and the SNWD project projected to cost twice that. Both projects have, or will continue to cause the dislocation of hundreds of thousands of citizens and the significant alteration of landscapes, including the destruction of arable land. Needless to say, both projects have required, or will require, massive inputs of concrete, steel and energy. Together, Three Gorges and SNWD point to an uncomfortable interrelationship between energy, water and food. Beyond the Yangtze, the "food-water-energy trilemma" represents a looming and complex threat to China's economic stability and national security.

Watergy

Climate change now stands front and center of energy and environmental agendas around the world. In virtually every case, the discussion of tackling climate change is centered on our energy system, specifically the need to replace our reliance on fossil fuels with cleaner sources of energy. A staggering 80% of China's electrical power is derived from highly polluting coal combustion. Meanwhile, the consumption of oil, half the domestic demand of which is met by imports, is rapidly increasing as vehicle ownership continues to make inroads on China's growing middle class. While keenly aware of the need to diversify its energy sources and reduce greenhouse gas emissions, China is starting to realize that proposed energy alternatives are running up against limits in water and food systems as well.

Let's start with water. Just about every traditional energy choice requires significant inputs of water. The reality is that the state of China's water supply is probably even more dire than its lack of energy self-sufficiency. China's per capita water resources is 2,200 cubic litres which is just one third of the world average. Even more startling is the utter imbalance of water resource distribution. Southern China, with 55% of the population and 35% of the cropland, has about 80% of the water resources. The north, by contrast, has to sustain 45% of the population and nearly 65% of all cropland with just 19% of the water.

This is not good news, especially for northern China, considering the various water demands of available energy options. The trade-offs between water and energy use has been dubbed the "water-energy nexus" or "watergy" for short. Any energy source that requires extraction, such as coal, oil, natural gas and uranium often result in significant contamination of water tables and depletion of groundwater. Power generation involving any of these fuel types also rely heavily on water inputs at various steps of the process, such as steam generation and systems cooling. Nuclear plants, in particular, can consume one and a half times more water than other types of plants due to their increased cooling requirements. Nonetheless, nuclear power is being favored as a major alternative energy strategy by the Chinese government.

Hydropower displays the most obvious link between energy and water. Although hydropower dams do not actually consume or alter the physical chemistry of the water, they do temporally disrupt their natural flows. With little by way of effective water rights management along rivers, the underpricing of water is leading to its overuse, especially by agriculture, which accounts for roughly 70% of all water consumption. Such over-exploitation threatens to deplete riparian water levels causing major rivers to run dry. In 1997, the Yellow River ceased to reach the Bo Sea for over 100 days, causing large economic losses in Shandong Province. The SNWD project and the increasing frequency of droughts will create uncertainty in water availability and threatens to undermine the long-term plan to more than double current hydropower capacity to 300 GW by 2020. Climate change, ironically, could have a countervailing effect. As the Himalayan snow frost melts due to climate change induced by the combustion of carbon-rich fossil fuels, water flows in southwestern China may actually get a medium-term boost. This complicated relationship of hydropower to water use and climate change speaks to the complexity of the water cycle which scientists are still trying to better understand.

Alternative transportation fuels such as biofuels and coal liquefaction also face serious limitations—the food versus fuel debate has given grain-based biofuels a black eye in the public imagination, while coal liquefaction emits large volumes of greenhouse gases. Both also require large volumes of water. As a result, China has sensibly halted the production of biofuels derived from grain-based feedstock and most of the proposed coal liquefaction projects.

On the flip side of the coin, the extraction, transportation, purification, distribution of water and treatment of wastewater is energy intensive. For instance, large-scale hydraulic infrastructure projects such as SNWD or any other large canals or dams (Three Gorges and others) for that matter, incorporate significant amounts of energy-intensive concrete and steel. Power plants that provide the electricity to operate water treatment facilities similarly require energy embodied in material inputs, such as concrete to build cooling towers, that are seldom considered when analyzing the water supply sector's consumption of energy.

The End of Food?

Agriculture accounts for 70% of all water use while contributing to just 15% of China's GDP. While the relative profligacy of water resources of the agricultural sector is often attributed to distorted water pricing policies—the agricultural sector benefits from grossly underpriced water (less than US$0.01 per cubic meter) compared to the industrial and residential sectors—some research indicates that a mere raising of agricultural water prices alone may have the unintended consequences of farmers reducing crop output or overexploiting groundwater in response to rising surface water prices. Instead, it is clear that any sort of integrated policy should also involve an upgrade of irrigation technology; current irrigation practices are so inefficient that only 40 to 45% of water applied ever reaches crops. The widespread use of modern drip irrigation technologies in Israel is a model to look at. Water distribution in urban areas register similar efficiencies; public investments in upgrading leaky pipes and taps in cities are sorely needed.

As is the case with water resources, China is also short on arable land. With 20 percent of the world's population, China has to feed itself with just 7% of the world's farmland. At current rates of growth, China will add 125 million to its population by 2025. In this scenario, China will have to expand its agricultural output by 25% to sustain this growth, yet this will have to be realized in the face of the pressures of increased urban and sub-urban development, which is encroaching on arable land. Food security will not only be threatened by increased urbanization and existing water scarcity, but by ongoing climate change induced by the ever growing dependencies on fossil fuels. Climate change will lead to increased temperatures, water scarcity and desertification, with a recent study commissioned by Greenpeace projecting a 23% decrease in food production by 2050. This downward trend is hard to square with the aforementioned needs to increase food output to match population growth.

Another overpowering demographic trend accelerating China's head-on charge towards the limits of its food-water-energy systems is the rapid pace of urbanization. In

1990, 26% of Chinese population lived in cities. This proportion has now risen to 45%. By 2030, it is projected that 350 million people will be added to urban centers. This largest rural-to-urban migration in human history is not simply a spontaneous demographic phenomenon, but a product of purposeful policies based on the premise that urban centers are engines of GDP growth. This trend reflects both the increasing economic outputs of cities—cities produce three quarters of the nation's GDP while housing less than half of its population—and declining economic contributions of agriculture as arable land becomes scarcer due to development or unsustainable farming practices. *also b/c of policy*

Yet as global economic prosperity starts to unravel, we are seeing the assumptions of the limitless growth potential of urban centers called into question, Earlier this year, 20 million migrant workers were repatriated from cities back to their rural hometowns, unable to find work. This occurred at the same time that northern and central China was experiencing one of the worst droughts in recent memory, affecting 10 million hectares of wheat crop and the drinking supply of 2.3 million people. Rural development has increasingly become an economic development priority of the central government; with urban center economic opportunities now hitting a "great wall," rural development policies are taking center stage. It is time to question the wisdom of policies promoting unabated urbanization and to reconsider the role of agriculture in China's economic and environment future. Regenerative agriculture represents a promising platform to rejuvenate the natural, social and economic systems of rural areas, while enhancing national climate, water and food security.

The Way Forward

As China seeks a cleaner, softer path of development, renewable energy sources such as wind, solar and geothermal are attractive not only because of their lower carbon emissions profiles, but because they use far less water than their fossil fuel counterparts. However, while displacing all fossil fuel power plants with solar and wind-farms is necessary in curbing the flow of additional greenhouse gases into our atmosphere, it does nothing to capture the prevailing stock of greenhouse gases that has already accumulated. While the fossil fuel industry tries its hand by spending billions of dollars of research on technically challenging solutions such as geological sequestration of carbon emissions from power plants, a natural solution which has been proven for hundreds of millions of years of evolutionary history lays before us—soils. Soil is a vast carbon sink, containing more carbon than all terrestrial vegetation and the atmosphere combined. Regenerative farming techniques, such as nutrient management, manure and sludge application, no-till agriculture, use of cover crops, and crop rotations, can rehabilitate degraded or desertified soils, which span a massive 3.57 million square kilometers in China, and correspondingly increase soil carbon sequestration. Such regenerative farming methods also address another crucial link between agriculture and energy, by reducing petroleum-based fertilizer and pesticide inputs. Reliance on such fossil-fuel inputs not only sustain oil dependency but also represent a major water pollution problem when they run-off into rivers. *good for health as well ✓*

not only that, but it is not feasible, nor sustainable

A second important way in which proper management of the food and agriculture systems can reduce its impacts on climate change is through a reduction in meat consumption. Livestock activities release significant amounts of methane, carbon dioxide and other greenhouse gases. Cattle manure, flatulence and belching, for instance, contribute a massive 30 to 40% of human-induced methane emissions. Moreover, meat, especially from cattle, represents one of the most inefficient ways to gain calories-it takes as much as twenty kilograms of grain feedstock and 15,000 litres of water to create one kilogram of boneless, edible beef. While pork and chicken fair with better ratios, their reduction in grain and water impact is still significant. To the extent livestock is not grain-fed but instead grazes on pasture, such land use comes at the expense of arable land. Growing meat consumption patterns in China will thus exacerbate grain and water security.

Thirdly, it goes without saying that sweeping reforms in water governance are needed. Institutional capacity must be built to manage water allocations among various regions and various uses, introduce water pricing coupled with a concerted outreach to educate end users, especially farmers, on water conservation technologies and techniques. *education*

The interactions between the energy, water and food systems are complex and, in China, especially urgent given the scarcities involved in all three systems. Integrated policies are essential; it is vital that a policy addressing any one of these systems pay heed to their linkages to the other systems. Thus, for instance, energy infrastructure decisions must be undertaken not only in consideration to carbon and air pollution constraints, but to the water and otherwise arable land resources that may be needed to support such choices. It means that in seeking to rationalize water pricing, considerations must be given to its effect on farmer's choices of crop output. It also means that in seeking to enhance food security, the energy, carbon and water footprint of food supply chains must be simultaneously considered. Holistic approaches that weigh trade-offs among the three resource systems is the future of natural resource management and, indeed, any sustainable economic or national security policy.

Julian L. Wong *is a senior policy analyst at the Center for American Progress in Washington, DC, a founder of the Beijing Energy Network, and author of the blog GreenLeapForward.com.*

SADOWAY, David

Spatial Sustainability in Urban Asia: Conservation, Eco-Modernization and Urban Wilding

The profound ethical lapses associated with the 2008-09 viral market failure appear to stem from poor financial assets management along with outright greed. A failure to manage planet earth's so-called "natural capital and assets" would certainly make the present economic episode appear trivial in comparison.[1] Sustainability is one avoidance strategy against potential earth systems catastrophe since it focuses minds on the long-term management of our common planetary assets: air, water, soil and biodiversity. Sustainability[2] is an ethic acknowledging the socio-ecological limits of human actions out of pragmatic concern for present and future generations. Applied to urban space, sustainability can include: energy management, waste reduction, green design, nature protection or restoration, mobility planning, environmental health and water management.[3] Arguably, spatial sustainability will also spark wild civic imaginations about the nature of a city's lived and virtual spaces.

This essay briefly explores spatial sustainability practices in the Asian Tiger city-regions of Hong Kong, Singapore and Taipei. These three cities arguably represent iconic urban role models, if not global brands shaping and reifying governance, cultural, production and consumption norms in rapidly urbanizing Asia[4] and beyond. This troika appears to comprise cases of advanced post-industrializing urban-regions—illustrating Manuel Castells' "spaces of flows" axiom, in that they act as urban nexus of people, capital, trade, ideas and communications.[5] While Hong Kong, Singapore and Taipei could be dismissed as vortices of high mass consumption—world cities that reached their zenith surfing late 20th-century global growth waves—all three have made impressive strides in allaying material poverty and generating economic wealth.[6] One audible argument is that these three cities' economic development resulted in net urban environmental and quality of life improvements alongside steady growth.[7] This argument, however, masks serious externalities or blind spots in that the urban metabolisms of Hong Kong, Singapore and Taipei cannot perpetually sustain growth premised upon: vast low-priced energy and water throughputs; discounted hinterland food and resource inputs; high growth middle-class consumption volumes; sizeable rural to urban population inflows and young demographics; and ongoing air, soil and aquatic outputs of pollutants and toxins within and beyond their urban bioregions.[8]

Given the extensive sustainability threats, what long-term developmental models remain possible for these now fast-graying Asian role model city regions?

Will green eco-modernization or perhaps slow growth models emerge as possible paths for metropolitan spatial development? These questions, especially in light of the 2008 Triple F crises—Food, Fuel and Financial—are cogent when discussing spatial sustainability in urban Asia.

Shadow Spaces and Sustainability

Oft hidden in the shadows of the fast-changing global city are serious threats to natural and built heritage. Shadow issues and shadow spaces represent urban problems denied, ignored, or forgotten and which may bite back in the future. Six spatial sustainability issues in Hong Kong, Singapore and Taipei are used to further illustrate. The first issue, air quality, is typically caused by an array of regional point and ambient air pollutants, sourced from industrial process and vehicular emissions, or forest burning. Urban heat island and air inversion effects illustrate how city form and location can concentrate air pollutants and their public health impacts upon the city's most vulnerable—youth and elders.[9] In addition to acid rain, CO_2/GHG impacts, and sunlight dimming, such threats have caused air quality and climate activists to identify scalar governance issues in the three city regions. For example, Hong Kong's air quality is impacted by and impacting-upon the massive industrialized Pearl River Delta (PRD) urban mega-region, now amongst the most populated on the planet—with approximately 45-48 million residents.[10] Similarly, urbanizing the Iskandar Economic Zone in Johore, Malaysia and forestry burning practices in nearby Indonesia illustrate adjacent international but regional air quality threats in Singapore's airshed. Likewise, industrial and vehicular emissions in Taipei City and surrounding Taipei County, directly impact the densely populated Taipei basin airshed. Achieving year-round unpolluted airsheds requires not only significant resources but collaborative leadership and coordinated inter-jurisdictional responses at varying spatial scales.

Second, traditional urban growth processes—typically reliant upon the construction of roadways, bridges, ports, channels, and other energy and carbon-intensive infrastructural networks—alters, channels or buries natural watercourses, harbours, wetlands and riparian ecosystems. Public access to water is also often relegated to the shadows in the name of efficiency, safety or hygiene. Calls have been made for ecosystems management and public access to waterfronts in Hong Kong and Singapore due to the cumulative impacts of harbor reclamations, port developments, water pollutants, and marine traffic.[11] Taipei's Danshui River—once a water trade route that shaped the city's post-aboriginal settlement history—continues to serve as a common open sewer for liquid effluent and even solid waste. Despite ongoing water quality problems, an emergent riverside system of parkways, trails, corridor wetlands and guerilla gardens—in Taipei City and County—exemplifies how residents can reclaim these vital public spaces. By reconnecting urban residents to waterfront spaces an intrinsic link to the natural world and watershed consciousness can be restored. With the impacts of climate and environmental change, integrated

Guerilla Gardening Spaces, Taipei County
Wilding the riverside: garden plots alongside the south bank of the Xindian Stream, Yonghe City, Taipei County

watershed and shoreline conservation practices will increasingly support crucial urban buffer spaces where waters lap the land.

Aravena

Third, questions of high ecological, carbon and waste footprints may be partly attributed to the rise of middle-class prosperity in each city. Associated with high material and energy consumption lifestyles—as the energy-intensive urban landscapes in the Americas demonstrate—is an insidious push for private automobility and its supporting infrastructure, often at the expense of urban public spaces.[12] This underlines the need for long-range zero carbon urbanity and mobility-exchange strategies. In all three cities automobility support systems threaten public health neighborhood safety, vitality and livability through air, noise and light pollution.[13] Public expenditures can also unwittingly cater to a roads-first transportation, urban design and engineering paradigm at the expense of public mass transit, pedestrians and cyclists. A key measure to track is the total outlays for capital and roads maintenance, including bridges, tunnels and parking, versus aggregate transit outlays. The

fact that all three high-density cities have invested heavily in mass transit bodes well for developing low energy development paths and may keep the powerful attraction to urban automobility at bay, at least in the short term.

A fourth shadow issue relates to the importance of a vibrant small, locally-owned, independent business sector. Like other cities shaped by modernity, Hong Kong, Singapore and Taipei as a troika of "world cities" feature iconic skyscrapers and denatured landscapes at the very heart of their global place-making endeavor. Whether the Taipei 101 complex, nestled amid the high-end shopping and office towers of Xinyi district; or I.M. Pei's iconic Bank of China Tower set amidst airborne commercialized private walkways in Hong Kong's Central District; or Singapore's vertical fossil-fueled Financial District and its horizontal high-end Orchard Road shopping district—the spatial vocabulary of narcissistic global mass consumption in these cities appears to cater to the efficient administration and rapid delivery/uptake of targeted financial and consumer products. This consumption-led urban development ethic has driven design for

San Francisco vs. Oakland
↓
gentrification along w/ cultural erasone

space that is often in denial of, or at the expense of, clusters of local, independent owner-operated businesses, community street markets and hawkers. Similarly, often ignored or maligned spaces like Hong Kong's Chung King Mansion—which serve as important global social nexus and economic incubators for immigrants, travelers and entrepreneurs—could provide useful clues for spatial and economic regeneration strategies elsewhere in the city.[14] Taipei's lively, enduring and anarchic night market spaces provide an interesting exception to trend towards regulatory containment of small businesses in tandem with increasingly dominant corporate and franchised spaces. The incremental erosion of traditional spaces for independent-owner operated businesses remains a shadow issue in all three cities.

Fifth is the shadowing of historical natural and built spaces. While the hypnotic, homogenized spaces of modernity previously noted, are commonly referenced in campaigns to attract tourist-shoppers, fragments of each of the three cities' historical patina and civility—whether parks, civic and festive spaces, neighborhood street and food markets, temples, waterfront spaces, forested spaces and historical structures—has sometimes been relegated to the shadows. These spaces often have shaky legal protections, poor maintenance and access; or they are ill-equipped to compete on a par with the design-build fetishized spaces favored by public agencies in new urban development projects. Sustainable spaces represent core real assets (as opposed to real estate assets) that reinforce the soul and character of a city and as such they need care—either through restoration, preservation, renewal or smart incentives—by governments, businesses, NGOs and residents alike.

Sixth, also lurking in the shadowlands—as with global cities elsewhere—remains the difficulties and shame associated with social polarization, whether among the poor, homeless, disenabled, un/underemployed or migrant workers.[15] Social sustainability in cities is often forgotten in the rush to urbanize, modernize and globalize. The issues of environmental and social justice, blind consumption, catering to automobility, the incremental loss of local small businesses to global franchises, and erosion of local knowledge systems and spaces all need to be brought out of the shadows into the light once again. The next section advances this discussion by examining three practices for addressing some of these concerns.

Potential Pathways to Spatial Sustainability

This essay highlights three spatial sustainability practices now detectable in Hong Kong, Taipei and Singapore. Rather than fixed categories these local practices illustrate a potential shift towards spatial sustainability. Instead of *sustained* urban development premised on short-term economic and political gain—in other words, "urban growth machine"[16] development with exaggerated public capital outlays and high ecological, energy and carbon-intensity—this sampling suggests *sustainable alternatives* to status quo urban development. The three examples include: *conservation practices*, where funtioning ecosystems and socially-defined heritage spaces are actually conserved; *eco-modernization practices*,

Tree & Temple, Taipei City
Conserved spaces: a heritage tree and neighborhood temple in Taipei near Guting MRT (subway) station

Shadowlands, Taipei County
At first glance beneath the bridge would seem to represent a lightless, troglodyte space. Elsewhere, on riverbank lands under the bridges residents have located markets, sports activities and even outdoor karaoke enjoying the shaded overhead spaces away from the scorching summer sun and heat

where functioning natural systems are bio-engineered into urban restoration ecology projects, or integrated into building systems and infrastructure; and _urban wilding practices_, that engage or catalyze local civic imaginations in critical, participatory and creative or wild thinking about the uses of urban space. The remainder of the essay discusses these three apparently emergent spatial sustainability practices.

Conservation Practices—Protecting Spaces in Flux

Local pride in place is illustrative of citizens' and civil society's concerns about the fate of city spaces—both natural and built. Given Hong Kong, Singapore and Taipei's relatively compact urban morphologies—compared with sizeable cities in the Americas—protected parklands take-on dual purposes. All three cities retain heavily used small-scale urban park systems inside their cores alongside peripheral ensembles of protected natural spaces or green belts. Hong Kong's Country and Marine Park system; Singapore's Nature Reserves, Reservoir Parks, Connectors and Wetlands; and Taipei's YangMingShan National Park, City and County Parks, local mountain and riverside trail networks—illustrate that these cities are not just concrete jungles, as might be the initial perspective from their core global city spaces. How to support additional green spaces within the existing dense urban matrix—while protecting peripheral natural spaces from constant incremental threats, ecological simplification and public access denials—remains a key challenge. Green roofing, daylighting buried water channels, and improving waterfront access are examples of practices that cities in Asia have employed in creating spaces within the existing urban fabric. Similar practices are discussed further below in relation to eco-modernization.

Citizens in all three cities have agitated over contested spaces deemed low-value heritage by state agencies and businesses. Examples in Hong Kong include: Star Ferry and Queen's Pier;[17] Lee Tung Street (Wedding Card Street) historic shophouse district;[18] or the traditional Graham-Peel-Gage Street hawker street market.[19] Contentious spatial issues in Singapore have included: redevelopment plans for the city's so-called Chinatown District;[20] the loss of the now demolished old Central Library—rationalized in order to accommodate a short highway tunnel and private college space;[21] development plans impacting Chek Jawa's unique mudflats and residential community; and demands to protect Cyrene Reef so as to avoid the impacts that urban development has already had on Singapore's native ecosystems.[22] In Taipei, recent examples include: re-development plans for the Losheng Lepers Sanitarium, a longstanding self-managed community;[23] the top-down planning process and loss of green spaces in order to accommodate a stadium and commercial development at the ex-Songshan Tobacco Factory;[24] development threats to the fragile Danshui northern mangrove ecosystem from an ill-conceived highway project;[25] along with a proposal to construct a tramway/gondola corridor and stations inside YanMingShan National Park—a space accorded the highest level of protection in Taiwan.[26] These spatial contests indicate that citizens in the three cities are demanding a greater say in urban development and

spatial planning processes, including the conservation of existing built and natural spaces. Clearly some urban residents are interested strategizing how to avoid the creation of further placeless places and soulless spaces.

Well crafted eco-conservation regulations and strategies mean little without the proper incentives and leadership, including community voices. Each of the three cities has unique formal and informal power constellations. Leadership not only emanates vertically from government executives, legislators and civil servants; but also horizontally, from neighborhood groups, clubs, associations, non-government organizations, conservation movements, activists, religious groups (such as temple associations), academia, and among local and international business communities. Judging from the various civil society discourses in the three cities, activists concerns are not about freezing space in time, but rather about fears of what might be lost, including the potential loss of—place identity, collective memories, local customs, and vibrant independent owner-operator economies. The urge to conserve distinct spaces appears as a logical horizontal reaction in the face of an unabated drive towards urban spatial modernization, limited consultation, and infrastructure or megaprojects that have the capability of eroding complex natural and community systems. Other types of practices may complement these civic concerns about spatial management, as the next two sections elucidate.

Eco-modernization Practices—Co-evolving Natural and Built Systems

If conservation espouses the protection of space, eco-modernization may be contrasted as a set of eco-development or ecological restoration practices that apply state-of-the-art green technologies to built and natural spaces. Eco-mod practices have appeal because their potential cost savings or profitability is linked to green spinoffs, such as improving urban biodiversity. Such practices involve projects at various spatial scales that minimize resource and energy use through symbiotic, integrated designs—from macro-scale mixed-use urban developments, to bio-mimicry in built structures; from ecosystems restoration technologies, to information technology applications in energy efficiency.[27] Eco-mod pilot projects and ventures proposed or actualized in the three cities have included transit-oriented developments, energy and water efficiency systems in buildings and districts; pedestrian and bicycle friendly urban designs; alternative agricultural food systems; and imaginative green skyscraper concepts, among others.

All three cities have also had a history of developmental governance with active state intervention in infrastructure projects, industrial incubation and housing/commercial developments.[28] With eco-mod this tradition could continue, albeit in favor of green collar jobs and explicit low carbon pathways. For instance, Singapore's use of state economic incentives for energy-efficient buildings, roof-top gardens and skyrise greenery[29] potentially integrates energy and water conservation and habitat restoration into otherwise sterile, energy-intensive spaces. An example of integrated spatial practices is evident in Singapore's planned 101 hectare Gardens by the Bay, a

Supertrees, Singapore
The Gardens by the Bay proposal features 18 tree-like structures (30-55m / 9-16 stories high). Essentially vertical gardens of tropical flowering climbers, epiphytes and ferns, these "supertree" structures also will provide canopy shading and shelter. Included in the supertrees design by landscape architects Grant Associates are sustainable energy and water technologies that serve to cool an on-site conservatory. Image courtesy National Parks Singapore

development managed by National Parks Singapore. Buildings and landscapes in this phased waterfront project will be required to conform to sustainability performance criteria. Proposed parcel designs include engineered ecosystems and solar-powered "supertree" structures that would link water circulation to biowaste and energy production.[30] While this site apparently has potential to be a high-visibility showcase for eco-mod technologies, it remains an open question whether social sustainability, affordability, public accessibility and full life-cycle sustainability can be achieved.

An entirely different project in Singapore, and the focus of eco-engineering—including bioclimatic and bio-mimicry advances—is evident in the Editt Tower proposal. Designed by tropical eco-architecture advocate Ken Yeang, this building, if completed, would feature rainwater harvesting, natural ventilation, biogas generation, waste-water recycling and alternative energy systems, along with hanging native plant gardens. The proposed structure would represent an important contribution to green high-rise architecture and bio-regionally-appropriate tropical urban sustainability design.[31]

Rooftop garden experiments currently underway at the University of Hong Kong and with the city's Mass Transit Rail Corp. may improve eco-mod rooftop gardening and building energy efficiency applications for high density, sub-tropical urban spaces. Also, upon completion, the proposed Hong Kong Special Administrative Region Government's Tamar waterfront office complex is expected to demonstrate energy efficiency by featuring solar panels, green roofing and natural ventilation, at the same time providing much-needed public open space adjacent to Victoria Harbour.[32] Meanwhile, Taipei city has demonstrated leadership in public procurement and the role-model effect by completing a duo of eco-friendly public library buildings in the Beitou and Shipai neighborhoods.[33] In addition, the publicly-funded National Taiwan Normal University features a renovated graduate school building acting as *in situ* sustainable green campus. This project—with a rooftop garden, recycled grey-water wetland system, solar hot water and photovoltaic systems—serves as an inspiring educational and public awareness model for urban sustainability technologies.[34]

Eco-mod practices may appear to be a panacea, or worse, public relations greenwash—particularly if

Supertrees, Singapore
Perspective view of the "cool dry" conservatory, Gardens by the Bay. The proposed conservation complex will feature "cool moist" (0.9 hectare) and "cool dry" (1.2 hectare) biomes, and "cloud forest/tropical montane" (Cloud Forest) along with other ensembles of native and non-native vegetation and flora. Image courtesy National Parks Singapore

awareness at what cost?

EDITT Tower, Singapore
Environmental Design in The Tropics (EDITT) is the moniker for a
26-story green tower that would feature native vegetation, biogas
and photovoltaic energy, rain and greywater collection amongst other
eco-mod features. Proposed by National University of Singapore.
Image courtesy eco-architect Ken Yeang/copyright T.R.Hamzah &
Yeang Sdn. Bhd.

Shihpai Library Branch, Taipei City
The 6740 sq meter Shihpai Branch of Taipei Public Library (台北市立
圖書館石牌分館), opened in 2006 includes a rooftop rainwater collec-
tion system, water-efficient washrooms, water permeable forecourt
surfacing and a rooftop garden. Image courtesy Kuo, Ying-Chao/Bio
Architecture Formosana

projects ignore social shadow issues, or if they mask the ongoing unabated destruction of wild spaces elsewhere in the city. Eco-mod as tools and technologies does not address contentious underlying issues of how conflicting "urban growth machine" interests and powers shape spatial development practices in global city spaces.[35] Still, for de-natured, denuded or toxic spaces, eco-mod options represent an urban green machine alternative for restoring or recreating natural ecosystem processes.[36] The examples already noted illustrate high visibility demonstration projects largely catalyzed by public leadership—and funds—that could potentially spurn further individual, business or non-governmental efforts. Besides conservation and eco-mod practices, an equally important aspect of spatial sustainability is an engaged citizenry (re)imagining and debating what an eco-city or wild city might look like, as the next section discusses.

3 Urban Wilding Practices—Civic Spaces that Enable Diversity

Without the spaces for diverse civic discourses and debates, governments and businesses can become complacent, or worse, potentially corrupt or autocratic. Arguably, a variety of practices are needed to unite a diversity of citizens in tackling spatial sustainability challenges.[37] Such practices might include exploring the meaning of what it is to be wild in the city, referred to here as wild spaces, wild civic imaginations and urban wilding.[38] Wild spaces in this context represent both *physical* or grounded spaces and *conceptual* or virtual spaces. Wild visions, ideas and alternatives to "business as usual" can generate public interest in spatial sustainability. The wilding tactics of ordinary citizens, activists, artists, academics, the media, and non-government organizations—that is civil society, along with political parties—have played increasingly important roles in advancing spatial sustainability discourses in Hong Kong, Singapore and Taipei. Wild cities also draw upon the longstanding local wisdom of residents including knowledge of rituals and customs, festivals, sacred sites or spaces, flora and fauna, waterways, agriculture and marine practices, local markets, food diversity and community histories.

Three examples in Hong Kong are noteworthy since in recent years there has been a groundswell of responses by citizen movements, organizations, associations and political parties in devising alternative spatial visions.[39] First, public space issues—whether the "wall effect" associated with the airflow dynamics of new residential tower developments; or the protection of historical sites of collective memories—involved articulating alternative spatial visions. In the latter case, a long-term sit-in and creation of a temporary autonomous zone at the now demolished Star Ferry and Queen's Piers in 2006-07 illustrated the passion felt about a site-specific spatial issue by heritage activists.[40] Contested public-private spatial access rights at Causeway Bay's Times Square—in the vicinity of one of the rare pedestrian-friendly districts of Hong Kong[41]—also illustrates how the micro-politics of spatial regulation and surveillance is linked to scalar issues beyond single sites in the city.

Second, concerns about land reclamations and the massing, scale and nature of developments alongside

Freedom Square, Taipei City
Top: Removing characters: 大中至正 ("great neutrality and perfect uprightness"), later changed to: 自由廣場 ("freedom square"). The later characters were attached to a gate in front of National Taiwan Democracy Memorial Hall (formerly named Chiang Kai Shek Memorial Hall) in December, 2007. Bottom: Public gathering in front of National Taiwan Democracy Memorial Hall (formerly Chiang Kai Shek Memorial Hall). This public square has served as a civic space for numerous protests, campaigns and sit-ins, including the 1990 "Wild Lily Student Movement" which campaigned for grassroots political reforms in Taiwan. More recently the "Wild Strawberry Movement" campaigned in 2008 against the criminalization of public dissent in Taiwan. Images courtesy David Reid, "David on Formosa Blog" (see: http://blog. taiwan-guide.org/)

Hong Kong's Victoria Harbour have been longstanding public issues. Legal activism stemming from reclamation concerns resulted in the 1998 *Protection of the Harbour Ordinance* which nominally keeps government and private developers at bay by minimizing infill, infrastructure and ill-conceived developments.[42] In addition, an alliance of 10 civil society groups—known as City Envisioning@ Harbour (CE@HK)—organized internet discussions, public forums, media campaigns and design competitions to support urban wilding efforts alongside Hong Kong's Central Waterfront. Designing Hong Kong's (DHKs) Waterfront Design Competition featured alternative public space configurations, habitat restoration and renewable energy systems, and so forth. It remains unclear, however, if these alternative visions actually influenced government intentions for this high visibility public space.[43]

Third, the fate of Hong Kong's famed street markets—such as Wan Chai and Peel-Graham-Gage Markets—became issues due to large-scale redevelopment plans by the Urban Renewal Authority (a statutory public developer) which threatened their demise. Spatial sustainability advocates and NGOs—such as the Conservancy Association—responded by working with merchants, artists, educators and designers in devising campaigns to protect these vibrant, auto-free, owner-operated network economies. Urban wilding campaigns, to win recognition for the uniqueness of these neighborhood markets included teach-ins, flash-mobs, public art exhibits and demos at public meetings.[44] These actions may have at least succeeded in reminding public officials of their duties and of desires for transparency, debate and constructive dialogue about the future of public spaces in Hong Kong.

While civil society in the city-state of Singapore is constrained in comparison with Hong Kong or Taipei, spatial sustainability discourses have involved residents, nascent campus green groups and a handful of dedicated NGOs, including the Nature Society of Singapore and the Singapore Heritage Society. In addition, virtual commons spaces—using social networking sites, weblogs, alternative news and campaign websites—illustrate an active civic discussion platform for built and natural sustainability issues.[45] Besides self-censorship in these virtual forums, sustainability questions sometimes instigate what Singaporeans refer to as "OB" or "out of bounds" issues, especially if assumptions behind the harmonious consumer-oriented society are questioned.[46]

Although rallies, political assemblies and protests of five or more citizens had long been considered out of bounds, or illegal without a permit,[47] one small and some suggest hopeful change for civil society in Singapore is Hong Lim Park's Speaker's Corner. Officially sanctioned by the government in 2000 for approved public gatherings, few were actually held since an overly restrictive permit-granting system and excessive policing deterred prospective speakers or protesters.[48] However, a recent liberalization of rules resulted in the use of this civic space for visible public dissent including human rights demonstrations, a domestic helper abuse rally, a gay rights protests and a gay rights gathering.[49] The creation of a pocket zone for approved dissent might be viewed as a top-down response to nascent activisms in Singapore. It remains to be seen, however, if Speaker's Corner is merely is a token form of state-sponsored dissent zoning on a par with Beijing's officially designated protestor park space during the Olympics. Arguably, spaces are not sustainable unless there is a degree of openness and civic access—including to virtual spaces—where citizens, media, academics, NGOs and activists may safely congregate, socialize and share collective memories or hopes, as well as vent healthy frustrations or undertake constructive criticisms without being branded as criminals.

In Taipei, the use of civic space has clearly transformed after the demise of martial law and with subsequent legalization of multi-party democracy and official NGO status in 1987.[50] In the two decades since the era of one-party rule in Taiwan a large range of spatial sustainability issues—whether land use, housing, aboriginal rights or environment and social justice—have become visible through the urban wilding tactics of citizens and political activists. Because Taipei is the capital and media center, early post-authoritarian era gatherings such as anti-nuclear, anti-incinerator and pro-housing rights protests involved wilding actions in urban spaces by movements and NGOs such as the Taiwan Environmental Protection Union and Organization of Urban Re-s (OURs), among many others. Taipei continues to witness a wide range of creative urban wilding activities—street protests, music concerts, petitions, creative parades and festivals—addressing any number of themes, whether political party sponsored rallies, or environmental concerns, redevelopment issues, human rights, anti-corruption, or gay-lesbian-bisexual-trans rights marches, for example. Such actions defy the stereotype of East Asian societies being fully compliant top-down, orderly, or conformist.

The politically-charged (re)naming of Taiwan Democracy Memorial Hall and Liberty Square in 2007—formerly named Chiang Kai-Shek (CKS) Memorial Hall and Square—illustrates the fierce contestations over symbolic spaces in Taipei. In this case the spatial contestation is between rival pro-localization (Taiwanese nationalists) and pro-Kuomingtang (Republic of China nationalists) factions. While some pro-KMT groups requested that the massive former CKS square, hall and park be retained intact as heritage sites without a name change,[51] pro-localization groups protested that this public space should no longer memorialize a dictator (i.e. CKS), but rather be dedicated to Taiwan's emergent post-authoritarian democracy.[52] Resolution of this issue—indicative of deep divisions within Taiwanese society—remained unclear at the time of writing.

The energy, public visibility and media attention generated by activist protest actions also distracts observers away from pragmatic associational activities taking place on a daily basis. For example, in Taipei groups such as the Homemakers Foundation—a women's environmental NGO—and Tzu-Chi Buddhist Foundation or urban *Li* (local neighborhood) groups have long been involved in recycling efforts and healthy community meal programs, illustrating ecological and social aspects of sustainability. These NGOs educational efforts to encourage waste reduction ultimately contributed to Taipei city implementing some of the most innovative and successful waste reduction strategies in urban Asia and have significantly reduced waste footprints and incineration.[53] These examples illustrate that civil society organizations undertake a wide range of activities—whether as government watchdogs, educators, innovators, social activists or pragmatists. Understanding their multifaceted contributions to spatial sustainability remains a complex research challenge.

The examples of wilding practices in the three cases illustrated how achieving sustainability requires imaginative discussions about city spaces. In all three cities an array of creative spatial visions are being articulated by individuals, movements and organizations. Considering the fate of city-regions beyond individual lived or ego spaces and even beyond neighborhood space appears

to be an increasingly critical issue. Arguably wild civic spaces provide platforms for conviviality, for visioning, as well as for debate or even dissent. The examples illustrate how local knowledge and civil society are serving as important watchdogs in keeping governments and businesses in check. Wilding practices in Hong Kong, Taipei and Singapore also demonstrate that urban wilding is not a dictated program or a fixed process, but rather it is a habit that comes about from an appreciation or even the love of a place and its myriad spaces.

Conclusion

By sampling site-specific issues and contestations in Hong Kong, Singapore and Taipei spaces this essay hoped to trigger discussions about pathways to spatial sustainability. If the Brundtland vision of "development that meets the needs of the present without compromising the needs of future generations" is to be realized, then the sustainability project needs spatial articulation at various city-region scales. In some respects, conservation, eco-mod and wilding practices envelop past, present and future time horizons by suggesting paths for—protecting natural and historical spaces inside the city-region; arriving at integrated responses to people's daily life needs in city spaces; and envisioning active citizenships inside the urban eco-regions of tomorrow. Ultimately the practices, definitions and measures of urban spatial sustainability will ideally stem from the citizens of a city, including from those residents and issues sometimes relegated to the shadows.

Imported utopian design discourses have influenced the perception and conception of urban spaces throughout these three cities' historic spatial transformations from agricultural to industrial spaces, and now to post-industrial urbanity. For example, Ebenezer Howard's Garden City and its antecedents continue to shape Singapore's post-colonial spatial planning.[54] The new towns and green belt zoning, associated with British regional planning, were colonial influences in Hong Kong's New Territories new town developments and the Country Parks system.[55] Japanese colonial town planning concepts (1895-1945), and the post-World War II and post-Chinese Revolution Kuomingtang government shaped spatial practices in Taipei and Taiwan.[56] Recent "smart growth" design practices and neo-traditional urbanisms like their colonial antecedents remain of questionable import in Hong Kong, Singapore and Taipei. These three cities already retain an inherent compact city advantage due to their island-physical constraints on space, historically high-density morphologies, and tight energy and mobility networks. This essay has suggested that learning from locally-grounded models and design experiments appears to be a hallmark of successful sustainability experiences worldwide. In this respect emergent Asian design discourses such as the New Taiwan Landscapes Movement[57] and the Ecological Design in the Tropics (EDITT) Movement (in Singapore and SE Asia)[58] are well situated for addressing local urban sustainability issues, complementing the numerous experiments of communities and local activists.[59]

Another paradox of sustainability noted in the essay is that problems are often nested within multiple institutional realities at varying spatial scales. The concept of mega-regionalization—the simultaneous interweaving and transformative urban growth processes within and between cities—will continue to have profound implications for built and natural spaces in Asia.[60] Inter-scalar spatial sustainability practices necessitate mega-regional and meso-urban knowledge, while remaining anchored in locally-grounded realities. Macro-scale strategies for conservation and development therefore need to mesh with socio-economic, energy, land use, mobility and infrastructure strategies, among others. Connecting plans and policies *to people* remains a crucial challenge for government. Without public voices in decision-making deliberations spatial plans can fail miserably and communities and ecosystems can pay the price of such failures for years to come. Devising how to link complex local knowledge systems to urban management also represents a key challenge for cities everywhere.[61] Such approaches might do well by starting to acknowledge the abiotic, biotic and cultural layers underlying city spaces.

Finally, while some may hope that government agencies and developers ought to take a lead in implementing urban sustainability projects, the current financial crisis reveals that besides goodwill or charity there has been little compelling managers to maintain their ethical responsibilities to shareholders let alone to the communities and ecosystems that give them life. The current market failure illustrates the important need for citizen voices in articulating tangible, ethical and alternative sustainable models of economic and spatial development. Whether rooftop gardens in Singapore; activist efforts to protect the independent-owner operated economy in Hong Kong; or partisan protestations against state corruption by marchers on Taipei thoroughfares and public squares—efforts to achieve spatial sustainability have been occurring at various sites within all three cities. These vigorous debates demonstrate the diversity of civic voices in urban Asia today. They also highlight the importance linkages between collective spatial memories, local ecological knowledge and visions for future spaces. Such complex connections and accumulated wisdom represent bridges to future generations and will continue to shape the struggle to conceive and design city-region spaces in harmony with nature, rather than against.

References

1. See: Homer-Dixon, Thomas F. Environment, Scarcity, and Violence. *Princeton: Princeton University Press, 1999, for discussion on the dangers of international conflicts due to resource scarcity and environmental threats. Also see: Costanza, Robert, Lisa J. Graumlich and Will Steffen (eds.).* Sustainability or Collapse? An Integrated History and Future of People on Earth. *Cambridge, MA: MIT Press, 2007, for Socio-economic-environmental collapse scenarios. Also see: Diamond, Jared M.* Collapse: How Societies Choose to Fail or Succeed. *New York: Viking, 2005, for examples of societal-induced sustainability collapses. Also see: Zhang, David et al, "Climate change and war frequency in Eastern China over the last millennium," in* Human Ecology, *Vol.35:4, pp. 403-414, 2007. pp. 403-414. Also see: Dyer, Gwynne.* Climate Wars. *Toronto: Random House, 2008, for examples of climate/environmental change historic and potential future links to resource warfare. Also see: Chew, Sing C.* Ecological Futures: What History Can Teach Us. *Lanham: AltaMira Press, 2008*

2. Oxford English Dictionary (OED), The Oxford Dictionary of Current English. *Oxford, England: Oxford University Press, 1986. Sustainability contains the verb "sustain," meaning to support, uphold or keep (OED, p. 758); and the suffix "ability," meaning, to be able to do something (OED, p. 2). Rapport, David J, "Sustainability science: an ecohealth perspective," in* Sustainability Science, *published online, Springer Science, Dec. 14, (DOI 10.1007/s11625-006-0016-3), 2006, pp. 1-8. Rapport suggests that sustainable development, refers to achieving "a symbiotic relationship between biological and sociocultural systems so that future options are not foreclosed"(Ibid, p. 1)*

3. These seven, were adapted from the core themes of the "Urban Environmental Accords," signed in San Francisco by city mayors and representatives. San Francisco Urban Environmental Accords—International Green Cities Declaration, 2005

4. Douglass, Mike. "The globalization of capital cities: civil society, the neoliberal state and the reconstruction of urban space in Asia-Pacific," p. 27-46 in K.C. Ho and Hsin-Huang Michael Hsiao. Capital Cities in Asia-Pacific: Primacy and Diversity. *Center for Asia-Pacific Area Studies, Academia Sinica: Taipei, 2006, p. 36. Also see: Rohlen, Thomas P., "Cosmopolitan cities and nation states: open economies, urban dynamics, and government in East Asia," paper for Asia/Pacific Research Center (APRC). APRC and Stanford, CA: Stanford University, 2002. Also see: Vogel, Ezra,* The four little dragons: the spread of industrialization in East Asia. *Cambridge, MA: Harvard University Press, 1991. These works discuss the role of the "Tiger" or "Little Dragon" economies including Hong Kong, Taiwan and Singapore, highlighting their massive export oriented growth in the 1960s*

5. Castells, Manuel. The Rise of the Network Society. *Oxford: Blackwell, 1996*

6. New Economics Foundation (NEF). The happy planet index: and index of human well being and environmental impact. *New Economics Foundation and Friends of the Earth: London, 2006, p.20. Also see: Warren-Rhodes, Kimberley and Albert Koenig, "Ecosystem appropriation by Hong Kong and its implications for sustainable development" in* Ecological Economics, *Vol.39, p. 347-359, 2001. These three cities' high ecological footprints (for Asian nations) are noted in these works.*

7. Marcotullio, Peter J. and Julian D. Marshall, "Potential futures for road transportation CO2 emissions in the Asia Pacific" in Asia Pacific Viewpoint, *Vol. 48:3, p. 355-377, December, 2007, for discussion on the "ecological modernization" thesis. Also see: Grossman, Gene M. and Alan B. Krueger, "Economic growth and the environment," in* The Quarterly Journal of Economics, *Vol. 110:2, p. 353-77, 1995, for a discussion of the "Environmental Kuznets Curve" (EKC) postulate*

8. For example, see: Ng, Mee Kam,"Governance for sustainability in East Asian global cities: an exploratory study," in Journal of Comparative Policy Analysis, *Vol. 9:4, p. 351-381, 2007. Also see: Ooi, Giok Ling,* Sustainability and cities: concept and assessment. *Singapore: Institute of Policy Studies and World Scientific, 2005. Wolanski, Eric,"Increasing trade and the urbanisation of the Asia Pacific coast" p. 1-14 in Eric Wolanski (ed.),* The Environment in Asia Pacific Harbours, *Dordrecht: Springer, 2006*

9. See: Hedley Index, 2009. Available at: http://hedleyindex.sph.hku.hk/pollution/home.php#s (03/20/2k9), for an example of air pollution related mortality rates and public health costs associated with Hong Kong air quality. Also see: Trumbull, Kate. Still holding our breath: a review of air quality policy in Hong Kong 1997-2007. *Hong Kong: Civic Exchange, 2007*

10. Data reported in: Yeung, Yue-Man. "Emergence of the Pan-Pearl River Delta," in Geografiska Annaler Series B: Human Geography, *Vol.87:1. pp. 75-79, 2005. Also see: The Greater Pearl River Delta website: http://www.thegprd.com/about%5Cpopulation.html*

(03/18/2k9). Pan-PRD Region data are difficult to affirm since they involve different jurisdictions and non-resident "floating populations"

11. Wolanski, Ibid

12. Paterson, Matthew. Automobile Politics: Ecology and Cultural Political Economy. Singapore: Cambridge Press, 2007. The term "automobility" is used by political scientist Paterson to refer to the rise of car culture and its concomitant environmental, social and economic impacts on society

13. Asian Pacific Energy Research Centre (APERC), "Urban transport energy use in the APEC region: trends and options." Tokyo: APERC and Institute of Energy Economics, 2007. Available at: http://www.ieej.or.jp/aperc/2007pdf/2007_Reports/APERC_2007_Urban_Transport.pdf (10/03/2k8). Also see: Poudenx, Pascal, "The effect of transportation policies on energy consumption and greenhouse gas emission from urban passenger transportation," in Transportation Research Part A, Vol.42:6, p. 901-909, 2008

14. See: ETH Studio Basel, "Chungking Mansions: 3D (in)formality," 2008, available at: http://www.studio-basel.com/Projects/Hong-Kong-08/Student-Work/Chungking-Mansions.html (04/29/2k9), for a fascinating series of visual floor socio-economic activity studies in Chung King Mansions

15. Tai, Po-Fen, "Social polarization: comparing Singapore, Hong Kong and Taipei," in Urban Studies, Vol. 43:10, pp. 1737-1756, September 2006

16. Jonas, Andrew E.G. and David Wilson (eds.). The Urban Growth Machine: Critical Perspectives, Two Decades Later. Albany, NY : State University of New York Press, 1999. This book is a retrospective on Molotch's original arguments about the political economy of urban development in US cities and his references to the city as an "urban growth machine."

17. See: Cheung, Anthony, "Policy capacity in post-1997 Hong Kong: constrained institutions facing a crowding and differentiated polity," in The Asia Pacific Journal of Public Administration, Vol. 29:1 , p. 51-75, 2007, for a discussion of heritage issues and environmental issues, including the Queen's Pier demonstrations in the year 2006

18. Lee, Joanna and Mee Kam Ng, "Planning for the world city," p.297-320 in ed. Yue-Man Yueng. The First Decade: the Hong Kong SAR in Retrospective and Introspective Perspectives. Hong Kong: Chinese University Press, p. 303, p. 315, 2008. The authors identify Wedding Card Street as a controversial issue that illustrates the importance of planning for sustainable "life space" in a world city

19. See: Conservancy Association (CA), "Taking action and making hard decisions now, for a sustainable future," submission by Conservancy Association prior to the Chief Executive's Policy Address 2006. Hong Kong, 2006. Also see: www.savethstreetmarket.com , (available 03/19/2k9)

20. Hin, Ho Weng, "Navigating the murky depths of architecture: ruminations of a neophyte," in Singapore Architect (SA), SA Online Magazine, Vol. 209:108, 2001. Available at: www.singaporearchitect.com.sg/magazine/209/108.html (03/19/2k9). Hin discusses the National Library, Chinatown District plans, the loss and reinstatement of street hawkers

21. See: Kwok, Kian Woon, Ho Weng Hin, and Tan Kar Lin (eds). Memories and the National Library (Between Forgetting and Remembering). Singapore: Singapore Heritage Society, 2000

22. See: Francesch-Huidobro, Marie (2008). Governance, Politics and the Environment: a Singapore Atudy. Singapore: Institute of Southeast Asian Studies, p. 210-213, 2008, for NGO-nature protection campaigns from the mid-1980s-2003. Also see: Hobson, Kersty, "Enacting environmental justice in Singapore: performative justice and the green volunteer network," in Geoforum, Vol. 37, p. 671-681, 2006, for a discussion of Chek Jawa [on Palau(Island) Ubin]. She refers to the

mudflats, where development and reclamation was deferred (for 10 years to 2012) due to a public outcry, as one of the "ubiquitous spatial struggles taking place in the country [Singapore]" (Ibid., p. 675). Also see: Chou, Loke Ming, "Marine habitats in one of the world's busiest harbours," p. 377-391 in Wolanski, Eric (ed.). The Environment in Asia Pacific Harbours. Dordrecht: Springer, 2006. Chou (Ibid, p. 383-84) discusses the threats to Singapore's reefs from harbour developments and traffic. Online social networking and blogging about Cyrene Reef can be found at: www.wildsingapore.com/places/cyrene.htm (available: 03/20/2k9). Also see: Corlett, Richard T. "The ecological transformation of Singapore, 1819-1990," p. 411-420 in the Journal of Biogeography, Vol. 19: 4, pp. 411-420, 1992

23. See: Loa, Lok-Sin, "Loseng 'meets' UNESCO criteria," Taipei Times, p. 2, March 8, 2009. Also see: Loa, Lok-Sin,"Losheng supporters demonstrate at DOH," Taipei Times, p.2, Oct. 4, 2008. Recently Losheng (Taipei County) residents and allied activists have attempted to gain UNESCO heritage status for the threatened Japanese-Colonial sanatorium community for Hansen's Disease (Leprosy) residents. Also see: Wang, Zuching (2006), "Losheng Sanatorium, Department of Health—future and past of a place with isolated body and memory" paper presented to Asian Youth Culture Camp, Doing Cultural Spaces in Asia. Session 13, Politics of Cultural Minorities and its Future. Asia Culture Forum: Gwangju, Korea. October 28

24. See: Taipei Times, "Residents rally against planned dome complex," p. 2, August, 24, 2008. Also see: Loa, Lok-Sin, "Green Party's Calvin Wen forced down camphor tree," Taipei Times, p. 3, March 1, 2009, for discussion about resident concerns and Green Party (ecology) of Taiwan actions

25. See: Lu, Meggie, "KMT legislator quizzes EPA over blocked expressway," Taipei Times, p. 2, March 19, 2009

26. See: China Post, "Activists threaten lawsuit over Beitou project," December 4, 2008. Available at: www.chinapost.com.tw/taiwan/local/taipei/2008/12/04/186082/Activists-threaten.htm (03/19/2k9). Plans to build a 4.8km gondola into Yangminghsan National Park met with opposition from green NGOs because of the impacts to the park and because the environmental impact assessment (EIA) process and safety concerns were apparently ignored

27. Virtual technologies present new frames of reference for interscalar visualization. For example, the ability to toggle, bird-like, between neighborhood-centric and regional-centric spatial frames using geographic information systems (GIS), or Google Earth, potentially enables holistic visualization. Virtual informatics technology is increasingly used for conservation and eco-modernization visualizations, spatial modeling, simulations, scenario-building, ecomonitoring, and interscalar sustainability activist social networking and mobilization

28. See: Douglass, Ibid; Rohlen, Ibid.; Vogel, Ibid

29. See discussion in: Ofori, George, "Clients' role in attainment of sustainability in housing: the case of Singapore and lessons for developing countries," in Journal of Construction in Developing Countries, Vol.12:2, p. 1-20, 2007, regarding green roofs/skyrise greenery incentives for housing developments in Singapore

30. For an overview see: Low, Calvin. "Green bequest: Singapore's gardens by the bay plan wows as it endows Singaporeans with an historic and strategic asset," in FuturArc, Vol.9, p. 32-39, 2008

31. Steffen, Alex. Worldchanging: A User's Guide for the 21st Century. Abrahms: New York: Abrahms, p. 245-246, 2006

32. A visual for the Tamar Development Project was originally available at: http://www.epd.gov.hk/epd/english/climate_change/public.html (03/20/2k9)

33. See: Tseng, Shu-hsien, "Green library design and evaluation: the Taipei Public Library, Taiwan," in New Library World, Vol. 109, p. 321-336, 7/8 2007, for an overview of energy and water efficient features

of the Beitou Branch of the Taipei Public Library. Also see: Culture Taiwan, "Taipei's green libraries: eco-friendly architecture making headway," in +culture.tw –Taiwan (online). August 28, 2007. Available at: http://www.culture.tw/index.php?option=com_content&task=view&id=242&Itemid=157 (03/20/2k9)

34. Chang, Tzu Chou, 2007, "Sustainable campus initiative," p. 35-40 in Rosalyn McKeown (ed.) Good practices in teacher education institutions. Education for sustainable development in action. Good Practices No.1. January. Section for Education for Sustainable Development (ED/UNP/ESD). UNESCO: Paris. Available at: unesdoc.unesco.org/images/0015/001524/152452eo.pdf (03/20/2k9)

35. For example see discussion in: Tang, Wing-Shing, "Hong Kong under Chinese sovereignty: social development and a land (re)development regime," in Eurasian Geography & Economics, Vol. 49:3,2008, p. 341-361. DOI: 10.2747/1539-7216.49.3.341

36. See: Weisman, Alan. The World Without Us. New York: Picador/Thomas Dunne, 2007, for speculation about the nature of a post-human collapse world, including estimated rates of decay for cities and various human technologies and products

37. Douglass, Mike, "Civil society for itself and in the public sphere," pp. 27-50 in Mike Douglass, K.C. Ho and Giok Ling Ooi (eds.) Globalization, the City and Civil Society in Pacific Asia: The Social Production of Civic Spaces, New York: Routledge, 2008. Douglass defines civic spaces as "socially inclusive spaces with a high degree of autonomy from the state and commercial interest" (Ibid, p. 27). Also see: Roseland, Mark. Towards Sustainable Communities: Resources for Citizens and their Governments. New Society Publishers: Gabriola Island, BC, p. 182-195, 1998

38. The concept draws inspiration from the Toronto-based non-profit group, The Society for the Preservation of Wild Culture. This loose collaboration of artists and environmentalists formed in the late 1980s to encourage urban ecological thought. Another inspiration comes from the Vancouver-based NGOs City Farmer and Farm Folk/City Folk

39. See: Chan, Elaine and Joseph Chan, "The first ten years of the HKSAR: civil society comes of age," in The Asia Pacific Journal of Public Administration, Vol. 29: 1, p. 77-99, 2007. The authors link Hong Kong civil society (movements and NGOs) to interest in "green issues," including land-use planning, environmental and heritage concerns

40. See: Cheung, Ibid., p. 64, p. 71. Also see Chan, W.K., "Urban activism for effective governance: a new civil society campaign in the HKSAR," paper presented at the conference on First Decade and After: New Voices from Hong Kong's Civil Society organized by Syracuse University in Hong Kong and Roundtable Social Science Society. June 9, 2007. Available at: www.hkpri.org.hk (03/19/2009)

41. See: Ng, Kang-Chung, "Call for people power to reclaim public space," in South China Morning Post, p.1. March 25, 2008. Community activists pressed the owner and government to ensure free access to the space at Times Square and other sites in Hong Kong where 'public open space' has been designated within privately owned sites

42. Ibid, Cheung

43. Ibid, Chan and Chan, p. 87-88. Also see alternative Central Waterfront Design Competition submissions may be found at the Designing Hong Kong website: http://www.designinghongkong.com (03/20/2k9)

44. See: Chan, W.K., "Urban activism for effective governance: a new civil society campaign in the HKSAR," paper presented at the conference on First Decade and After: New Voices from Hong Kong's Civil Society organized by Syracuse University in Hong Kong and Roundtable Social Science Society. June 9, 2007. Available at: www.hkpri.org.hk (03/19/2009)

45. For an example of online journalism in Singapore see: http://theonlinecitizen.com/blogs-sites/ (available: 03/20/2k9). Nature Society

of Singapore, ACRES, Wild Singapore also retain websites that address spatial sustainability issues

46. See: Gomez, James, "Online opposition in Singapore: communications outreach without electoral gain" in Journal of Contemporary Asia, Vol. 38:4, p. 591-612, 2008. DOI: 10.1080/00472330802311779. Also see: Lord, Kristin M. (2006), The Perils and Promise of Global Transparency: Why the Information Revolution may not lead to Security, Democracy, or Peace. Albany: State University of New York Press, p. 101-112, 2006, for her discussion on the limits of online activism in Singapore. They discuss state monitoring, sanitizing, scrubbing and depoliticizing of online civic discourse and political party speech via excruciating regulations backed by the threat of legal/libel action

47. Singapore Straits Times: Nov.28, 2008. A recent trial in late 2008 stems from a case over two years previously where six individuals spoke at Speaker's Corner and then were charged by police of attempting to march to Parliament without a permit.

48. See: Ooi's, "State-society relations the city and civic space," pp. 66-78 in Mike Douglass, K.C. Ho and Giok Ling Ooi (eds.), Globalization, the City and Civil Society in Pacific Asia : The Social Production of Civic Spaces, New York : Routledge, 2008. Her work discusses Speaker's Corner in the context of globalization, Asian state-civil society relations, public participation and civic spaces

49. Ibid. Also see: Wei, Jamie Ee Wen, "Hearty buzz at speaker's corner; many surprised it is stirring to life and serving its purpose, after ho-hum existence since it was set up in 2000," in Singapore Straits Times, Nov 2, 2008. Also see: http://www.csmonitor.com/2000/0421/p7s1.html (03/20/2k9)

50. See: Ho, Ming-Sho. Green Democracy: A study on Taiwan's Environmental Movement. Socio Publishing: Taipei. (in Chinese), 2006. Also see: Williams, Jack F. and Ch'ang-yi David Chang, Taiwan's Environmental Struggle: Toward a Green Silicon Island. Routledge: New York, 2008, p. 21, 29. Also see: Hsiao, Hsin-Huang Michael, "Environmental movements in Taiwan," p. 31-53, in Yok Shiu F. Lee and Alvin Y. So (eds.) (eds), Asia's Environmental Movements: Comparative Perspectives. East Gate Press: Armonk, NY, 1999

51. See: http://www.taipeitimes.com/News/taiwan/archives/2007/11/07/2003386620

52. The square has long been the site of protests of various sorts. Demonstrations and protests began in earnest at the square in Fall 2008 to seek the reform of Taiwan's Assembly and Parade Laws which govern the route and nature of protests in city spaces (see: http://www.taipeitimes.com/News/front/archives/2008/12/08/2003430569)

53. See Chen, Tsao-Chou and Cheng-Fang Lin, "Greenhouse gases emissions from waste management practices using life cycle inventory model" in Journal of Hazardous Materials, Vol. 155, p. 23-31, 2007. Also see: Fukushima, Yasuhiro et al, "Preliminary investigation of greenhouse gas emissions from the environmental sector in Taiwan" in Air and Waste Management Association, Vol. 58, p. 85-94, Jan 2008

54. See: Laquian, Aprodicio A. Beyond Metropolis: the Planning and Governance of Asia's Mega-Urban Regions. Woodrow Wilson Center Press: Washington, DC, 2005, p. 59-63, who refers to Howard's influences in Asian city planning. Also see: Velegrinis, Steven and Richard Weller, "The 21st-century garden city? The metaphor of the garden in contemporary Singaporean urbanism," in Journal of Landscape Architecture (JoLA), Vol. 07, p. 30-47, 2007

55. See: Lai, Lawrence W.C. and Winky K.O. Ho, "Low-rise residential developments in green belts: a Hong Kong empirical study of planning applications" in Planning Practice and Research, Vol. 16:3-4, p. 321-335, 2001. The authors (Ibid, 324) refer to Hong Kong's green belt policy and green belt zoning shaped by Patrick Abercrombie's post-

war (1948) British colonial era planning methods. They also note the use of exclusionary racial zoning against Chinese residents before the WWII. Also see: Castells, Manuel, L.Goh and Ry-W-Kwok, "The Shek Kip Mei syndrome: public housing and economic development in Hong Kong." Centre of Urban Studies and Urban Planning, University of Hong Kong: Hong Kong, 1986, for insights into Hong Kong's and Singapore's new town/satellite city housing strategies

56. Huang, Li-Ling, "Urban Politics and Spatial Development: the Emergence of Participatory Planning," p. 78-98 in Reginald Yin Wang ed. Globalizing Taipei: The Political Economy of Spatial Development. New York: Routledge, 2005. Huang (Ibid, 79-80) notes both Japanese planning/engineering ideas, as well as "garden city" town concepts introduced under the incoming Kuomingdang (KMT) that shaped planning in outer Taipei. Also see: Wu, Ping-Sheng "Phantasmagoria: A Study on the Transformations of Urban Space in Colonial Taiwan—Tainan and Taipei, 1895-1945," unpublished dissertation for Doctor of Philosophy in Architecture. Tainan, Taiwan. National Cheng-Kung University, p. 248, June, 4, 2007

57. Williams and Ch'ang-Yi, Ibid. p. 53. Also see: Phipps, Gavin, "Eco-technology paves the way without concrete: the Taiwan New Landscapes Movement is pioneering standards for public-works projects," in Taipei Times, Dec 12, 2004, p. 18

58. See: Yeang, Ken. Ecodesign: A Manual for Ecological Design. Singapore: Wiley-Academy, 2006. Also see: Yeang, Ken (1999), "Planning the sustainable city as the vertical-city-in-the-sky," p. 99-108, in (eds.) Ah Foong Foo and Belinda K.P. Yuen. Sustainable Cities in the 21st Century. Singapore: NUS Press. Also see: Soon, Tay Kheng. Mega-Cities in the Tropics: Towards and Architectural Agenda for the Future. Social issues in Southeast Asia. Singapore: Institute of Southeast Asian Studies. Loi Printing Pte., 1989. EDITT refers to both a 26-story building proposal and a movement. The former is proposed by TR Hamzah & Yeang and sponsored by the National University of Singapore. The movement includes the influence of architect Ken Yeang who has been an advocate of a "vertical city in the sky" (Ibid, 1999) in relation to Singapore and South Asia and whose work, Ecodesign (Ibid, 2006), introduces an ecological agenda for redesigning the traditional skyscraper and city

59. Also see discussion in: Lim, William S.W. Asian Ethical Urbanism. Singapore: World Scientific, 2005

60. Urban mega-regionalization processes—exemplified in the scholarship of: Hall, Peter, "The polycentric metropolis: a western European perspective on mega-city regions," paper presented at the International Symposium on Mega-City Regions: Innovations in Governance and Planning. Centre of Urban Studies and Urban Planning. Department of Urban Planning and Design: University of Hong Kong, 2008. Also see: Sassen, Saskia, "Novel spatial formats: megaregions and global intercity geographies," paper presented at International Symposium on Mega-City Regions: Innovations in Governance and Planning. Centre of Urban Studies and Urban Planning. Department of Urban Planning and Design: University of Hong Kong, HKSAR, 2008. And in the context of the Pearl River Delta Mega-region see: Yeh, Anthony G.O. and Jiang Xu, "Regional cooperation in the Pan-Pearl River Delta: A formulaic aspiration or a new imagination?", in Built Environment, Vol. 34:4, p. 408-426, 2008

61. Such local ecological knowledge might include wisdom about the changing seasons, plant or animal growth and natural cycles such as animal migrations, season or tidal rhythms, micro-climates, watersheds, shorelines or estuaries, amongst numerous other spheres.

The author would like to thank the University of Hong Kong and Academia Sinica (CAPAS) Taiwan for helping make this research possible.

David Sadoway is a PhD candidate at the University of Hong Kong in the Department of Urban Planning and Design. His research focus is on comparative urban sustainability and eco-governance in Asian cities. His Bachelor's was in Urban Planning (BES, Waterloo) and Master's in Resource & Environmental Management (MRM, Simon Fraser). He has worked as a manager/coordinator with a community economic development NGO on Northern Vancouver Island, BC; as a consultant with UNDP/Agenda 21, Mongolia; and had stints with urban planning firms in Toronto and Vancouver. He has also worked as a lecturer, tutor/teaching assistant, and researcher in universities in Asia and Canada. He is interested in learning about how we humans can overcome our fears, prejudices and greed to co-create sustainable organizations, institutions and cities for a healthy planet.

CHEN Zhuo and HUANG Keyi

CHINESE
CARNIVAL

CHEN ZHUO and **HUANG KEYI** are Beijing-based artists; both professors at the Digital Media Arts Studio at the Central Academy of Fine Arts. Their works are deeply influenced by China's mainstream culture since 1949. The images from the Chinese Carnival series are a painstakingly assembled tableaux of hundreds of doppelgangers interacting against the backdrop of a stimulated, synthesized reality, born of the shared imaginings of the artists. Although the general tone of the works is celebratory, even delirious, the duo has deliberately inserted darkly ironic references to a more conflicted Chinese history throughout the series.

Chen Zhuo and Huang Keyi, *Chinese Carnival No. 3*, 2007, C-Print, 90 cm x 250 cm, edition of 7

CHEN Zhuo and HUANG Keyi

Chen Zhuo and Huang Keyi, *Chinese Carnival No. 7*, 2008, C-Print, 90 cm x 250 cm, edition of 7. Following pages: Chen Zhuo and Huang Keyi, *Chinese Carnival No. 9*, 2008, C-Print, 120 cm x 180 cm, edition of 7

CHEN Zhuo and HUANG Keyi

一切反动派都是纸老虎

排除万难去争取胜利

为人民服务

AURORA

为人民服务

176

AYÓN, Angel, MARKS, Gerald
and WHITE, Sarah

ALONG TRAILS
AND SHORELINES

3-D Photographs by Gerald Marks

Bringing the reality of environmental distress out of the realm of abstraction and into the plurality of the senses was at the core of this artistic collaboration. Made possible thanks to a grant from iLAND (interdisciplinary Laboratory for Art, Nature and Dance), *Along Trails and Shorelines* brings together performance, lens and environmental arts in unique ways. Dead Horse Bay, the site chosen for the project, is an environmentally degraded area in southeast Brooklyn that defines the northern shore of the Rockaway Inlet. The site has had many incarnations since the 1800s, when it was transformed from a natural coastal marsh to a horse-processing industrial area—thereby gaining its name—and later to a landfill collecting New York City's refuse, a use it retained until the early 1900s. In the 1930s the former landfill was encapsulated with sand dredged from the bay as part of a development plan that included building the city's first commercial airport. Once WWII broke out, the development was halted and the area was used for military purposes. In the 1960s it was made part of the Gateway National Recreation Area.

Today, shoreline erosion has washed away much of the sand coverage, exposing hidden refuse at a rapid rate. Broken glass, ceramic shards, corroding metals, shoe soles, rubber tires and other discarded objects now litter the beach at Dead Horse Bay. The emergence of the site's past is today its most distinctive, intriguing and inviting feature. The gradually surfacing brownfield speaks of the forlornness of the site and portrays the persistent resilience of nature to the shortsighted intrusion of industry and waste.

Through public events using lens arts, dance and mind/body movement practices such as the Alexander Technique, we explored developing non-traditional models for raising environmental awareness and promoting discourse on the byproducts of human waste. Bringing people to the site, as opposed to taking the site to people through traditional media formats, the performances encouraged both dancers and audience to interact with the site using all perceptual faculties of sense, self, time and space. For the viewer, the presence of the dancers onsite—often moving amid, or lying atop, refuse—reinforced the existence of the emerging objects by coexisting with them in unexpected and at times contradictory ways. The audience's own potential risks at being onsite were reflected back on them in the more extreme gestures of the dance they were witnessing. The risk inherent in the dancers' movement served as a personification of the more subtle hazards involved in engaging in the area.

This method of involving people directly—spatially, sensorially, aesthetically and, ultimately, kinesthetically—revealed great potential as a creative model for expanding public education on, and understanding of, environmental issues. It showed that movement as an agent of change, both personal and collective, can be embraced as an instrument of environmental perception and advocacy.

SARAH WHITE is a dancer, choreographer, video artist, Alexander Technique teacher and massage therapist. She holds a BFA in dance from the University of Missouri in Kansas City, 1999 and an AmSAT recognized Alexander Technique Teaching Certificate from the Balance Arts Center in New York, 2007. She has been performing and choreographing in New York City for the last eight years. Her choreography and video art has been curated for shows and festivals in New York City, 5th Stop Open Studios, Monkeytown; Philadelphia, Philadelphia Fringe Festival; and Los Angeles, Fritz Haeg's Sundown Salon 2006 and Santa Monica Arts Center's Highways Performance Space, 2008.

ANGEL AYÓN is trained and experienced in architecture and historic preservation in both his native Havana and New York City. His work from the National Center for Conservation, Restoration and Museology allowed him to conduct design, research and conservation projects on several landmark-designated structures in Havana's historic center. Before leaving Cuba, Ayón was an adjunct professor at Havana's School of Architecture, where he taught and researched on topics of environmental design in hot wet climates. In New York City, his professional practice has included work on several historic buildings while at Li-Saltzman Architects, P.C. and WASA/Studio A, where he was the project architect for the recently completed exterior restoration of Frank Lloyd Wright's Guggenheim Museum.

GERALD MARKS is an artist working along the border of art and science, specializing in stereoscopic 3-D. He may be best known for the 3-D videos he directed for The Rolling Stones during their *Steel Wheels* tour. He has taught at the Cooper Union, The New School and the School of Visual Arts, where he currently teaches Stereoscopic 3-D as part of the MFA program in Computer Art. He was a visiting scholar at the MIT Media Lab, where he worked in computer-generated holography. His Professor Pulfrich's Universe installations are popular features in museums all over the world, including San Francisco's Exploratorium, the New York Hall of Science, and Sony ExploraScience in Beijing and Tokyo.

Free Viewing: To view these 3-D images, allow your eyes to focus on the page while aligning for a very close or far distance. The images are arranged Left-Right-Left so that the pair on the left allows for parallel viewing while the pair on the right is set up for cross eye viewing. When you focus on the wrong pair, the depth in the scene will appear in reverse, while the other pair will appear in glorious 3-D. This reversed depth can also be interesting. If you wear glasses regularly for distance, you may find you can do the trick more easily with your glasses off. If you have reading glasses, they will definitely help.

Top and bottom: Dead Horse Bay, second performance

Top: Dead Horse Bay, second performance; Bottom: Dead Horse Bay, third performance

AYON, Angel/MARKS, Gerald/WHITE, Sarah

Top and bottom: Dead Horse Bay, third performance

Top and bottom: Dead Horse Bay, third performance

AYON, Angel/MARKS, Gerald/WHITE, Sarah

Top and bottom: Dead Horse Bay, third performance

EDICK, Kipp, HILLYARD,
Chris and YUNG, Edward

REFLECTIONS ON HONG KONG'S WATERFRONT, AN EPILOGUE

Hong Kong's famous Victoria Harbor Waterfront is a shifting manufactured terrain, having been progressively reclaimed from the sea since early in the 20th century. Currently a government masterplan is being implemented for the Central waterfront, one that is legally defined as the last stage of this reclamation process, and the final resting point for the waterline of the city. Whilst a halt to reclamation has been a long-standing aim for many public advocacy groups, the nature of the government's proposal was perceived as sterile. Consequently, in summer of 2007, the Hong Kong public advocacy group *Designing Hong Kong* staged an international competition calling for alternative design ideas for this critical moment in the urban development of the city.

We now ask the question— how effective a role did design play within public advocacy? The shortlist of winning entries was startling in its diversity, projecting an ideological ambivalence from the progressive to the nostalgic. While this spectrum of solutions certainly opened new possibilities, it also lessened the cohesion of advocacy. Further, it might also be said to demonstrate a lack of conclusion over what constitutes sustainability in urban design practice today—does urban design necessarily have to take on the rhetoric of green, and distinguish its edges? In the end, the jury selected a project whose surface imageability was largely green,

Peak to Water Connectivity. Infrastructural platforms bypassing major highway and weaving through existing buildings to reconnect the hills to the waterfront

despite the fact that the final reclamation of Hong Kong's waterfront will be a manufactured social and physical ecology. Our project, simply titled *Hong Kong Waterfront*, which took second place, recognizes this inevitable artifice and is critical of green fever.

Our project also to a degree assumed a green mantle; yet more important to our concept of sustainability was the connectivity of the waterfront with Hong Kong's disjunctive infrastructure. In such a way the design treats sustainability as a social crisis as much as an environmental one. At present the Hong Kong waterfront is a disconnected patchwork, an unfortunate legacy of successive land reclamations and lack of public vision. It is severed from everything around it by infrastructures that serve circulation but not urban life. Rather than competing with the icons of Hong Kong's postcard skyline, our strategy weaves through the wall of skyscrapers to reintroduce the underlying and overlooked connection between the mountain behind the city and the water in front of it. Both as an infrastructural and social device, the new waterfront should effect the entire city.

We propose a topographical infrastructure contingent upon a host of existing connections—not an isolatable patch of development but rather an open system. To undermine the government's desire to ascribe zoned parcels we wove the ground in geometric forms, creating a territory for exchanges between private developer and public space. The undulating checkerboard alternates between hardscape and greenscape—reconnecting stratified layers and speeds and movement in the city, and creating a space for lingering. The section modulates locally to meet other infrastructural systems: dipping the merge with the subway, and rising to join overhead walkways. In plan the system inflects to mesh with existing patterns of development, while at the same time maintaining a unique spatial identity.

What happened in the aftermath of the public exhibitions, voting, commentary and presentations? To truly affect change for the ongoing waterfront development, it was important that the dialogue produced by the competition did not terminate at the moment the competition results were announced. One hopes that the effort of the competition galvanized the different the political, business and public constituents of Hong Kong, and yet it seemed the competition did little in sparking further review of current proposals. Today, new landfill and construction at the waterfront site continues uncontested.

CHRIS HILLYARD and EDWARD YUNG are recent graduates of Princeton University School of Architecture. KIPP EDICK is a student of Yale University School of Architecture. The *Central Waterfront Design Competition* was an international design competition held in 2007 by Designing Hong Kong, a non-profit advocacy group committed to urban development issues in Hong Kong. The entries and shortlisted finalists were exhibited at various public venues across Hong Kong in addition to an online gallery and voting system, and publication in Hong Kong's press.

System of Connectivity. A system that extends beyond the boundaries of the waterfront site to reconnect disjunctive patches of the city to the water

EDICK, Kipp/HILLYARD, Chris/YUNG, Edward

MARSHALL, Victoria

Onset, Event and Release

After non-linear dynamics were observed in ecosystems, ecologists began to introduce words into ecological literature to help explain this to a broader audience. To draw attention to the distinctions between efficiency and persistence, between constancy and change and between predictability and unpredictability, in 1973 "resilience"[1] was introduced by C.S. Holling. Later, in 1985, S.T.A. Pickett and P.S. White introduced "disturbance"[2] to describe events which have a slow onset, fast duration and quick release. This word communicated urgency as well as a sense of movement. Both a scarcity and an over abundance meet the definition of disturbance. Ecological resilience is now defined as the amount of disturbance that an ecosystem can withstand without changing self-organized processes and structures (defined as alternative stable states).[3] To explain what this meant to the practices of ecosystem science, we can say that there has been a shift from the study of the composition and functioning of ecosystems to the study of the processes of disturbance and to the evolutionary significance of such events.[4]

Urban design emerged as an innovative practice during a period of chaotic theoretical oscillations brought about by the collapse of Modernist master-planning.[5] Unlike the process of integration in ecosystem science through new viewpoints and definitions and frameworks, in the 1980s urban design was the result of a compromise position between the panoptic vision of city models, city growth and city transformation and the limited appeal of the "partial control" of the bottom up. It was defined as a middle ground, a world unto itself;[6] however theory has created a disturbance to this position via a release in urban design discourse from the linear understanding of nature as a unified whole that has an equilibrium seeking force toward a non-equilibrium understanding of uncertain multiple natures. Informed by three conferences on urban design in 2007-2008, this paper considers this most recent cycle of oscillations and the urban design practices that are emerging in parallel. Within each conference a manifesto was drafted. While the manifestos themselves did not create the disturbance to practice we will use them as a thread to link the events.

Urban Resilience in Ecology and Design Cary Conference 2007 was the 12th in a series of biennial conferences hosted by the Cary Institute of Ecosystem Studies in Millbrook, NY. The Cary Conference series is designed to focus on emerging issues and cross-disciplinary themes to help guide the development and application of ecology.[7] Early in 2008 The Council for European Urbanism (CEU) held its third international congress in Oslo, Norway. The congress discussed the global topic of *Climate Change and Urban Design*.[8] Late in 2008, the University of Pennsylvania hosted *Re-Imagining Cities: Urban Design after the Age of Oil*. The event marked the 50th anniversary of the 1958 Conference on *Urban Design Criticism*, whose participants included Jane Jacobs, Louis Kahn, Kevin Lynch, Ian McHarg, Lewis Mumford and I.M. Pei.[9]

These three conferences can provided a discourse between the following partners; urban design and science (Cary Conference), urban design and policy (CEU Conference), urban design and media (Penn Conference), with urban design and education as a common theme. The three conferences can also be organized in another way; Debates during break out sessions and dinner table post-mortems are common conference activities, however dilemmas, doubts and differences became legible in the collective writing of the conference manifesto. There was a moment of collegial divergence in each conference—not a riot—more like the marking of a slight barometric shift. While not all of the final manifestos have been published, below is a participatory account of each manifesto-in-development.

Orginally purchased by the Melbert and Mary Flager Cary in 1920 as a retreat from New York City, The Cary Institute of Ecosystem Studies (CIES) is located on 14 former farms. Since 1993 the focus of the institute has been on long-term study of ecological disturbance and recovery at all scales with the understanding that this knowledge provides sound basis for formulating sound public policy.[10] In 2002 as part of the Baltimore Ecosystem Study (BES), scientists from the CIES began parallel research with urban designers from Columbia University which signaled a shift away from policy and toward design.[11] Brian McGrath and Steward Pickett recently summarized the trends of this collaboration as "a shift from design of the city to design in the city and the understanding of ecology in the city to the ecology of the city."[12]

The 2007 Cary conference participants were challenged to identify and articulate the ecological principles, design imagination, and information needed to advance ecologically resilient urban design by first, addressing incomplete and out-of-date information, and then to identify innovative and emerging environmental research directions. After three days of presentations, shared breakfasts, lunches, walks and dinners as well as the scheduled *Group Reports* session Gene Likens, who is the Founding Director and President Emeritus of the Institute of Ecosystem Studies, made an announcement regarding ecology. Likens proposed to launch a research fellowship for ecologists on the topic of *Ecological Urban Design* in a wooded and remote location near San Francisco. The disappointed designers, in the spirit of the CIAM congress, debated and then voted to support this initiative with the qualifier that it includes a reciprocal offer for designers as well.

Founded in 2003 The Council for European Urbanism are no strangers to manifestos. Every international congress had produced one; *The Charter of Stockholm 2003*, *Declaration of Viseu 2004* and the *Berlin Declaration 2005*. Additional symposiums such as *Leeds 2006* and *Lisbon 2007* reinforced previous charters and recruited new members.[13] Following this ambitious trend, the 2008 Congress was located in newly oil-rich Oslo, Norway. It had an enticing title; *Climate Change and Urban Design* as well as a promise to address global issues. Touted as the birthplace of sustainability, this city where the Brundtland Commission was established in 1985, attracted scientists from around the world. The next international congress is scheduled for Havana in 2009.

The structure of the conference was organized into themes of Science: What we know, Policy: What we must do, Education: How we must develop and disseminate skills, and Best Practice: How we must implement these conclusions. Implied in this goal-oriented schedule is a narrow role of the scientist as the incontestable expert. In other words the scientist is seen as someone who has abstracted themselves and attained a perspective from a perceived place of neutrality to offer salvation which policy, design and education then implements. The CEU had recently embraced New Urbanism as a tool to carry this implementation out. This logic gently unraveled in the final plenary session. After several break-out groups had begun to draft the declaration, many scientists requested specific edits to clarify the use of science terms, proposed urban design models for rapidly developing countries, and finally made a courteous but pragmatic plea for cities to be included as a mitigating force for climate change in the Kyoto Protocol.

Unlike most Ivy League graduate design schools, PennDesign has a legacy of integration between urban design, landscape architecture and architecture. This was evident in the ambition and scale of the *Re-Imagining Cities: Urban Design after Oil* conference held in November 2008. With 78 invited speakers, occupying multiple halls, auditoriums, restaurants and hotels, as well as two exhibitions and seven bloggers, the conference registration quickly filled up and then re-opened offering overflow spaces with video feeds. Sponsored by PennDesign, the Rockefeller Foundation and the Penn Institute for Urban Research this no-fee conference also marked the transition of the school's Deanship to Marilyn Jordan Taylor, formerly of SOM. The break-out sessions were ordered according to scale; product design and engineering, building and landscape design and local urban design, city urban design, regional urban design.

The schedule for the final day of the conference was to forge an educational agenda in the form of a manifesto. In addition there was a parallel discussion on the need to update design education in general. The education of an urban designer was assumed to begin with the architecture student. Urban design is typically located as a final-year design project as it is considered complex and therefore only appropriate for mature students. In the *Agenda for Urban Design Education* session it was put forward that every first-year design project for architecture students should now be situated in a city and that every studio from then on must adopt an ecological point of view. For landscape architects this was an old idea but a truly welcome one and for the bloggers, it was newsworthy.[14] In the *Teaching Fundamentals* working group a short discussion began on the topic of how to integrate design fields within the education system and to integrate the design community with other fields of knowledge.

Sorting

What can be learnt from these three shifts in the understanding of urban design at the three conferences: The gracious acknowledgment of urban design at the science conference, that in turn excluded design from a new research opportunity; the voices of scientists asking to leverage the weight of a politically connected urban design group toward real policy change rather than simply voicing support for a design formula; and the slow opening of the isolation of formal design education to new types of design projects, topics of teaching and research partners? From what moments in time has the desire to write a manifesto come? Is it a desire to be perceived to be in control, to re-balance a bias or simply to make public a set of collective principles and desires?

One answer is to locate this collective desire to let go while not letting everything fall apart within the cycle of shock and trance that Andrew Revkin, (quoting President Obama) notes that the United States has lived in since 1988:

There've been two periods that could be construed as climate shocks along the 100-year trajectory of science pointing to human-caused heating of the Earth. The first came in the summer of 1988. Blazing heat and drought in the North, the combustion of Yellowstone and the Amazon, and warnings from scientists led by James E. Hansen led to a burst of headlines and scientific conferences, the creation of the Intergovernmental Panel on Climate Change, and the negotiating path toward agreement on the first climate treaty in 1992.

Then came the trance, acknowledged by former President Bill Clinton in a video interview. Low energy prices, the distraction of the first Persian Gulf war, and a temporary cool spell following the 1991 eruption of Mount Pinatubo in the Philippines all helped tamp down global warming as an issue through much of the 1990s, outside the brief burst of triumphant proclamations with the 1997 negotiation of the Kyoto Protocol, a stricter addendum to the faltering 1992 climate pact.

The second shock built slower and has lasted longer. It started with the European heat wave of 2003 and intensified from 2005 to 2007 as Hurricane Katrina and An Inconvenient Truth put climate in the headlines, the science pointing to a human hand on the planet's thermostat coalesced with the fourth I.P.C.C. report, and the Arctic Ocean sea ice peeled back in a way never observed before.

Many climate scientists have insisted that this is not a shock, but the opening salvo from nature in a new age of climatic destabilization: Global warming, they say, is no longer a "somewhere, someday" issue but here and now. Other serious researchers in the field, while convinced of the building long-term danger, warn that nature will almost surely jostle chaotically through cool and warm spells along the way to what Dr. Hansen calls "a different planet." They warn not to read too much into current events (particularly hurricanes) unless you're ready to explain the quiet seasons and cold snaps along with the tempests and heat waves.[15]

This feedback between human attention and ecosystem events is a circuit within which the moments of readjustment at each conference can be understood. To let go of equilibrium requires a corresponding release of a sense of control, which is frightening, for example, while images of the apocalypse were present in each conference, Nature's revenge was not. It seems that this more recent shock cycle has been accompanied by sophistication in the understanding of ecological processes as a sequential build-up of events rather than a symbol of human

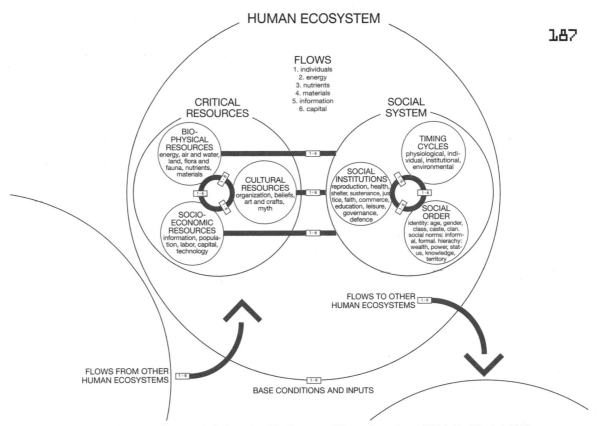

Human Ecosystem Framework. Redrawn from The Structure of Human Ecosystems, *V 05.2. Machlis et al, 2005*

failure or the hand of God. In addition, designers who have embraced non-equilibrium articulated the limits of existing normative models and frameworks, creating flexibility to risk new directions.

Another answer to the question of what is to be learnt from the shifts in the conference could be either more mundane or more radical. Could it just be the machinations of disciplinary fields learning each others language? Through the problematising of ruptures and articulation of rubs and synergies, is it simply part of an integration process? On the other hand we can also ask, are the ecosystem changes we are dealing with being fully comprehended and are existing urban design practices being defended with new words so as to keep them on the same middle ground? Gensko in writing about the work of Guattari, describes a *Transdisciplinary Metamethodoligy*—that is, a method that allows students from various disciplinary training skills to move beyond the compromises of interdisciplinarity into another mental ecology. That is beyond the perspective from an estab-lished discipline valorizing the between as an exciting place to visit and extend one core work. This objective is as Gensko writes "toward the rethinking of method rather than its migration across epistemological boundaries, supplementation/accessorization by 'other' methods, or simple multiplication of perspectives without adequate integration—a concern for theory and practice." The tools are; find ways to preserve singularity, expand refer-ential fields, open new lines of possibility, allow selves to mutate, auto-develop and redevelop.[16]

Some examples of rethinking of method could be seen at the conferences in the break-out sessions in the small rooms downstairs or across the courtyard. Separated from the seamless, spectacular and complete presentations in the large rooms were several contested, transparent and in-progress projects. At the Cary conference, Mary Miss presented *City as Living Lab*,[17] which positions artists, designers and other visualizers as significant catalysts for environmental, social and economic sustainability. Oslo Danai Thaitakoos' paper *Resilience and Adaptation* presented an aqua/landscape dynamic urban design model of the Chao Phraya River Delta in relation to the city of Bangkok. At Penn in the Product Design and Engineering panel, Robert Harris presented the *ISLES Project* for Trenton, New Jersey which engages eco-social equity through energy efficient retrofitting.[18] Each of these examples engages modes of practice which no longer rely solely on the greenfield and brownfield surfaces of the metropolis and megacity to design new sustainable cities. These new practice modes directly engaged the complex participatory processes of the meta-city with its rapid migrant flows, techno-intelli-gence and hybrid ecological structures and processes with decisive design intent.

The project of rethinking of method can also be translated into drawing, education and science. Brian McGrath's recent book *Digital Modelling for Urban Design* asks urban designers to work more with complex, interactive, reiterative and collaborative urban informa-tional feedback systems and less with bureaucratic,

Art Interventions

A   **Boundaries**
     Neighborhood
     & Park Permeability

B   **Circulation**
     heirarchy & usage

C   **Utilities**
     Hydrology and Energy

D   **Canyon**
     Microclimate & Biofiltration

E   **Wildlife Corridors/**
     Ecosystems

F   **Programs**

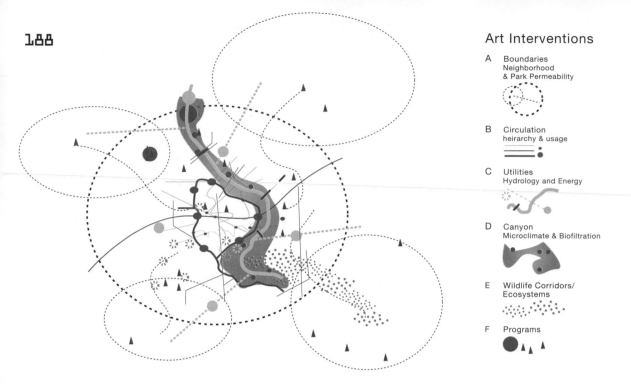

Opportunities

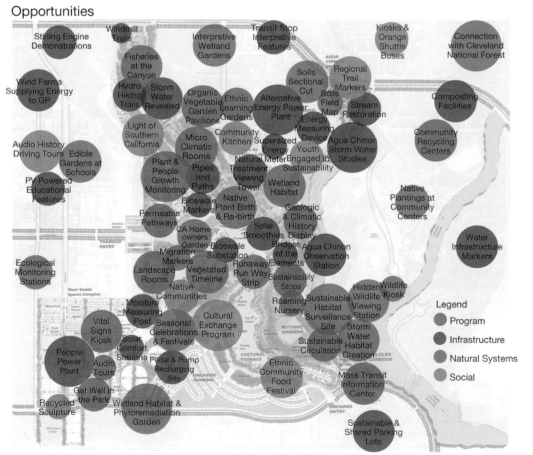

Legend
- Program
- Infrastructure
- Natural Systems
- Social

City as Living Lab: Sustainability Made Tangible, Mary Miss, 2006. Image Courtesy the artist

overly opaque and authoritative representations fixed in time.[19] McGrath argues that this practice is only possible when design education is released from mandatory solo exceptional invention. It is also possible when digital representation explores and makes tangible the spectacular psychological complexity of human and nonhuman interactions. Similarly ecologist Steward Pickett notes that given the changing forms of cities globally, novel ecological circumstances will probably emerge for which prematurely fixed codes and best management practices may not fit.

An example of change in design education is Parsons' New School for Design. Starting in 2003 the university as a whole recognized that the impact of "globalization, emancipatory movements, ecological crises and new media technologies dramatically shifted the perception of traditional disciplinary paradigms and their ability to both know fully and, more importantly, to engage with these issues."[20] These four *Wicked Problems* were then translated into three bridging themes; urban, sustainability and media which now allow students and professors with "expertise in specific disciplines to work together in multidisciplinary teams in an interdisciplinary process, in order to better address the complexities of a transdisciplinary issue or problem." This institutional design anticipates the increase in frequency of shocks and trances where on each iteration "issues become more complex, that is increasingly transdisciplinary, so the need for multidisciplinary approaches and interdisciplinary methods increases."

Finally, we can update the role of the scientist away from that of the expert consultant representing made science and engage in science in the making.[21] Scientists can be valued for "their ability to provide frameworks, models, instruments and equipment, their capacity to record and listen to the swarming of different imperceptible propositions that demand to be taken into account." It is "their ability to zoom in on an order of preference going from large to small that unblocks the situation by shifting the weight of the necessary compromises to other beings and other properties."[22] In other words their continual observation and theorization of the non-visual spectrum should not be an excuse to wait for the results. Nor should it be an excuse to not wait for the results but rather it could be taken as an invitation for urban designers to co-design ecological models that are conversant with the integrative frameworks that brought ecology together in the 1980s. This non-linear or non-hierarchical relationship between sciences and design is being tested in the BES. In this Long Term Ecological Research project, the watershed approach, patch dynamics and the Human Ecosystem Framework are used as integrative frameworks between sciences and design.[23]

Sensing

After the observation of non-linear dynamics in ecosystems, what the ecosystem scientists didn't do was choose names for the other types of ecological events. These events are made up of combinations such as: fast onset, long duration and quick release; fast onset, short duration and slow release; slow onset, long duration and quick release; slow onset, short duration and slow release,

and so on. The response options to these events increases the complexity of the understanding of an event, such as; immediate or lagged response to the onset, long or short duration and temporary or permanent release.[24] However patterns do exist. Our cities consist of attentive circuits between older, slower growth megalopolis that are rapidly retooling their oil-based economies and younger, rapidly urbanizing megacities that are hybridizing and mimicking the oil-based economies. Both the megalopolis and the mega-city are being transformed by the meta-city which is emerging in the cracks and voids in the old metropolis, in the formalization of the informal settlements of the mega-city and in a reconstitution of the landscape of sprawl.[25]

What cannot be addressed in the conference with a manifesto model of exchange is mega-city to meta-city feedback. The mega-city which emerged at the colonial periphery, post-World War II, is the result of a breakdown of the enforced controls of rural migrations to the city. It often consists of a highly efficient urbanism where resource scarcity, frugality and sweat equity may be more economically resilient than the subdivisions of suburbia.[26] William R Burch Jr from the Yale School of Forestry and Environmental Studies notes that humans are still learning to live in cities. Following his evolutionary time scale, everyday mega-city actors can be seen to have developed justified claims to specialized knowledge. Our next sequence of urban design forums needs to be designed to provide settings for these emergent identities to be taken into consideration, for shared imagination and action toward radically new modes of collaboration.[27]

This increasingly heterogeneous landscape is the wild ecosystem within which freshly attuned young and old urban designers are practicing today. Renewing the initial promise of urban design, they are developing the rare ability to see large scale-patterns with a simultaneous focus on small scale detail, incorporating feedback from the bottom up.[28] In addition they are developing the new skill of translating the meaning of ecological theory into cultural practice. Clearly it's going to take a while for urban designers and everyday urban actors to sort, sense or engage the non-linear dynamics of urban ecosystems into practices of sustainable action in relation to cities as resilient ecological systems. Informed by the cuts between the disjunctive frames that these three distinct conferences represent, as well as emerging urban design, education, science and collaboration practices, it seems possible.

Acknowledgements

This work has benefited from collaboration with Brian McGrath, Grahame Shane and Joel Towers as well as the the Baltimore Ecosystem Study, which is supported by the National Science Foundation.

References

1. C.S. Holling, C.S. Resilience and Stability of Ecological Systems, Annual Review of Ecology and Systematics, *1973, 4:1-23*
2. Pickett, Steward T. and White, P.S. The Ecology of Natural Disturbance and Patch Dynamics. *San Diego: Academic Press, 1985*

3. Gunderson, Lance H. Ecological Resilience—In Theory and Application, *Annual Review of Ecology and Systematics 31:425-39, 2003*

4. Pickett, pxiii

5. Shane, Grahame. Recombinant Urbanism. *London: Wiley, 2005, p. 151*

6. Shane, p. 74

7. http://www.ecostudies.org/cary_conferences.html

8. http://www.cityclimate.no/

9. http://www.upenn.edu/penniur/afteroil/index.html

10. IES Visitor Information flyer

11. McGrath, Brian et al. Designing Patch Dynamics. *New York: Columbia University Press, 2007*

12. Pickett, Steward T. et al. Urban Ecological Systems: Foundations and a Decade of Progress, Journal of Environmental Management, *(in review)*

13. http://www.ceunet.org/

14. http://americancity.org/afteroil/

15. http://dotearth.blogs.nytimes.com/2008/11/25/is-world-in-obamas-shock-and-trance-mode/?emc=eta1

16. Gensko, Gary and Guattari, Felix. Toward a Transdiscliplinary Metamethodology. *Angelaki Vol. 8, No. 1, April, 2003*

17. http://www.marymiss.com

18. http://www.isles.org/

19. McGrath, Brian. Digital Modelling for Urban Design. *London: Wiley, 2008, p. 14*

20. Martshall, Tim and Erlhoff, Michael eds. Design Dictionary. *Germany: Birkhauser Verlag, 2008, p. 134*

21. Callon, Michel; lascoumbes, P. and Barthe, Y. Acting in an Uncertain World—An Essay on Technical Democracy. *Cambridge, MA: MIT Press, 2001, p. 126*

22. Latour, Bruno. Politics of Nature: How to Bring the Sciences into Democracy. *Cambridge, MA: Harvard University Press, 2004, p. 137*

23. http://www.beslter.org/, http://www.lternet.edu/

24. Lecture notes; Steward Pickett, IDC, School of Design Strategies, Parsons, Nov 2008

25. McGrath, Brian and Marshall, Victoria. "New Patterns in Urban Design," AD Magazine. Ed. Mark Garcia, Nov/Dec 2009, p. 52,

26. McGrath

27. Latour, S.S. p. 130

28. Shane, p. 74

Victoria Marshall *is a practicing landscape architect and urban designer as well as an Assistant Professor of Urban Design at Parsons the New School for Design in the School of Design Strategies. Originally from Australia, Marshall completed graduate studies at the University of Pennsylvania in 1997 and has taught at that school as well as Columbia University, Pratt Institute, the University of Toronto and Harvard University. Her work has been published in AD magazine and her collaborative research into patch dynamics informs her practice. In 2002 she founded till design. www.tilldesign.com*

BRACKEN, Gregory

Something Rich and Strange

China's recent rise to global prominence has been startling, making this vast country one of the places to watch as the 21st century unfolds. China has long had the reputation in the West of being a strange and exotic land; but what will happen to familiar global capitalism as it takes on Chinese characteristics, particularly in light of the recent economic turmoil that seems to question the feasibility of the Wall Street model? Perhaps the neo-Confucian ethos that still underpins Chinese society can help a world that needs to focus more on sustainability of development rather than the simpler mantra of "greed is good," so savagely discredited in recent months.

China and its East-Asian neighbors may well be able to show the world a new direction for capitalism in the 21st century, neo-Confucianism tends to focus on communal harmony resulting in social comity, rather than on the individual and his or her need for conspicuous success. However, when Deng Xiaoping memorably admonished "some people have to get rich first" in the 1980s, he ushered in a leaner, meaner approach in China's engagement with the global market. More recently China's leaders have begun to be aware of the dangers of allowing inequality to creep into Chinese life—left unchecked it could lead to political instability. The Chinese Communist Party has even begun to implement policies designed to accelerate both the pace of farm-income growth in poorer parts of the country as well as kick-start economic development in some of its interior provinces, two areas of China that have certainly not been getting rich.

Part of this imbalance stems from the historical role played by China's coastal cities—the string of colonial enclaves and treaty ports developed by the Western powers in the 19th century. The brightest jewel in this coastal necklace was Shanghai, the engine room of China's economic growth as well as the test bed of the country's economic innovations during the colonial period. Shanghai is again the nexus of China's global ambitions. The city is attempting to reclaim its once pre-eminent position as Asia's regional hegemon, in short, it intends to become the New York of Asia.

The English word "modern" first entered the Chinese language in Shanghai. In 1842 the city became a Western colony and for the next century-and-a-half it was synonymous with the new, the innovative and the daring. Any change that happened in China during this period was seen in Shanghai before anywhere else. During the city's colonial heyday—the 1920s and 30s—Shanghai was one of the world's top five commercial centers, (London, Paris, New York and Tokyo being the others[1]); the city was also the second-busiest port in the world at that time.[2] After the lengthy hiatus of 1949-90 Shanghai's sudden scramble to rejoin the global market has led to urban redevelopment on a staggering scale.

Richard Turnbull maintains that "[b]y 2000 half the buildings from the late 1940s, the vast majority colonial, had been razed to make way for 200,000 high-rises."[3] Turnbull even refers to Shanghai as "the world's largest construction site."[4] The municipal government is investing heavily in urban infrastructure, what Darryl Chen calls the "hardware of any global city"[5]: Shanghai's first metro line opened in 1994 (it now has three, and is currently constructing three more); the city is home to the world's first commercial Maglev (magnetic levitation) line, which links the new Pudong Airport to the city; elevated motorways have also been snaking their way across the city since the 1990s, as have new river bridges and an outer ring road.

Darryl Chen calls Shanghai "…more a process than a static cityscape, with its explosion of object buildings tempered by new infrastructure, parks and conservation the city presents an almost unique control-model kind of urban subject matter among the world's major metropolises."[6] This can be disconcerting for the inhabitants of the city, with the dislocation and disorientation that has been captured in David Verbeek's film *Shanghai Trance* (2008) showing inhabitants of the city who seem to be no longer able to find their way around, with the result that they miss appointments and lose touch with loved ones.

Darryl Chen also warns against the danger of drawing hasty conclusions about a city like Shanghai, one that lends itself so easily to cliché and one whose presence in popular imagination is fuelled by what he calls "a mythologized past."[7] Nostalgia is something that has featured prominently in Shanghai's recent reinvention of itself; it seems almost to be a self-conscious distancing from what Ackbar Abbas calls the "culture of disappearance" in Shanghai's regional rival Hong Kong. Nostalgia is also something that is to be seen in most recent films set in Shanghai: *Shanghai Triad* (1994), *The White Countess* (2006), *The Painted Veil* (2007), and *Lust, Caution* (2007). All of these deal with the period of the 1920s to the 1940s, a time generally regarded as the city's golden age. This nostalgia can also be seen in urban redevelopments such as Xintiandi in the city's former French Concession, and also, and even more remarkably, in the One City, Nine Towns plan for its outlying areas.

One City, Nine Towns

Influenced by Britain's satellite towns of the 1960s, the One City, Nine Towns strategy was developed as part of the 2001 redevelopment plan for the greater Shanghai region.[8] It is an attempt to answer the increasing need for housing, particularly in Shanghai's manufacturing sector, which has been shifted to outlying areas in order to clean up the old city center. This shift is a part of the city's strategy to regain its world-city ranking, lost after the Communist takeover in 1949. The move of heavy industry to the periphery was meant to reduce pollution and noise in the city center, for the time being, however, these seem to have been replaced by even noisier building sites.

Under the redevelopment plan Shanghai was divided into five classes: the city (within the Ring Road); three major new towns; 11 minor new towns; 22 central rural towns; and finally general rural towns. These new towns

Existing suburban Songjiang

are being built on farmland and most of them lie on the outskirts of existing settlements. Some of these settlements are very large indeed (though perhaps in China they can be considered relatively small).

What sets these new towns apart from the likes of Milton Keynes or Harlow New Town in the United Kingdom is the fact that they each have their own manufactured identity, usually based on a Western urban articulation. The architectural and planning style of each is as follows: Anting (German), Buzhen (Euro-American), Fengcheng (Spanish), Fengjing (Canadian), Gaoqiao (Dutch), Luodian (Nordic), Pujiang (Italian), Zhoupu (Euro-American) and Zhujiajiao (Chinese water town). The decision to introduce Western-style architecture and urban planning is a break with China's traditional rural town development, which has tended to produce urban environments of unremitting grimness, but it is also intended to be a catalyst for future, more imaginative and—I will show—more sustainable development. The choice of these so-called "national" styles may seem at first glance somewhat arbitrary, but there is sometimes a link, for example the German theme for Anting probably relates to the fact that there is a Volkswagen factory there.

These new towns are elite developments and as such are beyond the reach of most of China's vast population. In fact the vast majority of China's citizenry would probably be denied access to them as many are gated and employ security staff. Some of the walled enclaves can contain other, smaller compounds, again with gates and guards, which means that to get home in the evening some residents have to pass through as many as three security checks. It is perhaps ironic that the very fact that a conscious effort has been made to build on Shanghai's colonial past means that these exclusive enclaves, located safely behind their walls and security gates, seem to reflect quite accurately the social order that was common in Shanghai prior to the Communist takeover of 1949.

The gated estate does not produce the sort of knee-jerk reaction of negativity it does in the West because the Chinese have a long tradition of living in family compounds, usually a type of courtyard house known as a *siheyuan*. This in turn influenced the development of the Beijing *hutong* as well as the Shanghai alleyway house or *lilong*. As a pattern it is very different from the West where the tradition now tends to site a building in the middle of a patch of open space; the *siheyuan* would have more in common with ancient Greek and Roman houses, where an atrium or courtyard nestled at the heart of the home.

Songjiang

Songjiang is the only city in the One City, Nine Towns plan. It is located approximately 40 kilometers to the south-west of Shanghai. Like most of the other so-called new towns, Songjiang already existed as a settlement. Founded during the Sui Dynasty (581-618 CE), it is home to some important Tang and Song Dynasty architecture, as well as a university and a science park. It is also an important manufacturing base. The new city zone is 60 square kilometers, with a core area of six square kilometers, within which is located a one-square-kilometer British zone known as Thames Town. Designed by the British firm of Atkins (who won a design competition for the commission in 2001), Thames Town has been lauded for successfully mixing elements from such dissimilar British cities as Oxford and Milton Keynes, (although apart from the fact that both of these cities are undeniably British, it is difficult to see what else might actually link them). Thames Town is the one part of this vast new city that seems to have been largely finished, though it has as yet to be fully occupied.

London telephone kiosk beside pastiche church

Songjiang is being linked to Shanghai via a new high-speed rail link, which should aid commuting, but as for working opportunities in the city itself, the only service that seems to be making any headway is the burgeoning wedding industry (also distinctly European in style). Thames Town is swarming with pretty Chinese models, male and female, all suitably attired and arranging themselves artistically in front of the various picturesque buildings for wedding catalogue photographs. Nothing else seems as yet to have been opened, though some of the shops and restaurants have been fitted out and appear ready to go for whenever people do eventually start to move in.

At the heart of the development is a stone-clad church, complete with spire, but this seems to have been built more as a Las Vegas-style wedding chapel than a religious institution. The building's facade is actually a cladding system designed to look, from a distance, like massive gothic blocks (providing a suitably authentic-looking backdrop for weddings photographs). In addition to this are picturesque red telephone boxes and security guards sporting jaunty red Guards uniforms. Along with the church, the pubs and the squares, this cultural *mise en scène* has been imported wholesale from the West, yet what exactly is it that China is importing? The traditional British cathedral town, such as Salisbury or Canterbury? Or is it something less authentic, like Quinlan Terry's Richmond Riverside? (Although this latter is also undeniably British). Thames Town brings to mind the sort of Britishness more associated with Enid Blyton's Toytown than Edinburgh's New Town, but as a town it does seem to have a good mix of uses and scales (as well as an attractive balance between them).

The new town is a pleasant size and well-designed, but there is a certain sense of dislocation when moving from zone to zone, particularly the link from Thames Town to the circular center of the rest of the enclave (which has a distinctly Postmodernist feel). As a sensation it is not unlike

Pastiche Victorian-Tudor architecture, Thames Town

Neo-classical pastiche, Thames Town

moving from the Main Street USA of Disneyland into Fantasyland. Even in the more straightforward residential areas the air of unreality never seems to quite dissipate, the streets look uncannily like a set for *Desperate Housewives*.

Lake in new park with facsimile of Drakensteyn in the distance

Gaoqiao

Gaoqiao is a large industrial town and port, located on the coast about 20 kilometers north-east of Shanghai. It faces Changxing Island and is close to where the Huangpu debouches into the sea at the mouth of the Yangtze. Like Atkins architects in Songjiang, Rotterdam-based architects KuiperCompagnons have opted for a mix of more straightforward pastiche (this time in the national style of the Netherlands) with some more modern architectural articulation (waterfront villas, courtyard houses and multi-storey apartment buildings). The pastiche elements consist of parallel streets of 17th-century-style canal houses, as well as numerous references to famous landmarks from Dutch architecture, such as the Scheepvaartsmuseum (which contains a Chinese restaurant), Drakensteyn (overlooking a marina), and, of course, the inevitable windmill and drawbridge; they are even building a facsimile of the Amsterdam branch of the famous deBijenkorf department store.

From a distance these pastiche streetscapes give quite a startling feeling (something used to quite telling effect in David Verbeek's film *Shanghai Trance*), as indeed do all the historical references in these new towns.

But up close, seemingly Dutch streets reveal a grasp of neo-classical detailing that is sketchy at best. But then, if one were to take a Chinese person into the grounds of an English or French country house of the 18th century they would probably recoil in horror at the Chinese pagodas to be found there.

BRACKEN, Gregory

Facsimile of Drakensteyn at the new marina

Traditional-looking Dutch windmill overlooking new park

16th-century-style Dutch houses

Traditional-style Dutch drawbridge in new park

Traditional-style Dutch houses overlooking new park

Detailing on the traditional-style Dutch houses

Traditional bridge, old town

Anting

Anting is a sprawling industrial town of just under 70 square kilometers. Located in the Jiading district, about 35 kilometers west of Shanghai, it is known as the International Automobile City because it is home to car manufacturing plants as well as Shanghai's Formula 1 racetrack and Tongji University's new engineering faculty. The town itself has one main thoroughfare, a lot of recently built industrial and residential development, and one pretty pagoda. The German-themed development is located at the eastern edge of the town (the Shanghai side—making it convenient for commuting). Intended as a core residential area it is actually quite peripheral, perhaps the planners mean "core" in the sense of being a new way of thinking about planning? The developers are Albert Speer und Partner, after winning the commission they set up an office on Yan'an Road in Shanghai.

Intended to be home to 40,000 residents, this new town is actually little more than a suburban residential zone, albeit a large one (covering 236 hectares—which would actually make it a moderate-sized residential development by Asian standards). Based on the dimensions of the traditional German medieval town, this new

extension to Anting has the architectural expression of the Bauhaus (though in a far more colorful articulation). There has been a good attempt to mix the uses of the different blocks, and a pleasant civic center has been built at the heart of the development. The irregular and winding roadways, presumably the part of the plan based on the medieval typology, makes for a pleasant layout, with the whole development being beautifully landscaped. A well-thought-out mix of scales has been achieved but the whole enclave feels anything but urban; the most that could be said of it is that it has urban pretensions.

Anting is proving popular with buyers, presumably the managerial-level expatriates based here or local executives with families, which would seem to make the medieval walled-town model particularly appropriate given that the entire compound is gated. Entrances are few and heavily guarded. It will be interesting to see how the civic center gets used. Sadly, it may never achieve anything more than the somewhat flaccid buzz of a suburban shopping center—It is hard to imagine the sort of liveliness seen in a medieval town on market day.

limits to mimicking urban design of Western world w/o incorporating the policies that make it successful

BRACKEN, Gregory

Main entrance, new town

Square, new town

Housing block, new town

Main roadway, new town

Main roadway, new town

Civic center, new town

Housing block overlooking spontaneous street market

Pujiang

Pujiang is the Italian new town, unique in that there was no existing settlement here, neither was there any industry, despite the fact that the site is located on the eastern bank of the Huangpu 15 kilometers south of Shanghai, which makes this the new town closest to the city. This will be important when the World Expo begins in Shanghai on the May 1, 2010, and even after the Expo has ended, this degree of proximity to the city center should help ensure Pujiang will be an attractive prospect for Shanghai's commuters.

Designed by Gregotti Associati International of Italy, a 2.6-square-kilometer plot was first worked out in detail, followed by the construction of a 47-hectare sample area. Several other Italian design firms—such as Battisti, Cellini/Cordeschi, Galantino, Pascolo and Rizzi—were invited to participate on various parts of the plan, designing houses and apartments, with Gregotti Associati acting as overall coordinators of the 10.3-square-kilometer scheme. Another interesting feature of this scheme is that it follows a rigorously rational planning typology rather than the theme-park like designs of most of the rest of the new towns. (This eschewing of nostalgia could be the result of

Greggoti Associati's unsuccessful competition entry for the Grand National Theater competition in Beijing in 1998, where they rather self-consciously imitated traditional Chinese forms—even mimicking roof styles and making lavish use of the color red.)

Unlike most of the new towns cited in this paper, a large proportion of this town's plan has been built, and seems to be well-inhabited. Its schools are operational, as are its shops, offices and restaurants. Oddly enough, it is the least lively. Perhaps when more of the scheme has been built (there are plans for a golf course, a stadium, a swimming pool, playgrounds and bicycle paths) it will lose some of its aridity. The scheme is crossed by a rigid grid of streets and avenues, some of which have canals running down their center (the existing network of irrigation canals between Puxing Road and the Huangpu has been retained and improved). The infrastructure is good but many of the streets lead to dead ends, especially the ones running perpendicular to the river. Bridges and landscaping are in place, but there is no real town center. An Italian-Chinese Square has been completed, also known as a "cultural plaza," it is in reality little more than an attractive open area, with a bell tower, arranged around a shallow carp pool. This, in turn, is overlooked by

BRACKEN, Gregory

Pastiche Italian palazzo

Spontaneous street market

Canal

Main avenue

Canal

Plaza at cultural center

an information office, exhibition center and an Italian restaurant.

Pujiang appears to be popular and is selling well. However, while there are some attractive-looking houses on the new waterways, most of the new town of Pujiang seems to consist of slabs of apartment buildings, which, despite their bright colors, impart a distinctly drab and somewhat arid atmosphere. One odd flight of fancy is the Italian-style palazzo, complete with formal garden, which strikes a distinctly surreal note at the heart of what is otherwise a rigorously rational design. The only part of the whole scheme that seems lively and pleasant is the impromptu street market that has established itself on one of the east-west avenues, showing that even in the most rigorously planned of spaces, the Chinese will still find a way to allow street life to flourish (long may this continue).

Sustainable Development?

Firstly, we need to question the feasibility of building a new town's identity on an old and foreign style. The national styles on which these new towns are based were built up slowly over centuries, even millennia, while these new pastiches are being built, like much of the rest of Shanghai, virtually overnight. As a result they are bound to lack something of the originals. From a distance these streetscapes have a startling effect, up close, however, they soon reveal the emptiness at the heart of the concept. As urban developments they are nothing short of remarkable, but perhaps no more remarkable than what happened in Shanghai between 1842 and 1949, the only difference now is that these borrowed ideas are being imported rather than imposed.

Are these new urban models working? It would seem not. While the developments are providing homes and jobs for some people, they remain enclaves for a small and wealthy elite; and while they are a commercial success, they are being bought by people who do not much care for interacting with one another in the street. Had the towns' designers made more of an effort to incorporate some of China's more traditional housing typologies then perhaps something more interesting and useful might have resulted. This was the case in the 19th century when the traditional Chinese *siheyuan* or courtyard house was reinvented as a Western terraced house, producing an urban typology of immense richness, the alleyway house or *lilong*. These new towns cannot be described as cohesively functioning urban communities in comparison to the *lilong*.

It is perhaps ironic in a city so synonymous with the modern that Shanghai should find itself so obsessed with its past. The increasingly nostalgic view of Shanghai's past is a dangerous road to follow, particularly in a city that wants to reinstate itself at the forefront of Asia's global economy. In a word, the One City, Nine Towns plan is surreal. It takes wealth and imagination to do what Shanghai is doing, and wealth is something the Shanghainese have in abundance. For imagination, these new towns indicate an eagerness on the part of municipal authorities to achieve the sense of urban identity that the colonial-era parts of the city have, against the backdrop of recent less successful approaches.

References

1. Fishman, Ted C. China, Inc., 2006
2. Ibid
3. Ibid
4. Chen, Darryl. "View from Shanghai," Architectural Review, February 2003
5. Ibid
6. Ibid
7. Over the course of a week in April 2007, I visited some of the remarkable new settlements that have been created outside of Shanghai, namely the city of Songjiang as well as three other towns, Gaoqiao, Anting and Pujiang. It was while researching Shanghai's place in the international network of global cities for my PhD in architectural theory at the Technical University of Delft in the Netherlands that I came across the One City, Nine Towns plan for the outlying parts of the city. While this was not actually central to my enquiries, I found these new towns so fascinating, in what they were doing, and more especially how they were doing it, that I felt I simply had to draw attention to them.

Dr. Gregory Bracken *successfully completed a Ph.D. at the Architecture Faculty of Delft University of Technology in the Netherlands in June of this year. His thesis was titled "Thinking Shanghai" and is available at http://www.library.tudelft.nl. Gregory got his B.Sc.Arch. in Bolton Street in 1992 (with distinction in thesis) and an M.Sc.Arch. at TU Delft in 2004 (graduating cum laude). He has lived and worked in Asia since 1993 and has travelled extensively in the region. He also speaks Chinese (Putonghua).*

HEMPEL, Adina

Is *Going Green* another Utopia?

Recently sustainability has made an impressive transformation from a hippie ideology to a universal idea. It seems the word sustainable is filled with new content and used for everything; from being economically, politically and socially aspired to, to anything that is labeled as being fair and green.

The word sustainability has hardly a precise definition and its meaning can only be understood when looking at its use over time. The concept of sustainability (*Nachhaltigkeit*) was commonly used in forestry in the 18th century and was related to the amount of timber that had to be felled per year in order to sustain a vital growth for the following year. This so-called *Nachhaltigkeitsprinzip* (principle of sustainability) was first written down in 1894 as part of the general economic policy for the Federal Prussian Forestry Administration. In general the *Nachhaltigkeitsprinzip* suggests few or no interventions in the natural environment in order to sustain the natural cycle. The last one would save nature completely but eliminate civilization. Civilization, with its technologies and developments, is generally anti-nature. Since the United Nations' Brundtland Report in 1987 environment and development have become partnered fields.[1] Therefore, what seems contradictory from the beginning has kept architects, urbanists and academics discussing and developing new prototypes for sustainable settlements.

Jumeirah Islands. Photo courtesy Micro Urban

Emirates Hills. Photo courtesy Mirco Urban

Greening the desert

The Gulf Region is in the midst of becoming the test field for new sustainable technologies and eco-friendly settlements. How can one speak of sustainability when urbanizing and developing waste areas of desert land? The United Arab Emirates (UAE), in particular is better known for its rapid growth and fast, outward and efficiency oriented mega-projects. Those projects have tried to overcome the traditional properties of the Arabic city. Whereas the old, traditional Arabic city was built around human needs and activities, and had developed a repertoire of urban characteristics for harsh climatic conditions, such as wind towers and courtyards, the 21st century city is witnessing a development, which has abandoned density, concentration and connectivity, in favor of high maintenance communities.

Developments spreading along the coastline and into the desert transform the land into perfectly manicured lawns, water fountains and high-rise communities. Those images of natural scenery from developments such as Jumeirah Islands, even though they may be artificial, lead to local and global investments and sustain the wealth of the local community. The power of the image is directly influencing its marketability and therefore the value of the project. Huge desert projects have not only contributed to one of the largest

Masdar City, architects Foster + Partners. Image courtesy Foster + Partners

real-estate markets, but also to the largest ecological footprint in the world. Urbanizing the desert and building the worlds tallest high-rise and biggest mall are undeniably connected to one of the highest consumptions of energy and, moreover, to the highest use of water for irrigation systems in the world. As a reaction to numerous critics and the recent aim of changing the existing image of the UAE, various LEED[2] certified buildings and zero emission projects, such as Masdar City by Sir Norman Foster, were announced and construction commenced. *Going Green* or *Blue*, as per Nakheel's[3] campaign, has become the synonym for a new sustainable ideology for urban development in the UAE.

Green Utopias

With the newly created identity of *Going Green* or *Blue*, developments trigger attention and higher profit, fueling the continued desire to build large-scale projects. LEED plays a major role in the so-called *green* campaign, as the aspired green-building rating system achieves about 18 percent more profit for the owner.

LEED was established in 1995 in the US and since then about 1,500 buildings have been LEED certified with another 3,000 pre-registered. Compared to the British system BREEAM[4] which has accredited about 100,000 buildings since 1990 on a relatively smaller market, the expansion of the brand LEED seems to be more important then establishing LEED as a sustainable building code.[5] Similar effects can be monitored in the UAE, where investors are generally more interested in the logo LEED and its grade "platinum" than in sustainability itself. LEED until now has not become an overall building regulation, but a private support system for those who prefer and are able to build sustainably. Generally environmental building guidelines should not be an add-on, but a government registered building code, that relates to local climatic conditions.

A major "sustainable" project in the UAE and good bet for the LEED platinum certificate is *Masdar City*, a new zero emission city for 50,000 inhabitants. Located on the outskirts of Abu Dhabi, Masdar City is envisioned as a car free eco-city. Unlike one of the most exclusive and secluded communities in Dubai, Emirates Hills, with its wide open green lawns and huge mansions, Masdar City will revive the ideas of vernacular architecture in the Middle East, such as narrow, shaded walkways and dense urban housing.

HEMPEL, Adina

Through its unique and distinguishable urban concept Masdar City will attract rich investors and wealthy inhabitants in equal numbers. In addition, Masdar City aims to have as close to zero carbon emission per capita as possible. An in-house research team at the newly established Masdar Institute of Science and Technology will develop strategies to reach this quite aggressive target. However, isn't the pure construction of a zero emission city in the desert already consuming an immense amount of energy prior to the objective of zero emission per capita?[6]

Not so *green* realities

Masdar City aims to apply some of the latest building technologies and new energy sufficient methods, some of which make use of local and sustainable building materials, sustainable food and a sustainable transportation system. These methods are not significantly new sustainable practices, and most are already suggested in the currently used green building rating systems. Further, it is to be questioned if Masdar will achieve its zero emission target, when considering the energy consumed by people traveling between Masdar City and Abu Dhabi, as the resident work force is only envisioned for one third of the total inhabitants. Even though Masdar City is set up as a clean and energy sufficient zone, its surroundings operate on a totally different standard. Wouldn't it be more sustainable to build several mini-Masdar cities within existing urban voids instead of one mega bubble in the middle of the desert?

In order to achieve its green goals Masdar City appears to be a controlled sustainable zone offering an aspirational lifestyle for its inhabitants. This differs from the spontaneous mix of lifestyles and loose forms of building that are found on the outskirts of Dubai. Here buildings change as the needs of the inhabitants change; Masdar leaves little room for the adaptation of structures by its inhabitants. Can sustainability only be achieved through an architecture of control and political regulation?

Since industrialization, growth and wealth are a direct consequence of energy use and Masdar City is no exemption to this premise. The Middle East, through the plenty of its natural resources and therefore its economical and political power, has long played a mayor role in terms of the economical, political and social (in)stability of the rest of the world. In order to support social sustainability, stability and the equalization of global wealth, an immense amount of energy support will be required. On the other hand the energy consumption needed for this undertaking will increasingly influence the wealth of the bourgeois society.[7] Given the sheer growing number of expatriate societies in the Middle East and their natural concern with social, cultural and political justification, is an eradication of wealth boundaries between the rich and poor possible at all?

Although Masdar City will be a gigantic long-term test ground for new sustainable technologies with its research center for new methods of energy saving systems ensuring it will be a forerunner of sustainable technology and engineering, it highlights the crisis of architectural vision in sustainable design and urban development. Masdar proves once more that vernacular typologies can keep up with the challenge of environmental sustainability and are therefore widely reused. It seems the concept of sustainability has given the already struggling field of architecture and its search for purpose in the 21st century new meaning. Debates about sustainability arrived at just the right time and place, in order to justify the current developments in architecture and urbanism. Dangerously, the attention given to the concept of sustainability could turn into a generalized attitude towards architecture which overlooks its social, cultural, political and aesthetical dimension and reduces its impact to pure material performance and design decision. The concept of Masdar City, despite its controversial aspects, demonstrates the need for research on new urban and design prototypes within existing urban fabrics and empty quarters.

Apartment blocks on the outskirts of Dubai. Photo courtesy Micro Urban

References

1. Various. Was Bedeutet, Platin? Zur Entwicklung von Nachhaltigkeitsbewertungsverfahren. *Bauphysik 30, 4, pp. 244-256, 2008*

2. LEED (Leadership in Energy and Environmental Design) is the US Green Building Rating System

3. Nakheel is one of three mayor developers (Emaar, Dubai Properties) in Dubai and responsible for mainly all offshore projects, including the Palm Jumeirah and the World Islands

4. BREEAM (BRE Environmental Assessment Method) is the most widely used building assessment method for environmental standards for clients, developers and designers

5. Various. Was Bedeutet, Platin? Zur Entwicklung von Nachhaltigkeitsbewertungsverfahren. *Bauphysik 30, 4, pp. 244-256, 2008*

6. Fernández, John E. Beyond Zero. Volume 18, 2008, p. 6-12

7. Kraft, Sabine. Zeitenwende. Archplus, 2007, p. 24-29

Adina Hempel *is an architect and researcher who is currently based in Dubai after having worked in offices in Hamburg, Berlin and Basel. In 2008 she co-founded the interdisciplinary think tank pr0gress, dedicated to research in architecture and urbanism in the Gulf Region. pr0gress initiated a series of studio based research projects in Dubai, alongside a number of workshops, lectures and exhibitions to support cross-cultural exchange as well as an experimental approach to architecture and urbanism.*

Hempel graduated with distinction, receiving a Master in Architecture from Technical University of Dresden in 2006 and a nomination for the Kurt Beyer Preis. She was an independent research fellow at the American University in Sharjah for her research project "Dimension Dubai," which has been included in a range of publications. She won the Scholarship of the Kulturstiftung Dresdner Bank and studied at Columbia University in New York City focusing on Urban Studies, as well as at the New York Film Academy, specializing on digital filmmaking. She has lectured widely and participated in various conferences, including the AA London, American University of Sharjah, University in Brisbane and University of Kassel.

LI Shiqiao
The Economy of Desire

A development develops two economies simultaneously: the economy of goods and the economy of desire. The economy of goods—which may be seen to be an analogue of natural ecology—seems to be finite and fundamentally sustainable, although we are still finding ways to attain sustainability. The economy of desire, on the other hand, is complex, cultural, libidinal, limitless; it is created not by a simple desire such as hunger which is capable of being fulfilled, but by an abstraction of desire (perhaps through a suppression of the simple desire) which is not sustainable. Under normative conditions, the potentially sustainable economy of goods becomes the surrogate for the economy of desire; putting a finite and sustainable framework around the economy of goods must also involve a parallel but very different endeavor to mitigate the trajectories of excess and obscenity inherent in the economy of desire.

While the prospect of an unsustainable future is recent, its fundamental driving forces have long been in the making. These forces are grounded, among other things, in two basic activities of human life, the production of goods and the fulfillment of desire; but today they are also much more than these. In the late 19th century, Karl Marx showed us that the production of goods was not a simple matter of making with a useful purpose as the goal, but part of complex mechanisms created by the logic of the capital. In this process, the capital alienates humanity in pursuit of its own interests in accumulation and circulation. Sigmund Freud revealed, at about the same time, that human desire is an unpredictable outcome precariously balanced between fulfillment and suppression. The obvious desire and its fulfillment mask an unconscious and insatiable double, which is rooted in libido and manifests itself in various excessive ways. The 20th century has brought a highly vigorous social form that incorporated these two fundamental forces as its grounding principles. This social form—a gigantic and amorphous amalgamation of goods and desires—has deliberately cultivated a separation between human life and all meaningful processes of production and usages of resources, which contributes significantly to the prospect of an unsustainable future. The built environment, it is worth emphasizing, comprises one of the most visible and highly valued social activities, which has tremendous impact on the natural environment. According to the US Green Building Council, buildings consume 72 percent of electricity and account for 39 percent of energy use.[1]

The Abstraction of Goods and Desire

Over the course of the 20th century, we can perhaps see two crucial changes leading towards the current social form. The first is that goods have left their medieval craft tradition, and have become a "system of objects." We live in the midst of this system of objects. In his *System of Objects* (1968) and other writings, Jean Baudrillard points out that the production of signs has replaced the production of goods in the 20th century; goods, in this sense, have become abstracted, and a greater value has been assigned to these abstracted goods. High fashion is an example of this system of abstracted goods; the value as a sign of style far outweighs its usefulness as clothing. Often the abstracted and highly valued goods are referred to as goods with "added value." Baudrillard stresses that the production of goods has entered a new era in which "need" is no longer grounded in use value; need is increasingly constructed. Understood in this way, the definition of sustainability by the Brundtland Commission in 1989, "to meet the needs of the present without compromising the ability of future generations to meet their own needs," would seem to be a dangerous grand delusion. The way we design and construct buildings is an example of this system of objects; buildings are some of the most powerful objects—Dubai can be seen to exemplify today a willful creation of buildings as a system of objects—which are pregnant with endless and long-lasting symbolic values. Construction and destruction of buildings and cities carry deep meanings in the minds of citizens and their enemies. The destruction of the Acropolis by Persian armies and its reconstruction by Pericles and Phedias still mark perhaps the most significant milestone in the history of architecture; the destruction of the World Trade Centre two and half millennia later reinforces the symbolic value of buildings while at the same time announces

Consuming the image of Venice, The Venetian, Macau

a significant shift of the loci of the symbolic values from buildings of faith to buildings of trade.

This constructed need is perhaps best understood as an "image;" in this sense, every product comes with an image which is highly valued. The separation of goods from its craft tradition has placed an extraordinary importance on the value of the image, leading to a condition which might be described as "image culture." Through the electronic and printed media, this image culture generates an "imagined reality" of its own, partially grounded in the reality of goods but partially sustained by the logic of the image—its singularity, excess and reproducibility. Friedrich Kittler, in his important account of the history of media as the history of image production, *Gramophone, Film, Typewriter* (1986), placed Thomas Alva Edison before philosophical and literary figures such as Nietzsche and Goethe as the true hero of our contemporary culture. As in many other aspects of life, the image culture features prominently in contemporary architectural discourse. For instance, Rem Koolhaas's *S,M,L,XL* (1995) is essentially an image of the book. As it is, *S,M,L,XL* subverts reading (too bulky to hold, too digressive to contemplate, too provocative for the coffee table); instead, it reinforces the image of the sacred book in an over-compensated form without actually becoming one. Together with its rich content, *S,M,L,XL* contains an image of research in the forms of observation (stark photography), documentation (statistics) and analyses (maps of connecting lines)—the appearances of the hallmarks of conventional science. This image of research is tremendously attractive to architects who have always desired a greater credibility of architectural knowledge, particularly in the current context of quantity-based quality assessment systems sweeping through global universities. Architectural research has

Standard habitation: luxury apartments in Tung Chung Crescent, Hong Kong

acquired a new vigor in the age of electronic media: it is visible, it is in books and it is guiding architectural practices.

The second change is that desire has left its subsistential biological roots on a mass scale, and it can be seen to have been motivated by the libidinal force; the evidence of this departure, in Freud's formulation, was that desire is capable of moving beyond the pleasure principle, into the realm of a destructive "death drive." In Lacan's analysis, desire is created by an abstract cause (*objet petit a*) which is an inherent lack in human life that does not have a real existence therefore can never be fulfilled. Nevertheless, this abstract cause of desire plays a crucial role in the formation of subjectivity. The democratization of rights and wealth in the 20th century has also brought about a "democratization of desire;" once exclusively the privilege of a small part of the population in traditional societies (hence the bourgeois association of psychoanalysis), desire now becomes a feature of mass culture. This is an extraordinary change.

The social form that sustains a proliferation of desire requires an understanding of desire as having a range, from simple desire (such as hunger) to complex desire (such as *objet petit a*); in this case, we can conceive a middle range (perhaps equivalent to the notion of the middle class between the very rich and the very poor in economic terms) of normative desire which lies between the simple and the complex. Simple desire is closely mapped on to the biological functions of human life, while normative desire departs from them significantly as a psychological formation. Although psychoanalytically uninteresting, normative desire is nevertheless crucially important in the social form brought about partly by the democratization of desire; unlike forms of dysfunctional neurosis, the manifestations of this normative desire take place as a form of mass cultural trends—sexual, romantic, narcissistic and material desires which find surrogated forms in the system of objects, endlessly and instantaneously multiplied and amplified through the printed and electronic media. They arise and intensify—without becoming clinical—from what may be described as a mild form of suppression of simple desire.

The Economy of Desire

Goods and desires, in their abstract forms, have made a crucial alliance with the capital in the 20th century. This is an extraordinarily robust alliance that produced our contemporary consumer society; it has created an "economy of desire." The key to the success of consumer society lies in the production of the laborer, an educational process which may be seen as a mild form of systematic suppression of simple desire. As Hannah Arendt explained in *The Human Condition* (1958), the capital demands laborers, not workers: the laborer labors to the beat of biological necessity and produces, through fragmented labor, consumable products, while the worker works over and above biological necessity and produces long-lasting artifacts. The production of the laborer was achieved through the eradication of the worker. Adam Smith, in his *Wealth of Nations* (1776), already foresaw the economic potential in the production of the laborer in his analysis of the division of labor. The 20th century has produced what Arendt calls the "society of laborers;" in this society, labor is alienating and fragmented toil, and efficiency and discipline are highly valued virtues. Through standardization of curricula, our educational systems serve the purpose of the production of the laborer, rehearsing the realities of standard careers in the interest of the logic of the capital and suppressing aspects of human life that do not comply with this logic. The mild form of suppression of simple desire that gives rise to the fundamental virtues of the society of laborers places an endless demand on the system of objects as ever changing surrogate sites for normative desires on a mass scale. In this context of abstract goods and desire, the laborer, over the course of the 20th century, has successfully been transformed into the consumer; the meaningless and fragmented labor is therefore best compensated by the activity of excessive consumption. For the laborer, purchasing fragments of culture, to follow Arendt, provides a powerful illusion of creation as the image of the worker at his/her productive best. This same fragmentation of labor severs links between all meaningful processes of production, leading to "abstract externalities" where resources and wastes would not be understood and cared for deeply.

education

The dominance of the consumer culture in our daily lives perhaps explains the intensity of its critique. Horkheimer and Adorno, in *Dialectics of Enlightenment* (1944), characterized the mass culture of consumption and the capitalist mode of cultural production as a "culture industry." The mechanical reproduction of the work of art—the birth of the mediated image conceived through its mechanical reproducibility—laid down the foundation of the culture industry. Guy Debord regards the system of objects (abstracted goods and desires) as more than just false consciousness; it has become a new "social relation," a "bad dream" of humanity in *The Society of the Spectacle* (1967). It is a new reality that is entirely fabricated and capable of distorting the real lived world, a *hyperreality*. Debord describes bleakly a world of countless abstracted and exchangeable forms of aspects of human life, propelled by its own destiny of ever-increasing abundance: "commodities are now *all* that there is to see." The more we produce images—and details of life replicating these images—the more we are separated from life, the more we are subject to the manipulation of capital (and the power on its behalf).

The impact of the economy of desire is not just cultural; more importantly, it is also environmental. The economy of desire has promoted and advertised a fetish of limitless growth, and propagated a tremendous fear of shrinkage and reduction gloomily named "recession." Growth, in the history of the human settlement, has only become important recently, with the rise of capitalism. For the medieval city, "God" can perhaps be seen to be the key word; cities, following St Augustine's imagination, were conceived and constructed as a form of mediation between the human and the divine. From the Renaissance to the 18th-century, cities can probably be seen to be sites of propriety, where virtue as proportional relationships between fellow humans (derived but also departed from those between humans and the divine) were formulated, and where art grounded in the aesthetics of proportion displayed a parallel propriety. In this sense, many ancient Asian cities were also results of different schemes of hierarchical propriety. None of them conceptualized growth as having a virtue of its own. However, the 20th century had abandoned God and proportion and given rise to the notion of city as limitless growth; "development"—labeled as sustainable and otherwise—became and remains the key word for our cities in the 21st century. Development is primarily related to

Themed clubhouse, Palais Monaco at Mount Beacon, Kowloon Tong, Hong Kong

the expansion of cities, as the word "developer" indicates. Banks are often presented as development banks, countries are either developed (awaiting redevelopment), developing, or undeveloped. It is as if there is no other reality in urban formation outside the framework of limitless growth. Development as limitless growth is connected to the accumulation and circulation of the global capital in its perpetual search for sources of cheap materials, labor and products. This is a development process that is largely dedicated to the generation of profit, propagating an aesthetic of abundance and symbolic happiness—as our department stores and amusement parks testify—which are some of the essential hallmarks of the society of laborers.

The economy of desire invests huge resources in the technologies of limitless growth. These include efficiency technologies such as mechanization of production, standardization and digitization as a ways of minimizing human errors and increasing quantities without increasing cost; they include circulation technologies such as aviation, shipping, motorized transport and vast stretches of land, sea and air monopolized for their use; they also include hygiene technologies such as antibiotics and proliferation of antisepsis to anticipate the consequences of growth—pollution, dense urban environments, resilient bacteria and viruses. Above all, they include military technologies which open and protect markets and trading routes of goods and supplies. The economy of desire also invests huge resources in constructing needs instead of meeting innate needs. Almost all successful players in this economy run large budgets on advertising; through ubiquitous printed and electronic media, advertising focuses on the construction of abstracted goods and desires. It is here—be it artificial beauty or excessive horse power—that the abstracted goods and desires can be manipulated. Most important of all, it is here that growth becomes endless.

City of endless abundance, Sai Yeung Choi Street, Hong Kong

It is the libidinal roots of the economy of desire that subverts the biological principle of equilibrium and legitimizes limitless growth; in unmediated forms, the endless permutations of libidinal energies could only become swollen to ever larger proportions towards excess and obscenity, like those of Marquis de Sade. Excessive growth—in the form of biological cells (cancer) or species (dinosaur)—is clearly an unwise and unsustainable strategy in the natural ecology. In the fast expanding cities of Asia, the deteriorating quality of our commons—water, soil, air, vegetation—also points to the same destructive potentials of excessive growth. There was a much older form of excessive growth in imperialism and colonization as a legitimate and highly admirable accomplishment, which once resulted in extraordinary increases of wealth and power for colonizers; but it is the 20th-century democratization of desire—motivated by the unfulfillable *objet petit a* and the death drive on a mass scale—that has created the human conditions for limitless growth and the prospect of a destructive future. In today's economic context, growth is still seen as a benign and legitimate cousin of imperialism and colonization, and the global market—seen through the customary speeches of its political and business leaders—continues to legitimize growth by seeking "sustainable development strategies."

If the economy of desire is constructed, there should be a way to construct it differently. Desire on a mass scale perhaps demands a new form of psychoanalysis in the form of critical intellectual and innovative cultural productions. Critical cultural strategies could serve as the mediation for the libidinal energies of desire before they enter into the surrogates of goods on a mass scale, always threatening their own existence with their own death drive. There seems to be a correspondence between the vibrancy of the economies of desire and low reflexivity and the freedom of humor in cultural developments: the phenomenon of commercial cities with thin and market-driven cultural activities; furthermore, the economy of desire resists reflexivity, turning many critical forms of culture into simulacra, in order to protect growth. We often observe how quickly an avant-garde strategy of resistance to capitalism is transformed into a marketing strategy, or a subculture turned into a sellable style. The stake is very high in this contestation between critical culture and the economy of desire. Critical cultural strategies can shift the focus of education from that of the laborer to that of the reflexive producer. Particularly in the educational context of Asian societies, openness towards creativity, freedom of wit and humor, and simple desire, rather than a determined emphasis on efficiency and discipline, would mitigate the powerful process of the production of the laborer. With a possible reconstitution of goods and desires, we can begin to reformulate the scaling down of the force of economic production not always as recession, and the scaling up of critical cultural production not always as the burden of tax-payer's money. Under this assumption, growth would only make sense when it is accompanied by decay of similar magnitude, and development would also acquire connotations conceived through the qualities of human life instead of those conceived through the logic of the capital and the profitability of concrete, steel and glass within the economy of desire.

References

1. http://www.usgbc.org/DisplayPage.aspx?CMSPageID=1718, accessed 19 May 2009

Li Shiqiao *is associate professor at the Department of Architecture, the Chinese University of Hong Kong. He studied architecture at Tsinghua University in Beijing and obtained his PhD from AA School of Architecture and Birkbeck College, University of London. His research is focused on modernity and architecture. His writings appeared in international journals:* Bauwelt, Domus China, World Architecture, Cultural Politics, Theory Culture & Society, Cultural Studies (Wenhua Yanjiu), The Journal of Architecture, Journal of Architectural Education, Architectural Theory Review, *and* Journal of Society of Architectural Historians, *and his books include* Architecture and Modernization *(Beijing, 2009) and* Power and Virtue, Architecture and Intellectual Change in England 1650-1730 *(London and New York: Routledge, 2007). He is External Examiner for PhD degrees at the RMIT University and University of New South Wales, and was International Judge for RIBA President's Medal for Dissertations in 2006. He has been keynote speaker at Peking University, University of Johannesburg, RMIT University, Melbourne University, Southeast University and Beijing Normal University, and lectured at Bartlett School London, University of Pennsylvania, Harbin Institute of Technology, Tsinghua University, and Nanjing University. He practiced architecture in Hong Kong, and taught at AA School of Architecture and National University of Singapore. His architectural designs have won several design awards.*

The Clean Development Mechanism: Tactics of Aggregation

As a developer of projects under the Clean Development Mechanism (or CDM) we at Caspervandertak (CVDT) Consulting position ourselves at the crossroads between companies that implement green projects in developing countries and the providers of financing and technology from industrialized countries. Through assisting such projects to obtain CDM status we enable our clients to obtain an additional revenue stream through the sale of carbon credits, which is key in making such projects financially viable. Getting complex projects off the ground requires a local presence, which is why we locate our offices in the key emerging markets of Asia with our main offices in Beijing and Singapore.

CDM has emerged over the past few years as a substantial source of funding for sustainable projects that aim to achieve a reduction of greenhouse gas emissions. To date, the beneficiaries of CDM funding have mainly consisted of large-scale single installations such as grid connected power projects. Smaller and more distributed emission reduction activities, such as renewable energy and energy savings at the residential level, have been much talked about on the United Nations level but have received relatively little attention from the carbon markets.

The Kyoto Protocol and CDM

The CDM is together with Joint Implementation[1] one of the so-called flexible mechanisms under the Kyoto Protocol that allow greenhouse gas emitters in industrialized countries to offset their emissions at home by supporting emission reduction projects abroad. The idea behind these mechanisms is that emission reductions may be achieved at less cost in developing countries and therefore allow a more cost-effective reduction of greenhouse gas emissions globally.

The CDM focuses on projects in developing countries that do not have a cap on their emissions and provides the framework regulating the eligibility of such projects which ultimately have to be approved by the Executive Board (EB) of the United Nations Framework Convention on Climate Change (UNFCCC). A strict set of rules has been devised to assess the eligibility of projects, which centers around two key elements.

Firstly, a project needs to demonstrate that it reduces greenhouse gasses below the so-called baseline scenario, i.e. what would have happened in absence of the CDM funding. A project can then claim the difference between emissions in the proposed project scenario and the baseline scenario and sell these in the form of carbon credits on the carbon market. Examples include: renewable energy projects displacing fossil-fueled power generation; the prevention of methane emissions from landfills through the utilization of landfill gas; and the reduction of power consumption by increasing energy efficiency.

The second eligibility requirement involves a demonstration that the project could not have happened without CDM funding. This requirement is known as the *additionality* of a project and is generally demonstrated by showing that the baseline scenario is economically more attractive (i.e. has a higher return on investment) or that the project scenario faces barriers that can only be overcome through CDM funding.

Example: Development of the Chinese Wind Sector
The Chinese wind farm sector was almost non-existent prior to the availability of CDM. Wind energy, being substantially more expensive than energy produced by burning coal, generally suffers from a low return on investment. As wind power produces clean energy a typical Chinese wind farm reduces CO_2 emissions by about 100,000 tons bringing in about US$1 million in additional revenues each year through carbon trading.

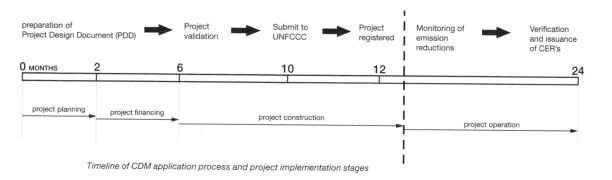

Timeline of CDM application process and project implementation stages

CDM application process

CDM applications involve a rigorous process of approval and verification, which is aimed at ensuring that emission reductions are additional, measurable and verifiable. The first step in the CDM cycle consists of preparation of the Project Design Document (PDD) which describes the proposed project and which needs to be written in accordance with a specific format approved by the UN. This PDD is subsequently submitted for third-party auditing that is carried out by accredited auditing companies known as Designated Operational Entities (or DOEs). When the auditors have established that the project describes the project accurately and meets all criteria for CDM eligibility, the PDD is submitted to the UNFCCC for approval. The final verdict on the project's eligibility then rests with the Executive Board of the UNFCCC which decides whether or not to grant CDM registration status to the project.

Projects can only claim emission reductions under CDM after they have achieved registration status and the actual emission reductions are based on precise monitoring of the project's performance and emissions in accordance with a detailed monitoring plan contained in the PDD. The results of the monitoring process will then be periodically submitted for DOE and UNFCCC approval, upon which Certified Emission Reductions (CERs) are issued.

Development costs and the issue of scale

The CDM application process is costly due to the complex procedures and engagement of specialized expertise in the development and auditing process. These costs easily add up to 60,000 EUR or more until the moment of registration with further costs down the line for verification and issuance. As project size has only a limited impact on the CDM development costs, it is only natural that large projects receive most attention. In addition, the complexity of managing a portfolio of many small projects presents an extra obstacle for small-scale projects to compete with large-volume projects.

However, with the CDM market maturing and more than 1,000 CDM projects having achieved registration status and about 4,000 more projects in the process, there are fewer opportunities for large emission reductions. The attention is therefore changing towards smaller activities,

and mechanisms have been emerging that allow for the aggregation of smaller activities and economize substantially on development costs.

Aggregation mechanisms

With the growing realization that small-scale activities form an untapped potential for achieving emission reductions, several approaches for the aggregation of small-scale projects have been developed recently.

The most straightforward approach towards aggregation consists of bundling several projects under a single CDM project activity. The bundled approach basically stays within the framework developed for regular CDM project activities and applies the same rules. This is, on the one hand, an advantage as the rules for regular CDM projects are relatively clear and experience with such projects has accumulated.

On the other hand, a major drawback to the bundled approach is that it requires all of the project activities to be validated at the same time, which means that precise information on the activities should be available with local government approvals in place. This is often a problem with projects that involve a stage-by-stage scaling up where the details of the project may change during implementation. Most bundled projects have therefore been limited to a relatively small number of activities, and it remains difficult to develop projects that involve the combined emission reductions of hundreds or thousands of installations under the bundled approach.

Example: Bundled CDM development in animal manure management. The treatment of animal manure by letting it decay in deep lagoons is common practice in many developing countries. A side effect is the release of substantial volumes of the greenhouse gas methane as a result of bacteria decomposing the manure. A solution to this problem is the installation of biogas reactors that capture the methane and allow the farms to use this gas as a clean fuel for cooking, heating or the generation of electricity. Such projects are however limited to the availability of manure at the farm and often do not reach the scale necessary to benefit from CDM. However, by applying the same technology across a number of farms and bundling them as one CDM project, these projects are finding their way through the CDM process, bringing additional revenues to the farmers.

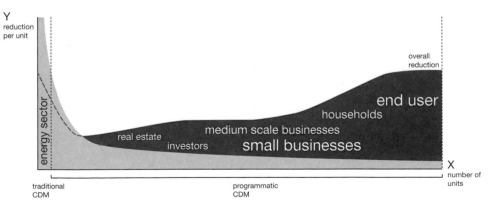

Increased potential for reductions based on Programmatic CDM

An alternative aggregation mechanism that has emerged since 2008 is the Programmatic CDM approach (or pCDM). Under pCDM a Program of Activities is formulated which enables a large number of activities to take place through providing incentives that are made possible through CDM funding. These incentives can include a discount on the procurement of equipment; below market price leasing arrangements, free maintenance; or in some cases even providing a product or service without any cost to the users. The pCDM approach requires the program to define the project activities but does not need to describe the details of implementation. The advantage of this approach is that it allows for the unlimited expansion of the program with new activities as long as these fall within the defined scope of the overall program.

Example: Programmatic CDM enabling the distribution of solar panels. Solar panels for off-grid power in remote villages have clear benefits for sustainable development in poor areas across the developing world. As the impact of one set of panels is tiny, their combined impact can be substantial. Such projects have however suffered from the fact that they are rolled out over several years and are difficult to describe under the regular CDM rules that require the implementation to match exactly the description of the application documents. The programmatic CDM approach makes it possible to benefit from CDM even though the individual impact of one set of panels is too small by defining it as a program. The program defines the specification and conditions under which the panels are placed and allows the program to grow over time as more panels are being placed.

The emergence of aggregation in the carbon markets opens up opportunities for small-scale project activities in a variety of sectors, from the installation of energy efficient light bulbs to small-scale biogas installations, or from solar water heaters to energy efficiency measures in residential buildings.

Although the CDM process formally allows small-scale projects to be developed and benefit from CDM funding, the procedures are generally considered complex and time-consuming. Also, CDM has been struggling with the concept of additionality, which is clearly understood in a theoretical sense but has proven to be difficult to demonstrate and assess in practice. The challenge for the future of CDM lies in the development of mechanisms that make the process less cumbersome and shift the focus from large projects to more distributed activities that have a stronger impact on local sustainable development.

With the COP 15 UN conference at the end of the year new ideas are being brought up in the discussion of a post-Kyoto treaty after 2012. One new concept being proposed is the use of benchmarks, instead of the project-based additionality requirement, allowing firms and projects to claim emission reductions below a set emissions target. Technology is also expected to play a bigger role in the future scheme, as well as incentives to implement emission reduction projects in the poorest countries. The Kyoto system is expected to change from the system that is currently in place, but it seems likely that reforms will be beneficial to smaller projects, creating opportunities for small-scale energy efficiency and renewable energy activities.

References

1. The Joint Implementation (JI) mechanism is aimed at emission reduction projects in countries that have a reduction commitment under the Kyoto Protocol. Therefore such projects are limited to industrialized and transaction countries while CDM is targeted at developing countries.

Joost van Acht is managing director for Southeast Asia at CVDT Consulting, a carbon advisory firm with a focus on Asia. CVDT Consulting works together with local project developers to obtain additional revenues through the CDM process. Since 2004, Joost has been working on projects in China that involve renewable energy, industrial energy efficiency and bio-energy. In 2008 he established the company's Southeast Asia Office in Singapore from where he provides a wider range of carbon advisory services to clients in the region. With climate change a 21st century reality, CVDT Consulting's clients demand a wide range of services. For technology companies this could mean strategic advice on how to benefit from the growing carbon markets, while other clients may need solutions to address and reduce their carbon footprint. The fast paced economic development in Asia provides both an opportunity and a challenge to Climate Change and project development therefore remains a central element of day-to-day activities. By providing emission reduction advice, investment brokerage and technology matching services he assists clients in the implementation of projects that contribute to the sustainable development of Asia.

Regular CDM — Mechanism (carbon credits / revenue from sale of credits) — Market (trading)

Bundled CDM — Mechanism (carbon credits / revenue from sale of credits) — Market (trading)

Programmatic CDM — Mechanism (emission reductions / incentives — Co-ordinating entity — carbon credits / revenue from sale of credits) — Market (trading)

expansion

Different tactics of the Clean Development Mechanism

LIAUW, Laurence

Urbanization of Post-Olympic Beijing

In order to comprehend the effects of the 2008 Olympic Games on Beijing's urbanization, one should look both at its preceding urban development context and future potential post-Olympic strategies needed to sustain it. The 2008 Games as an event catalyst has transformed Old Beijing into New Beijing. Many questions remain for Beijing's future planning now that the spectacle is over. Would Beijing succumb to the same slump that affected many other post-Olympic cities, or could the Chinese capital be radically different in the urban trajectory it now chooses?

Beijing urban development before the 2008 Olympics

Prior to Beijing winning the Olympic bid in 2001, it had held two mega-events that had transformed the city through urban development and spectacle. The 1990 Asian Games and the 1999 People's Republic of China (PRC) 50th Anniversary Celebrations, both had heavy political overtones and an Orwellian precision that characterized China's transformation from a socialist to a market economy over the past 30 years. Since Mao had literally destroyed the Old to establish the New China in Beijing since 1949, urban transformations linked to such mega-events were meant to heal and beautify the city as a political Chinese icon.[1] After membership of the World Trade Organization (WTO) and the failed 2000 Olympic bid, Beijing subsequently rebranded itself as an international metropolis with avant-garde architectural icons symbolizing contemporary China's arrival on to the world stage. This called for a massive overhaul of the city's urban fabric and infrastructure leading up to and after the 2001 bid for the 2008 Games including: 22 new stadiums, 15 renovated facilities, two new Ring Roads, 142 miles of new infrastructure, eight new subway lines, 252 new star-rated hotels, 40km of cleaned rivers, one million new trees and 83km of planted greenbelt.[2] Even an artificial mountain and lake, at the scale of the projects of the Qing Dynasty Emperors, were built in the Olympic Park to symbolize celestial harmony along the extended North-South Axis. The Olympic Park itself is three times the size of New York's Central Park, and the North-South Central Axis linking the Olympic Park with Tiananmen Square is conceived by no less than Albert Speer Jr.[3] Entire new Central Business Districts have sprung up in the vertical image of Hong Kong and Shanghai.

These vast additions to Beijing have come at the expense of older *hutong* streets and housing fabric being forcibly demolished, or socialist-era factories relocated, releasing huge tracts of land—all land is state-owned—for urban renewal. In the post-1998 real estate boom housing prices rose between 400 and 600 percent between 2001 and 2008. With Beijing's vernacular fabric cleared in the same way that Baron Haussmann cleared Paris in the 1800s, recent urban developments have become a global stage for theatrical set pieces complete with neo-traditional gentrified restorations and futuristic landmarks, supported by the Stalinist maxim that *you can't make an omelet without breaking a few eggs*.

An estimated 1.5 million Beijing residents have been relocated to suburban satellite new towns as part of a Modernization Policy,[4] and entire migrant workers districts have been literally erased as officials felt they presented an unsightly image to tourists and Olympic Committee members alike. It is ironic that the hundreds of thousand of migrant workers that literally built the Olympic developments were sent home unable to witness their own creations. Meanwhile the city's population swelled to officially 18 million (with an estimated seven million extra unregistered migrant workers) causing urban development bottlenecks so typical of major Chinese cities today: highway expansion; traffic congestion; air pollution; housing shortages; income gap increases; displacement of locals to peripheral suburbs, and in the case of Beijing, architectural heritage destruction and architectural stylistic confusions.[5] These presented challenges to planners and architects leading up to 2008, with lessons to be learnt from preceding post-Olympic Games cities as well as the experience of the 1990 post-Asian Games.

2008 Olympic Bid and Legacy: Mega Event, Policy and Utopian Tradition

The Olympic Bid Legacy is to make the 2008 Games the biggest and the best ever. Branded as the *"Green Olympics"* the *"Technological Olympics"* and the *"Peoples Olympics"* the claim of the legacy is designed to justify the colossal budget of $42 billion[6] (10 times 2004 Athens' budget and three times London's for 2012).

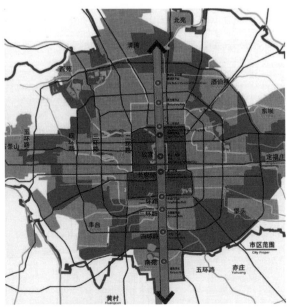

Beijing City Structure Plans showing expansion and N-S Axis, Beijing Municipal Planning Commission. Image courtesy Beijing Tsinghua Planning Institute, 2008

This echoes Chinese grand tradition since Mao to build extensive monuments and infrastructure as physical propaganda to the world to demonstrate political ideologies and give Chinese face, thereby purging historical wounds. Developing Beijing for the 2008 Games at such scale and speed has been likened to a building a new Great Wall. This manifestation of China's biggest ever coming-out party celebrated not only sporting prowess, (winning most gold medals), but also its global economic ascendency and political pride for its own population after recent tragic natural disasters, (such as the 2008 Sichuan earthquake and Lunar New Year snowstorms).

Such massive development to create New Beijing also follows a more brutal urban tradition of Chinese utopias being created through wholesale destruction and rebuilding of both society and cities (Classical Utopia, Soviet Utopia, Modern Utopia as classified by scholar Zhou Rong).[7] Mao's ideological void had been replaced by Olympic development for everyone through the slogan "One World One Dream." The Olympic Games Park in rural northern Beijing and other Olympic sites now acts

as a *tabula rasa* strategy to impose a new ideological order over the chaos of 1990s urban development.

Olympic cities sustaining development—at what cost to the city?

Recent history of such mega-events as an urbanization tool could be traced back to the world fairs and expos of the early 20th century in the US and Europe. However the Olympic Games themselves, despite their scale and prestige, have not always yielded similar successes with respect to sustainable development. 1960 Rome and 1964 Tokyo built new infrastructure projects, 1972 Munich built social housing, while Atlanta and Los Angeles refurbished existing sports facilities. The 1996 Barcelona and 2000 Sydney Games were successful urban regenerations, while 2004 Athens and 1976 Montreal were deemed unsustainable failures leaving behind unused stadiums and huge debts. We need to question both the sustainability of the Olympic Stadium typology and the mechanisms of the Olympic funding model. The Barcelona Effect where debts are recovered quickly through further investments and tourism, as opposed to the Montreal Effect where financial debts took 30 years to pay off. Funding models vary: Munich relied mainly on government funding linked to a social welfare mission; while Los Angeles was sponsored by private finance and made a profit.[8] Financial costs to each city must be balanced with sustained urban growth models, so that new stadiums do not lay idle requiring large, annual maintenance budgets. Currently the Birds Nest™ National Stadium requires annual maintenance of US$15 million, with entrance ticket sales declining from 80,000 daily to 10,000 daily within eight months of the Olympics closing.[9] There are rumored plans to revive the Olympic Opening ceremony extravaganza within the Birds Nest as a show to boost revenues, after discussions to transform it into a hotel and football stadium failed.

Expiry of Olympic types and Sustainable Development—Is Beijing different?

The difference with Beijing is that investment is going into mostly new development rather than redevelopment or regeneration projects compared to other Olympic cities. Furthermore, China is still a developing country with high growth rates compared to other past Olympic cities in more mature economies.[10] Social costs and knock-on effects to nearby regions such as Tianjin Bohai region should also be accounted for. In Beijing's case the service industry was overhauled, communication and energy networks improved, much technological transfer in construction industry included "green building" designs,[11] and certain media freedoms prevailed during the Games.

A housing boom with millions of square feet built per annum in Beijing prior to the Olympics, has created a more mature real estate market, but also vastly inflated home prices and unaffordable housing for locals as well as forced evictions. Inequitable distribution of housing since China's housing reforms in 1998—market-driven private housing was introduced and social housing provision stopped—have been exacerbated by local government taxation laws related to property. Beijing has created

Beijing City Model, 2008—Olympic Green/CBD

Fireworks of the opening ceremony of the Beijing Olympic Games held in the National Stadium, also known as the Bird's Nest, in north Beijing, China. © Erich Schlegel/Dallas Morning News/Corbis

brand new urbanized districts from former agricultural lands in a rapidly rising property market. However the 130,000 hotel rooms built were not fully occupied during the Olympics as predicted and will suffer unless Beijing can continue to boost its tourist industry, especially on the China domestic front, (locals are spending three times the foreign tourist total per annum). Of the $42 billion total Olympic budget, $15 billion was spent on infrastructure with 25 percent spent on upgrading existing facilities. Investment on environmentally polluting road networks was balanced by building new cleaner metro lines and intercity rail links. Radiating developments will spread Beijing's growth outward to integrate the region while de-densifying the city that still has an average living space of only 18 sq meters per person. Due to the scale and speed of construction, Beijing's Olympics is estimated to have created over two million new jobs, compared to the only 150,000 for Sydney and 135,000 estimated for London.[12] These extra jobs are temporary, related to new hardware of the city, while the software of the city needs to continue growing to sustain new job creation after the Olympics.

The "Green Olympics" initiated nearly $17 billion investment into environmental initiatives to clean up the city prior to and after the 2008 Games. Examples include the 83km greenbelt with one million trees planted around Beijing, water recycling, solar heating and geothermal

heat pump systems. Venues such as the Watercube Aquatics Stadium deployed energy-efficient designs and recyclable materials. However what remains to be seen is whether the Clean Air Days (an enforced halving of cars on streets during the Games and rain-inducing chemical rockets from the army) and green building technologies, can themselves be sustained in Beijing's post-Olympic development. Some new stadiums have been integrated into university campuses, or will be converted to other uses after the Games (the Olympic Media Centre was designed to be converted into a much needed convention center with hotel).

The Beijing Olympics have also been called the "world's largest single urban development since the Pyramids"[13] by Prof John MacAloon, so long-term urban planning and investment must be considered in a self-sustaining manner to reduce the burden on future generations. Beijing's Deputy Mayor and the Beijing Olympic Organizing Committee were advised by international experts on sustainable Olympic urban development as a "once in a lifetime opportunity to change the way the city operates, the feeling citizens have and the perception of the rest of the world towards Beijing and China." Policy recommendations included "looking hard at essential future stakeholder needs of the city and questioning what type of facilities/infrastructure to build. Opportunities for Beijing include transportation emission controls, water conservation, waste management, energy efficiency, improving air quality, sustainable building design, etc."

Society of the Spectacle, Soft Monuments and City Branding

But would these "Green and Technical Olympics" really provide what the "Peoples Olympics" need in a sustained manner beyond the pride and spectacle of the Games themselves? The opening and closing ceremonies of the Beijing Olympics within the Birds Nest National Stadium are now legendary for their Zhang Yimou-directed extravaganza that celebrated Chinese culture with hi-tech special effects.

Notwithstanding the huge production cost and media coverage of this "event as Olympic architecture," China for 17 days in 2008 became a *Society of Spectacle to the world*, either real or fabricated (including lip-synched theme songs, digitally rendered fireworks, and staged participants in Tiananmen Square). Arguably the Chinese people had been waiting for 100 years for this

Beijing Urban Masterplan 2005-2020. Image courtesy Laurence Liauw/CUHK

glorious moment, and the legacy of this event should be sealed in our collective memory through images and symbolic monuments at all costs. Rumored to have cost over $300 million,[14] Chinese people interviewed on the street generally applauded the mythic quality of the Olympic ceremonies held amid a national fervor not seen since the Cultural Revolution. Such temporary visual spectacles created by architectural events are what urban theorist Paul Virilio calls soft monuments as opposed to traditional hard monuments. He describes them as "disembodied electrical signals that dissolve solid forms" and as "petty narrative(s) of practical opportunity" characterized by the "contemporary monumentality of installations."[15] In this sense, the Olympic events at the Birds Nest and Water Cube are no different from those created in Tiananmen Square by the Communist Party in previous years, except that Olympic development exists within an ideological trap of a depoliticized slogan: "One World One Dream." The National Stadium architects Herzog de Meuron have even likened it to the Eiffel Tower of Beijing.[16] Architecture has become part of city brand-ing machine through mediated imagery, and no longer related to Aldo Rossi's typological permanence.[17]

Endless City, Keeping the Dream Alive and the People's City

Pre-Olympic masterplans (2005-2020) for post-Olympic Beijing reveal that most of the surrounding context of the Olympic Park will remain unchanged, and approximately 2.3 million sqm GFA of land within the Olympic Green, (which is the 2.5 sq km rectangular park containing most of the main Olympic venues including the Birds Nest and Water Cube) is planned for new development into a commercial and cultural zone, complete with under-ground shopping malls. Various real-estate swaps and the redevelopment of Olympic facilities will render many into non-sporting venues aimed at tourism and mass-market commercial developments.[18] Stadiums will house new tourist and leisure programs. The copyrighted Beijing Olympic brand is no doubt a strong one in the Chinese consciousness, but how will such typical developments and monumental scale of the Olympic Green keep the (Chinese) Olympic Dream alive? One needs to ask if this dream is worth maintaining through memorializing the Olympic Park. Should it be returned to Beijing's citizens as accessible city fabric as part of the *The People's City*?[19]

Pre-Olympic urban problems listed previously have returned to Beijing after the Games' temporary solutions, and it is time for more permanent measures to sustain Beijing's development in a coherent manner. The eventual expiration of Olympic types is unavoidable, and the best way forward is to gradually dissolve them and keep urban-izing the city through its refabrication (see our proposal below). Richard Burdett and Deyan Sudjic's new book *The Endless City* describes the megacities of our future as globally competing metropolises bursting with both potential and urban problems.[20] If Beijing became one of the projected megacities with over 30 million inhabitants, it would signal a return to *Dadu* (Great Capital) when Yuan Dynasty Imperial Beijing was the biggest and grandest city in the world. While other cities in the developed economies are shrinking, China's cities continue to expand. Beijing

溶解奥林匹克公园-梦想远去，还于市民

Dissolving the Olympic Park /
Landscape Infrastructure
溶解奥林匹克公园/景观基础建设

Dispersing the landscape is dispersed /
local scale fabric emerges and grows
分散景观/本土比例的肌理出现和生长

Urbanization process of Mesh Densification
evolves over time
网状密度随时间发展的都市化进程

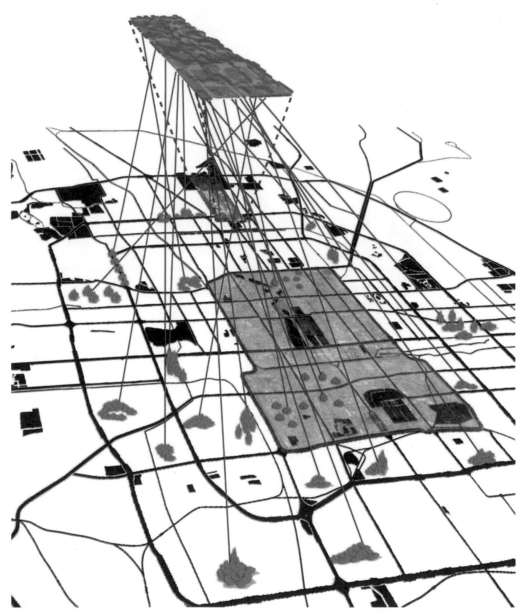

Proposed 4 Stages of Post-Olympic Urbanization Process—Dissolve, Urbanize, Disperse, Re-Fabricate. 1. Dissolving the Olympic Park/Landscape Infrastructure. 2. Dispersing the landscape is dispersed/local scale fabric emerges and grows. 3. Urbanization process of inhabitable mesh densification evolves over time. 4. Fully urbanized urban fabric around monumental types re-fabricates the city. Image courtesy Laurence Liauw, Ray Wong, Andrew Yu, 2008

Dissolving and refabricating Beijing Olympic Park back into the city. Variable type fabrication as urban strategy for sustainable development.
Image courtesy Laurence Liauw, Ray Wong, Andrew Yu, 2008

has now a golden opportunity to fulfill its potential again through sustained urbanization, as long as it can coherently accommodate differences in scales, types and programs.

Dissolving and Refabricating Beijing — Urban Manifesto As New Idea of City

In response to this Post-Olympic challenge, I have produced a collaborative project proposal (with Ray Wong and Andrew Yu at the Chinese University of Hong Kong) to dissolve the Olympic Park back into the city (as landscape catalytic infrastructure) and fully urbanize the Olympic Green as a new district for mixed income living-leisure.[21] With our intensification strategy on re-fabricating the Olympic Park as city through evolved typological transformations and variable proliferation, public land and green space is freed up to be redistributed to much needed areas in other parts of Beijing. We are fundamentally opposed to the idea of concentrating so much open space in one Olympic Green area whilst the rest of the city is choking, for the sake of preserving a monumental dream. Through multiple strategies of density exchange, public green space creation, environmental infrastructure,

neo-mat urbanism,[22] multi-scalar renewable types, anti-monument, variable courtyard fabric as new landscape, accretion and open participation, we believe that Beijing can sustain its current development path to overcome some of the urban problems that have plagued it since the 1990s. This project proposes an urban manifesto that can once again ideologically influence the course of urbanism in Beijing beyond mere market dynamics. Beijing will evolve (as Rome has over time) into a new polemical idea for the city through continuous, variable and catalytic development that recognizes the limited lifespan of the Olympics and recharges the People's City for future generations.

Do the 2008 Olympics represent the apex of Beijing's current development or will the inevitable expiry of unsustainable Olympic types lead Beijing down the path of Ancient Rome. Reformulating long-term prospects of post-Olympic Beijing must start with the premise of questioning of how Olympic urban fabric and landscape was made in China — at rapid speed, iconic, symbolic, generic, political and decorative — without much concern for the social, cultural and architectural qualities of the city. Our proposal's new urban paradigm of dissolving landscape and variable type fabrication could be implemented over

6. Walters, M; Kumar, P. & Lim, M. *Beijing Beyond the Olympics. Urban Land Institute, Feb 2008*

7. Rong, Zhou. *"AD New Urban China,"* Architectural Design, vol 78 No 5, 2008, p. 36-39

8. Walters, M; Kumar, P. & Lim, M. *Beijing Beyond the Olympics. Urban Land Institute, Feb 2008*

9. *"All Form, No People" article, Newsweek, April 6-13, 2009*

10. *Ibid*

11. *United Nations Environmental Program (UNEP) reported on Beijing's $17bn invested in clean air initiatives since winning the bid in 2001*

12. Chernushenko, David. *"Sustainable Development through the Olympics: Using Partnership to Seize the Opportunity," presented to the Beijing Olympic Organizing Committee, 2005*

13. *"Delivering the Olympic Dream," ch10, Professor MacAloon is an Olympic anthropologist in Kellog on China, Northwestern University Press, 2004*

14. *http://english.ntdtv.com, Aug 21, 2008, interview with China analyst Jason Ma*

15. Virilio, Paul. *The Virtual Dimension. Princeton Architectural Press, 1989*

16. Lubow, Arthur. *Quoting Herzog de Meuron in "The China Syndrome,"* New York Times, May 21, 2006

17. Rossi, Aldo. *The Architecture of the City. MIT Press, 1984*

18. *Xin Ao Group is a property developer linked to local government who is leading post-Olympic development of the Olympic Green, Jones Lang Lasalle White Paper, April 2008*

19. Wang Jun and Shi Jian. *"The Peoples City" essays in* AD New Urban China, Architectural Design, *vol 78 No 5, 2008*

20. *Endless City. Eds. Ricky Burdett & Deyan Sudjic. Phaidon, 2007*

21. *"Refabricating Post-Olympic Beijing" proposal is a collaboration by Laurence Liauw, Ray Wong and Andrew Yu assisted by Chen Yue, Li Jingwen, Wong Ka Wing*

22. *Mat Urbanism refers to a 1960s movement in architecture that uses thickened 2D mat surfaces as a primary device to generate 3D form. Typified by projects such as Le Corbusier's Venice Hospital and Candilis, Josic, Woods' Berlin Free University, this way of conceptualizing architecture as continuous mat form is currently enjoying renewed interest in contemporary architecture.*

Laurence Liauw Wie-wu *is an associate professor at the School of Architecture, Chinese University of Hong Kong, a UK-registered architect who practiced in the UK, Malaysia, Mainland China and Hong Kong after graduating from the Architectural Association School in London. His main area of interest is contemporary Chinese urbanism, typological evolution and post-generic cities, through research publications, and consultancy work. Professional practice has included building arts and social institutions, residential and planning projects in UK, China and Malaysia. Published internationally, he research-produced with the BBC a program on the rapid urbanization of the Pearl River Delta in 1997. He was guest-editor of 2008 publication AD: New Urban China and 2007 World Architecture publication Hong Kong Good Bad and Ugly 1997-2007. Liauw has won competitions and awards for his architectural projects, and has exhibited internationally, including at the 2006 Venice Architecture Biennale, the 2007 Shenzhen-Hong Kong Biennale, and at the New York Skyscraper Museum, 2008. He has lectured at AA London, Columbia University, Harvard GSD, China-India Institute New York, Tsinghua University, Central Academy of Fine Art, and was an invited jury critic to AA London, GSD, Columbia GSAPP, Cooper Union and MIT.*

the next 30 years as Beijing becomes a truly global city having the ideological power to influence the development of other cities. This would close the chapter on the 2008 Beijing Olympics and start a new page in the future of contemporary Chinese urbanism.

References

1. Liauw, Laurence (ed.) *AD New Urban China, Architectural Design, Vol 78 No 5, 2008, p. 8*

2. Christensen, Ben and Hand, David. *Accelerating Towards a New Beijing, Jones Lang Lasalle White Paper, April 2008, p. 5*

3. *Albert Speer Jr's father was Albert Speer, Adolf Hitler's chief architect, a member of his inner circle. Speer had made plans to reconstruct Berlin on a grand scale, with huge buildings and wide boulevards centered around a three-mile-long grand boulevard running North-South Axis, which Speer called the Prachtstrasse, or Street of Magnificence, which was never built.*

4. Campanella, Thomas. *The Concrete Dragon, Princeton Architectural Press, 2008, p. 127.* Author Laurence Liauw witnessed an overnight erasure of an entire migrant worker village on 3rd Ring Road en route to Beijing Airport in 2008.

5. *Ex-Mayor of Beijing Chen Xitong favored all major new buildings to have "Chinese style upturned roofs" on modern facades, prior to his*

PIPAN, Tomaz

Three Sustainabilities

Peri-urban condition in the vicinity of Dongguan, Guangdong Province, Pearl River Delta, China

Apart from the bustling new cities of China that extend into the domain of metropolises and are the new economic centers of Chinese developments, there is another kind of reality. This reality exists in the shadow of these prosperous new cities, and if it were entirely up to the Chinese, it would be hidden from foreign sight. These are places without which the Chinese economical reformation would not be possible at all: places like Dongguan—a peripheral-urban basin in Guangdong Province. This peri-urban landscape consists of kilometer upon kilometer of fragmented parts—interlocking low-end housing, industrial assembling plants and agriculture.

Dongguan basin is one of the biggest producers and exporters of consumer goods (mainly electronics, toys and garments), in Guangdong and in China in general. It is highly dependent on foreign capital investments and global markets. With this fact in mind, it is not hard to understand that a decrease of consumption in the Western world as a direct consequence of the credit crunch could have a devastating effect on mono-functional production oriented areas such as Dongguan. "About 20 percent of the small [toy] factories in Dongguang closed this year"[1] and the economical forecast for the near future is not optimistic. Furthermore, if we couple this idea with the fact that people living in these peri-urban areas come from the lower end of the social strata, we get a volatile mixture of events and conditions that could lead to a huge socio-economical crisis.

This brief text offers some alternatives to the mono-functional developments as exemplified by Dongguan. It examines ways to make this environment more sustainable in three major areas—society, economy and spatial form. It explores these three intricately connected fields and offers a more sustainable alternative for each. Apart from offering new alternatives it also looks for the imbedded potential of these spatial configurations that could be harnessed as a sustainable advantage; making the area more resistant to drastic economical fluctuations as exemplified by the current economic crisis.

Before venturing into the possibilities a definition of the peri-urban condition is needed.

Peri-urban condition

Dongguan's peri-urban basin is a mono-functional re-development of a rural area geared towards labor-intensive manufacturing that proliferates a completely new type of landscape. As mentioned, this landscape consists of great areas of fragmented parts—interlocking low-end housing, industry assembling plants and agriculture. It is a domain of hard working people, laboring day and night in assembly and production plants. It is home to China's strength—lower-class diligent workers and farmers—the production force of the new Chinese economy.

New lower-class housing grows between industries and villages. The *checker blocks* are usually four to six storeys high with just a few meters between each block. The new typologies disregard the traditional spatial and social practices, furthermore, the economic standard of people living here is not great, and the consequences ripple throughout the social and physical landscape. Most common public space is the street, dominated by trucks and cars. Scarce and degraded public spaces with only rudimentary services and no leisure activities are combined with only basic education facilities—no universities, no theaters or cinemas. A vast population of millions, that can easily rival any European city in area and density alike, is living in village-like conurbations.

When confronted with this peri-urban condition on such an immense scale, some very vital questions start to surface. Why did the fabric stay in this stage of development? How is it that there are no internal processes or catalysts that could transform it into a more urban and social environment? Part of the answer lies in the nature of the *traditional economical model*. Alternatives should be found (if momentarily only academic ones) that can bring about better economical and therefore also social sustainability of these areas.

Economic sustainability

The *traditional economical model* advocates the economical and social transformation of society on the basis of the main production sectors. It follows the logic of economy and capitalism and could be argued is a linear model whereby agricultural production is replaced by industry and sequentially by services and tertiary sector production. The leap from one stage to the next only happens when the current mode of production is not economically viable anymore, and a more profitable one is needed in order to sustain its development. In the case of the peri-urban industrial areas of Dongguan, this has not yet happened; the industrial production is still the main vehicle for development, so there is no need to establish a new one.

There are many repercussions of this kind of urbanization; notably that during the agricultural and industrial stages the social and spatial structure is really poor. The financial situation of the farmers and workers is not

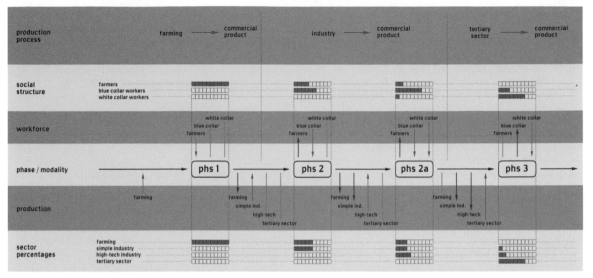

Traditional economic model

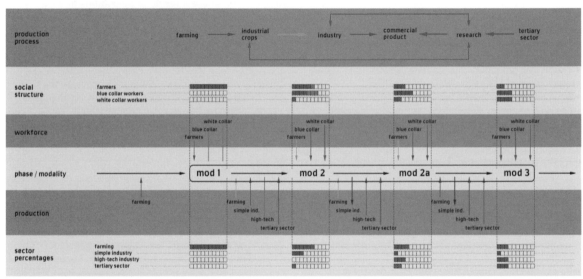

Sustainable economic model

sufficient for the development of sophisticated leisure and services. Another serious problem is the mono-functional orientation which leads to economical and spatial unsustainability. For example, the car industry in the United States until the late 1970s gave rise to a vast amount of industrial cities, of which Detroit is the most famous. When the car industry crashed, the repercussions on the social and spatial strata were devastating. We can ask ourselves quite legitimately, what will happen to Dongguan in the light of the current economical crisis? Will a vast majority of the population be without a job when the crisis deepens and the export of consumer goods like electronic gadgets, toys and other luxury goods decreases?

The self-organized "Darwinian" model will always face these kinds of problems; it will always be unsustainable as it favors the fittest on the basis of capitalism and economical drive.

By understanding this process, a different kind of economic model can be put forward that accommodates for better social and spatial conditions and facilitates a more sustainable development strategy. This sustainable model has to start to blur the sharp boundaries between phases and work against the short-sighted economical drive. By dissolving the boundaries, different phases of the model start to mix and interact, creating modalities of one phase rather than distinctively different phases. This is done through linking the now separate production of different stages into one interdependent loop where each stage contributes to the final product of the other stage or, in turn, uses the product of another stage. This model argues for a dynamic and interdependent side-by-side development of the previously mentioned three basic production sectors (agriculture, industry and services).

Social sustainabilty

The switch of the economic model enables a better social sustainability as well. A good precedent can be set through introducing the tertiary sector into the mix. By adding the educated and economically more affluent class, an environment that is economically more capable is generated; therefore, it brings about a better service sector and consequently better amenities and open spaces for everyone. This is in turn beneficial to the less well off. One of the more suitable programs for the integration of the tertiary sector is research and development (R&D) geared towards innovation. By addressing the industrial and rural environment, this innovation has to be accordingly targeted; it should focus on research of industrial crops, agricultural cultivation and industrial production techniques.

This outlined sustainable model is clearly idealistic with numerous obstacles that must be overcome. The most apparent drawbacks are as follows:

• The spatial proximity of sectors from an economic point of view is irrelevant as the contemporary technological advancements in transportation and communication can more than compensate.
• The higher educated classes have little interest in living in peri-urban areas and mixing with workers.
• R&D and science parks need premier research universities as innovation generating institutions,"[2] something that production oriented areas like Dongguan chronically lack.
• The only input to R&D comes from educated classes, thus the importance of the worker class is diminished.

On the surface, it seems that the presented model is indeed hopelessly idealistic, but the switch from a capital based, "natural selection" model to a sustainable one requires acknowledgment of more profound benefits that are strategic in nature and not immediately obvious.

• Innovation can substantially benefit from the local context as knowledge is embedded in culture and culture is always regional and specific.
• By retaining agriculture and industrial production in the mix, crucial inputs are retained in the form of skills that inform the innovation environment geared towards researching these sectors. Agriculture also reduces food miles contributing to a more sustainable system.
• By extending the scope to three sectors, the area gains in economical sustainability as an urban entity making new fabric more flexible.
• By bringing workers and farmers into the R&D process they can be educated, thus helping the local economy, and more importantly, the local community.

Even with all of these benefits, it should be taken into account that R&D in this kind of environment could not be expected to produce great breakthroughs right away. Rather, it is a long-term strategic investment and a mechanism for social stabilization.

The change of the economical model would not bring about better definition, hierarchy and structure to the already existing fabric. To make this fabric more sustainable and liveable, there has to be a significant change in governing policies, and maybe even more importantly, a change in the way the peri-urban condition is understood. A change of mindset is required to find a *new urbanity* within the existing condition.

Spatial sustainability

Firstly the existing fabric and spatial organization is examined and looked at from the point of view of sustainable urban form. Later a proposal is made that examines additional organizational principles that can enhance the already existing rules.

Although the physical reality of these areas is rather grim, the pure formal and morphological organization tells a different story. The inherent potential that could be harnessed as a main design tool for a next generation of sustainable developments is situated beneath the hard everyday exterior of these areas.

One of the more intriguing spatial features is the proximity of different fabric organizations and their adjacency. This unplanned development and interlocking character of fabric gives rise to a unique spatial condition, mixing dwelling, industry and agriculture. This spatial logic is completely different from a Western zoning logic. It is a difference that Richard Sennett in his paper *The Open City*[3] describes as a difference between the "open city" (mixed, permeable, flexible and open to change) and a "brittle city" (controlled, defined and rigid).[4]

In spite of the outlined strong fragmentation and close super-imposition, there still is a natural separational logic that manifests itself in a very useful way. Production (mainly industries) accumulates along the infrastructural grid. Dwelling ecology develops in between the industrial production corridors, spawning from existing villages. The latter, more loosely connected configuration could be seen as a local dwelling system. This separational logic of tightly woven corridors gives the system spatial flexibility. Both corridors negotiate for space and can accommodate more or less fabric, depending on the need. The first system, called the Regional Corridor, accounts for freight transport and regional connections. The second system, called the Local Corridor, accounts for all the activities connected to everyday living.

When these two systems intersect they tend to develop new organizations that usually account for rudimentary services and can be seen as the beginnings of urbanity. These instances of programmatic mixing can be understood as nodes linking both systems together. Furthermore, they can be used as nodal elements so that both systems can be controlled simultaneously. With new strategies and policies in mind, they can be redeployed as growth control mechanisms in similar spatial conditions to Dongguan.

In the Regional Corridor, the prevailing organization is the enclosed, aggregation of different parts. Although being enclosed and mono-functional, these clusters are good organizations in how they bring together different parts and organize them around common open space. This creates a dense, varied and above all, highly adaptable organization that can accommodate change easily.

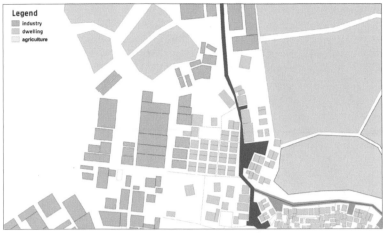

Legend
- industry
- dwelling
- agriculture

Spatial proximities and adjacencies of the existing fabric

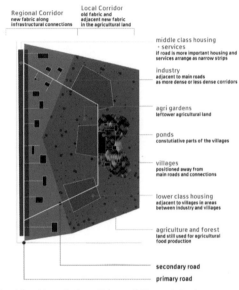

Regional Corridor
new fabric along
infrastructural connections

Local Corridor
old fabric and
adjacent new fabric
in the agricultural land

middle class housing
+ services
if road is more important housing and
services arrange as narrow strips

industry
adjacent to main roads
as more dense or less dense corridors

agri gardens
leftover agricultural land

ponds
constutiative parts of the villages

villages
positioned away from
main roads and connections

lower class housing
adjacent to villages in areas
between industry and villages

agriculture and forest
land still used for agricultural
food production

secondary road

primary road

Local and Regional Corridors, their spatial negotiation and structure

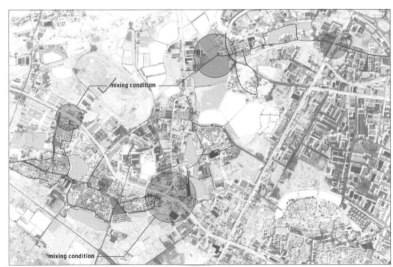

mixing condition

mixing condition

Corridor intersections generate program mixing conditions that can be redeployed as growth control mechanisms

Enclosed clusters as predominant organizations of Regional Corridor

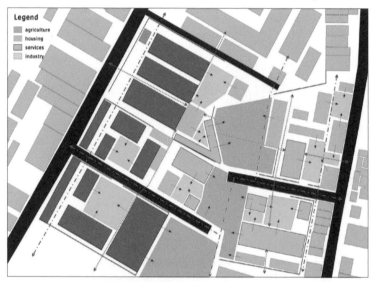

Reconnecting the infrastructural grid opens new possibilities of use

The potential of small-scale spaces that is vital to urbanity (right) is unexploited in peri-urban environments (left)

Clusters operate as individual cells and do not engage the surrounding fabric resulting in the intermittence of the infrastructural grid. By changing the permeability of clusters and their orientation, the disconnected network could be reconnected and a better organization of areas could be envisioned. The permeability would enable much more varied and interconnected environment mixing different production sectors with housing and services to create *a new kind of urbanity of peripheral areas*.

After critically examining the existing fabric organizations, the form of the current fabric reveals itself to be highly adaptable and versatile—much more so than a traditional zoned city of the West. Taking the argument one step further, a legitimate question could be posed: Could this type of fabric because of its capacity to embed change and allow for differentiation be perceived as better than a strictly planned and rigorously regulated one? Due to its adaptability is this type of fabric strategically better positioned to deal with the upcoming economical uncertainties?

However, this view of the existing peri-urban organizations should be challenged as there are real problems; not just socially and economically but also spatially and morphologically speaking. One of the biggest problems is that the current urbanization and development of these areas is largely perceived on a large scale. Consequently, planning these areas remains at this scale resulting in the formation of large, monofunctional areas that are not suited for small-scale urban living. Planning at this scale has a direct repercussion in that *the stitches*—the spaces between planned areas—remain unresolved, degraded and unused. These are the spaces that have the most potential to make the area more urban, defined and structured.

If we compare this condition with the city environment, we can see that in the city these kinds of spatial fragments take the most prominent role as generators of public, urban space. The reason that the city environment uses these elements so efficiently lies partly in the fact that the urban space "construction" and definition in the city is derived from a much smaller scale which is in part possible due to the fact that the tertiary sector elements that usually constitute these fragments (bank, post office, church, shop, cinema, etc) do not require much space. A tightly packed and varied city program generates a lot of activity in a very limited space. This creates urbanity, nodality and hierarchy—all the ingredients needed for dense urban space. In the peri-urban condition on the other hand, the primary and secondary production sectors of agriculture and industry require large areas to function and cannot develop dense, varied and contained spaces.

Proposition

To enhance the current urban organization of peri-urban fabric like Dongguan, a new proposal has to upgrade the current spatial organization and integrate concepts of urban construction that are used in the city environment. The *stitched* areas of the peri-urban fabric should be resolved on a smaller scale with finer detail. However, there are no spatial elements like the tertiary sector that can generate urbanity. Instead, we must look into processes within the sectors that are spatially not so demanding

and could be taken out of these areas and assembled into a tighter spatial relation. In this way *a new kind of spatial experience* is generated, similar to the urban experience found in the city. Along these lines and on the basis of the city's existing spatial organization, the proposal puts forward dense mixing nodes of rural-urban systems that structure and consolidate this vast landscape.

For example, a local agricultural node could be structured as follows. First it is necessary to define the elements and parts of the agricultural process that are spatially not so demanding and can be detached from agricultural land. These elements can be then put together as a node as generators of public space. Such elements could be: hydroponics, allotments, rice milling processing, crop storage and preparation, field machinery, tool storage or a local food market.

To define the mixing node, the organization and workflow of the processes has to be understood. The diagram shows the functional system of a food production cycle that is connected to local distribution (market) and global distribution (wholesale). The systems are kept apart so that the global distribution does not obstruct the local market activities. The organizational diagram shows an application of the food production cycle diagram within an agricultural node.

Drawing on existing local material intelligence and enhancing it with finer resolution in the newly designed mixing nodes, a better defined and structured fabric is proposed. The emerging large-scale gridded network is composed of all three basic sectors and dwelling: agriculture (as the initial substance), industry (aggregated along the Regional Corridors), services (clustered in mixing node organizations) and housing with daily activities (dominating the Local Corridor). The proposal creates a completely new kind of dense environment—intertwining production and dwelling in a structured, hierarchical way, yet making it flexible and designed to accommodate market fluxes. Through this the fabric becomes much more sustainable and robust.

Conclusion

Peri-urban production oriented areas in China like Dongguan are areas of lower social strata—workers and farmers. Although these areas have their disadvantages with respect to social conditions, the fabric's ability to accommodate change and its character offers a lot of potential. With minute changes in the way these spatial configurations are understood, new set of policies and design approaches can be devised that turn the area's disadvantage into an unprecedented opportunity. The inherent character of the area that manifests itself in the never finished, interlocking character of spatial parts is a great starting point to drive the urbanization into a completely different, more sustainable direction. By attaching spatial possibilities to the non-linear sustainable socio-economical model, these areas can be offered an alternative future to the one currently pursued.

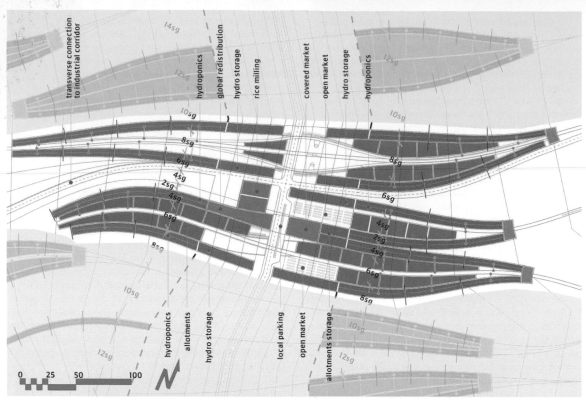

Image labels (top to bottom, left to right):

transverse connection to industrial corridor · 14sg · 12sg · hydroponics · global redistribution · hydro storage · rice milling · covered market · open market · hydro storage · hydroponics · 12sg · 10sg · 8sg · 6sg · 4sg · 2sg · 4sg · 6sg · 8sg · 10sg · 8sg · 6sg · 4sg · 2sg · 4sg · 6sg · 8sg · 10sg · 12sg · hydroponics · allotments · hydro storage · local parking · open market · allotments storage · 12sg

0   25   50   100   N

Organizational diagram of agricultural node

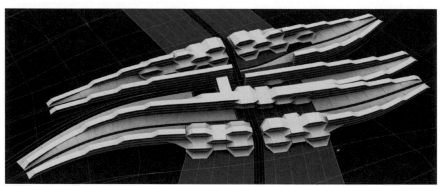

Spatial (design) diagram of agricultural node

References

1. http://www.newsgd.com/news/guangdong1/content/2008-11/06/content_4690858.htm

2. Walcott, Susan M. *Chinese Science and Technology Industrial Parks.* Ashgate Publishing Limited, 2003, p. 176

3. http://www.urban-age.net/0_downloads/Berlin_Richard_Sennett_2006-The_Open_City.pdf

4. Although Sennett does not talk about primary and secondary production sectors, the organizational principles indicate that there is a way of making industrial and agrarian areas part of the new urban experience and that these peri-urban organizations are more flexible and accommodate change better than traditional city like organizations.

Tomaz Pipan is an urbanist and an architect. He understands the city as a dynamic intertwining of spatial, economical and social processes. He seeks how to understand and manipulate these processes in order to devise and create new and better urban living environments. His work is a bifurcation of theory and praxis, and ranges from architectural and urban projects to teaching and research.

After finishing undergraduate program in Urbanism at the School of Architecture in Ljubljana in 2005, he worked as a part-time assistant at the University. He also worked for Elastik where he was engaged in projects ranging from architectural to urban designs. After moving to London in 2006 he worked at Chora, an architectural and urban research laboratory, mainly on urban projects and was a design assistant at London Metropolitan University. In 2008 he finished an MA course in Landscape Urbanism at the Architectural Association School of Architecture in London. His general research direction dealt with spatial urban organizations and the performance of urban fabric. Currently he is working in the landscape architectural office of Gustafson and Porter in London.

TERREFORM

NEW YORK CITY
(STEADY) STATE

www.terreform.info

This large-scale inquiry seeks to answer the question: Can New York City
become self-sufficient within its political boundaries? Intended to be an
alternative masterplan for the city's
future, this study investigates the
possibility for urban self-reliance
in such areas as food, energy,
waste, water, air supply and quality,
manufacture, employment, culture,
health and transport. The predicate
of the study lies both in questions
of the limits of sustainability and in
a response to the failures of democratic autonomy in an increasingly
globalized economy. The study aims
to produce not simply a dramatic
new plan for the future of New York,
but to compile an inventory of best
practices that are relevant to cities
around the world.

TERREFORM is a non-profit (501.C.3) organization dedicated to research into the
forms and practices of just and sustainable
architecture and urbanism. Founded in 2005
by Michael Sorkin, and located in New York
City, Terreform undertakes self-initiated
investigations into both local and global
issues and is a resource for community and
other organizations to support independent environmental and planning initiatives.
Current Terreform researchers include
Brian Baldor, Auptha Surli Dev, Aleksandra
Djurasovic, Shirish Joshi, Max Mecklenburg
and Francis Milloy.

Single-family house at present

Single-family house, 5-10-yr scenario

Single-family house, 30-yr scenario

In a low-density, single-family house scenario, yard space ceases its decorative role and becomes essential ground for steady-state practices. In this example, a typical outer-borough house and yard have been refitted for water harvesting, bee-keeping, wind power generation, and hydroponic greenhouses. To maintain year-round food production, windows, staircases and exterior vertical surfaces are converted into small-scale greenhouses and 20% of interior space is utilized for aeroponic food production. Adjoining impermeable street and sidewalk surfaces are replaced with permeable paving and rainwater is stored in underground cisterns. The roof is not simply greened but furnished with wind turbines and photovoltaic and solar hot water panels.

Apartment building present situation

Apartment building, 5–10 yr scenario

Apartment building, 30-year scenario

This medium-sized apartment building deploys a range of sustainable technologies and practices that will allow it to become a near-autonomous organism. It grows its food, treats its waste, harvests energy, and collects and recycles water. The rooftop becomes a particularly intensive production site, where food is grown in greenhouses, energy is harvested by wind turbines and solar panels, and rainwater is collected and channeled to the apartments. Within the building, food is grown hydroponically and water and waste are recycled and re-used. The proposed system separates and reuses yellow and black water, which become fertilizer and other raw materials. Adjoining buildings are connected via aerial greenways which function as both circulation devices and greenhouses. The vertical surfaces of the building are also active farming ground.

Hamilton Heights block at present

Hamilton Heights block, 5-10-yr scenario

Hamilton Heights block, 30-yr scenario

The scale of the block allows attainment of a very high level of autonomy, closing the loop of production, distribution, and consumption for its population. As the city comes to use walking, biking, and public transport as its primary means of movement, 50% of the street surface will be opened up for intensive agriculture (and other public uses), fed by recycled grey and waste water. The buildings of the block will also become productive areas as living and working are mixed and new technologies of self-sufficiency are introduced. The rooftops of the block will be furnished with solar panels, wind turbines, greenhouses, and aquaponic tanks. Interior spaces will house small and medium scaled hydroponic systems. The existing centralized municipal waste water system will be replaced by a local, distributed, biologically-based operation, to reuse, recycle, and compost this valuable commodity.

CHU, Yan

SUSTAINABLE DEVELOPMENT AND ARCHITECTURE

What is sustainable development for architecture? The United Nations Brundtland Report of 1987 defines sustainable development as "meeting the needs of the present without compromising the ability of future generations to meet their own needs." Such a definition requires a consideration of the overlaps of social, environmental and economic concerns.

The Geo Data Portal, an environmental database produced by the United Nations Environment Programme, serves as a basis for environmental assessments. The following graph illustrates all available regional variables from the database, which is further sub-divided to illustrate the correlative effect of each region's social, environmental and economic performance. If the success of China's economy comes with environmental devastation, but also a positive progression in social standards, then how is one to mediate these consequences towards a sustainable model of development?

Seen together, this data provokes the following questions:

Is such a model of sustainable development plausible? How can architecture assume a definitive role within this complex web of relationships? How can one begin to translate this intangible information into productive tools for architects?

If sustainable development by definition eludes conclusive resolutions, how is one to begin?

YAN CHU received her Masters in Architecture from Princeton University.

highest energy production 2004

highest GDP per capita

most electrical output from nuclear power reactors

highest total carbon dioxide emissions

highest emissions of CO2 from transport

highest forest average annual change

highest forest average annual change

highest total CO2 emissions

highest urban population

most wetlands of international importance

highest population growth rate 2005 - 2010

highest urban population

most animal species threatened

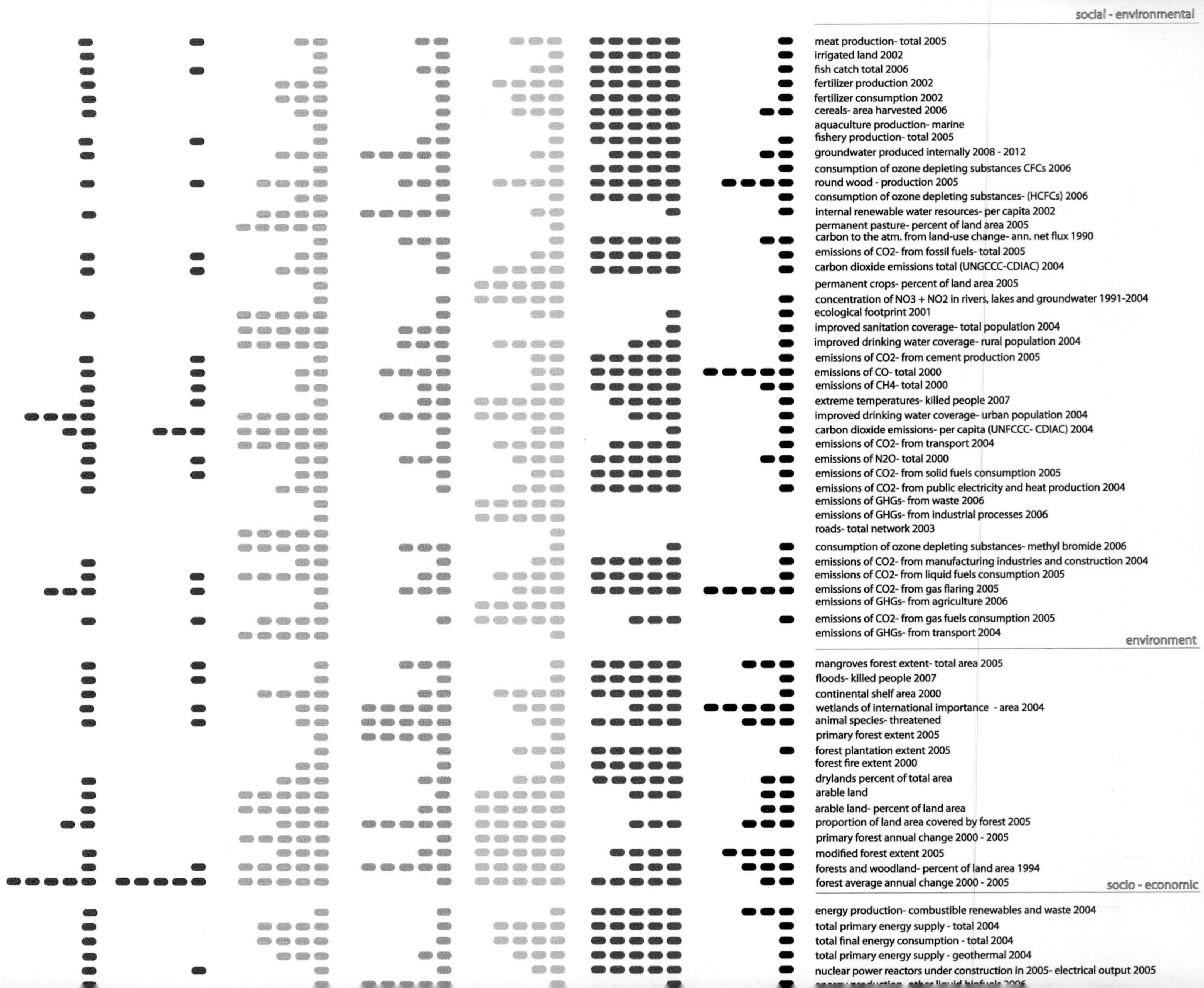

- meat production- total 2005
- irrigated land 2002
- fish catch total 2006
- fertilizer production 2002
- fertilizer consumption 2002
- cereals- area harvested 2006
- aquaculture production- marine
- fishery production- total 2005
- groundwater produced internally 2008 - 2012
- consumption of ozone depleting substances CFCs 2006
- round wood - production 2005
- consumption of ozone depleting substances- (HCFCs) 2006
- internal renewable water resources- per capita 2002
- permanent pasture- percent of land area 2005
- carbon to the atm. from land-use change- ann. net flux 1990
- emissions of CO_2 from fossil fuels- total 2005
- carbon dioxide emissions total (UNGCCC-CDIAC) 2004
- permanent crops- percent of land area 2005
- concentration of NO3 + NO2 in rivers, lakes and groundwater 1991-2004
- ecological footprint 2001
- improved sanitation coverage- total population 2004
- improved drinking water coverage- rural population 2004
- emissions of CO_2 from cement production 2005
- emissions of CO- total 2000
- emissions of CH4- total 2000
- extreme temperatures- killed people 2007
- improved drinking water coverage- urban population 2004
- carbon dioxide emissions- per capita (UNFCCC- CDIAC) 2004
- emissions of CO_2 from transport 2004
- emissions of N2O- total 2000
- emissions of CO_2 from solid fuels consumption 2005
- emissions of CO_2 from public electricity and heat production 2004
- emissions of GHGs- from waste 2006
- emissions of GHGs- from industrial processes 2006
- roads- total network 2003
- consumption of ozone depleting substances- methyl bromide 2006
- emissions of CO_2 from manufacturing industries and construction 2004
- emissions of CO_2 from liquid fuels consumption 2005
- emissions of CO_2 from gas flaring 2005
- emissions of GHGs- from agriculture 2006
- emissions of CO_2 from gas fuels consumption 2005
- emissions of GHGs- from transport 2004

- mangroves forest extent- total area 2005
- floods- killed people 2007
- continental shelf area 2000
- wetlands of international importance - area 2004
- animal species- threatened
- primary forest extent 2005
- forest plantation extent 2005
- forest fire extent 2000
- drylands percent of total area
- arable land
- arable land- percent of land area
- proportion of land area covered by forest 2005
- primary forest annual change 2000 - 2005
- modified forest extent 2005
- forests and woodland- percent of land area 1994
- forest average annual change 2000 - 2005

- energy production- combustible renewables and waste 2004
- total primary energy supply - total 2004
- total final energy consumption - total 2004
- total primary energy supply - geothermal 2004
- nuclear power reactors under construction in 2005- electrical output 2005

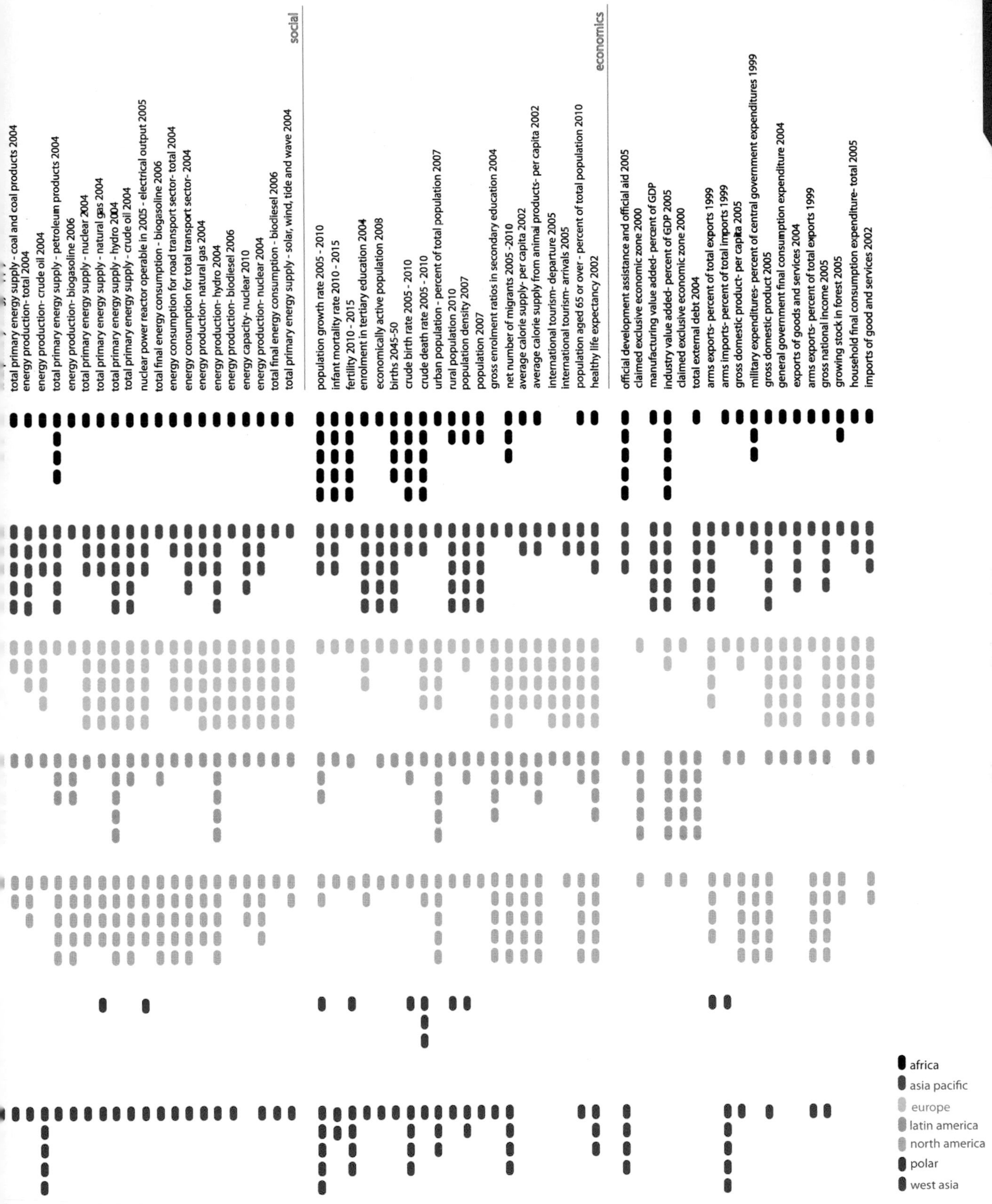

Column labels (social):
- total primary energy supply - coal and coal products 2004
- energy production- total 2004
- energy production- crude oil 2004
- energy production- biogasoline 2006
- total primary energy supply - petroleum products 2004
- total primary energy supply - nuclear 2004
- total primary energy supply - natural gas 2004
- total primary energy supply - hydro 2004
- total primary energy supply - crude oil 2004
- nuclear power reactor operable in 2005 - electrical output 2005
- total final energy consumption - biogasoline 2006
- energy consumption for road transport sector- total 2004
- energy consumption for total transport sector- 2004
- energy production- natural gas 2004
- energy production- hydro 2004
- energy production- biodiesel 2006
- energy capacity- nuclear 2010
- energy production- nuclear 2004
- total final energy consumption - biodiesel 2006
- total primary energy supply - solar, wind, tide and wave 2004
- population growth rate 2005 - 2010
- infant mortality rate 2010 - 2015
- fertility 2010 - 2015
- enrolment in tertiary education 2004
- economically active population 2008
- births 2045-50
- crude birth rate 2005 - 2010
- crude death rate 2005 - 2010
- urban population - percent of total population 2007
- rural population 2010
- population density 2007
- population 2007
- gross enrolment ratios in secondary education 2004
- net number of migrants 2005 -2010
- average calorie supply- per capita 2002
- average calorie supply from animal products- per capita 2002
- international tourism- departure 2005
- international tourism- arrivals 2005
- population aged 65 or over - percent of total population 2010
- healthy life expectancy 2002

Column labels (economics):
- official development assistance and official aid 2005
- claimed exclusive economic zone 2000
- manufacturing value added- percent of GDP
- industry value added- percent of GDP 2005
- claimed exclusive economic zone 2000
- total external debt 2004
- arms exports- percent of total exports 1999
- arms imports- percent of total imports 1999
- gross domestic product- per capita 2005
- military expenditures- percent of central government expenditures 1999
- gross domestic product 2005
- general government final consumption expenditure 2004
- exports of goods and services 2004
- arms exports- percent of total exports 1999
- gross national income 2005
- growing stock in forest 2005
- household final consumption expenditure- total 2005
- imports of good and services 2002

Legend:
- africa
- asia pacific
- europe
- latin america
- north america
- polar
- west asia

source: United Nations Environmental Programme, Geo Data Portal

GATTEGNO, Nataly

RECOMBINANT ECOLOGIES: RESILIENT INTERVENTIONS IN ATHENS, GREECE

Wallenberg Studio, University of Michigan, Taubman College, Winter 2009

This studio explored potential for resilience in urban Athens; resilient urban interventions, capable of adapting, flourishing, recombining and synthesizing with the urban fabric and infrastructure. The studio took the position of un-fortifying, opening and decentralizing the city's university structure by proposing a new Athens Urban University; a transparent, networked ecology in contrast to the fortifications of current university structures; highly integrated and open—a place for urban exchange and education. The studio explored the potential for resilience to be achieved through the synthesis and hybridization of urban elements as opposed to the careful sequestering of our urban habitats. These recombinant ecologies perform at multiple time scales, seasons and phases. What is the potential of occupying these fluctuating scenarios? Can these synthetic recombinations of program, infrastructure, energy, site and systems become robust urban habitats? When do they optimally perform? What emerges at the junction of architecture, landscape architecture, ecology and hydrology? What are the latent possibilities within these recombinant ecologies?

What was once a US military base four miles from the Acropolis and the site of mass airlifts from the Middle East and Northern Africa is slated to be developed as public space. This studio explored ways of strategically and opportunistically intervening on the site of the old Ellinikon airport. It proposed a series of spines, arteries and programmatic scaffoldings to occupy the site and explored the potential for these conduitsto become programmable sites and remediating channels, knots within the urban landscape. We experimented with permanence and temporality, performance and phasing, the capacity for program to change and adapt, to yield gradients of possible environments—in other words, to be resilient and productive.

This was studio was funded by the University of Michigan to travel to Athens visit the site and participate in Ecoweek—an international design conference and charrette.

Active Energy/Landscape Systems
Anemoi Pier

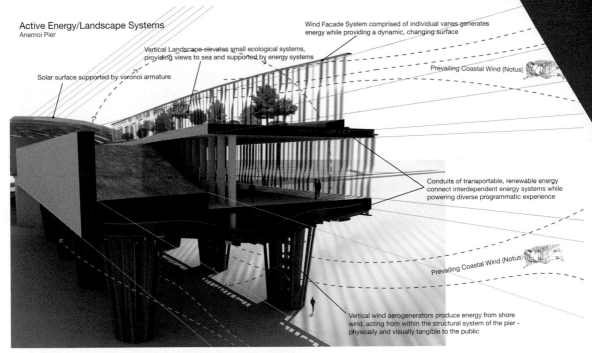

Wind Facade System comprised of individual vanes generates energy while providing a dynamic, changing surface

Vertical Landscape elevates small ecological systems, providing views to sea and supported by energy systems

Solar surface supported by voronoi armature

Prevailing Coastal Wind (Notus)

Conduits of transportable, renewable energy connect interdependent energy systems while powering diverse programmatic experience

Prevailing Coastal Wind (Notus)

Vertical wind aerogenerators produce energy from shore wind, acting from within the structural system of the pier - physically and visually tangible to the public

Active energy and landscape systems calibrated to the prevailing wind direction

Andrew Zyrowski, Anemoi Pier

Anemoi Pier is an urban intervention connecting the city to the sea. The pier constantly harnesses the turbulent wind conditions of the site, processing raw energy. Wind is the catalyst for economical and social change within Ellinikon and the surrounding area of Athens—through the progressive development of energy systems literally powering public space.

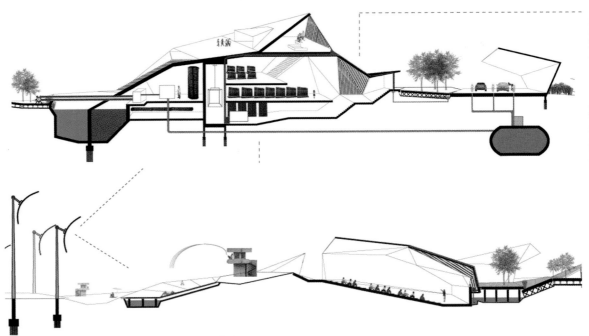

Rick Cosgrove, Algacultural Catalyst

Large groups of locals infiltrate the Ellinikon site in Athens, cranking wrecking balls into the air with gantry cranes to smash up the useless concrete runway of the old airport. New ideas arise: the resulting rubble could be contained with wire mesh cages to create pervious surfaces to facilitate water collection. That water can be harnessed and transformed into algae growth for biodiesel and clean water. A new face develops for Ellinikon: a park for recreation, schooling, and interaction. The park continues to contribute positive energy through algaculture to the city of Athens.

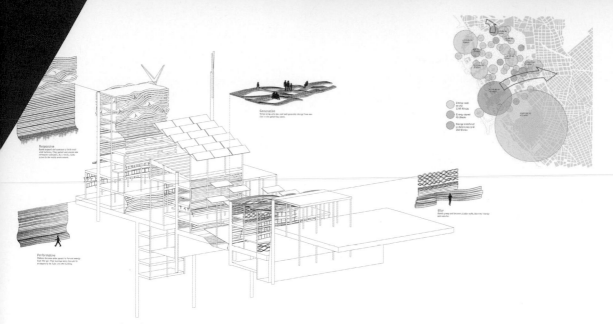

Productive Ribbon Axonometric. Strip of the energy system highlighting the bands which create enclosure and define space. They function to collect energy from the environment, generate power and blur boundaries between interior and exterior, above and below ground and building and landscape.

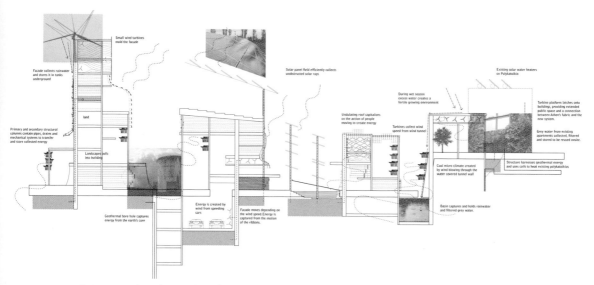

Systems Section. Diagram of the integration of energy collection systems with landscape and the built environment. The systems recombine with the surroundings to generate space and create new ecologies.

Amanda Winn, Tensioned Energies

Sited in the homogenous city of Athens, Greece, Tensioned Energies uses an incremental development strategy currently existing in the city to blur the boundaries between landscape, energy and the built environment. The exchange between the three capitalizes on the everyday flux of activities Athens offers while allowing for variance and performability. The framework facilitates a gradient of enclosure between landscape, building, energy, and politics; it looks at the relationship between aboveground and underground, and uses energy systems as connectors between the two. From collection, to storage, to usage, the systems allow for continual exchange between the ground and the atmosphere, exaggerating the "above" or producing a new "under."

Tensioned Energy also examines and challenges the relationship between activities associated with above and underground; Open and public versus secret and avant-garde. Subtle shifts push these programs next to one another, creating new interactions. The tension generates a dynamic atmosphere, continually adapting to changes in energy flows. The project strives to engage in the current political energy Athens offers while integrating energy systems, landscape and architecture.

ZOTES-LOPEZ, Marcos

poroCITY

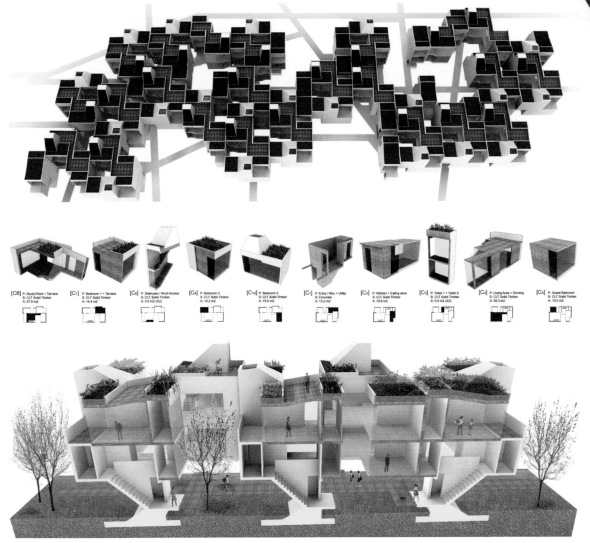

[C6] P: Study/Work + Terrace S: CLT Solid Timber A: 27.6 m2
[C7] P: Bedroom 1 + Terrace S: CLT Solid Timber A: 14.4 m2
[C8] P: Staircase / Roof Access S: CLT Solid Timber A: 3.0 m2 (X2)
[C9] P: Bedroom 2 S: CLT Solid Timber A: 13.2 m2
[C10] P: Bedroom 3 S: CLT Solid Timber A: 15.0 m2
[C1] P: Entry / Rec + Utility S: Concrete A: 13.2 m2
[C2] P: Kitchen + Eating area S: CLT Solid Timber A: 15.6 m2
[C3] P: Toilet 1 + Toilet 2 S: CLT Solid Timber A: 5.0 m2 (X2)
[C4] P: Living Area + Dinning S: CLT Solid Timber A: 35.3 m2
[C5] P: Guest Bedroom S: CLT Solid Timber A: 10.0 m2

Flood housing prototype

For many people around the world, the dangers associated with flooding are serious. Climate change is causing heavier precipitation and sea levels are rising as the polar ice caps melt, threatening not only coastal areas, but also low-lying cities and entire countries.

The project originates as a reaction to the current housing and planning strategies affecting large suburban areas in the Thames Gateway zone in the UK, where thousands of new, ordinary homes have been planned for areas that are at high risk of flooding. In these scenarios, the endless repetition of identical housing units along linear streets creates monotonous cityscapes, lacking in character and having little to offer. The monofunctionality of such schemes produces deserted streetscapes in which social interaction and community life is reduced to a minimum and the use of the car becomes an essential element of the everyday life.

poroCITY presents a housing prototype that challenges the conventional implications of the family home and offers a new suburban lifestyle in a very dynamic and unique environment. Keeping its impact onsite to a minimum, the project aims to preserve the

natural conditions existent in the floodplain and to promote a sustainable approach to collective living. Rather than using standard flood defenses along the riverside, the project's flood mitigation strategy does not present a threat to existent reedbed habitat. The proposed offsite manufacture construction technique developed in the project seeks to contribute to the ecological well being of the natural environment by minimizing carbon emissions and encouraging energy conservation.

The housing typology generates a public ground that is filled with different levels of activity, becoming a catalyst for social interaction. The continuous, unexpected encounter between residents and visitors is encouraged by the addition of different programs within the structure.

Public squares, playground fields and vegetated areas are interlocked within a network of pedestrian paths, providing public access to all people. In contrast to the public and natural conditions of the ground plane, the roof terrace creates a platform for semi-private outside-spaces and artificially vegetated areas that in return supports and enriches the existing local wild life.

The project presents a dynamic urban planning system in which clustered elements are developed over time through certain evolutionary processes. Different densities are adapted within the structure by the combination of different housing types and unit sizes. According to user group requirements, the spatial requirements are achieved by managing different modular assemblies.

MARCOS ZOTES-LOPEZ is a practicing architect who graduated from London Metropolitan University with distinction in 2008, receiving an award by Ryue Nishizawa (SANAA) at the SPACE Prize for International Students of Architecture. Marcos has collaborated with architects CHORA/Raoul Bunschoten, Urban Future Organization and Newbetter, in London, and VA Arkitektar in Reykjavik. In 2008 Marcos joined the Office for Metropolitan Architecture in Rotterdam, where he worked on several projects, most notably the Cordoba Congress Center in Spain, Coolsingel Cube in Rotterdam, Koningin Julianaplein in The Hague and Zayed National Stadium in Abu Dhabi. In 2009 he was awarded the "la Caixa" full fellowship in residence for postgraduate studies in the USA.

DC on the High Seas

Wal-Mart Plans to Build 1,800-Acre Distribution Center in the Pacific

by Jesse LeCavalier

Almost exactly 200 miles off the Northern California coast, Wal-Mart Stores, Inc. is at work on a new building project ambitious even for a company known for its size and audacity. Wal-Mart has been secretive about their experiment in the Pacific but a recent press release confirms that skyrocketing oil prices are forcing the company to significantly change its policy concerning Chinese imports. Officially, Wal-Mart will no longer be paying to ship merchandise manufactured in China to its North American retail outlets.

However, the record-high WTI price is not just affecting Wal-Mart. China is one of its largest trading partners and post-Olympic increases in Chinese quality of life have made the nation's economy increasingly dependent on its exports to the US. The rising costs of manufacturing in China, the country's reliance on Wal-Mart's revenue stream, and untenably high fuel costs led Wal-Mart to make a radical proposal to its Chinese trade partners: meet us halfway or we stop importing from you.

As extreme as this bargaining position may seem, the Bentonville-based retailer has done its homework. While the company would prefer to maintain its supply of Chinese-made products, its accountants estimate that, given the price of fuel, it would actually be less expensive to buy the equivalent merchandise in North America and ship it over land (due in part to the increase in Chinese labor costs and to the decrease in American ones as a result of the 2009 depression). While this is one option, Wal-Mart has found an even cheaper solution that both their board and their suppliers can tolerate.

Wal-Mart will still pay for Chinese imports but will not pay for their transport. Wal-Mart, for their part, will use the opportunity to overhaul their supply chain network and distribution system through the development of a massive logistics complex 200 miles off the coast of California. The retailer is wagering that the revenue saved by the combination of increased efficiency, reduced fuel costs and new prediction software will make the effort worthwhile.

The Arkansas company made its plans public recently with a press release in which CIO and former head-of-logistics Rollin Ford states, "Wal-Mart will continue to put the needs of the customer first by lowering the costs of the things they need to save money and live better. This new distribution center will allow us to streamline our operation, reduce costs associated with increasing fuel prices and unnecessary overstock, and benefit from increasingly accurate logistics dynamics enabled by CPFR collaborations."

CPFR, or Collaborative Planning, Forecasting, and Replenishment, forms a series of guidelines intended to enable collaborative supply chain coordination. As the logistics industry becomes increasingly deregulated, the market for third party aggregators—companies that take care of collecting, sorting, and managing their clients' materials—has become more competitive thus driving down costs.

For Wal-Mart, this increased coordination means an opportunity to retool its distribution network. Previously, with Chinese suppliers for example, cargo ships would drop their containers at a port facility to be placed on transport vehicle

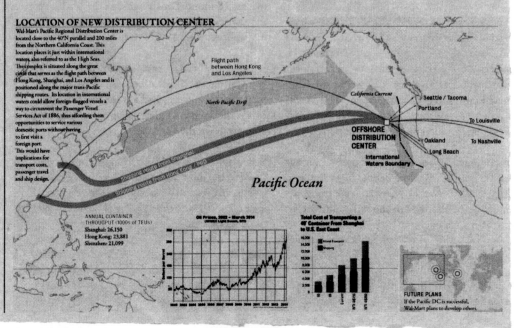

LOCATION OF NEW DISTRIBUTION CENTER

Wal-Mart's Pacific Regional Distribution Center is located close to the 40°N parallel and 200 miles from the Northern California Coast. This location places it just within international waters, also referred to as the High Seas. The complex is situated along the great circle that serves as the flight path between Hong Kong, Shanghai, and Los Angeles and is positioned along the major trans-Pacific shipping routes. Its location in international waters could allow foreign-flagged vessels a way to circumvent the Passenger Vessel Services Act of 1886, thus affording them opportunities to service various domestic ports without having to first visit a foreign port. This would have implications for transport costs, passenger travel and ship design.

Flight path between Hong Kong and Los Angeles

North Pacific Drift

California Current

Seattle / Tacoma
Portland
To Louisville

OFFSHORE DISTRIBUTION CENTER

Oakland
Long Beach
To Nashville

International Waters Boundary

Pacific Ocean

ANNUAL CONTAINER THROUGPUT (1000s of TEUs)
Shanghai: 26,150
Hong Kong: 23,881
Shenzhen: 21,099

FUTURE PLANS
If the Pacific DC is successful, Wal-Mart plans to develop others.

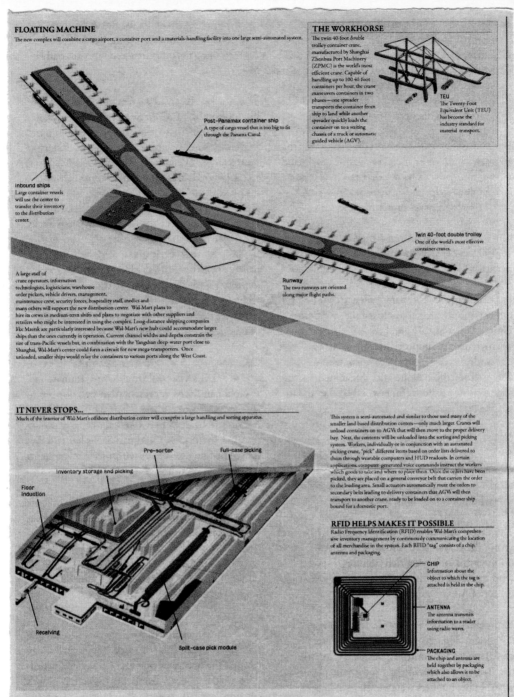

FLOATING MACHINE

The new complex will combine a cargo airport, a container port and a materials-handling facility into one large semi-automated system.

Post-Panamax container ship
A type of cargo vessel that is too big to fit through the Panama Canal.

Inbound ships
Large container vessels will use the center to transfer their inventory to the distribution center.

A large staff of crane operators, information technologists, logisticians, warehouse order pickers, vehicle drivers, management, maintenance crew, security forces, hospitality staff, medics and many others will support the new distribution center. Wal-Mart plans to hire its crews in medium-term shifts and plans to negotiate with other suppliers and retailers who might be interested in using the complex. Long-distance shipping companies like Maersk are particularly interested because Wal-Mart's new hub could accommodate larger ships than the ones currently in operation. Current channel widths and depths constrain the size of trans-Pacific vessels but, in combination with the Yangshan deep-water port close to Shanghai, Wal-Mart's center could form a circuit for new mega-transporters. Once unloaded, smaller ships would relay the containers to various ports along the West Coast.

Runway
The two runways are oriented along major flight paths.

Twin 40-foot double trolley
One of the world's most effective container cranes.

THE WORKHORSE
The twin 40-foot double trolley container crane, manufactured by Shanghai Zhenhua Port Machinery (ZPMC) is the world's most efficient crane. Capable of handling up to 100 40-foot containers per hour, the crane maneuvers containers in two phases—one spreader transports the container from ship to land while another spreader quickly loads the container on to a waiting chassis of a truck or automatic guided vehicle (AGV).

TEU
The Twenty-Foot Equivalent Unit (TEU) has become the industry standard for material transport.

IT NEVER STOPS...

Much of the interior of Wal-Mart's offshore distribution center will comprise a large handling and sorting apparatus.

Pre-sorter

Full-case picking

Inventory storage and picking

Floor induction

Receiving

Split-case pick module

This system is semi-automated and similar to those used many of the smaller land-based distribution centers—only much larger. Cranes will unload containers on to AGVs that will then move to the proper delivery bay. Next, the contents will be unloaded into the sorting and picking system. Workers, individually or in conjunction with an automated picking crane, "pick" different items based on order lists delivered to them through wearable computers and HUD readouts. In certain applications, computer-generated voice commands instruct the workers which goods to take and where to place them. Once the orders have been picked, they are placed on a general conveyor belt that carries the order to the loading area. Small actuators automatically route the orders to secondary belts leading to delivery containers that AGVs will then transport to another crane, ready to be loaded on to a container ship bound for a domestic port.

RFID HELPS MAKES IT POSSIBLE
Radio Frequency Identification (RFID) enables Wal-Mart's comprehensive inventory management by continuously communicating the location of all merchandise in the system. Each RFID "tag" consists of a chip, antenna and packaging.

CHIP
Information about the object to which the tag is attached is held in the chip.

ANTENNA
The antenna transmits information to a reader using radio waves.

PACKAGING
The chip and antenna are held together by packaging which also allows it to be attached to an object.

---

bound for a supplier's warehouse. The various goods would be assembled into another container and taken to the local Wal-Mart distribution center (DC) to be once again unloaded, resorted, repicked and reloaded on to a carrier bound for a local retail outlet.

With the new system, the containers bound for individual stores will be prepared on the new distribution center at sea. This will eliminate most of the intermediate steps between supplier and shopper. CPFR coordination efforts and increasingly sophisticated software allow accurate forecasting at an immense distance: a single 20-foot container bound for an individual store can be loaded 200 miles off the coast without any need for further distribution.

To date, Wal-Mart has used its smaller distribution centers to process material through what is known as "cross-docking." With cross-docking, the merchandise in transit does not actually get stored in the warehouse but is simply switched from one carrier to another, minimizing the need to stockpile. Wal-Mart's new complex in the Pacific operates with a similar imperative, only at a much larger scale.

(See WAL-MART, Page E8)

WAL-MART

(Continued from Page E1)

One might wonder how it will be possible to maintain Wal-Mart's "just-in-time" ethos of supply delivery from a distribution center in international waters. As the new DC will be just over the "high seas" threshold, it is estimated that Long Beach, for example, is less than a two-day journey. Maritime travel combined with overland travel could have an item on the shelf of any western or mid-western Wal-Mart supercenter in less than four days. By supporting this with advances in information technology, including improved RFID implementation, more sophisticated predictive software and improvements in the coordination of their "fuzzy transportation" system, Wal-Mart is convinced that sorting all their inbound merchandise offshore will reduce their bottom line significantly.

The location in the high seas also allows the Arkansas retailer to undertake an enormous territorial operation with hardly any tax contributions. There is also the possibility that Wal-Mart will benefit from the difficulty of enforcing labor laws in international waters.

Critics point out the numerous problems they see with such a scheme including its intensive resource use, dubious labor practices and potentially negative environmental impacts. Regarding labor rights, some believe that, though the offshore site will prevent union formation, it could indirectly consolidate the power of the ILWU (International Longshore and Warehouse Union) on-shore because they will be processing containers already loaded and bound for very specific stores. This could leave Wal-Mart few options if there were another strike like the one in 2002 that crippled incoming container traffic to West Coast ports for several months.

Wal-Mart's high seas distribution center is positioned at the edge of other regulatory conditions. For example, though Wal-Mart is a US-based company, their new complex is not technically part of US sovereign territory. Among other things, this allows Wal-Mart to circumvent the relatively obscure Passenger Vessel Services Act of 1886 that relates to cabotage (the transport of goods or passengers between two ports in the same country) by foreign-flagged vessels and prevents them from travelling directly between US ports. Though a technicality, a major logistics hub just out of reach of US legislation would allow foreign-flagged vessels to shuttle passengers (and material) between many of the West Coast ports. They would also be able to act as shipping relays to supply these same cities.

This would produce a more nimble delivery response time and would allow shipping companies to continue researching deep-sea vessels. For example, since the completion of the Yangshan Deep Water Port connected to Shanghai via the 32.5-km Donghai Bridge, trans-Pacific shipping corridors have seen an increase in so-called "Post-Panamax" ships (vessels too large to pass safely through the Panama Canal). The Yangshan port is far enough out to sea that it could accommodate much larger vessels. However, there has been no equivalent deep-sea port on the Pacific coast until now.

One daunting question that Wal-Mart is facing has to do with energy requirements for their new location. Since former CEO Lee Scott outlined the company's aggressive sustainability campaign in 2005, Wal-Mart has surprised critics by becoming a leader in the field. From eliminating packaging, to helping industries become more environmentally friendly, to redesigning their trucking fleet, Wal-Mart has been responsible for numerous innovations that have satisfied environmental advocacy groups and the company's shareholders.

In a similar spirit, Wal-Mart is using its new distribution complex to pursue alternative energy sources at a large scale. One such system, known as Ocean Thermal Energy Conversion (OTEC), will provide much of the station with is power. OTEC relies on the dramatic temperature differences between warm surface water and cold deep water to run to a heat engine that drives turbines to generate electricity. Since the system relies on economies of scale to increase its productivity, Wal-Mart hopes to take advantage of the size of their new complex. Similarly, as one of the by-products of OTEC is an abundance of cold seawater, various fisheries can be farmed that would be impossible to sustain in its otherwise temperate location, including salmon and lobsters.

Wal-Mart's new Pacific Ocean distribution hub begs the question of the fate of its many land-based DCs. Indeed, most of them will ostensibly become redundant if the stores' replenishment orders are picked and sorted offshore. However, Wal-Mart plans to keep most of the distribution centers "on call" in case of some kind of unexpected delay. In a similar approach to the US military's development of a redundant and polycentric network, the large retailer needs to ensure that its distribution will be able to sustain unpredictable disruptions. The company will also keep many of the distribution centers in the eastern part of the country functioning as usual—at least until they can build a similar offshore hub in the Atlantic.

JESSE LECAVALIER is an architect currently pursuing a doctoral degree at the Swiss Federal Institute of Technology, Zurich.

SEAVITT, Catherine

On the Water: Palisade Bay

"At the end of a hundred leagues we found a very agreeable location situated within two prominent hills, in the midst of which flowed to the sea a very great river, which was deep at the mouth."
—Giovanni da Verrazano, 1524

The transformation of the city during a flood event, the movement of the liquid datum along the vertical axis, creates radical planar reconfigurations through a simple horizontal sheet of water. The city of Rome is marked in many ways with the presence of the Tiber River and its historically relentless floods. Throughout the city are markers and hydrometers, registering the heights of extreme floods and measuring water depth during the flood event itself. Venice, during its periods of *acqua alta*, is radically transformed as wooden plank platforms are strategically placed to create new pathways. The movement of water along a vertical scale draws attention to the subtle realities of topography, and the consequential horizontal extent of flooding. During a flood, the section gives rise to new configurations and understandings of the city. Today, flooding has become synonymous with the impact of global sea level rise, and the threat of rising waters has taken on a new urgency.

Studying the planar transformation that takes place during a time of high water is an opportunity to reinvent and redesign the 21st-century city, and to consider new notions of urban and ecological development. Sea level rise will impact infrastructures, environments and coastal communities around the world. The New York New Jersey metropolitan region is no exception. The region is an economic powerhouse, with 20 million people living within a 50-mile radius of its central harbor and an expected increase of almost one million more residents in New York City's five boroughs alone by 2030. The harbor itself is home to a rich but fragile estuarine ecosystem. Both the built and the natural elements of this tenuous relationship would be radically affected by global climate change and its consequences. Red Hook and Bayonne, for example, would be massively transformed by a three-foot rise in sea level. In fact, substantial portions of these two neighborhoods on the Upper Bay would disappear.

By 2050, it is likely that the mean sea level in the New York New Jersey area will rise by between six inches and two feet as a result of warming oceans. And given the potential widespread melting of the Greenland and Antarctic ice caps, it is quite possible that the relative sea level in the area could rise by three feet by 2080.[1]

Sea level rise is the static part of global warming's impact. The dynamic aspect is the depth and extent of flooding produced by storm surges. Because of higher global and local water levels, it is likely that the frequency and extent of flood damage due to severe storms—hurricanes and Nor'easters—will increase dramatically.

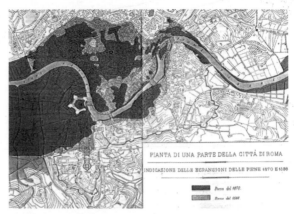

Plan of Rome depicting the extent of the 1598 and 1870 floods. The flood of 1870 led to the implementation of the massive Lungotevere embankment walls along the Tiber's urban course at the end of the nineteenth century, an infrastructural solution that essentially depressed the river below the level of the city

A marble hydrometer from 1821 inlaid on the exterior wall of the Chiesa di San Rocco, near the former Ripetta port and the Temple of Augustus, Rome. A fixed vertical axis that measures the depth of a flood event, the hydrometer is also marked with the heights and dates of significant flood events at this location

Venice's Piazza San Marco with the Doges' Palace under the acqua alta of 1 December 2008. This was the city's most significant flood event in the last twenty-two years, with the waters rising five feet before beginning to recede. Courtesy Andrea Pattaro/AFP/Getty Images

GIS-generated composite aerial view of the New York-New Jersey Upper Bay. Dataset by the US Geological Survey, 2006. ©2007 Latrobe Prize Team

GIS-generated inundation analysis of 100 and 500-year floodplains. The 100-year floodplain is indicated in yellow; the 500-year floodplain indicated in red. Dataset by FEMA. ©2007 Latrobe Prize Team

GIS-generated image of the New York-New Jersey area's high-density landcover. Dataset by the US Environmental Protection Agency. ©2007 Latrobe Prize Team

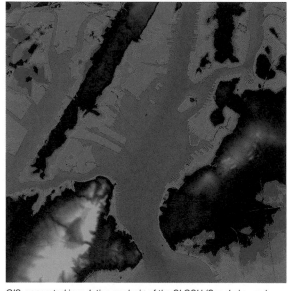

GIS-generated inundation analysis of the SLOSH (Sea, Lake, and Overland Surges from Hurricanes) zones. Category 1 hurricanes are indicated in dark green, Category 2 in light green, Category 3 in orange, and Category 4 in red. Dataset by the National Hurricane Center. ©2007 Latrobe Prize Team

What is currently considered the 100-year storm flood will recur every 19 to 68 years, and the 500-year storm flood may recur closer to every 100 years.[2] Furthermore, higher ocean temperatures could increase the frequency and severity of hurricanes, and thus increase the chance of extreme storm surges.[3] Storm surge levels could reach up to 24 feet in the New York area with a Category 3 hurricane.[4]

The hazards posed by climate change, sea level rise and severe storm surges make this the time to transform our coastal cities through adaptive design. The conventional response to flooding, in recent history, has been hard engineering—fortifying the coastal infrastructure with seawalls and bulkheads to protect real estate, at the expense of natural tidal wetlands and ecosystems. This approach has been proven environmentally damaging, unsustainable, and often ineffective. The failure of levees and other coastal protection structures facing Hurricane Katrina in 2005 is a dramatic example of infrastructural inadequacy. The unexpected ecological effects of the Eastern Scheldt Storm Surge Barrier in the Netherlands also indicate the risky nature of such systems. A core premise of our research and proposal is the transformation of hard engineering practice into soft infrastructural development.

Significant research into the risks of climate change in the New York New Jersey area has led to several proposed solutions to the problem—most notably, a system of four storm surge barriers.[5] But the shortcomings of such conventional systems should provoke a comprehensive reconsideration of coastal planning. It is time to invent a new approach that can not only be sustainable from an environmental, technical and economic standpoint, but also improve the quality of urban life.

On the Water: Palisade Bay is a project funded by the 2007 Latrobe Prize, the American Institute of Architects' College of Fellows biennial research grant. It reflects the initiative of a group of engineers, architects, landscape architects and planners, working collaboratively to imagine the transformation of the New York New Jersey Upper Bay in the face of certain climate change. The project's selected study area is framed by the Bayonne Bridge at the western edge of the Kill van Kull (the tidal strait separating Staten Island and Bayonne), the Holland Tunnel and the Manhattan Bridge at the north, and the Verrazano-Narrows Bridge at the south. The surface area of the Upper Bay is approximately 20 square miles, and it measures almost four miles across at its widest point. The Upper Bay has been chosen as the site for our proposal because of its potential to create a unified regional place for New York and New Jersey, a body of water creating a geographic urban center based on shared ecological and physical boundaries, rather than one divided by the arbitrary lines of political districting. We imagine the Upper Bay as a kind of Central Park for the region, a re-centering of the city away from Manhattan to the boroughs and adjoining New Jersey counties. We envision the potential of the Bay as a common "ground," a figure that could be for the region what the Bacino di San Marco is for Venice—a meeting place and cross roads on the water.

The word "palisade" frames the argument of our proposal for the Upper Bay of New York and New Jersey—the term refers to plant ecology at a cellular level, geological formations, and man-made fortifications. Palisade derives from the Latin *palus*, meaning stake, and by extension, boundary. The possibility of creating porous boundaries, across both politically staked borders, and specifically along the edge of water and land, deeply influences this research and our design proposal.

In the cellular structure of a leaf, the cylindrical palisade cells are arrayed vertically below the upper epidermis of the leaf, and contain the chloroplasts necessary for photosynthesis, absorbing light and harnessing the maximum amount of energy from the sun. The geological term palisade is physically manifest here along our site—The New Jersey Palisades. These are the vertical cliffs rising steeply above the western bank of the Hudson River, a geologic palisade sill. This sill is a Triassic period rift uplifted during the breakup of Pangea. The cliffs were formed by the intrusion of molten magma upward into sandstone, later eroded by water. The Lenape people, the original denizens of the region, called the columnar cliff formation "we-awk-en", meaning "rocks that look like rows of trees." As a fortification, a palisade is a wooden fence or wall made of tightly arrayed small tree trunks aligned vertically, historically used as a defensive structure. The tops and the bottoms of the trunks were sharpened and driven into the ground. Protecting small forts or military camps, the palisades were often reinforced with earthworks.

This notion of the fluid boundary of our palisade development involves more than the invention of an adaptive strategy to address sea level rise and a protective approach to flooding and storm surge. It is equally focused on the development of urban place, as well as enriching estuarine health, diversifying habitat, and transforming our understanding of water in the urban condition. The figure of the water of the Upper Bay might again be seen as fluid, entering the city, retreating, giving residents a sense of tidal variation and the transformations that might occur with controlled flooding. We are developing ideas for both the fresh (rainwater and river) and marine (saline and tidal) components of the estuarine mix, harnessing each for appropriate uses.

We propose three adaptive strategies to transform the physical characteristics of the Upper Bay, reduce flood risk from both sea level rise and storm surge, and challenge current development strategies among water, land, and shelter.

• Create an archipelago of islands, shoals, and reefs in the Upper Bay to both reduce the impact of storm-induced wave energy and improve the ecology of the estuarine environment. The bathymetrics of the bay will be modified, but current shipping channels will be maintained. We are exploring the possibility of harnessing the wind and waves to produce energy.

• Create a soft but resilient thickened coastline edge, combining tidal marshes, public parks and finger piers and slips for recreation and possible development, and determine where to selectively place protective seawalls.

• Create flexible and democratic zoning formulae for coastal development that evolve in response to climate change and storm events to increase community welfare and resilience to natural disasters.

Together, these three strategies—on the water, on the coast, and in the coastal communities—form a radical proposal to transform the Upper Bay into the Central Bay of the region. The Upper Bay has the potential to become an ecologically sound archipelago park, a place that will be for the New York New Jersey region in the 21st century what Central Park was for Manhattan in the late 19th century.

The historic role of the upper New York New Jersey harbor as a site of distributed maritime use with conventional break-bulk shipping was gradually lost as the shipping industry shifted to the more concentrated container-based ports of Elizabeth, Newark and Bayonne in the 1960s. This subsequently led to the near total demolition of the piers that once lined the edges of Manhattan, Brooklyn and Staten Island. This clean-up of the disused waterfront opened the way for recreational,

Bacino di San Marco, Venice *by Canaletto (Giovanni Antonio Canal), about 1738. Oil on canvas (124.5cm x 204.5cm), Museum of Fine Arts, Boston. Abbott Lawrence Fund, Seth K. Sweetser Fund, and Charles Edward French Fund. 39.290. Photograph ©2009 Museum of Fine Arts, Boston*

Structured piers along the Hudson River on the west side of Manhattan, about 1930. These piers lined much of the perimeter of lower and midtown Manhattan with a projective fringe. Courtesy New York City Municipal Archives, Department of Ports and Trade, neg. 32

SEAUITT Catherine

residential and commercial use and gave the impression of progress, renewal and redevelopment.

Yet in fact, this conversion led to the degradation of existing habitats and, in some areas, an increased vulnerability to flooding. Because it most often resulted in a hard sea-walled edge, any ecosystems that may have gathered around or in the shadow of the piers were displaced or destroyed, and any sense of tidal variation was lost. Any protective advantage of the piers in the event of storms was eliminated. And at the same time, valuable real estate was pushed to the waterfront, often privatizing access to the water.

A principle hypothesis of this research is that a softer shoreline—a more gradual transition from land to water—provides a more resilient edge, better able to contend with sea level rise and increased storm surge flooding. A fingered edge like the repetitive piers of the former working waterfront would offer a buffer zone of breakwaters and relieving structures in case of flood events. These pier structures could also be adapted to create a graded edge of tidal wetland terraces or other sloped surfaces, rather than a hard vertical edge. A softer shoreline and broader edge zone are likely to prove more sustainable and resilient.

This thinking also extends to the water of the Upper Bay itself. In addition to the establishment of a hard waterfront edge, the shift to container shipping led to the dredging of deep channels providing ship access to Bayonne and Red Hook, through the Kill van Kull and up the Hudson River. This dredging continues today in order to maintain and even deepen many of these channels to accommodate deeper-draft vessels around the Upper Bay. Some of these channels may no longer be necessary, given current traffic levels, and might in fact act to funnel storm surges.

We propose filling in some of the channels and recovering the shoals, anchorages, and oyster beds of the bay's original bathymetrics, particularly along the Jersey City and Red Hook shores. These changes would not only enrich the bay ecology but would serve as breakwaters to diminish wave action and thus the extent of storm surge flooding. Our scheme for a matrix-like field of caisson islands—an archipelago of shoals, oyster beds, artificial barrier reefs and low islands—would transform the bathymetrics of the Upper Bay into a nature preserve on the water, enhancing its ecology and improving storm protection for the region.

This transformation of the edge—thickening it from the solid line of the seawall to the mucky width of tidal wetlands and the fringe of piers and slips—is central to our proposal. This thickened edge is also seen as new habitat, improving the health of the estuarine ecosystem. We draw much of our formal inspiration from the *informe* post-industrial debris and decay in evidence around the bay today. The aerial view of Shooters Island, a 43-acre island at the end of the Kill van Kull, displays just this condition. Remnants of wooden ships and piers are gradually disintegrating into the water. These are the only relics of the several shipbuilding companies that formerly operated here from approximately 1860 through 1918. The island was later abandoned and in the late 20th century was acquired by the NYC Department of Parks and Recreation as a bird sanctuary. The island now supports

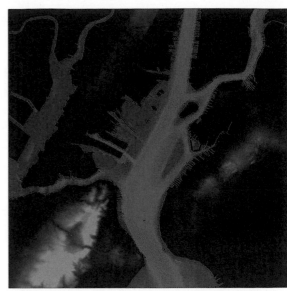

GIS-generated bathymetric model of the Upper Bay. Deepest areas are indicated in green, shallowest areas in red. Note the deep Verrazano Narrows, the shallow Jersey Flats to the west, the Bay Ridge Flats to the east, and the straight dredged shipping channels cutting through the Jersey Flats. ©2007 Latrobe Prize Team

Finite-element model of current direction, speeds, depths, and water temperatures in the Upper Bay using ADCIRC dynamic analysis software. ©2007 Latrobe Prize Team

habitat for nesting pairs of wading birds such as herons, ibis and egrets, as well as double-crested cormorants.

In addition to protecting and revitalizing the harbor ecology, we imagine the water as productive as well. We hope that by bringing the unique rich ecosystem of the Upper Bay back to health with these soft infrastructures, the bay will become a place teeming with life—not just with human population but also with crustaceans, fish, birds, phytoplankton, marsh grasses and plants. How can we use this infrastructure to solve the issues of combined sewage overflows, and potentially collect filtered storm water runoff to be used as fresh water irrigation for food crops along the thickened coastline margins? How can we use crustaceans such as mussels and oysters not only to clean and filter the currently polluted waters, but also to ensure that the waters become so clean that we may again eat them? We imagine a thriving aquaculture in the waters of New York once again. We envision the

Tracings of a century of coastline transformations. Edges, flats, shoals, and anchorages extracted from a series of NOAA (National Oceanic and Atmospheric Administration) historic nautical maps and charts. ©2007 Latrobe Prize Team

Shooters Island, aerial view showing the semi-submerged detritus of the former shipyard. Courtesy United States Geological Survey, High Resolution Orthoimagery for Coastal New York

Eastern end of Shooters Island seen from Staten Island's Mariners Harbor. ©2004 Matthew Trump

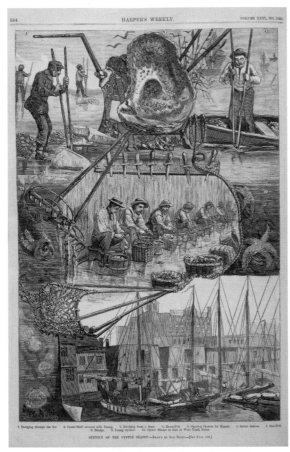

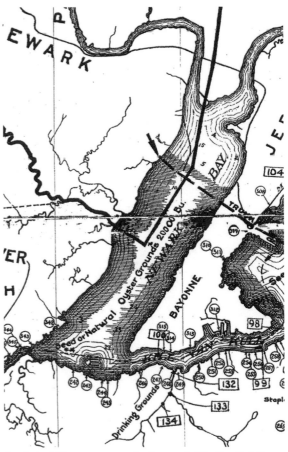

Daniel Beard's illustration "Opening of the Oyster Season," from Harper's Weekly, *September 16, 1882, illustrating the process of oyster harvesting, shucking, and delivery to the oyster barges once docked at lower Manhattan, where they were sold wholesale and to the public. Courtesy Collection of the New-York Historical Society, neg. 82152d*

Detail of a 1905 map accompanying the report of the New York Bay Pollution Commission, entitled *Outline Map of New York Harbor and Vicinity, showing Main Tidal Flow, Sewer Outlets, Shellfish Beds and Analysis Points. The report documented the volume of sewage discharge into the harbor and analyzed water samples and shellfish for contamination.*

Upper Bay's potential transformation into the belly of New York and New Jersey.

The transformation of the Upper Bay will be studied both as an urban landscape design strategy and as a plan for flood protection. We will test its design elements using computational fluid dynamic models to evaluate their effectiveness as storm breaks and barriers. The extent of flooding predicted by these models will then be used in GIS-based economic analyses to determine damage and cost consequences.

Our Palisade Bay masterplan proposal addresses the Upper Bay as both an urban landscape design strategy and as a plan for flood protection. The design elements of the masterplan have been incorporated into a fluid dynamic model to evaluate their effectiveness as storm breaks and barriers, given specific storm models. The extent of flooding predicted by these storm models may then be used in GIS-based economic analyses to estimate damage and cost consequences.

We propose to implement this transformation using the most cost-efficient and environmentally sound methods possible. One strategy for achieving the desired bathymetric changes involves the use of clean dredge spoils from current and future dredging projects. The Harbor Deepening Project—the largest such undertaking for the Port of New York and New Jersey—will make available an estimated 40 million cubic yards of dredged material. Striving for habitat restoration and environmental improvement in conjunction with dredging projects—authorized under federal law and a major goal of the Army Corps of Engineers' Dredged Material Management Plan—is a mutually beneficial endeavor.[6]

Costs and feasibility for the use of dredge material in the creation of caisson island fill, mudflats, dredged rock reefs and oyster beds are promising.[7] Likewise, the use of recycled materials such as decommissioned subway cars to create artificial reefs has proven economical and successful on other waterfronts.[8] Other possibilities for fill material include clean garbage and construction debris, as well as the enormous volume of earth and rock that will be removed for the Metropolitan Transportation Authority's Second Avenue subway project. Given the economic and environmental costs involved in the construction and maintenance of traditional flood protection methods, unconventional methods like these may in fact be the most sustainable.

MARTEL'S NEW YORK CENTRAL PARK.

An 1864 aerial view of New York's Central Park, a void within the void of an undeveloped Upper Manhattan. Lithograph by Joseph C. Geissler after Pierre Martel, dedicated to the Park Commissioners. Courtesy Collection of the New-York Historical Society, neg. 4384

The inversion of the model of Central Park in Manhattan, whose planning and development predated the growth of the city around it, serves as the metaphor for our view of the Upper Bay today. Here, we have the fully developed regional city, framing a void within itself. We see this as the time for the region to rediscover and reinvent its locus as a place for the development of 21st century ecological infrastructure—and like Frederick Law Olmstead's conceptual vision of Central Park, in the support of democracy.

The Palisade Bay proposal seeks not merely to protect the New York New Jersey region from sea level rise and storm surge flooding, but also to reconceptualize the relationship between adaptive infrastructure and ecology in the 21st-century waterfront city. It is an attempt to reconcile the relationship between stewardship of the environment and infrastructural development, a proposal that transforms clean construction debris and dredge spoils into a support for new habitat and a healthy ecosystem. With looming climate change as catalyst, we aspire to develop a new and versatile system of coastal planning, to enrich ecology and the health of the urban estuary, and to create methods of making a vital urban place on the water.

References

1. Gornitz, Vivien; Couch, Stephen and Hartig, Ellen K. "Impacts of Sea Level Rise in the New York City Metropolitan Area," Global and Planetary Change 32, 2002, p. 72

2. Gornitz et al, p. 85

3. The Intergovernmental Panel on Climate Change establishes that it is "likely" that tropical cyclones will be more intense in the future. See Climate Change 2007: Synthesis Report. Contribution of Working Groups I, II and III to the Fourth Assessment Report of the Intergovernmental Panel on Climate Change, eds. R.K. Pachauri and A. Reisinger (Geneva, Switzerland: IPCC, 2007), p. 47

4. Gornitz et al, p. 66

5. Bowman, Malcolm J. et al, "Hydrologic Feasibility of Storm Surge Barriers to Protect the Metropolitan New York-New Jersey Region": Final Report to HydroQual, Inc, Marine Sciences Research Center, State University of New York, Stony Brook, NY (March 2005). See also: Bowman, M. J. and Hill, D. "Bracing for Super-Floyd: How Storm Surge Barriers Could Protect the New York Region," Briefing for the New York Academy of Sciences, www.nyas.org/ebriefreps/splash. asp?intebriefID=415.

6. Yozzo, David J.; Wilber, Pace and Will, Robert J. "Beneficial Use of Dredged Material for Habitat Creation, Enhancement, and Restoration in New York-New Jersey Harbor," Journal of Environmental Management 73, 2004, p. 39-52

7. Yozzo et al, p. 39-52

8. Urbina, Ian. "Growing Pains for a Deep-Sea Home Built of Subway Cars," New York Times, 8 April 2008

SEAVITT, Catherine

Preliminary design strategies for an adaptive intervention of wetlands, windmills, reefs, oyster beds, island fields, extended piers, detached piers, and extracted slips. ©2007 Latrobe Prize Team

The 2007 Latrobe Prize team was awarded to Guy Nordenson and Associates (GNA), Catherine Seavitt Studio (CSS), and Architecture Research Office (ARO). **Guy Nordenson** *PE SE, Professor of Architecture and Structural Engineering at Princeton University's School of Architecture and partner at GNA, was the overall project director. Nordenson worked with Professor* **James Smith***, of Princeton University's Department of Civil and Environmental Engineering, and* **Michael Tantala** *to direct the engineering analyses and infrastructural design. CSS principal* **Catherine Seavitt** *AIA and ARO principal* **Adam Yarinsky** *FAIA oversaw the urban planning, architecture, and landscape design. Seavitt also provided the ecological analyses. Additional key team members included ARO principal* **Stephen Cassell** *AIA and GNA associates* **Lizzie Hodges** *and* **Marianne Koch***.*

DECOSTERD, Jean-Gilles
The Osmotic Territories

Architecture needs to engage with the possibilities of sustainable development and the reconciliation of development and sustainability, through the exploration of strategies that go beyond *the mere advancement of green technologies.*

For a long time, the notion of development in architecture had been a synonym for technical progress and its measurement was made strictly quantitatively. Today's requirements and regulatory controls are to minimize energy consumption, to increase the insulation of buildings and to reduce waste. But these technical solutions are simply not enough to construct an architecture of sustainability. Architecture cannot be reduced to pure technique.

In the same way, ecology, which asks the question of our relationship to the environment, has the tendency to be reduced to the dimension of green technologies. Sustainable development, beyond a quantitative scale, must be able to address a qualitative balance. This question must then take into account the two scales that are intrinsic to architecture: the body and the landscape.

As architecture can only exist according to a specific location, I postulate that the site—the place or context—can no longer be defined in an immutable manner in relation to a static ground.

As climate change is becoming a defining reality of our times, I consider architecture to be a climatic answer to a climatic context through parameters such as technology, phenomenology and ecology.

The notion of territory, today too simplistic in its strict morphological dimension, must extend to a more generous context regarding ecological, climatic and physical immersion. I'm defending an "architecture of territorial resources" that is highly contextualized in order to place the local context within the global and more dynamic realities of ecology and climate.

My work focuses on how energy and climate qualify space rather than on formal mechanisms. Air, light and heat are regularly summoned in my projects as a material, first definition of space. Simultaneously, this architecture is physically linked to its specific, territorial context.

In fact, new ways of research and practice open up the possibility to consider architecture in terms of immersion, with respect to the body's immersion into architectural space and the immersion of architecture into a climatic and physical territory. In this sense, Architecture can no longer be apprehended from a single aesthetical point of view; it becomes a straightforward connection between the body and the territory.

Kenneth Frampton, in the 1980s, theorized the revival of context in architecture. It was about opposing the unifying and globalizing tendency of Modern Architecture through the creation of a "critical regionalism." Today, things are more complicated.

We can ask ourselves if this critical regionalism has "found the means to resist without falling into nostalgia or demagogic strategies of kitsch with political or cultural consequences of capitalist theory."[1] In other words, if, through "introducing an ontological dimension to place rather than space," this point of view or attitude could transcend the results of a simply aesthetic stance or style.

There is no doubt that issues of ecology and economics viewed as a series of crises over a longer historical period, have not increased. How can architecture, as an architecture that has attempted to come to terms with issues of context and the local, deal with this historical inevitability? The relationship between the external characteristic of architecture, its relationship to space and its internal characteristic has become more complex. This relationship can no longer be limited to its local and regional dimension, nor to its material and constructive traditions.

Site, place, environment, resources—words which all apply to the question of context—all help move beyond a poetic representation towards a sphere of study and action to discuss the condition of the present.

Historically, architecture was forced to return to a form of local rootedness and place as a counterpoint to the generic globalism of modernism and steamroller capitalism.

The triumph of the 1990s and globalisation could lead one to consider this attitude as utopian or naïve. I believe nevertheless that a form of resistance and rootedness in

Three examples of architectural projects involving territorial resources

Offices For Academia

Jean-Gilles Décosterd was commissioned to re-design the offices of the Swiss Railway Company Academia Building. The key issue is how a room may facilitate collective work. The study links work with rituals, furniture with space, the office with the territory. The linking element is water and mosses.

The pretext of a collective ritual is organized around the consumption of water, a reason to take breaks and for casual exchanges. Specific furniture that contains plant mosses and water distributors that generate their own fluorine light are developed for the project. From the building's physics point of view, the surfaces of plant mosses introduced within the offices have the capacity to filter air, to regenerate it and to improve the hygrometry of the workspaces in a passive manner.

Through introducing natural samples into the workspace, the project makes reference explicitly to the northern Alps of the Swiss territory. Plant mosses taken from the four Swiss versant basins reveal the geological and hydrological qualities of the different locations. Historically, the railroad networks were constructed in close relation to the pipeline of the streams on the valley floor: the superposition of the hydrographical network maps and the railway network is striking.

Distribution of mosses limits the need for ventilation or cooling systems in the offices. The corporate identity of the Swiss Railway Company offices is given simply by promoting social exchanges and regenerated air. Via the purifying mosses, the outside territory of the company is "invited" to act in the inside space of the office, the natural materials linked to artificial spaces create hybrid architecture.

context and landscape for architecture must operate within a framework which defines new modes of action and a new definition and understanding of landscape itself.

From our perspective today, the question of landscape as a place is not only to be viewed in its cultural or historic dimension. The climatic dimension has carved a role in the definition of context. In these terms a new definition of landscape considers air quality, light, water, physical, chemical or fluid mechanics.

In this sense there is a change in the paradigm of territory, a new reading grid of the territory that superimposes itself to the former and inflects it: in other words, a passage from the *territoire-paysage* to the *territoire-climat*, which is also a *territoire-énergie*.

This postulates that the nature of territory has simply evolved: it has expanded with a new climatic and energetic dimension. Climate and energy is our contemporary way of relating to the territory. It is here, in the notion of climate and territorial resources, that we look for a territorial anchoring for contemporary architecture.

These layers of new territorial realities, those of climate and of energy, are of direct interest to architecture by linking the inside space and the outside place in terms of fluxes (or streams).

In my sense, the benefit of that new territorial paradigm consists in the redefinition of the usual boundaries or limits of context. Architects who are concerned by contextual notions usually refer to cultural areas, political boundaries or visual landscape limits. Working with climatic determinations of a place means to think of local conditions as part of a global flux. It means also to think interior space as a climatic extension from the outside.

Modernity in architecture attempted to take the step of emancipating itself from outdoor climatic conditions to the benefit of a climate created from nothing in order to maintain the most "purified" territorial inscriptions: orientation and the view. The machine, allied to the pure laws of optics, created an architecture essentially retinal in its apprehension and its relationship to territory.

How is architecture thought of today, when our definitions of the territorial matter change? Or to put it in another way: what happens when architecture and territory are considered with respect to climate and energy, and situated within a paradigmatic shift from a *territoire-paysage* to a *territoire-climat*?

From this last modality that I call "an architecture of territorial resources," is one that operates as both a climatic and energetic reading with concomitant scales of references: the territory, the city and the inner space. In this way, architecture isn't just an object with a visual dialogue with the landscape, but a *thing*, submerged into a climate that extracts its own living environment. Energetic continuum and climatic submergence are crucial recurring themes.

A double entrenchment: the human body inside the body of architecture, inside the body of the territory, opens the possibility for new architectural designs as well as new means of construction. It promotes architecture as the science of setting relations, beyond the average production of forms. Architecture, thus seen predominantly as what links, becomes (once again) ecological, in the first meaning of the word, as invented by Ernst Haeckel in 1866 in his work *General Morphology of Organisms*: "the science of relations of organisms with the surrounding world, that is to say, in a large meaning, the science of existing conditions."

Could there be a more beautiful definition of architecture than this *science of existing conditions*?

In a text written in 1967, *Heterotopias*, Michel Foucault addresses the question of the nature of *outside* space throughout its historical evolution. He observes the passage from *localization*; a prioritized set of formed and autonomous places which originates from the Middle Ages, to the notion of *location* peculiar to our time and which relies more on the relationships between singular points within a neighborhood: "we live a time where space is given to us under the form of relationships of locations." It might be that this territorial conception applies also today as a consideration of the linkages between spaces from the inside to those of the outside, as ordinary points of a climatic and energetic continuum.

This way of thinking about the territory corresponds to a way of physically building these *inside* spaces. The building materials and techniques of today directly engage with this climatic and energetic continuity between inside and outside. Constructive Modernity taught us to think about building in terms of specific layers, superimposed to respond to a succession of problems: bearing the static load, containing the water vapour, insulating from the temperature, waterproofing the façade; all designed as segregation processes. Today new materials could ensure comfort and energetic savings through a kind of climatic permeability and continuity between the inside and the outside.

Thermal insulations in the future authorize hygrometric migrations; indoor paints and outdoor rough coats are embedded with photo-catalytic properties, which improve the quality of gaseous exchanges. Materials with phase-changing properties regulate thermal variations. These materials with passive regulation emerge from nano-technologies, powered by catalysts not consuming any energy. They announce the decline of mechanical conditioning technologies of indoor climate in favor of materials, which failing being intelligent, will be smarter.

So if a field of research opens at the crossroads of materials and state-of-the-art technologies, including high-tech answers to ecological and climatic questions, there is also another domain, low-tech in nature, which resurfaces in architecture. It is the rediscovery of a whole repertoire of techniques and materials, coming from traditional or vernacular architecture, whose use had been overshadowed, if not demoted, by Modernity. It is therefore why we re-discover straw and adobe construction, lime coating plaster and vegetal insulation. It is a matter of finding in parallel the knowledge and the know-how often only transmitted orally and which has disappeared in the leap of a generation, swept by a blind confidence in technological modernity.

The radical opposition between high-tech and low-tech and the dominance of the hi-tech has, for a long time, been made possible through the modern ideology of the *tabula rasa* and the desire to constantly renew the architectural language. Indeed, low-tech materials often dictate, by their needs of implementation, a constructive expression that is in opposition to the diktats of Modernity. Modernity is digested as a granted historical fact and architecture should be able to reposition itself on other issues that are less aesthetic and more essential, which touch public health and energy saving. Today the traditional antagonisms between high tech and low tech approaches are no longer valid: combinations of highly engineered nano-technologies can be integrated with passive heating or ventilation methods as well as lower tech building components.

The only reason to choose one or the other depends on the energy consumption entailed in each specific situation. The question is no longer about confronting ideologies or aesthetics but about finding smart organizations of techniques and materials in order to answer the legitimate climatic *non-tranquillity* that has seized the (re)territorialized question of architecture.

The very matter of architecture evolves towards this organic dimension that builds climatic phenomena in collaboration with the outdoor climate, more than by artificial creation. The energetic supplies follow the same evolution, which summon the sun and wind in order to extract energy. A decreasing architecture announces itself, breaking off from the all-consuming technologic of Modernity in order to elaborate *a construction of climates within the climate*.

References

1. Frampton, Kenneth. Modern Architecture: A Critical History. *London: Thames and Hudson, 1993*

Jean-Gilles Décosterd *was born in 1963 in Lausanne, Switzerland. Over the last 15 years he has been developing architectural research on the energetic and climatic definition of space. Air, light and heat are often used as the substance and elementary material for his architectural projects. This strategy was applied to the interior space in several well-known projects such as Hormonorium, the Swiss pavilion he designed in 2002 at the Venice Biennale with his former associate. Other projects, such as the Omnisport Hall, were acquired by the Modern Art Museum, Centre Pompidou in Paris. Décosterd considers architecture as a climatic answer to a climatic context through parameters such as technology, phenomenology and ecology. In 2008, with architect Catherine Cotting, and civil engineers Guscetti & Tournier from Geneva, he won the international design competition for Egremont Castle in England. Décosterd is currently teaching architecture in Switzerland and has been running his own office in Lausanne since 1993.*
Further information: www.climats.ch and www.decosterd.net

Egremont Castle Competition

*In Egremont in Britain's Lake District, the structural design is
considered together with the wind factor—one of the major climatic
definitions of the site.*

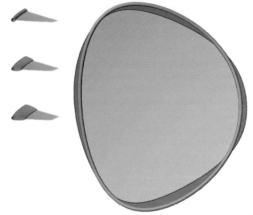

*Our research aims is to bring together a conceptual contempo-
rary structure and an 800-year-old construction. Historically, the usual
response to entropy was to apply heavy materials and thick walls to
construct premeditated forms. The castle itself illustrates such a strategy against external forces such as gravity, wind and rain. Nowadays,
high tech materials are available that have the ability to react to
internal deformation and external conditions. The formal definition of
the structure is dependent on this climate contextualisation.*

*In order to deal with the wind factor, the whole structure has
the ability to minimize the wind's impact. Hydraulic masts permit
height and angle adjustment accordingly to lessen its flying surface.
The round cylindrical beam made of carbon fiber, which sustains the
sail border, has a variable geometrical design. The part of the round
cylindrical beam that is most exposed to the dominant winds bears an
elliptical design, whereas the least exposed part has a circular shape.*

*Lastly, the central coverage material made of armed foil can
be used as a filter for daylight. For that reason, we aim to transform
the quality of daylight by warming it throughout our main architectural
feature. Northern European homes use colors and light to warm up
their interiors to counterbalance the grayness of their weather. The
coverage could gain a new function by "warming up the daylight."
During the night, the bottom of the coverage will act like a big reflec-
tor, disseminating the projected light as a diffused ambience.*

*Architecture remains a simple interface between territorial
conditions and human needs. The formal proposition could not exist
without the specific climatic conditions of Egremont. The architectural
project uses territorial resources to modify elementary climate conditions—shield from the rain, expand the light and deflect the wind.*

Grizedale Arts in the Lake District: Lawson Park and Park Amoor

Grizedale Arts, an international research and development agency for artists based in the Lake District National Park, was looking for an architectural strategy to transform Park Amoor Farm. With both a pragmatic consolidation of the existing building, and the addition of a rammed earth technical structure, we aim to develop links between our architectural intervention and the material and climatic determinations of the territory. For the isolated existing buildings, which are not connected to energy networks, the project produces solar and wind energy towards the dual objectives of auto-subsistence and having a minor impact on the site. It makes use of present technology as well as low-tech materials. When used without an existing building, the structure produces energy and stores it briefly, just as it preserves the raw materials for domestic needs: wood for cooking and food production. It is linked to an experimental agriculture program developed under the auspices of the Grizedale Foundation. One lives there as in a shelter, nestling in a hollow, an empty space with a domestic vocation, a vertical dormitory that is not a house, and is at most a refuge for backpacking tourists

The project is a landmark in the countryside on the scale of the landscape. The establishment of a new isolated shelter responds to a simple territorial rule: each is built at a distance of six hours walk from the next. Solar energy is used for the night lighting. The shift phase of energy reproduction is 9 hrs 30 minutes indexed on the sun's course. The aeolian energy feeds the heating in real time; the temperature obtained varies in accordance with the force of the wind.

Rammed earth which forms the walls of the built structure of this energy annexe is of interest to the project in more than one aspect. As a link with the land, it is simply the local application of resources present at the site: mud that is compacted and mixed with lime, itself present in the chalk deposit of the subsoil. This lime was at the origin of energetic autonomy of the area in the 18th century, making it possible to produce with coal, the fuel which fed the foundries. It is particular to the geological subsoil of the region, which unites the crystalline volcanic rocks with chalk sediments. It is this mixture of volcanic and sedimentary

rock which produces the bio-diversity which today characterises the region and produces the richness of the flora. The rammed earth will be enriched with organic residue from the filtering of barley: the malt draff is rich in azotes and was traditionally used as agricultural manure and for feeding livestock. In the construction, this additive plays the role of catalyser for the vegetal colonisation of the rammed earth by mosses and lichens.

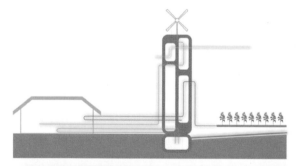

DECOSTERD, Jean-Gilles

BISHOP, Elizabeth

Nothing Runs Like a GPS-Navigated Deere: Cedric Price and the Precision Farming Industry

Cedric Price once asked, "Technology is the answer—but what was the question?"[1] A radical architect who actively attempted to incorporate cutting-edge technology into his designs, Price was also aware of sustainability issues and viewed the landscape as a changing infrastructure that interacted with architecture.[2] Price's views about technology and the landscape unexpectedly resonate with more recent developments in the farming industry. In fact this resonance is not arbitrary: agricultural elements of Price's entry for the Parc de la Villette competition in 1982 foreshadow recent developments by the John Deere Company in the realm of precision guidance systems for tractors. In the Parc de la Villette entry Price situates farming—which, as the John Deere example shows, is intertwined with technology—within the realm of architecture and design, and in so doing establishes a framework for architecture's role as a harbinger of future technologies.

Price was interested in design that maintained a balance with the environment, although he eschewed the idea of sustainability as "social do-goodery."[3] His views about sustainability often had to do with architecture being flexible enough to accommodate changes in its surroundings. Change and time were part of Price's architectural palette. For example, in the plans for the Fun Palace, Price designed a deep framework above the project that "…could manipulate all the required changes from above. Thus a richer, more valuable mix, requiring little long-term planning, was available to the user."[4] The landscape, an infrastructure of constant change, was met with a receptive architecture. Other projects addressed farming in a more literal sense. 181 Serre I/II, for example, is a design for a structure described as a "secret garden" for growing roses. Price used a greenhouse typology in this project to maximize the benefits of the sun. As in plans for the Fun Palace, the architecture could flex and change as the user required. In Serre I/II, the flowers growing and changing had an impact on how the architecture was experienced. The internal structures were also intended to "adapt and change to both usage and occupancy."[5] In this way the surrounding environment was part of the design. In Price's buildings, architecture, technology, and the landscape had interactive relationships.

Today, farms all over the world similarly reference a changing landscape infrastructure. In recent years, technologies developed in disciplines such as aeronautics and the defense industry have been deployed in the farming context in order to increase the precision of farming.[6] This resonates with Price's belief that technology was to be used in conjunction with the natural environment to accommodate users' needs.[7] In the case of the John Deere Company, systems of linked satellite and terrestrial networks are used to map and predict the production and yield of farms. Specifically, Deere's Green Star and Star Fire Ag Management Solutions have connections to both global networks and to the landscape.

Farmers today who use the GreenStar Guidance system interface with three main elements: The GreenStar Display, the Mobile Processor and the StarFire iTC position receiver.[8] The Mobile Processor attaches to the GreenStar Display and provides the information that is represented graphically by the display. Described as the brains of the system, the processor uses John Deere-developed software to track the metrics of entire growing seasons. Information about the farm, the field, various crops and the position and location of the tractor is transmitted or entered and then stored in the processor.[9]

The third part of the system is the StarFire iTC position receiver. This receiver uses signals from Global Positioning System (GPS) satellites and corrects the error in these signals via a terrestrial network of relay towers erected by John Deere. Originally developed (and still owned) by the United States Department of Defense, the first GPS satellite was launched in 1978 for military purposes.[10] Today a variety of industries use information from the GPS satellites in conjunction with a system of terrestrial radio beacons called Differential GPS, or DGPS, which correct errors in the signal from the satellites. The US government has an array of 86 terrestrial DGPS receivers that covers most of the US, but John Deere maintains its own terrestrial network of radio beacons.[11] In the US today, GPS is nearly ubiquitous, "woven into our technology infrastructure, just like the power grid

In the landscape of the Central Valley of California, between Los Angeles and Santa Barbara, one finds the following: solar arrays, almond shelling and husking, planting, hay storage, train and grain, tomato harvest, oil harvest, spinach and gantries

BISHOP, Elizabeth

or the water system."[12] StarFire, John Deere's terrestrial network, is used in conjunction with the government-owned network of GPS satellites as a guidance system for farm equipment. The StarFire receiver pinpoints the location of the farm, the field and the tractor within the field using this large satellite and terrestrial network. An accurate ground speed can be calculated from this information as well.

All of this information comes together on the GreenStar Display which uses small, full-color screens mounted in the tractor to present data. The plans or overhead views that are generated reflect the shape of the field as well as the paths the equipment is following. The yield of a crop can be estimated in real time as the field is being harvested. The calculation of the amount of rows harvested, for example, to give a specific yield to be sold at a certain price in order for the farmer to break even is performed by JDOffice software (also developed by John Deere) in conjunction with the StarFire System. The software takes into account certain infrastructures—market and economic networks, transportation and positioning networks, and to an extent the infrastructure of the landscape. Additional information can be shown overlaid on top of the base information. Changes in elevation are mapped and displayed against the latitude and longitude and area of the field. Terrain and yield are joined, with colorful displays showing the areas of low yield juxtaposed against areas of higher yield. Color-coded maps are created and overlaid on the plan of the field to show seeding or harvesting information, application of fertilizer or pesticide, and harvest yield rates.[13] This mapping process resonates with many of the computer modeling exercises that architecture and related fields have used to understand the landscape.[14] In this context, the graphic element of the full-color real-time display screen is one element of the larger system of precision farming.

The connection of farming to infrastructures beyond the farm as developed by John Deere resonates with the masterplan that Cedric Price developed for the Parc de la Villette Competition. Price describes this design for the park as "…a giant, city-center food factory; the content and nature of which is totally unknown at the time of design."[15] The design includes horticultural elements, fish farms and a market place, in addition to the elements stipulated by the competition brief. To Price, "parc" can mean garden or agricultural field. The design for Parc de la Villette is supposed to be a "lung for the city,"[16] as Price writes in the competition report, but this does not mean the design is constrained to the picturesque. The landscape is put to work producing food as well as providing enjoyment. "The growing, harvesting and consumption of vegetables and fish on the site logically interweaves with the production and dissemination of music and science."[17] Seasonal changes to the landscape alter the design, and Price expected that "[t]he tradition will become that of change and the new."[18]

Huge mechanical gantries that rove automatically across fields in Price's design presage the John Deere tractors that today use technology to harvest information as well as produce as they move across the landscape. Price considered his gantries to be a form of urban entertainment. Passengers could ride on the gantry as it passed over the fields, observing a spectacle unfold below. Price writes in the competition report that "[t]hese gardens, straddled by mobile feed, control, measure, and observe gantries, can accommodate and reinforce open, sheltered, and totally enclosed growth patterns."[19] It was not clear exactly how the gantries were to drill seed, fertilize, water, or harvest the crops that they moved over, but it was clear that this process was to be automated, and that people visiting the site were to gain enjoyment and entertainment from interacting with the process.

The images from the report show what looks like stadium seating attached to the side of a mechanical arm. In Deere's StarFire system there are no leisure-seeking passengers taken along for a relaxing ride, only the operator who still has to turn the machine at the ends of rows (If there are obstacles in the field, such as trees or buildings, the equipment's path can be programmed to avoid them). Plans of different fields and their equipment-path patterns can be stored in the system for future use. When in use, the farmer is alerted if the tractor veers off path, and the overlapping of rows already plowed, seeded, or sprayed with fertilizer is reduced. According to John Deere's website, farmers that access the StarFire RTK network can expect accuracy of less than 1 inch within a 12-mile radius of the StarFire transmitter.[20] If information harvested from the field shows that certain areas of the crop need more water or fertilizer, the Green Star system calculates the required flow-rate and the speed of the tractor can be reduced as the flow is increased over these specific areas. Irregularities are addressed with a calculus that is designed to reduce the risk and unknown quantities of nature.

John Deere subjugates many of the unknown factors of the field to technology. Price embraced the use of technology to allow users to control the built environment

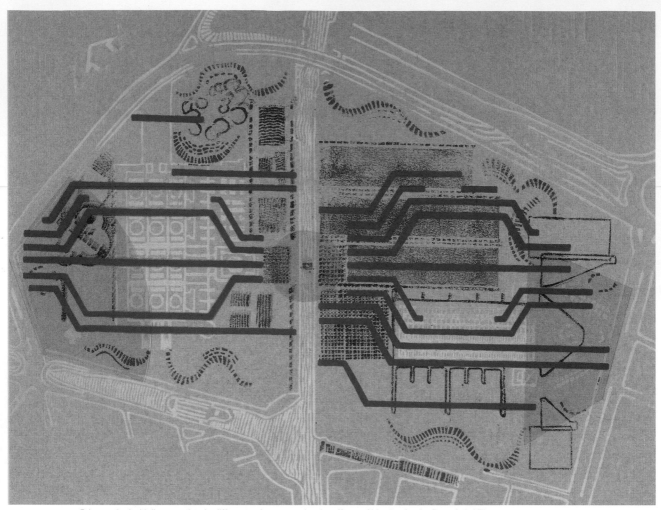

Price worked with linocut prints in different colors to overlay the effects of his plan for the Parc de la Villette on the landscape. Parts of the linocuts were cut out and overlaid on each other as needed. Each color had a specific meaning as was explicated in the key. Light blue = Site and Retained Structures; Red = First Stage: Horticulture, Earthworks, Information; Black = Subsequent Stages: Pisciculture, Gantries, Flora; Dark Blue Lines = Overlaid Public Routes. Image courtesy Fonds Cedric Price, Collection Centre Canadien d'Architecture / Canadian Centre for Architecture, Montréal

and add an element of flexibility or change to buildings, introducing unpredictability and change into architecture. In the Parc de la Villette, mechanized elements interact with a landscape infrastructure that is expected to change as time passed. A degree of flexibility is designed into the masterplan for the park. Price writes that "[i]t is therefore essential that any new or existing buildings are over-provided with access zones for goods, people, services, and maintenance"[21] in order to accommodate future changes to the park. This commitment to accommodate change in the design is apparent elsewhere in the brief, where the architect notes that "[t]he tradition [of the park] will become that of change and the new."[22] In 1982, Price championed an approach to the landscape that allowed the architecture to be mutable. Rather than waiting to study the eventual affects of technology on the park in the future, Price developed an open design which would allow technology to be incorporated as needed.

What the juxtaposition of Price's Park de la Villette entry with John Deere's GPS technology offers architecture is a reversal of the "technological determinism" equation. As Stephen Graham explains it, technological determinism tends towards the belief that "new telecommunications technologies are seen to directly cause urban change."[23] What Price's design suggests is that architecture could become the forerunner, exploring technological solutions before technology can catch up. It is possible then that these

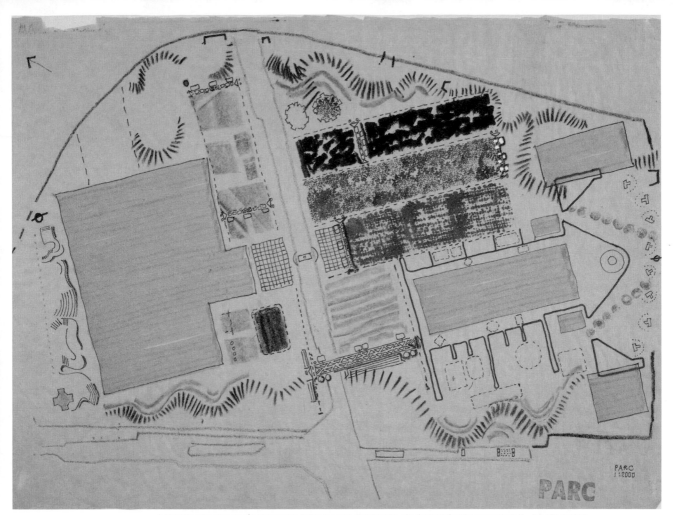

A black and white study of the competition entry. Price writes in the text for the entry that, "… it is likely that the most valuable activities generated by this park will be those resulting from the content and operation for the Park itself and for which there are as yet no names." This plan uses different textures to suggest the differing purposes of the landscape without explicitly defining the use of any particular area. Image courtesy Fonds Cedric Price, Collection Centre Canadien d'Architecture / Canadian Centre for Architecture, Montréal

technologies that are currently being deployed in the landscape can become part of the architect's repertoire. If technology is the answer, could architecture be the question?

References

1. See John Frazer's essay in Samantha Hardingham, ed. Cedric Price Opera. *New York: Wiley, 2003, p. 47*
2. In this context the word "landscape" borrows Denis Cosgrove's definition from Social Formation and Symbolic Landscape *"… landscape denotes the external world mediated through subjective human experience… Landscape is not merely the world we see, it is a construction, a composition of that world. Landscape is a way of seeing the world." Human subjectivity is part the landscape. See Cosgrove, Denis.* Social Formation and Symbolic Landscape. *London: Croom Helm, 1998, p. 13*
3. 181 Serre 1 was a proposal for a greenhouse in the Parc de la Villette that Price described as "… literally green = growth, not green = social do-goodery. A greenhouse depends on the sun. It is not a justification for it." See Samantha Hardingham, ed. Cedric Price Opera. *New York: Wiley, 2003, p. 10*
4. Price, Cedric. The Square Book. *New York: Wiley, 2003, p. 54*
5. Hardingham, Samantha (ed). Cedric Price Opera. *New York: Wiley, 2003, p. 10*
6. Changes in farming technologies have a real effect on cities, towns, and villages. For an interesting account of changes in farming technologies on the East Anglian Fens in England, Robert McFarlane's article "Ghost Species." McFarlane writes that "[t]he application of the internal combustion engine to agriculture

meant that the horse was usurped by the tractor, that the boundaries of the village exploded and that the number of people required to work the land was enormously reduced." McFarlane, Robert. "GhostSpecies," Granta no. 102, summer 2008, p. 113

7. In her introduction to Supercrit #1 Cedric Price: Potteries Thinkbelt, Samantha Hardingham quotes Cedric Price as saying, "Architecture should have little to do with problem-solving—rather it should create desirable conditions and opportunities hitherto thought impossible." Hardingham, Samantha and Rattenbury, Kester (ed). Supercrit #1 Cedric Price: Potteries Thinkbelt. New York: Routledge, 2007, p. 11

8. http://www.deere.com/en_AU/equipment/ag/ams/GreenStar-Guidance.html Accessed 20 December 2008

9. http://www.deere.com/en_AU/equipment/ag/ams/mobilecomponents.html Accessed 12 January 2009

10. In the early days of GPS, civilian use was intentionally made inaccurate with Selective Availability (SA), which caused random interference. In 1998 SA was turned off and today civilian GPS is as reliable as the GPS the military uses, especially when terrestrial transmitters in the Differential Global Positioning System (DGPS) are used to correct the satellite signal

11. http://www.navcen.uscg.gov/dgps/default.htm has maps of the locations of radio receivers

12. Ganapati, Priya. Quoting Paul Kintner, director of Cornell University's GPS Laboratory in "Researchers Demonstrate How to Spoof GPS Devices" in Wired magazine, 29 September 2008. See http://www.wired.com/gadgetlab/2008/09/researchers-dup/. For Wired magazine's timeline of GPS technology, see http://www.wired.com/science/discoveries/news/2008/12/dayintech_1208. GPS came in at number 6 in the "Top Technology Breakthroughs of 2008" by Wired in 2008. See http://www.wired.com/gadgets/miscellaneous/news/2008/12/YE8_techbreaks?currentPage=all

13. http://www.deere.com/en_AU/equipment/ag/ams/GS2/GreenStar_2_OnScreen_Mapping.html Accessed 28 December 2008

14. Shane, Grahame. "The Emergence of Landscape Urbanism" in the Harvard Design Magazine, No. 19, Fall 2003/Winter 2004, p. 4. In an essay discussing the genesis of Landscape Urbanism, Grahame Shane writes about the various methods of using graphics to understand the American landscape. "Computer modeling, Geographic Information Systems, and satellite photography formed part of this research into the patches of order and patches of 'disturbances'...that help create the heterogeneity of the American landscape."

15. Price, C. op. cit. 54

16. See Cedric Price: Parc de la Villette Competition Entry Report (unpaginated) #156 PARC 1.3.3 at the Canadian Centre for Architecture (CCA), Montreal

17. Ibid

18. Ibid

19. Ibid

20. See John Deere's website: http://www.deere.com/en_US/compinfo/index.html

21. Ibid

22. Report, op. cit. (unpaginated)

23. Graham, Stephen. "Towards Cyberspace Planning: Grounding the Global Through Urban Telematcis Policy and Planning" Electronic Working Paper No. 26, p. 3. Accessed 12 February 2009, http://www.ncl.ac.uk/guru/assets/documents/ewp26.pdf

Elizabeth Bishop is a recent graduate of the MED program at Yale. She lives in London where she works for Zaha Hadid. She would like to thank Michael Powers for his help in the archive.

EDNIE-BROWN, Pia

Feeling Green: Plastic Transformability and Generative Critique

Any thinking about green design involves, whether implicitly or explicitly, an image or idea of the environment and our relationship with it. This relationship is becoming increasingly complex, partly because our capacity to actively manipulate the world (and ourselves) has zoomed into unprecedented dimensions and domains. Living things are no longer cultivated and manipulated only at the level of the organism, they are genetically *ch* engineered, chemically altered and affectively farmed. Globally networked systems have us swimming like fish in a turbulent sea. Production as tangible as vapor infuses the landscape. Flocks of nano-bots are assembling, joining the swarm of living organisms that inhabit our bodies and take part in its functioning. We *are* ecologies, no less than we are inseparable from the ecologies we inhabit, and all ecological assemblages are continually altering, adapting and collapsing in both cacophonic and tuneful concert with the instruments of human activity. The environment seems less and less like a divine, natural other.

Richard Sennett has made the important point that while the word sustainable "suggests living more at one with nature… establishing an equilibrium between ourselves and the resources of the earth—an image of balance and equilibrium… this is an inadequate, insufficient view of environmental craft; to change both productive procedures and rituals of use requires a more radical self-critique."[1] If our buildings and clothes (our constructed skins) are instruments through which we modulate our relationships with the environment, what might happen if we test bringing these environmental relationships uncomfortably close to home? Might this encourage related design practices to develop something akin to the radical self-critique Sennett speaks of? In other words, if we fold these constructed skins back into our biological bodies, and then back out again, would such an intimate design encounter elicit more self-critique?

These questions propelled *The Biospatial Workshop*, a design research project assembled in the School of Architecture and Design and the Design Research Institute at RMIT University in Melbourne in 2007. This project aimed to explore the problematic relationships that shape our sense of environment and their relation to the problem of green design, or sustainability. Works of architecture and fashion, strange domestic products, films and writings were generated by third and fourth year students from architecture, fashion and environmental science, with input from a number of design practitioners (Pia Ednie-Brown/onomatopoeia, Tim Schork/mesne, Adele Varcoe), and an artist in residence (Boo Chapple). The students engaged in three courses: *Contaminated Life* (a design seminar elective), *Cultivating Life* (a design studio and science project), and *Contagious Life* (a Generative Components scripting seminar).

Feeling Green?

The Biospatial Workshop emphasized the capacity of aesthetic ways of knowing for approaching contemporary environmental issues. By "aesthetic," I don't mean simply what something looks like, but rather a form of knowing that pertains to the experience of relation or, more colloquially, the way in which we feel relationships of all kinds. Aesthetics in this sense becomes inseparable from ethics. As such, there was less of a focus on the technological operations of (sustainable) systems than on negotiating the complex assemblages of often contradictory, competing relations that become implicated in the operation of any system.

For instance, the complexity of contemporary environmental relationships became emphatically felt as we confronted the work of the environmental science students.[2] These students did some experiments related to ecotoxicology which, broadly speaking, concerns how organisms are affected by chemicals released into the environment by human activities. Specifically, they were exploring how organisms may be utilized to monitor and remove chemical toxins from environments: a growing field referred to as bioremediation. They set up controlled environments in which earthworms and sunflower

address ing post problem vs. prevention

Death X, *Jen Wood, 2007*

*Class dialogue had picked up on MX, a free Melbourne newspaper that
is read and thrown away by around 700,000 Australian commuters daily,
as an example of obscene waste. Wood responded to that dialogue
by manipulating a picture of a girl picking up a copy from a dispenser,
in a way that captured the fervor and feeling of horror that had swept
through the class in those early weeks, as they digested literature on
bleak futures in the face of environmental change.*

seedlings lived and grew in soil spiked with heavy metals. After grinding up the worms
and plants that lived in those contaminated environments, they could measure their
bioavailability—or the uptake of metals into their tissue.

It was not without discomfort that we found earthworms dried to a crisp after making
seemingly desperate attempts to escape the more highly contaminated containers of soil.
The more stunted, yellowish, less vibrant plant specimens, valiantly struggling to grow
in overdoses of metal contaminants, induced some sadness. Turning living organisms
into vehicles for analysis and de-contamination felt ethically confronting, and highlighted
the problematic aspects of many of our scientific, and increasingly biotechnologically
informed practices. What is done in the name of cleanliness often has a faintly unpleas-
ant smell. Processes such as bioremediation complicate any cartoon-like distinctions
between insides and outsides, clean and dirty, sacred and profane.

If, as William Taylor has argued,[3] our historical attempts to accommodate nature
within the design of cultured spaces shaped our idea of environment, then it makes
sense that the quite radical micro-logical accommodations of *culture into nature* through
bioremediation, genetic modification and the like, surely leads to changes in that idea,
and our awareness of it. If the environment is changing, what are we trying to sustain
as we strive to act more sustainably? Are we in danger of sustaining patterns that are
already out-of-step with what's happening?

If there seems to be a lingering aroma of sickliness in the environment of late, it is
perhaps illuminated by Samuel Beckett's comment that: "Habit is the ballast that chains
the dog to his vomit."[4] We are always out-of-step with even our own actions, innovations
and transformations, the implications of which take a while to realise. The half-second
lag between, say, pricking your finger with a pin and the conscious perception of both
that event and your response to it has been well documented. In socio-cultural collective bodies, the lag between doing something and knowing about it is somewhat longer,
and our habits can take a while to shift, even when the conditions for which they are
patterned have changed.

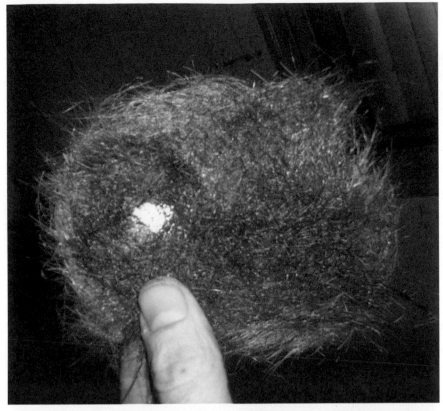

Felted Beard, *Stephen Mushin, 2007*

Mushin Writes: Where does all of our hair go, and could we begin to cultivate it? Would it be a useful fiber being so coarse? Could we make clothing or other textile-based household items or would its use be limited to fiber/resin composite materials and heavy duty sacking? For the purposes of envisaging uses for human hair, let's focus on the production of clothing and work with a double thickness weave for greater strength (the woven fabric could also be felted for strength). Every day I produce 32.4 meters of hair. It's astounding but true.

This figure is comprised of 3.6 meters of head hair (An average of 90,000 hairs at .4 mm per day), 25 meters of beard hair (20,000 hairs at .1 mm per day) and around 5 meters of pubic, arm, leg and other bodily parts hair (250,000 hairs at .2 mm per day). Of this fiber making capacity, 90% of the follicles are in active growth mode every day. Based upon the above figures and accepting that that it would be difficult to cultivate more than 50% of our hair production, we could estimate that each male could produce 4 square centimeters of this double thickness woven human hair fabric per day. In a week this would give us 27 square centimeters, and in a year 1460 square centimeters; about enough for a scarf.

How fantastic! Our own, not home made, but me-made scarf to mark each year, complete with an environmental log of everything that we have come in contact with from food to chemicals, happiness and love to fear and stress.

Seed, Jen Wood, 2007
Wood observed that as the chemical constitution of semen can be slightly altered by the consumption of certain foods, men might potentially affect the growth of their seedlings through a disciplined diet.

The Biospatial Workshop began with a 12-week seminar, *Contaminated Life*, with students from architecture and fashion design. In picking through the politics and poetics of excreta and pollution, our investigations called up the other meaning of "green": feeling unwell, nauseous, unstable. The twisted forces and anxieties about waste and toxicity, that squirm and flutter through so many activities and objects we actively desire, offer up a rich compost material for approaching the problem of lifestyles grounded on toxic practices.

Fairly early on, we decided the term "sustainability" required some adjustment. To sustain implies maintenance, or a keeping-things-going. As it seemed clear to us that we needed to change quite radically rather than maintain current practices, we decided to replace sustainability with *transformability*: the ability to transform. Transformability suggests life cycles in which there is no grave, influenced by McDonough and Braungart's *Cradle to Cradle* approach.[5] Approached with an emphasis on the self-perpetuating and plastic properties of living systems, we tapped into the material processes of embodiment, guiding our own bodily activities into ways of transforming waste and/or toxicity. This led to an emphasis on self-farming. After all, if we can use the processes of other living entities to combat environmental problems, such as in bioremediation, then surely our own bodily processes could be open to utilisation as well?

Stephen Mushin experimented with the farming and felting of human hair. He estimated that every day he produces 32.4 meters of hair across the different parts and hair types of the body.[6] He cut hair from his head, added 5 percent beard hair for texture and color, and felted it through a process of agitation with hot water and soap. Ear wax, he informed us as an aside, was another substance worth collecting, for its effectiveness in polishing timber furniture. We learnt that the practice of drinking urine, which apparently contains on average about 95 percent water, has a long and diverse history, and that urea is a very common ingredient in cosmetics.

Jen Wood's *Seed* project researched the potential of semen as a nutrient for sprouting plants. *Seed* is an idea for ribbed and studded condoms where the studs are embedded seeds which germinate in the spent semen after the condom has been used, enabling men to spread their seed in a new way.

Stephen Mushin's *The Loop: Urban Nutrient Banking* reconfigures the usual rejection of waste into systems that allow that waste to be directed and transformed into the production of new life. *The Loop* is an idea for a public toilet franchise that offers a user credit and rewards system. At *The Loop* one makes a deposit (of urine and/or faeces) which is used to produce fertile soil in which food produce is grown. After accumulating a certain amount of credit, there are rewards to be redeemed, such as a glass of orange juice squeezed from oranges grown with our organic capital. These amenities are imagined as glasshouses in which the produce is grown, and where the place for making a deposit is designed to offer a stimulating spatial experience.

These creative works helped establish and flesh out a design emphasis on life-cycles, feedback loops and their actual (rather than mimicked) engagement with living processes. The loops threaded through and connected often habitually disassociated materials and activities, raising transformative potential as they did so, particularly for the recasting or destabilisation of (unsustainable) habits or taboos. Through a focussed attention on the intimate and the bodily, these environmental assemblages bought the issues they raised extremely close to home.

Plasticity

"Plasticity, *then, in the wide sense of the word, means the possession of a structure weak enough to yield to an influence, but strong enough not to yield all at once. Each relatively stable phase of equilibrium in such a structure is marked by what we may call a new set of habits…* the phenomena of habit in living beings are due to the plasticity of the organic materials of which their bodies are composed."
—William James[7]

In a climate of change, this plasticity becomes more explicit. We are currently in a very plastic world: in the process of adapting and shifting from one set of habits to another. These habits do seem hard to break, but this is perhaps because they are plastic. Rather than break, they gradually yield, change shape, restructure. Changing habits involves mobilizing our plasticity and ability to transform, without falling apart. It is how best to skilfully and critically direct our plasticity which becomes a crucial issue. If, as theorist Sylvia Lavin has claimed, "plasticity is at the core of the contemporary architectural project,"[8] it also operates at the core of our environmental challenges.

As I have discussed at length elsewhere,[9] many contemporary design practices are making some fairly emphatic statements about qualities of plastic transformability, in ways both promising and problematic. Our way of defining (and generating) entities, is changing *in nature*, and design has been articulating this plasticity in wordless (formal and processual) ways. Might these wordless articulations of plasticity have anything to offer the challenge of climate change? It may seem a long bow to draw, but we set out to explore this question in the *Cultivating Life* design studio in the second part of the year.

The studio began by developing physical models that embodied a plastic system of relationships defined, as James put it, as "weak enough to yield to an influence, but strong enough not to yield all at once." These material plastic systems were then taken into a parametric scripting seminar with Tim Schork. Parametric scripting operates as a system for describing co-dependent relationships and their variations. Within this system there are no objects to be found directly, or bluntly. Objects, in other words, primarily become a system of intricate, plastic relations where wholes become inseparable from an intricate multiplicity of interacting constituents.

While scripted descriptions are infinitely reduced in complexity to any related thing in the analogue world, especially living ecologies, they offer us usefully plastic, diagrammatic models of (and therefore a tool for knowing) systems of co-dependent variation. It is in this way that these ways of working resonate with the complex environmental relations discussed earlier, and the climate of change in which we currently live. The usefulness of such a design exercise, in other words, is not necessarily *instrumental*, in the sense of being a tool that directly leads to sustainable outcomes. Rather, the value is carried via resonance, in that it encourages ways of thinking and doing that loop or fold back into our capacities for negotiating complexity. It is in terms of this feedback loop that these systems are not unlike the less precise and full bodied, but more socio-politically rich self-farming projects from *Contaminated Life*.

While the projects produced are all quite diverse in nature, they all have a crucial thing in common: they usher a problem into a resonant feedback system such that this very problem is both highlighted and transformed. They raise awareness, but always problematically. As they do this, they all enact transformations upon an existing situation and space that loops back on itself, such as, for instance, where the produced becomes the consumed, waste becomes generative, and cleanliness becomes dirty. Often this

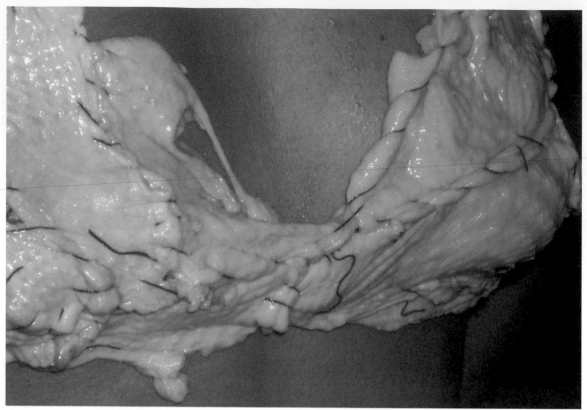

Chicken Skin Bra, *Sarah Martinus, 2007*

Martinus confronts us with an intimate example of the environmental violence hidden behind the manufacture of the majority of clothing and bodily products made in the name of beauty, and the impending stench of these activities.

looping unfolds into a growing concern for how the boundaries that define environments might become thick and active sites for the housing of transformational processes.

To return to Sennett's call for "a more radical self-critique," what I have just described in the previous paragraph is a type of critique that is not purely reflective, nor entirely analytical. Rather, the act of reappraising a situation occurs through the act of generating or designing something new. It could be seen as a *generative critique*. This does not occur by placing oneself at a distance from problems, fears and discomforts, or by trying to control or escape them, but by *engaging* with them in order to transform them and/or ourselves. This form of critique highlights problematic issues while using them to generate something compellingly poetic, useful and provocative in the same gesture. Repeatedly, and via a number of routes, the aim was to fold abstract and large scale problems into the very close-to-home. In this sense, it is not irrelevant that these design investigations often made us laugh, gasp and sigh, our bodies opening up, squirming, or exhaling as we did so. For it was in moving through tangles of affective responses, that we were tickled by micro-instances of the very thing we sought to achieve: transformability, or the ability to transform.

References

1. Sennett, Richard. The Craftsman. *New Haven and London: Yale University Press, 2008, p. 12-13*

2. Supervised by Associate Prof. Dayanthi Nugegoda and Associate Prof. Barry Meehan in the School of Applied Science at RMIT University

3. Taylor, William. The Vital Landscape: Nature and the Built Environment in Nineteenth-Century Britain. *London: Ashgate Publishing, 2004*

4. Beckett, Samuel. Proust. *See: http://en.wikipedia.org/wiki/Proust_(Beckett_essay)*

5. McDonough, William and Braungart, Michael. Cradle to Cradle: Remaking the Way We Make Things. *New York: North Point Press, 2002*

6. See Stephen's blog entry: http://liveness.org/contaminated-life/?p=228

Chew, *Sarah Martinus, 2007*

Chew is a collection of garments that become part of a parametric system for bodily transformation—being designed for muscular restraint, exercise and weight loss, while also for openly excessive, narcissistic consumption. Clothing, usually largely defined by relationships between textiles and bodies, here becomes also threaded into internal processes of consumption and absorption, and external processes of narcissistic engagement that, in turn, loop into one another. Chew is a self-feeding system that enables excess by countering its effects, and enables processes of transformation while paradoxically maintaining an ongoing need for these very processes. Critiquing the narcissistic cycle of excessive consumption and over-production of the fashion industry, Sarah has produced something that is, paradoxically, all waste and all production.

Breath Catchers, *wearable breath recycling and carbon offset systems, Boo Chapple, 2007*
Among other works Chapple, Biospatial Workshop 2007 artist in residence, attached nostril pipes to plastic bags to condense exhaled moisture and channel the drips into collection devices for drinking or watering plants; and developed a wearable urine collection device with a detachable carbon filter for extracting drinkable water. The absurdity of these scenarios act as a critique of the logic of self-sufficiency. More profoundly, Chapple's work brings into view the very mechanistic logic embedded in most sustainability systems, which become somewhat incompatible with the actuality of living processes and their intrinsically ecological, collectively involved operations.

7. James, William. The Writings of William James, *John J McDermott (ed), London: The University of Chicago Press, p. 10, 1977*
8. Lavin, Sylvia. "Plasticity at Work," Mood River, *Ohio: Wexner Centre for the Arts, p. 80, 2002*
9. Ednie-Brown, Pia. "Plastic Super Models," Fibreculture Journal, Issue 12: Models, Metamodels and Contemporary Media, *Andrew Murphie and Gary Genosko (eds), 2008, http://journal.fibreculture.org/issue12/*

Dr. Pia Ednie-Brown *is a writer, designer and educator based in Melbourne, Australia. She works at RMIT University where she is a senior lecturer in the Architecture program and a research leader in the Spatial Information Architecture Laboratory (SIAL). Her texts and projects have been published and exhibited internationally. Her work negotiates emerging modes of organization and related architectural design practices via a focus on embodiment, presence and new technologies. Current research explores ethics and aesthetics as key drivers of innovation, with an emphasis on design and the biotechnological. Her diverse, transdisciplinary research activities are encompassed under her practice, onomatopoeia.*
http://www.onomatopoeia.com.au/practice

Sbstititsue, *Sarah Martinus and Sophie Braungartner, 2007*
Martinus and Braungartner played with the idea that we are suffocating in the toxic substances that fill most Western domestic environments. In re-purposing domestic fabrics into a fashion collection, they recycled this toxicity. Suffocation was embodied by a set of garments that literally restricted one's breathing; an uncomfortably powerful beauty. Their pale, submissively poised models, dressed in reworked carpet and plastic table cloths, had their shoulders drawn forward by garments made to be tight across the chest. Combining a sense of deathly claustrophobia with delicacy and fragility, Sbstititsue manifests the (re)cyclic movement from "cradle to cradle," while nestling within it the pallor of the grave.

Arid

Aridness and the lure of the arid climate is based on the rejection of a seasonal sense of time. The predominant motivation for migrating to arid zones has for a long time been retirement, and with it an attempt to escape the ritual-heavy existence of cyclical time of more northern climates. French sociologist Henri Lefebvre has observed that along with the migration of rural workforce into industrialized cities came a sense of separation from seasonal time to be replaced with the year round and 24-hour continuum of mechanized environments.[1] For different reasons the move from seasonal to arid climates produces a similar change in the perception of time in leisure pursuits, relaxation and changes in lifestyle.

In order for this to appeal to the leisure classes, cities like Los Angeles, Las Vegas and Phoenix had to engineer a transition in the perception of the desert from a hostile wilderness to an Arcadian idyll. Overcoming the fear of brutal landscape was initially engendered by soothing images of citrus groves, then suburbia, and subsequently retirement ex-urbs like Sun City and Anthem. This transition has occurred with marked contrast in different generational perceptions. In 1849 the Bennett-Arcane Party named Death Valley on leaving after months of struggle to cross into California. By marked contrast Superstudio's "Life and Supersurface"[2] presents naked families within a seamless landscape refocusing the myth of American settlement. While this image is often regarded as a high point of the architectural avant-garde in the 1960s it may also be seen as partly responsible for propagating another myth of arid landscapes, an avant-garde form of real estate speculation based on the idea of an endless unobstructed terrain that is entirely compliant and serviced for consumption. In effect (rather than appearance) this scenario has come to pass in the suburbs of Phoenix and Las Vegas. "Fundamental Acts"[3] can be closely matched to the today's serviced grids stretching out across a flat landscape at the borders of southwestern suburbia. For many years arid zone cities were regarded as supreme achievements of water engineers, sheer willpower and expansionistic zeal. However, recently this ethic seems to have turned sour under zeitgeist of environmentalism. What was once boosterism has turned into a loss of confidence along with a desensitized sense of expanded space. Today the images of golf courses in the desert are just as likely to be used as warnings against profligacy as they are as selling points for new communities. Similarly the image of bermed lawns flooded by former citrus irrigation channels does little to improve Phoenix's attempts to address use of water resources.

These twin aspects of endless terrain and suppression of seasonal time are key factors in the make-up of arid zone cities.

However retirement and leisure are by no means the only form of arid expansion. Today's new emergent demographics have brought with them the possibility of a departure from the city's predominantly excessive image.

Phoenix, Arizona. Bermed lawns are periodically flooded by the former citrus grove irrigation system

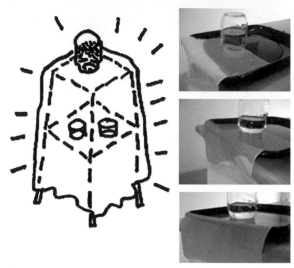

Desert fridge and evaporative cooling model

Under the title the "New American University" Arizona State University is projected to expand to 100,000 students by the year 2020,[4] having extended its campus from Tempe to three new locations in greater Phoenix.[5] Along with the title "New" comes renewed interest in educational environments within arid zones that is coupled with a rejection of profligacy of physical expansion. This new university campus offers a departure partly in its physical nature but more drastically in the temporal and episodic use of space. While this may currently be a less visible attribute of the arid zone campus it is potentially its strongest benefit. While the more seasonal universities of the Midwest, A&M's and rural campuses appear to be conditioned by traditions and rituals of cyclical events (football seasons, spring break events, fall bonfires, etc.) the ASU campus appears less "event driven." A considerably less spectacular sense of seasonal change is replaced with a year round continuum of good weather and outdoor existence. This sense of a continuum may also offer a marked contrast from the way seasonal campuses delineate between enclosed learning environments within buildings and external space as predominantly zones of transition, (romantic landscaping, processional routes). In arid zone universities this delineation may be less defined and instead focus on the nuances of different cooling techniques for each condition. Here the distinction lies between evaporative cooling as an alternative to AC and forced air systems. In some senses this distinction presents a departure from the prevalent notion of hermetically sealed interior (along with an enclosed learning environment) and a less defined cooled zone.[6] It is the latter that presents the greatest opportunity in terms of alternative places of learning. Similar to other arid zone universities, the ASU campus has the potential to regard its interstitial spaces as extended learning zones. Additionally, those interstitial zones may also offer an ideal location for the much sought after locus for cross-disciplinarian academic production. In short it may become both physically and academically transitional.

Recently these forces have lead the university to adopt specific policies with regard to water conservation and the use of external spaces that are part of their wider campus sustainability initiatives.[7] Offshoots of these initiatives are found in the university arboretum and campus-grown foods that deploy flood irrigation systems for water conservation. In terms of architecture recently commissioned buildings have turned towards design of outdoor spaces through evaporative cooling systems as the corollary of indoor AC-cooled spaces.[8]

One such initiative currently under proposal suggests the development of a series of Freshman Dining Pavilions[9] that comprise of 10 temporary structures across the campus that focus on a dining ritual for incoming students. This project has become the subject of a prototype cooling structure that offers an assimilation of evaporative cooling systems as architectural narration of water use and cooling processes. The project aims to communicate its themes through both a haptic and symbolic understanding of evaporative cooling around the rituals of outdoor dining.[10]

Desert Fridge: A Dining Pavilion at ASU

"When you look at a building what do you see?
The modification of those rhythms and their inscription in space by human means"[11]
—Henri Lefebvre

To the east of Johnson City, TX, is the Lyndon B. Johnson family home. Part of the Johnson Estate[12] is given over to a working farm circa 1870 that presents various aspects of domestic practice from that era. This includes a desert fridge, which is a simple four-legged structure with a slightly battered profile that is draped in calico. Its principle is simple; water from an upturned jar is drawn by osmosis down the sides of the calico where it evaporates in wind currents drawn though a "dog run" between two log cabins. Cooled air circulates within the structure where cheese and milk are kept fresh during the summer. The desert fridge is a simple system that reaches a state of equilibrium through the natural process of evaporation.

This biological process offers a system that is then projected both upon the dining ritual and the composition of the building. The following text explores a sequence of levels by which the structure, via digital production process, provides an educational narrative on sustainability. This communicative quality is portrayed by a prototype pavilion in direct biological terms, through tacit knowledge,

perceived phenomena, lexical and mechanical systems. The text also describes how these digital production processes were used in the pavilion's design and fabrication. These range from an empirical prognosis of evaporative cooling effects, fluid dynamics, heat mapping and solar radiation analysis through to sheet steel laser cutting, folded plate construction and fully associative variable models of standard steel construction. The aim of the pavilion is to create an environment that presents the evaporative cooling message at a multiple of levels that will concentrate the visitor in a complete understanding of the processes imbued within the building.

For invited freshmen the experience of the dining pavilion begins prior to actually arriving at its site. Each dining event is preceded by an invitation that is sent to the students in a simple glass jar. The jar contains instructions printed on a clear plastic sheet that describes not only the event but also what to do with the jar:

"THIS JAR IS AN INVITATION TO DINE AMONG FRESHMEN. PLEASE BRING IT ON (date) TO (campus location). WHEN YOU ARRIVE FILL THE JAR WITH WATER AND INVERT IT ON TO THE CLOTH STRIP WITH THE PLASTIC STRIP PROVIDED."

Using the jar in this manner is a deliberate appropriation of familiar dining rituals, i.e. a glass of liquid at each setting. However when the jar is inverted, water gradually seeps out of it and is drawn under osmotic pressure through the canvas. This canvas, like the inverted jar, shares affiliations with the dining ritual. Like the tablecloth it conveys a sense of a formal event. However, like the jar, the cloth is estranged from this familiarity—it hangs inwards and invites the controlled accident of split liquid.

Cooling Function and Iconography

The jars and the cloth present two elements in the chain of events that make up the pavilion. A series of other technical and iconographic components make these events functional. At the center of the pavilion is a 16" aluminum fan that hangs below the surface of the table. The fan is driven is driven by a roof-mounted 50-watt direct current PV panel[13] (For the prototype structure the PV fan was hardwired to the DC motor although in the final proposed version solar generated electricity would be stored in batteries concealed below the floor structure) and drives air downwards on to a diverter and then horizontally through the inverted tablecloth. Air is cooled through the evaporative process and then blown on to the legs and midriffs of the students dining at the table. The students dine in the cooler micro-environment as the water level in the jars gradually recedes in front of them, prolonging the event and engendering interactions. The system achieves a considerable drop off in ambient air temperature up to six feet from the table's center.

However the empirical nature of this project is not, in itself, enough to directly communicate the message of the buildings system. This scheme is also arranged to communicate, via a sequence of physical components, several levels of comprehension of the buildings core concept. Each component of the building transcribes its particular role in the larger scheme in ways that assist the

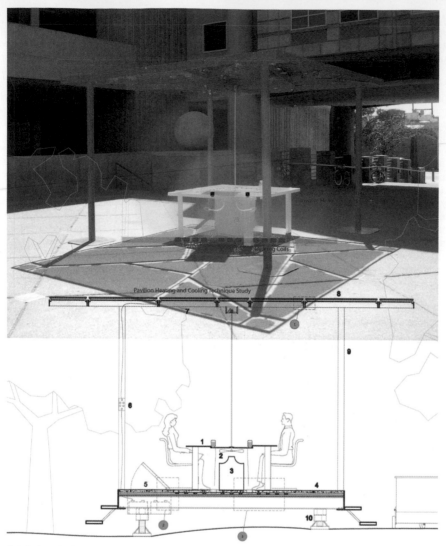

Detailed section/photograph of pavilion and cooling table showing temperature drop off

visitor in a tacit and visual understanding of the buildings message and performance.

Providing the visitor with the sight of a jar of water that gradually empties offers a direct visual and quantative experience of the building's process. Henri Lefebvre writing in the *Production of Space* describes "the modification of those rhythms and their inscription in space by human means"[14] In so doing he refers to those acts, events and flows that occur within a building but are not considered architectural material *per se*. Lefebvre argues that such experiences are equal if not greater among architectural experience but commonly considered ancillary to conventional architectural discourse—a building may contain a swamp cooler although it is rarely considered as an architectural element. The change in state of a body of water passing through it is even less architectural. In this respect this pavilion exposes similar aspects of the actual flows within the building and brings them into the architectural experience, engaging and informing visitors about hidden environmental systems that lie within.

While the role of the fan, like the jar of water, is crucial to the operating system of the design it is also a key iconographic element in visually translating the pavilion's theme. At times the iconographic power of the fan exceeds its ability to perform effectively.[15] This "both and"[16] interpretation is apparent in the design of the dining table. The functional necessity of the under-table air forces the fan out of sight and below the table and ensures that it plays a subservient role as a communicative architectural element. The design of the table addresses this issue through a perforation pattern of enmeshed fans arranged to make up the table surface. This pattern is laser cut into ¼" paintlock mild steel sheet that is then bent and formed into the table.[17] The level of perforation is designed to allow the passage of cool air through the table and on to the diners. The perforation also borrows from the functional typology of outdoor furniture that is perforated to allow rainwater to pass through it and also to reduce its thermal mass in hot temperatures. In this

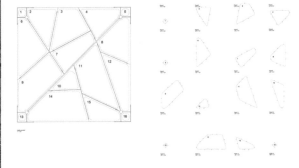

Above and top: Pavilion roof structure and perforated panel pattern formed from standard steel sections

Roof structure and perforated panel pattern generated from assimilation of fan image and diagram of fan axes

way the fan pattern acts as a visual communicator and simultaneously a functional element.

The size of the pavilion means that it can only effectively communicate its performance within close visual proximity. It is too small to propagate its message to the wider context of the campus. This scale of communication is broadened by the shade structure that sits above the table. Here again the iconography of the fan is used to generate a mesh of primary and secondary structural beams and perforated infill patterns. The underbelly of the structure (lit at night) projects this pattern language at various angles around the campus. The structure is designed to support a sequence of PV shade panels. These panels are set above the perforated shade panels and comprise polycrystalline PV elements laminated between sheets of toughened glass. Each panel is designed to directly charge batteries stored below the suspended floor.

The arrangement of these patterns is specific to the location and orientation of each individual pavilion. Each pavilion site is chosen for its proximity to existing shade on campus and its exposure to direct sun, the locations themselves derived from a set of solar radiation studies.[18]

The Aesthetics of Green

Today green architecture produces either a technology driven functional aesthetic or an undeclared system of green iconography. The worst excesses of bolt-on green signifiers attract criticism as "greenwash" while a purely technological approach produces an anti-aesthetic or non-aesthetic result. Either way, neither position fully recognizes the importance of the emblematic and as such undermines the movement's ability to make a complete response to all aspects of architecture. Raoul Bunschoten, writing in the *OASE Architectural Journal*,[19] asserts that architecture propagates itself through a diagram of its idealized condition. This diagram, generated as an abstraction of the ideal is also present in architecture in emblematic form. Both the artifacts and the processes that are essential to any particular culture are embedded within one another in a manner that raises both function and décor together inextricably. How might green architecture be seen in this light? What are the implications of this upon the movement and what is emblematic of its ideal state?

An overview of sustainable architecture today reveals a sequence of signifiers (either functional or not) that seem to consistently symbolize "green." Quasi-naturalistic finishes, global associations, organic form and omnipresent vents and fans are but a few. That these appear to represent a consensus either consciously or not may allow them to feature as a lexicon of signifiers that might ultimately be used deliberately within architecture. In the ASU Dining Pavilion function, message, and associated iconography are drawn together to convey its environmental system. From the function of natural evaporation ramify a series of results that are portrayed through the building's composition, fabrication, structure and environmental effects.

The ASU Dining Pavilion is a prototype for a building that is designed to engender social discourse among freshman students on entering the university. Its formal aspects connect the project to the wider cultural context of arid zone campuses. The building is set up to mix user and education in the interstitial spaces between the more conventional learning environments of an enclosed building. This scenario is symptomatic of an emerging condition in places like Arizona where the conception of a non-seasonal continuum allows architects and university planners to delineate space in news ways born of the idiosyncrasies of an arid climate.

References

1. Lefebvre, Henri. Rhythmanalysis: Space Time and Everyday Life. Continuum, 2004, p. 51-56

2. Lang, Peter and Menking, William. Fundamental Acts 1972, Superstudio: Life without Objects. Milano and New York: Skira. Distributed in North America and Latin America by Rizzoli International Publications, Inc. through St. Martin's Press, 2003, p. 179-184

3. Ibid

4. http://asunews.asu.edu/20080131_campusgrowth

5. http://asunews.asu.edu/20080131_campusgrowth

6. Problems associated with evaporative cooling i.e. air-borne pathogens, matrix maintenance, etc make it less desirable to high tech and domestic interiors which favor highly automated and manageable ac systems. Evaporative cooling system and swamp coolers tend to appear in older houses, industrial sheds and exterior spaces.

7. See http://sustainability.asu.edu/giosmain/news/gios-news/bonny-sustainability

8. Richard and Bauer. See ISTB1 - http://www.richard-bauer.com/istb1.htm

9. The brief for the project was proposed by former dean Duke Rieter in collaboration with Bruce Mau. All detailed design and fabrication work carried out in collaboration with students from ASU's School of Architecture and Landscape Architecture. Kelvin Hsuan, Terrance McMahon, Jack Spalding, Amy Loeschen, Nicole Melde, Carrie Miller, Brian Bissonnette, In Young Kim, Matt Ihms, Mike Goetz, Kasey Zantos, Mark Meyers.

10. The pavilion is intended as a gathering point and a place of interaction for ASU freshmen. The long-term aim of this project is to provide a multiple of these pavilions across the campus that will be the locus of a sequence of dining events over a "dining season" during the fall and spring semester.

11. Lefebvre, Henri. The Production of Space. Wiley-Blackwell, 1992, p. 117

12. Lyndon B. Johnson State Park and Historic Site. Hwy. 290 E. at Park Road 52, Stonewall, TX 78671

13. DC Motor: Permanent Magnet, Totally Enclosed Non-Ventilated, HP 1/35, RPM 2350,Voltage 12 DC, Full Load Amps 3.8

14. Lefebvre, Henri. The Production of Space. Wiley-Blackwell, 1992, p. 117

15. For example the RIBA center in Portland Place, London proposed a wind turbine on the roof

16. Venturi Scott Brown Izenour. Learning from Las Vegas. MIT Press, p. 72

17. For 20 gauge the laser ran at 2900 mm/minute at 3600 Watts while for the ¼" ran at the same feed rate but at 3600 Watts

18. http://squ1.com/products/ecotect

19. "Stirring the city," OASE Architectural Journal. No.48/1990

Jason Griffiths gained his professional qualification at the Bartlett UK and is a partner of Gino Griffiths Architects in collaboration with Alex Gino. He began teaching in 1994 at the Bartlett and then went on to teach at Oxford Brookes and University of Westminster as a senior lecturer. His teaching career is paralleled with 11 prize-winning competitions including first prize in both the AAFab 2009, Temple of Laughter and the Millennium Café competitions. In 2003 Jason and Alex came to the US to conduct a sabbatical research/lecture tour of North American suburbs. Prior to joining ASU he worked in Texas, Nebraska and Iowa. Griffiths' teaching explores the design build studio as a vehicle for research interests in both digital fabrication and contemporary iconography. His completed works in this field include an Arts Pavilion for Iowa State, Sioux City Bus Stops and ASU Dining Pavilion. He is currently building a house in Mojave Desert in collaboration with Alex Gino. Jason has been published in many academic and professional journals including the Journal of Architecture, Architecture, Sunday Times, World Architecture, Building Design and AJ. He has lectured in Spain, Italy, Mexico and the US for institutions that include ESTAM, In-Arch, UNAM, Rice, Sci-Arch, the AA and the Bartlett.

Laser fan pattern functions to allow passage of cooled air through the steel table and to reduce thermal mass

DMZOO

A. Democratic People's Republic of Korea; B. Republic of Korea; C. People's Republic of China; D. East Sea (Sea of Japan); E. Yellow Sea; F. Demilitarized Zone; G. Jeju-do; H. Seoul; I. Pyongyang; J. Taebaek Range; K. Baekdu Mountain; L. 38th Parallel

An investigation into the relationship between man and the built environment, the DMZOO envisions a new paradigm for the 21st-century zoological garden empowered by the technological process of cloning. Dystopian tradition serves as the conceptual framework for examining the interdependence of nature and artifice as manifest in the regeneration of the ecosystem in the Demilitarized Zone, the corridor separating the two Koreas. The project confronts the paradoxical complexity of national reconciliation in the Korean peninsula in an attempt to reveal potential problems facing normalization of the territory.

Established in 1953 at the end of the Korean War, the 250km long, 4km deep Demilitarized Zone (DMZ) continues to operate as a boundary between two hostile nations that were once culturally unified. Korea's bipolarity has engendered an intermediary zone defined by conflict and contradiction. Although initially created as a neutral buffer free of military presence, the DMZ is currently the world's most militarized border with an estimated 1.2 million troops stationed within 100km of its limits. Four tunnels dug by the North Korean army in preparation for invasion exist underneath one of the most heavily mined areas in the world. No official peace treaty has been signed to this day; the United States and South Korea are technically still engaged in war with North Korea.

Due to the hostile nature of the DMZ, only a very small number of humans—usually unauthorized military personnel—have entered its official boundary. This minimal level of human intervention during the past half century has caused drastic changes in the physical landscape. The natural regeneration of the ecosystem has created an ecological sanctuary; the DMZ and its contiguous Civilian Controlled Zone (CCZ) are now host to 52 animal species, 201 bird species, 28 amphibian reptiles, 67 inland fish species and 1,194 plant species.[1] More than 100 of these species have been classified as either rare or endangered by the IUCN.

The rapid development of South Korea encroaches upon the previously uninhabited area around and within the DMZ. Joint economic ventures between North and South Korea—in the form of industrial parks and tourist sites—are emerging in close proximity to the DMZ. With 70 percent of the Korean peninsula covered in mountain ranges, arable and developable land is a valuable resource. The renewal of biodiversity and animal life in the DMZ has resulted in the urging of environmentalists and ecologists to maintain the zone as a natural reserve or to set up a system of national parks. The DMZOO, through the process of cloning, offers a solution to mediate the overlap of these two conditions.

References

1. Shore, William B. "Sanctuary: For Nature and for the Dead." World Watch Magazine, Nov.-Dec. 2004, p. 34

David Yang is an architect working in New York. Born in Seoul, South Korea and raised in New York, he received a Bachelor of Architecture from Cornell University in 2006; DMZOO was his senior thesis project. He is currently pursuing his post-professional degree at the Yale School of Architecture.

From left to right: Remove specimen from habitat; Extract DNA; Store in genetic bank; Destroy original (optional); Clone ad infinitum

The genetic data of all plants and animals living within the DMZ are collected and stored within the Frozen Zoo. The genetic bank archives all building information necessary to clone and recreate animals that were previously threatened or endangered. South Korea, spurred by the breakthrough cloning of Snuppy the Afghan hound, is currently at the forefront of animal technology. Ongoing research at the DMZOO laboratories is dedicated to producing and breeding superior specimens.

 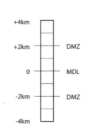 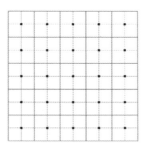  

From left to right: Identify location of intervention; Analyze site conditions; Distribute and allocate; Divide; Connect

Located in the middle of the Korean peninsula, Cheolwon County served as its capital during the Silla Dynasty from 57 BCE to 935 CE. Its relative flatness—a result of its situation between mountainous zones—renders the area ideal for manipulation.

The DMZOO, delineated by eight contiguous square kilometers, straddles the Military Demarcation Line. Four of the squares occupy the 4-kilometer depth of the DMZ while the remaining 4 squares are equally divided between the two countries: two to the north and two to the south. Each of the larger squares is subdivided into 100 smaller modules. The ARCC + Gatelodge facility splits the DMZOO in two, and functions as the mediator of the two zones. In order to mediate faster travel speeds across the immense site, the SKYFARI is constructed along the lengthwise median of the site.

  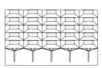

From left to right: Skyfari; Skyway; Shell; Wind turbine; Branching enclosure

YANG, David

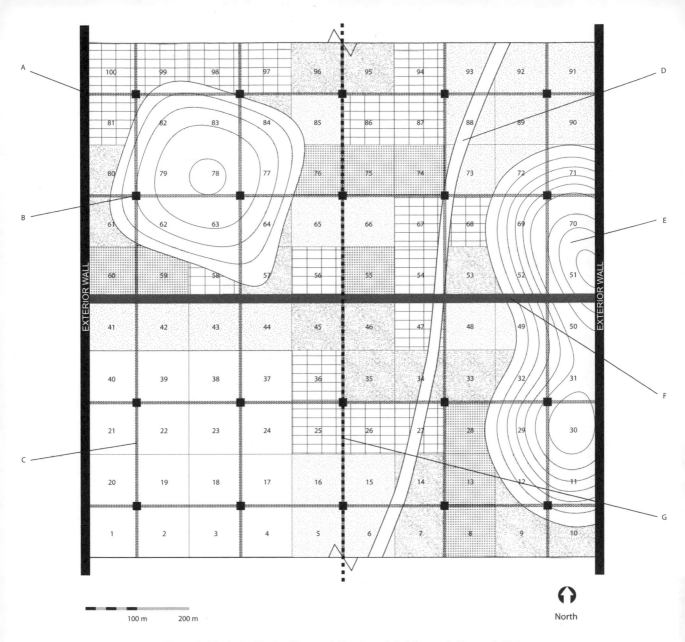

Theoretical Zoological Garden Diagram: A. Exterior wall; B. Infirmary; C. Skyway; D. Highway;
E. Topography; F. ARCC and Gatelodge; G. Skyfari

Skyway, Shell, Infirmary, "Random"

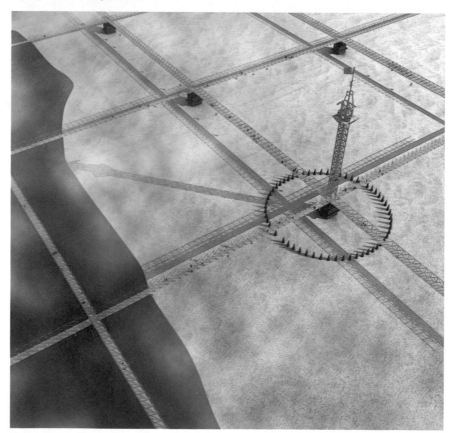

Skyfari, Skyway, Circular Array, Infirmary

YANG, David

MOTODA, Hisaharu

REVELATION AND INDICATION

Japan is often associated with bucolic tableaus. Images of nature figure as prominently in my nation's historic cultural identity as in our contemporary tourist economy; but today bucolic Japan is a convenient myth for a land that suffers from widespread environmental disruption. Behind beautiful Japan lurks another that is less often seen but no less present. Recently, ecology has been a theme of local and government initiatives, but are the Japanese people really aware of their own nature?

Scenes from nature figure largely in Japan's long tradition of printmaking: the power of a wave or a rainstorm, the presence of a mountain, the fleeting delicacy of a blossom. Today the majority of young people in Japan don't know much about their own culture. I was born not into an image of natural bounty, but into one of unprecedented economic growth and technological advancement. I have been searching for a way to express the disassociation of my environment from my culture through printmaking. My work seeks something of *Wabi* and *Sabi*, the twin concepts of the Japanese Tea Ceremony. *Wabi* means "austere refinement" and *Sabi* means "quiet simplicity." There is a Japanese saying "everything is impermanent." I simply want to send these same messages through my work; the beauty and refinement of fragile things.

HISAHARU MOTODA has exhibited internationally in Egypt, Canada, Hungary and Thailand, as well as in his home country of Japan. He holds a BA in printmaking from the Department of Fine Art, Faculty of Arts, Kyushu Sangyo University and a MA in printmaking from the Faculty of Fine Arts, Tokyo National University of Fine Arts and Music. His series *Revelations* and *Indication*, featuring famous sites in Tokyo reduced to ruins, were presented in a solo exhibition at Gallery III at the Contemporary Art Museum Kumamoto in Kyushu, Japan.

Electric City, Hisaharu Motoda, lithograph, 55x91cm, 2004

MOTODA, Hisaharu

Niijyuku, Hisaharu Motoda, lithograph, 90.5x69cm, 2001

MOTODA, Hisaharu

306090 13

Town, Hisaharu Motoda, lithograph, 91.5x187cm, 2003

MOTODA, Hisaharu

294

Hashima 6, Hisaharu Motoda, lithograph, 75x160cm, 2002

MOTODA, Hisaharu

306090 13

180 degree view of BAR-3 DEW Line Site, Tuktoyaktuk, Northwest Territories, Canada, 2009

STANKIEVECH, Charles

THE DEW PROJECT

www.stankievech.net/projects/DEW

A border is not a connection but an interval of resonance, and such gaps abound in the Land of the DEW Line. The DEW Line itself, the Distant Early Warning radar system installed by the United States in the Canadian North to keep this continent in touch with Russia, points up a major Canadian role in the 20th century, the role of hidden ground for big powers. Since the United States has become a world environment, Canada has become the anti-environment that renders the United States more acceptable and intelligible to many small countries of the world; anti-environments are indispensable for making an environment understandable.
—Marshall McLuhan, "Canada: The Borderline Case"

Since the arming of the jet, and especially since the arrival of artillery on the scene, warfare has not only created a landscape by defensive constructions, by the organizations of fronts and frontiers, but it has also competed successfully with natural forces; firearms, explosives, smoke screens, and gasses have contributed to the creation of an artificial climate… pollution, saturation, and biological disequilibrium.
—Paul Virilio, *Bunker Archeology*

With the centenary of the North Pole's discovery on April 6, 2009, the Arctic region has never been more of a global concern. A melting ice cap has refocused the world's attention on the Arctic, partly as an index of the global warming crisis and partly as an economic opportunity from the opening of new shipping trade routes and new access to the region's wealth of natural resources. Mid-way

between the North Pole's discovery and current times, the Arctic served as a theater for the Cold War. Nuclear attack delivered across the North Pole brought new fears for both Russia and the US in a mounting arms race. As much ideological deterrent as defense infrastructure, the Distant Early Warning (DEW) Line constructed between 1954 and 1956 was a joint venture between the US Air Force and the Royal Canadian Air Force. A long distance radar and communication system, the DEW Line created an electromagnetic boundary able to detect airborne invasion while making problematic Arctic sovereignty—an issue once again at stake. The Cold War might have been a successful negotiation over the frozen landscape of the Arctic but will the current battle over natural resources and sovereignty in a rapidly developing world share the same quiet fate? A germane topic today, sustainability is not just a question concerning

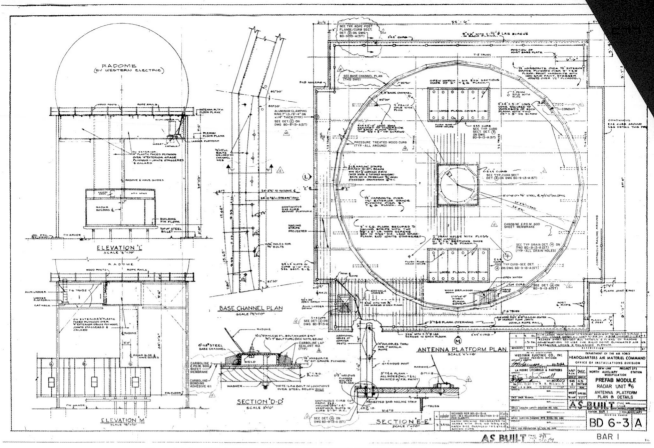

Blueprint for BAR-1 DEW Line Radome, Yukon Territory, Canada, 1956

a particular architectural design but the infrastructure and networks between nation states that will determine not only what—but who—is sustained in the future.

The *DEW* project revisits the issue of boundaries—both in regards to the environment and sovereignty—while observing how communication technology plays a pivotal role in the definition and delivery of such ideologies. Sheltered in a geodesic dome, *DEW* is a remote radio station positioned on the Yukon River outside of Dawson City, Yukon Territory, Canada. The radio station monitors the sounds of the river's ice and underwater flow on a continual basis, transmitting the signals to Dawson City where the field-recordings are processed and broadcast via the internet. Parallel to the radio broadcast, a parabolic projection screen displays a video in the SOVA gallery. The screen's design echoes the billboard form of a troposcatter

antenna originally used to communicate the radar data between the DEW Line stations and NORAD. Composed from footage of the Arctic landscape and various communication technologies used throughout the Arctic's history, the video spans a period from the Klondike Gold Rush to the present day, including infrastructure such as the telegraph, civilian radio, military radar, microwave and satellite. A live performance on April 6, 2009 incorporates a real-time audio feed from the ice pavilion mixed with electromagnetic recordings from the BAR-3 DEW Line site for the audience, who are able to listen to the concert with small transistor radios in the gallery and the surrounding landscape.

Funding provided by the Canada Council for the Arts, Hydrophones supplied by Aquarian Audio.

CHARLES STANKIEVECH works at the intersection of art, architecture and theory. Through aesthetic experimentation and rigorous research, he reveals latent histories while questioning conventional boundaries. His writings have been included in several academic journals, such as *Leonardo Music Journal* (MIT Press), numerous artists' catalogues and translated into French, Italian and German. His work has been exhibited in the Biennale of Architecture (Venice), Banff Centre for the Arts (Canada), Subtle Technologies (Toronto), Eyebeam (New York), and the Planetary Collegium (UK). Stankievech holds an MFA in Open Media and BA (hon.) in Philosophy and Literature. He is represented by Galerie Donald Browne in Montreal. Currently developing the new KIAC School of Visual Art in the Canadian Arctic, Stankievech is also a researcher in the Digital and Media Arts network for the University of the Arctic.

North Warning System Radomes, historic site of BAR-3 DEW Line, Tuktoyaktuk, Northwest Territories, Canada, 2009

STANKIEVECH, Charles

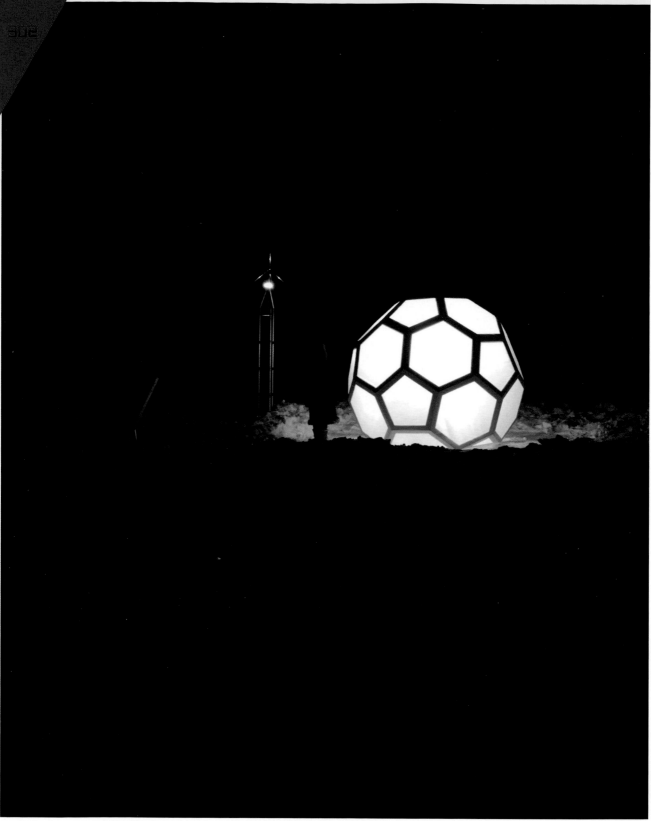

The DEW Project, (installation view), Confluence of Klondike and Yukon Rivers, Yukon Territory, Canada. 64°03' N, 139°27' W

STANKIEVECH, Charles

LING Fan

SITTING ON A FLOATING GREEN

The lawn represents social common-wealth, an urban substitute for the productive soil of the rural environment. An ambiguous surface, infill for urban designers' master plans, palliative for the scourge of urban development. Green looks great filling the spaces between buildings on all those drawings, but once those lawns are seeded do we all have to "Keep Off!"? Lawns are benign, hygienic and controlled; they cover all the horror, squalor and uncertainty of the ground. Lawns are a tactic on the battlefield between power and democracy — occupying and sometimes also inhabitable!

Lawns are a visual representation of nature in an urban context; but they are anything but natural. The lawn is an engineered product genetically enhanced, mass produced in rolls, cut into uniform strips, transported in a truck and installed on-site by hard human labor. Lawns are a little like urbanism in China; they consume little material, and cover large areas in a short time.

Floating Green, a public art installation located in Shanghai Pudong Zhangjiang Hi-tech Park, detaches the flat lawn from the earth it covers, folds it and structures it to form inhabitable urban furniture. Instead of "Keep Off!" we are encouraged to "Hop On!" and touch it, smell it, use it and sense it however we please. The thin structure shakes gently when people sitting on it burst into laughter. An architectural artifact is usually singular and monumental, while a city emphasizes density and multiplicity. *Floating Green* rejects sculptural iconography in favor of an urban surface articulated in diverse parts.

LING FAN is an architect and critic based in Beijing. He is Assistant Professor at the School of Architecture at the Central Academy of Fine Arts, Beijing.

Floating Green, Ling Fan, Zhangjiang Art Park, Pudong, Shanghai, 2008. Four 2 × 1.5 × 1.2 meter stainless steel units are assembled and topped with turf on-site

Floating Green, Ling Fan, Zhangjiang Art Park, Pudong, Shanghai, 2008. Four 2 x 1.5 x 1.2 meter stainless steel units are assembled and topped with turf on-site